Canadian Families:

Ethnic Variations

Edited and with an Introduction by **DR. K. ISHWARAN,**
Professor of Sociology, York University

McGRAW-HILL RYERSON LIMITED

Toronto   Montreal   New York   St. Louis   San Francisco
Auckland   Bogotá   Guatemala   Hamburg   Johannesburg
Lisbon   London   Madrid   Mexico   New Delhi   Panama
Paris   San Juan   São Paulo   Singapore   Sydney   Tokyo

CANADIAN FAMILIES: Ethnic Variations

Canadian Cataloguing in Publication Data

Main entry under title:

Canadian families

Bibliography: p.
ISBN 0-07-077884-1

1. Family—Canada—Addresses, essays, lectures.
2. Canada—Population—Ethnic groups—Addresses, essays, lectures.*
I. Ishwaran, K., date.

HQ560.C35   306.8'0971   C79-094869-9

12345678910 D 9876543210

Printed and bound in Canada

Care has been taken to trace ownership of copyright material contained in this text. The publishers will gladly take any information that will enable them to rectify any reference or credit in subsequent editions.

Contributors

1. Ann W. Acheson, formerly at Department of Sociology & Anthropology, Bowdon College, Brunswick.
2. Alan Anderson, Department of Sociology, University of Saskatchewan.
3. Kwok Chan, Department of Applied Social Science, Concordia University.
4. Peter D. Chimbos, Brescia College, University of Western Ontario.
5. Leo Driedger, Department of Sociology, University of Manitoba.
6. Philippe Garigue, Department of Anthropology, University of Montreal.
7. K. Ishwaran, Department of Sociology, York University.
8. Larry Lam, Department of Sociology, York University.
9. John S. Matthiasson, Department of Anthropology, University of Manitoba.
10. Minako K. Maykovich, Department of Sociology, Sacramento State College.
11. F. M. Mealing, Department of Anthropology, Selkirk College.
12. Karl Peter, Department of Sociology & Anthropology, Simon Fraser University.
13. Henry Radecki, Department of Sociology, Laurentian University.
14. Joel S. Savishinsky & Susan F. Savishinsky, Department of Anthropology, Ithaca College.
15. Franc Sturino, Department of History & Philosophy, Ontario Institute for Studies in Education.
16. Michel Verdon, formerly of the Department of Sociology & Anthropology, University of Guelph.
17. Ravi Verma, Population and Social Statistics, Central Statistics Bureau, Victoria.

Contents

Preface

Ethnicity, whether we focus on urban or rural areas, is one of the most important components of social reality in Canada. This ethnicity is not simply bicultural; it relates to all the immigrant groups, drawn from various parts of the world, which have made Canada their new home. It serves as a major component of the Canadian social reality because it plays a definite role in the cultural survival of the immigrant groups. This, however, is so not only in Canada but in all multi-ethnic societies. In all such societies, the family operates as one of the crucial institutions for the transmission of ethnic values which, however, are adaptively modified by the integrative factors that may be operative. The tension between ethnicity and integration is expressed in different multi-ethnic societies in different ways which are influenced by historical, geographical, economic, demographic, and political factors. It is with this wider awareness of ethnicity in relation to the family processes and patterns that this volume examines the Canadian situation on a scientific basis.

The basic value-orientation of this volume as a whole is that ignorance of the life of Canada's ethnic groups cannot promote effective integration, while it may generate resentment among such groups for the high price they are forced to pay by sacrificing their cultural identity in the process of making their home in Canada.

I am indebted to the contributors whose researches made this volume possible, to Dr. K. Raghavendra Rao, Panchu Ganguly, Lawrence Lam and Dr. Ravi Varma for editorial assistance, and to Janette Rife for secretarial assistance in the preparation of this volume.

Finally, I am indebted to Canada Council for Leave Fellowship Award (No. 451-780100), which enabled me to write my Introduction and the paper to the volume, and to the Minor Research Grants of York University for providing me funds to do my fieldwork in the Holland Marsh area.

K. Ishwaran

York University
Downsview

To
My Dutch Relatives
who have made their homes all
over the world

I

1. FAMILY, ETHNICITY, AND RELIGION IN MULTICULTURAL CANADA

K. ISHWARAN

Multicultural nations like Canada, historical products of complex efforts at creating new societies out of culturally diverse immigrants in alien lands, pose a continuous problem of integration. In understanding the processes by which such immigrants, arriving at different times and from different cultural contexts, become integrated into a viable national society and polity, it is necessary to identify the key variables in the situation. One of the basic assumptions of this volume is that there are, indeed, such key variables, and one of them certainly is the family. The family, as the main socializing institution in each ethnic community, is likely to perform a crucial role in three ways. On the one hand, it ensures the cultural identity of the ethnic group. On the other hand, it helps the group face up to the existential problems of multiculturalism. Eventually, it enables the group and its individual members to adapt themselves to the situation without loss of ethnic identity.

If culture is defined as the sum total of the ways of acting and thinking in a group, considered as a historical continuum, then the family is a fundamental part of the cultural system. This is because a cultural system is sustained by a cultural process in which the family performs the strategic function of socialization. In performing this function, the family becomes virtually a microcosm of the wider socio-cultural system, encapsulating the wider culture as mediated by the ethnic group's culture. It becomes the dynamic bearer of the various aspects of the cultural system, such as the marriage institution, the courtship patterns, parent-child relations, and husband-wife role interactions.

Since the Canadian society is a class society as well as a society characterized by a plurality of interest-groups, the culture of a family reflects significantly this social reality. As a result, the family functions

1

within a specific class context. Its members become socialized systematically into a class culture. It develops and shapes the values and attitudes of the individuals around a class focus, enabling them to be conscious of their own class and of the other classes. Thus, class mediates and is mediated by the family within the framework of the overall socio-cultural system. However, it would be a naive mistake to cast the family exclusively or even primarily in a conservative role, the role of maintaining the *status quo* at all costs. This is because the family as a social institution is also called upon to handle the problem of socio-cultural change.

The widespread notion that modernization drastically erodes religious values and institutions appears to be more an ideological assertion than an empirically tested proposition. Evidence is mounting that modern societies do not discard religion in all senses, even as they are involved in an apparently escalating process of secularization. For instance, a collection of essays devoted to this problem[1] demonstrates beyond doubt that the religious culture to which an individual or group or family belongs continues to exert significant influence on societal processes in general, and on family life in particular. In fact, like class culture, religious culture affects family life systematically insofar as it determines the patterns of family culture.

Besides class and religion, language also is an important constituent element in the formation of cultural patterns at different levels. Language is a basic behavioural institution, and it is the very basic stuff of group-culture since much of cultural life tends to express itself in a basically linguistic modality. Language is more than a mere mechanism for socio-cultural communication within a group and between groups; it is the elemental structure of group life, attitudes, values, and behaviour. In its role of cultural communication and innovation, language becomes another important variable in understanding the interrelationship between socio-cultural processes, ethnicity, and family life.

Our discussion has been moving towards a major variable in the sociology of multiculturalism, and that is ethnicity. Socio-cultural processes, as mediated by the family, are generally located within the bounds of ethnicity. A recent survey by George Murdock[2] revealed that as many as 892 ethnic groups were scattered in the nation-state systems of the world. A more recent study[3] draws attention to the dramatic fact that virtually every country in the world today has squeezed within its political bounds at least five ethnic groups. It also points out that hardly one-fifth of the world's nation-states today enjoy any significant degree of cultural homogeneity. Therefore, ethnic heterogeneity and diversity seem to be the rule in the nations of the world today. It underlines the fact that, in the last three decades, the most frequent source of political conflict and violence has been internal, intra-state, and ethnic, rather than international or transnational.

If multi-ethnicity is an incontrovertible fact of modern life, then there is an imperative need to understand it in sociological terms. According to some recent projections,[4] it has been estimated that, by the end of this century, more than half the nation-states will have experienced political conflicts, whether internal or international, traceable to ethnic factors. Canada, the focus of this volume, is a clear case of multi-ethnic nationality. Its record in respect to inter-ethnic conflict-management appears to be not altogether discouraging. On the whole, peaceful Canadian efforts at such management have mostly adopted a strategy of either minority suppression or of accommodating reluctant minorities to get absorbed within the framework of dominant ethnic groups.

i

Sociological theory has yet to come to real grips with the phenomenon and concept of ethnicity. Ethnicity has apparently been the victim of what may be called disguised neo-evolutionism. It has been relegated to a supposedly primitive, pre-modern stage with which are associated primordial and prerational sentiments and primitive socio-political organizations.[5] The underlying assumption of this orthodoxy is that ethnicity tends to disappear as societies become more modernized. Whatever residual ethnicity that might persist in a modern society would be a marginal survival from a pre-modern, pre-rational past or a reversion and retrogression to such a past.[6] But this orthodoxy has not remained unchallenged in recent times.[7]

Further, empirical evidence seems to challenge the theory of equating ethnicity with premodernity. The case of Quebec is very much to the point in this context. Even after a century of political stability and economic prosperity, Canada seems not to have succeeded in integrating politically its Quebec population. Today Canada's very existence as a political system seems to be threatened by this issue. The separatist movement to secede Quebec from the Canadian Federation in order to constitute it into a separate sovereign state has gained a special momentum and a disturbing significance with the election to the Quebec provincial government of the separatist militant party, the Parti Québécois, on November 15, 1976. Of course, the question of political separatism cannot be dissociated from the question of economic viability. It seems very unlikely that the Québécois bid will succeed in the foreseeable future. But the problem of integration is there, and the role of the French Canadian family in contributing to such integration should not be underestimated.

The case of Quebec leads us to the question of what John C. Calhoun[8] formulated as the problem of permanent minorities in a society. A permanent minority is based on an ethnic subcultural group identity. It is a structural feature of a society, and not temporary like the changing political minorities of the classical model of party democracy. They constitute a perpetual and serious challenge to a numerical majority. If their rights and aspirations are denied to any significant extent, they may embark on action that would erupt in political violence, eventually damaging the body politic beyond repair. The limits to which such a minority group with the added advantage of ecological concentration in a historically well-defined region may be pushed is problematic. The political skill and management needed to locate the limits and deal with them may prove too much. There is, therefore, need to understand in depth more structural, sociological mechanisms that underpin the ethnic minority politics in multicultural societies such as the Canadian society.

Before we move on to a consideration of the Canadian specifics, we should undertake, however briefly, a preliminary operation of conceptual clarification. It is sufficient here to examine briefly some of the main terms used in our formulation of the problem. Let us take up first the term "ethnic group." The word "ethnic" is etymologically traceable to the Greek term *ethnikos*, which bears the meaning "people" or "nation." Therefore, we may use the term to denote any of the most basic group-characteristics or their combination. Ethnicity is both a subjective and an objective condition, because it involves both a subjective awareness on the part of the group and a systematic perception of its identity by others. To put it in sociological terms, an ethnic group is one which is a collectivity of individuals sharing unique socio-cultural traditions which are inter-generationally transmitted. According to the 1971 Census, the ethnic or cultural group refers to ethnic or cultural background traced through the father's side. This should not be confused with citizenship, which refers to the country to which the person owes allegiance. Language spoken by the person or by his paternal ancestor on first coming to this continent was a guide to the determination of ethnic or cultural group in some cases.[9] This concept has to be distinguished from the more complex and related concept of "peoplehood." In the modern world, for a variety of reasons, peoplehood has been splintered into a large number of disconnected group identities based on other criteria, such as class or political ideology. This does not mean that the process of people-formation has died out. Quite the contrary. Today, this process, as in Canada, for instance, has been going on, but it draws substantially from the core ethnic identity related to race, language, or religion, or a combination of the three.[10]

The second concept that needs examination here is minority group. It has been one of the most debated, controversial, but least satisfactorily settled issues in the social sciences. For our limited purposes here, a majority group is one which exists in a relationship of dominance to some other group within a common political framework. Though this necessarily involves numerical superiority, it also involves socio-cultural, economic, and political dominance as well. Being a minority group entails a certain status characterized by such features as citizenship, culture, number, or religion. But the essence of the matter is that a minority group tends to suffer social, cultural, economic, and political subordination. Therefore, the two basic ingredients of the minority position are social status and political power. This has to be distinguished conceptually and empirically from ethnicity. While ethnicity implies shared socio-cultural uniqueness and is manifested in a distinctive identity, minority group status implies political deprivation and social inferiority. Ethnicity becomes a minority characteristic through a political process of increased consciousness and action based on such consciousness. Therefore, the ethnicity of an individual or a group does not automatically become a minority issue. This happens only when there is a political attempt by the dominant ethnic group to subordinate other groups and when the subordinated groups attempt to act counterpolitically.

ii

Turning to our main theme, ethnic diversity in Canada, it is more meaningful to discuss it in terms of separate provinces than in terms of the country as a whole. This is because Canada is politically a federal system and it is a vast country about which overall generalizations are difficult to make.

Newfoundland is ethnically the most homogeneous and compact of all the Canadian provinces. About 94% of its population in 1971 is from a single ethnic stock, and it is all of British origin. At the other end, Quebec and Nova Scotia also present a very low level of ethnic diversity, as they are dominated by a population originating from a single ethnic stock. While in Nova Scotia the British account for 78% of the total population, in Quebec the French constitute about 79%. The prairie provinces are ethnically the most heterogeneous and fragmented. Here a large variety of ethnic groups, mostly non-British and non-French, find themselves within common provincial boundaries. The maximum British population in any prairie province is well under 50%. Thus, every province presents, with three exceptions, a veritable mosaic of ethnic-cultural diversity.

The distribution of the main ethnic population is also quite complex. The British predominate in the Atlantic provinces, Ontario, and British Columbia. The French dominate in Quebec and New Brunswick. The Germans are concentrated in all the western provinces, whereas the Ukrainians are mostly packed in the prairie provinces. The Jewish population is relatively more concentrated in Manitoba, Quebec, and Ontario. The Italian immigrants, especially the post-war ones, are mostly concentrated in Ontario. The Chinese are mostly to be found on the West coast, and the more recent Chinese immigrants have followed this pattern.

One finds that the most recent immigrant groups also have tended to display a pattern of spatial concentration, and quite understandably their concentration has been in *fast-growing provinces*. Most of the East

Indian groups are to be found in Ontario and British Columbia. The West Indians have mostly gravitated to Quebec and Ontario, although Quebec's population is growing more slowly. In short, one finds that ethnic diversity for Canada as a whole is also accompanied by a complex demography of spatial concentration. This is a situation that has naturally raised the issues of dominance and minority status. Thus ethnicity has the potential for social and political conflicts.

iii

A deeper look at the Canadian ethnic situation shows that the cultural patterns rooted in ethnicity are significantly affected by the religious culture of ethnic groups. In fact, we find a systematic relationship between religion and ethnicity. There is, for instance, a congruence of religious identity, ethnicity, and regionalism in Canada. The French Canadians of Quebec are predominantly Roman Catholic; British Canadians tend to be followers of the Anglican or the United Church. The Canadian Catholic population has always been substantial, and it has increased from 43% of the population in 1871 to 49% in 1971. The different Protestant groups account for 44%. The rest of the population is distributed as follows: 1.3% Jews, 0.1% Buddhist and Confucians, 1.4% other unspecified religious groups, 4.3% claiming to have no religion.

Within the major religious division of Catholics and Protestants, there are further denominational subgroups. Such denominational identities, both Protestant and Catholic, become greatly strengthened because of the pattern of spatial concentration. Here again, like the ethnic situation, the denominational distribution in spatial terms presents a fascinating mosaic of diversity. The larger Catholic denominations are concentrated in Quebec mostly, followed by New Brunswick. The Anglican groups are mostly to be found in Newfoundland and British Columbia. The lesser Protestant denominations are localized. The somewhat exclusivist Hutterites, rigidly attached to a well-defined religious way of living, are essentially a rural group and they find the rural situation highly congenial to their way of life. As many as 96% of them live in the three prairie provinces. With the exception of the Baptists and the Salvation Army, the Protestant sects live mostly in the western provinces. Some Protestant groups—Mormons, Mennonites, Doukhobours, Hutterites, Christian Scientists, and Evangelical United Brethren—are markedly absent in the Atlantic provinces. In view of these facts, it is difficult to pinpoint and characterize an *average Canadian* in terms of religious identity—a problem more baffling than that of identifying him in ethnic terms. The intermeshing of religious and ethnic identities heightens very sharply the picture of Canadian diversity.

This diversity is not a mere question of describing the existing population; it exerts a profound impact on the population dynamics of Canada, determining its social and political demography on a continuing basis. This is because the fertility patterns of the ethnic groups vary widely, due to the differing impact of religious beliefs, the social structure, the value system, the group traditions, and the changing socioeconomic condition. For instance, the fertility varies from 2,283 children for 1,000 women ever married, 45 years of age and over for the Jews, to 6,267 children for 1,000 ever married Eskimo women for the native Indians. On the higher fertility side are the French, the Asians, and the native Indian.[11] In terms of religious identification, the Roman Catholics, the Mennonites, and the Hutterites show relatively higher fertility rates: 4,052 and 4,890 children born to 1,000 women ever married, 45 years of age and over respectively, as compared to the Jews (2,117) and Protestants (2,480) (1971 Census of Canada, Table 32, Bulletin 1.5-11).

iv

In the process of group identity, whether ethnic or religious, language seems to be playing a crucial role. A group's commitment to ethnic identity and culture is directly proportionate to its capacity to preserve its linguistic identity. The strategic function of language in maintaining ethnic group identity in Canada was clearly recognized by the Royal Commission on Bilingualism and Biculturalism, which noted, ". . . language is a necessary condition for the complete preservation of a culture. . . . The life of two cultures implies in principle the life of two languages. . . ."[12]

While a great deal of attention has been paid quite legitimately to the central role of language in the preservation of the distinct culture and community structure of the French, its role in the persistence of other ethnic group culture should not be ignored. But its role does not seem to be the same for both the dominant and non-dominant language groups. For the dominant groups, linguistic identity is more a positive expression of power, whereas for others it might be the result of a compulsion generated by weakness.[13] For instance, between 1931 and 1971, the French Canadian population has registered a sharp decline in some provinces such as Prince Edward Island (from 77.3% to 45%), Nova Scotia (67.7% to 46%), Ontario (77.4% to 61%), Manitoba (86% to 63.4%), Saskatchewan (78.5% to 51.1%), Alberta (70.4% to 44.2%), and British Columbia (48.5% to 33.3%), and New Brunswick (94.9% to 87.6%). This situation has understandably worried the French Canadians.

In their capacity to retain their mother tongue, the Italian Canadians come next to the French. However, they, too, have a very low retention rate in the Atlantic provinces and British Columbia. It is also an interesting fact that the Italians in Quebec, among the non-French, constitute the largest users of French at home.

Though in overall terms, the linguistic picture of Canada might appear to be static in its basic patterns, this could be misleading. The French Canadians in Quebec are merely the most dramatic and politically explosive indication of the changing situation, but dynamic factors and forces might well be at work for other linguistic minority groups.

V

It is necessary to work out briefly the implications of Canadian multi-ethnicity. Historically, multi-ethnicity is a product of interaction over a period of time between different ethnic groups. But this interaction may generate different patterns for different groups, and for the same groups during different historical periods.

Underlying this process, of course, are the demographic processes involving the systematic and continuous displacement of the native peoples by immigrant European ethnic groups, and the political process involving the conquest of New France and the eventual political unification of English and French Canada.

The fact has to be squarely faced that the native Indian peoples have been the worst sufferers historically. As Patterson has demonstrated, the Indians have been subjected to a process of political and cultural disintegration, with devastating effects on their family system.[14] In recent times, these groups, especially the Cree, Iroquois, and Haida, have fought with cultural rearguard action in trying to preserve their ancestral patterns. Apart from some degree of cultural revivalism, one may also note a more modern political movement aiming at a better group identity and group status in the context of a competitive modern ethos. The two, of course, are not mutually exclusive, since group identity does imply cultural revivalism.

If the native Indians at one end represent the weakest ethnic minority, at the other end the French Canadians are the strongest in terms of their capacity to maintain their cultural, linguistic, and historical integrity as an ethnic unit. But the deeper implications of this situation needs to be carefully examined, especially from a political perspective. In short, what has been happening recently is a radical transformation of the older French Canadian identity into a politically more explosive "Québécois" identity. The French ethnic situation, therefore, has become complicated by the presence of two apparently opposed strains. The Québécois have cast the other French Canadians in the supposedly uncomplimentary role of being less genuinely French and hence "lost." The other French Canadians, on their part, tend to characterize the Québécois as less progressive, unrealistically "closed."[15]

As for the non-dominant ethnics, four distinct phases have been identified.[16] The first phase dates from the seventeenth century to 1901, covering such groups as the Blacks, the Chinese, the Germans, and the Icelandic. The second phase, from 1901 to World War I, is concerned mainly with the settlement in the West, comprising such groups as those from Ukraine, Poland, Norway, Russia, Germany, Japan, Iceland, and Italy. The third phase, from the Depression to World War II, involved small numbers settling all over Canada, but more especially in Ontario and Québec. This wave comprised Ukrainians, Germans, and Scandinavians. The fourth and final phase, stretching from World War II to the present, included a bewildering variety of immigrants from Europe, Asia, the West Indies, and Africa. They have mostly concentrated in the leading centres—Toronto, Montreal, and Vancouver—thus escalating the ethnic diversity of Canada's metropolitan population.

In terms of numbers, according to the 1971 Census, the two dominant groups account for 73% of the total population (English Canadians 44.6% and French Canadians 28.6%). Of the rest, the most numerous are the German Canadians (6.1%), followed by the Italians (3.4%), the Ukrainians (2.7%), and the Dutch (2%). The native Indians account for 1.4% and the Inuit represent about 0.1%.

These figures contain an element of ambiguity insofar as they point to a situation of multiculturalism and biculturalism co-existing. The fact that two ethnic-cultural groups are so overwhelmingly powerful in relation to the other ethnic groups has an inevitable tendency towards biculturalism, overshadowing the interest and claims of other groups. So far, the French Canadians have been sustained on an axiological system traceable to the Catholic Church and the liberal-humanistic system of education. The English Canadians have developed their value system within the framework of Protestant ethics, resting on such values as competition, individualistic achievement, and so on. But really, sociologists have left this important aspect of Canadian ethnicity virtually unexplored. The pattern of socialization and institution-maintenance in the other groups seem to be considerably variegated. They also seem to differ at different points of time. To use Raymond Breton's[17] original concept of "institutional completeness," it may be suggested that a major source of ethnic diversity in Canada is the different degrees of institutional completeness displayed by the different ethnic communities.

The native Indian people present a special problem. It has been shown that modernization in education tends to destroy the capacity of the Eskimo children to understand and appreciate their own culture and its institutions.[18] The northern educational system injected the new value system based on individualism, competition, and success symbols, driving the children towards a situation of cultural alienation from their own people. A Winnipeg study by Leo Driedger and Glenn Church[19] established that French as well as Jewish Canadians had achieved a substantial degree of institutional completeness. It was found that the Scandinavians, spatially more dispersed, were not successful to any significant degree in this regard.

When one examines the basic mechanism and process of such institutional completeness, one finds that five factors appear to be relevant. The first is religion. For a group which has a strong religious tradition, the ethnic churches offer a comprehensive context for solidarity group activities. This is the case, for instance, with the Ukrainian Catholic and orthodox churches, which contribute greatly to cultural ideology and group identity. They also reinforce the group's linguistic identity. The second factor is the school. In fact, the group develops its own schools only when its language and cultural ideology become salient to group life. The schools offer programs that strengthen group cultural identity, specific religious, social, and economic ideologies. This may be done through such cultural forms as music, dance, and craft. The Royal Commission[20] mentions the existence of some five hundred part-time schools run by sixteen cultural groups, more than two-thirds being German, Ukrainian, and Polish. In terms of student population in such schools, around 65% belong to ethnic schools run by Germans, Ukrainians, and Jews. But there are also full-time schools which provide a combined program of formal education and cultural recreation, and they are the main sources for future community leadership. Such schools exist for Mennonites, Jews, Ukrainians, and Greeks.[21] The fourth factor is the mass media which help strengthen ethnic diversity. The ethnic press, for instance, plays an invaluable role in this regard. It also helps maintain links with the original homeland. The Lithuanian press runs five periodicals, catering to some 28,000 members. The Chinese, Hungarians, and Ukrainians have their own press.[22] Lastly, there is a proliferation of ethnic voluntary institutions meant for specific purposes, such as mutual-aid societies, health-care units, employment counsel agencies, recreational and leisure organizations.

As the Porter study demonstrates, the ethnic situation significantly correlates with the Canadian system of stratification.[23] Continuously for three decades, 1931-1961, the English Canadians were over-represented in the top categories, while the French Canadians were underrepresented for the same categories. In this, the role of English language as a means to social mobility has played a crucial part. In fact, the French Canadians have been persuaded to acquire facility in the use of English, at least to the extent necessary for material success.[24] But such adaptation has not been without considerable resentment towards cultural dominance of English. As for the other groups, the Jews are over-represented in the top categories. But it should be noted that there is also a tendency over a period of time for such discrepancies to diminish, however small in scale. A key factor in this is the educational level of the group. When it rises, a group is likely to rise in social scale. For instance, the underrepresentation of the Dutch has been reduced from −1.1 in 1931 to −0.9 in 1961. For the Germans, it declined for the same period from −2.2 to −1.8. For the Asians, in this time, their under-representation of −4.3 changed dramatically to an over-representation of +1.7. Thus, there is considerable inter-generational social mobility in ethnic groups. From this perspective, the most deprived and underprivileged are the native peoples. Whatever the objective criteria, they find themselves at the bottom of the social ladder.

Around 40% of Indians and Metis earn an income less than $1,000 per annum, whereas, for the overall Canadian population, this figure is only 13%. Among the native groups, only 25% attain the educational level of sixth grade, and most of them get no education whatsoever. In terms of infant mortality, pre-school mortality, and general health level, these groups are considerably less favorably placed than the average Canadian.

vi

As already noted, the role of the family is crucial in two respects. On the one hand, it helps sustain ethnicity through its socialization and solidarity functions. On the other hand, as a socio-economic and political unit, it helps enable the ethnic communities to face up to the challenge of change. In the context of a highly mobile and dynamic society such as the Canadian society, both the roles are important. The family in all ethnic groups has been undergoing change over the years.

Though the pace of this change has increased in more recent years, even during the earliest historical times the family has not been a static institution and change took place then also in the context of great ethnic diversity.[25] There was, for instance, noticeable difference between the French Canadian family in Quebec, the English Canadian family outside Quebec, and the family of the native peoples in the border areas of Canada. Each ethnic community was equipped with its own set of beliefs, attitudes, and behaviour patterns, going back to the original home-land tradition. However, in the new Canadian world, these became significantly modified without losing a core identity, as revealed in the studies in this volume. Because of such persisting patterns of ethnic diversity, it is difficult to identify anything as the Canadian family. Not only ethnicity, but the other associated variables, such as class, language, or religion, have accentuated this sense of diversity.

Nonetheless, sociologists can, and perhaps should, identify in broad terms a reasonably comprehensive model of the Canadian family, cutting across the diversities. The broad framework of this model would be industrial, democratic, and predominantly Christian, and perhaps this could cover the wide range of family forms in Western society. A suggestion on this line was made three decades ago by Ernest Burgess.[26] Among the sources of change in the ethnic family has been the process by which it has become increasingly "atomized," that is, individualistically oriented. This process, however, has slowed up considerably due to the counterpressure generated by the persistence of kinship networks. An important sociological task is to trace the direction of nature and the path of this movement of change. One suggestion is that the cumulative effect of this process of change is towards the emergence of an overall Anglo-Saxon family model. But there is nothing known about this model. In fact, this suggestion involves what Ralph Linton[27] characterized as the "calm ethnocentrism," a product of the nineteenth-century colonial evolutionary thinking. Eventually, its source is the colonial European epistemology of duality—the "primitive they," and the "civilized we." Though in this crude form the evolutionary frame has apparently been discarded, neo-evolutionary thrusts have recently emerged.[28]

The second framework for analyzing family change is the Marxian evolutionism, postulating a uni-directional historical process. In its extreme version, perhaps never accepted even by Marx himself, this leads to oversimplified economic determinism. Only uni-directional influence, that flowing from the economy to the family, is considered, and no room is provided for the flow of influence from the family to the economy.[29] There are less deterministic and simplistic frames which are sensitive to the mutuality and interdependence of family and other societal institutions.[30] What emerges from the studies assembled here is a framework of institutional interdependence and multi-dimensionality of change.

We now briefly focus on an important mechanism through which any social institution, including the family, maintains itself, adapts itself, or radically alters itself. The mechanism consists of the system of values which guides individual and group action, provides criteria of evaluation of such action, and also finally provides a basis for legitimizing such action in normative terms. Values, therefore, motivate behaviour and help understand human attitudes and behaviour. The ethnic values, whether intrinsic or instrumental, tend to be sustained, as illustrated by many of the studies in this volume, through the ethnic family. Among the values socialized through the family, there may be intra-ethnic marital alliances, family stability, kinship loyalties, equality between partners, male dominance, parental authority, small family norm, large family norm, and ethnicity itself. But the family derives its value system from two important contexts in Canada—ethnicity and religion. In macrosociological terms, one significant thrust of the interdependence of the family, ethnicity, and religious culture is that the individual is provided considerable insulation from the wider societal processes, and hence he tends to derive psychological and material security from ethnic family. For instance, Peter Chimbos in this volume shows how the Canadian Greek family is structured around the values of kinship and ethnicity. For the Polish family in Canada, Radecki demonstrates that the original value of patriarchalism derived from the homeland undergoes a perceptible modification. The family, then, performs the function, through socialization, of maintaining the ethnocultural identity, and thus indirectly a basic cultural continuity between the homeland society and the immigrant groups. The studies in this collection clearly testify to this aspect.

It follows from what has been said above that ethnic diversity tends to be preserved. The result has been the evolution of what Leo Driedger[31] has characterized as "the Canadian ethnic mosaic." In other words, the ethnic family strengthens the ethnic identities of the various

Canadian ethnic groups while it simultaneously deepens the diversity between the different groups. One primary aim of this volume is to draw attention to this ethnic heterogeneity, and, more important, to the nature and sources of this heterogeneity. In fact, the essence of ethnicity is distinctive individuality and diversity, which pervades the totality of group life-situation values, attitudes, lifestyle, customs, rituals, and psychic patterns. Their overall status in the context of biculturalism accentuates, if anything, this socio-cultural pattern. Basically, it seems to derive its support from a variety of sources—ethnic-nationality, homeland culture, religious identity and racial origins. The ethnic situation in Canada does not conform to the American model of what has been designated "the melting pot," a term first suggested in 1908 by Israel Zangwill. The assumption underlying this term is that in the United States, the various ethnic groups have become substantially fused and homogenized. But this has been recently challenged.[32] If this challenge has any validity, then the alleged differences between the Canadian and the American ethnic models require considerable critical attention. The fact seems to be that there always is an unmeltable, residual ethnicity, which even the highly integrated market of the industrial economy cannot eliminate. To describe the American situation, there seems to be a tendency to change the metaphor of "the melting pot" to that of "the salad bowl." The latter phrase seems to apply even more to the more pluralistic Canadian ethnic reality.[33]

The central issue, in terms of sociological theory, in both these ways of conceptualizing ethnicity, is clearly the concept of integration, more loosely referred to as "assimilation." However, using here the more familiar term assimilation, we find that there seems to be a mystique attached to it in the American sociological perception of the American social reality. If the mystique is ignored, one finds that the concept is highly ethnocentric, assuming as it does that the host American culture is so overwhelmingly superior to the incoming immigrant ethnic cultures that the latter are discarded almost automatically. No doubt, there is some sociological substance in this idea insofar as the modern, industrial, market economy and the historical matrix of the modern nation-state tend to counteract ethnic diversity. Nonetheless, we have to reckon with residual, unmeltable ethnicity. So far as Canada is concerned, the challenge posed to ethnicity has not been in terms of a "melting pot" model. As we shall see later, here the challenge comes from a bicultural model. But it must be admitted that biculturalism, itself based on the French Canadian challenge to the unstated Anglo-Saxon melting pot ideal, has prevented ethnic groups from the assimilationist fate. Today, in Canada at any rate, ethnic minorities are political units, whose existence can scarcely be ignored. Yet one gains the impression that there is still in operation a process of ethnic discrimination, as a result of which certain ethnics are systematically downgraded in the employment market by being associated with dirty work or drudgery. But the Canadian as well as the American record challenges the myth that ethnic minorities are biologically and culturally disqualified from occupying the higher rungs of the economic levels. The Chinese, the Japanese, the Dutch, and the Germans have demonstrated overwhelmingly that the ethnics are fully qualified to compete successfully in the market for jobs. One political consequence of such developments has been the civil rights movement in the United States, whose impact has been felt throughout the American political system, public life, and the socio-cultural framework.

vii

Though this volume professes no explicit concern with the political aspects and dimensions of Canadian ethnicity, it can hardly ignore them altogether. They are present by implication in most of the studies. But they are, even more importantly, structurally bound up with the major theoretical concerns of these studies. We believe that the fundamental issue is the political process by which the traditional Canadian biculturalism may be transformed into a genuine multiculturalism. In such a political transformation, Canadian sociology can and should play a role. This volume is intended to provide a sociological insight and some of the data on the basis of which a multicultural policy may be effectively implemented.

We need here to go into the issue of multiculturalism in some depth. First, we need to distinguish between multiculturalism as an empirical phenomenon and as a value. A society may be historically and empirically multicultural and multiethnic, but from this it need not follow that such a society actually accepts this situation as a desirable one. In other words, a multicultural society need not accept multiculturalism as a desirable goal, as a value. The second distinction is between multiculturalism as a societal value and as an object of policy, as determined by the political system. The point so far has been that multiculturalism is a more or less basic to the structural framework of the "Canadian people." It may also be suggested that, in contrast to the United States, the Canadian society has historically evolved in a direction of biculturalism with potentialities for multiculturalism. One may legitimately infer that the Canadian society has in some sense accepted this as a desirable situation, and hence as a value. No doubt, this might well have been a pragmatic response to a developing situation, but a pragmatic response does not necessarily preclude its becoming over a period of time a community goal. However, there is need for much historical and sociological research on this problem.

By 1971, Canada had a population of seven million, which did not belong to the two founding ethnic groups—the English and the French. Bilingualism, however, had received official recognition to the extent that a Royal Commission was set up to examine its implications. But the Federal Government, while accepting the overwhelming reality of bilingualism, did not merely limit itself to biculturalism. The Government's action on the report of the Commission was to accept the position that Canada is a bilingual, multicultural society. No doubt, it would be more accurate to call Canada also multilingual, but this would be merely a pedantic accuracy. In a more significant sense, the Government was justified in emphasizing bilingualism as long as it did not ignore the fact of multiculturalism. The Government recognized the fact that one-third of the country's population, mostly located in urban, metropolitan areas, consisted of around forty ethnic groups. In its response to the Royal Commission's report, as tabled in the House of Commons on October 8, 1971, the Government declared its position as follows:

> ". . . We believe that cultural pluralism is the very essence of Canadian identity. Every ethnic group has the right to preserve and develop its own culture and values within the Canadian context. To say that we have two official languages is not to say that we have two official cultures, and no particular culture is more 'official' than another. A policy of multiculturalism must be a policy for all Canadians.
>
> Vibrant ethnic groups can give Canadians of the second, third and subsequent generations a feeling that they are connected with tradition and with human experience in various parts of the world and different periods of time.
>
> The Government regards this as a heritage to treasure and believes that Canada would be poorer if we adopted assimilation programs forcing our citizens to forsake and forget the cultures they brought to us. . . ."[34]

The policy has had the expressed support of the opposition parties, the Progressive Conservatives and the New Democrats. Programs to implement this policy have been initiated under the auspices of the office of the Secretary of State. For the fiscal year 1975-76, for instance, the expenditure for these programs was $4.5 million or about 0.34% of the Secretary of State's total budget. The programs in question included Multicultural Project Grants, Multicultural Centers, Non-Official Language Teaching, Ethnic Press Analysis, Immigrant Orientation Conferences, and the Canadian Consultative Council on Multiculturalism. The Government programs, including the types indicated above, have not satisfied apparently a considerable number of ethnics. For instance, M. Carole Henderson, a specialist in minority folklore, has faulted the policy for not promoting genuine minority identities.[35]

If minority cultural life, as any cultural life, can be examined in terms of three levels of functioning—the superficial morphological level, the deeper ritual practice level and the most basic level of values—then it appears that the Multicultural Policy has failed to penetrate beyond the first level. In other words, the ethnic groups are allowed to enjoy individuality only to a limited extent, while they suffer the dominance of the English Canadian culture at deeper levels. One must also note that there is yet another dominance, the American dominance, radiating from across the border and engulfing the English culture. In the context of modern political systems, in sharp contrast to the pre-modern ones, culture becomes highly politicized. But this process should not be confused with the process by which what Almond and Verba[36] call "political culture" is created and sustained. When we refer to political culture, what we are referring to is the system of attitudes, symbols, and values which structure around the political system of a society. When one talks of *politicized culture,* what one really refers to is the political *use* of a culture—either to perpetrate political-cultural hegemony or to challenge such dominance. There is little doubt that the English culture in Canada has become politicized in order to serve as a significant component of the system of English political hegemony. It may be equally asserted that the Canadian French culture has been politicized to carry on a political struggle against English hegemony.

The issue of cultural hegemony, the assimilationist doctrine, and minority cultural exploitation cannot be simply dismissed as political. It has seeped, no doubt subtly and even unconsciously, into serious, academic, sociological interpretation of Canadian social reality. A very distinguished Canadian English sociologist, John Porter,[37] for instance, has mounted an attack on multiculturalism. He based this attack on the ground that multiculturalism offends the liberal political theory of individual rights. It is a moot point whether this is a deliberately disguised attempt to provide a theoretical underpinning to cultural hegemony. Further, Porter has suggested that there is an inherent contradiction between biculturalism and multiculturalism. His overall thrust is to argue that multiculturalism is less compatible than biculturalism with the post-industrial world. In a truly liberal spirit—spirit which justifies individualism on broad theoretical grounds, while at the same time conceding that individualism in a context of group inequality may be unfair—Porter, with unconscious candour, declares:

> ". . . Most liberal social scientists viewing this phenomenon of ethnic stratification assumed that over time processes which they called absorption, assimilation and acculturation would eliminate this relationship between national or ethnic origin and economic condition and they advocated policies that would lead to such a result. . . . The emphasis was on individual achievement and . . . it meant forgetting ancestry and attempting to establish a society of equality where ethnic origin did not matter. Some fears were expressed, of course, that these liberal assimilationist values would require a large measure of Anglo-conformity on the part of 'non-Anglo' groups. In a large measure these fears were probably justified, but it could also be said that what was being advocated was conformity to the values of societies leading to the modernizing process. . . ."[38]

What Porter is suggesting, in essence, is that English is modern, modern is right, and hence it is good and right for everybody to fall in line. The irony of it is that, not only does Porter admit in the above passage that "Anglo-conformity" is involved, but he has also elsewhere[39] provided abundant evidence for the relationship between Canadian inequalities and Canadian ethnicity. In view of this, there is an urgent need for sociological theory to examine without ethnocentricity the issue of multiculturalism. It would enable the political elite in Canada to face up to the implications of a policy and theory of multiculturalism. It has been one of the major assumptions of this volume that modern sociology has the ethical framework and the technical competence to tackle such issues.

viii

Recapitulating what has been so far stated, we may sum up our broadest concern in these studies: (1) to examine the reality of the Canadian ethnic diversity and heterogeneity as a context for individual ethnic groups; (2) to examine for each specific group the role of the family in maintaining ethnic cultural identity, but also its role in enabling the ethnic group to meet the challenge of an external environment; (3) to pinpoint the socio-religious bases of ethnic community life; (4) to raise, within the context of individually examined ethnic communities, broader issues of cultural dominance, dependence, and equality; and (5) to discuss to the extent possible in highly specific studies the very general issue of multiculturalism.

While the individual scholars have been free to work in their own styles, both methodological and theoretical, we have started with a few broad initial assumptions. The first is that Canadian multiculturalism is a central sociological reality of Canadian national life. The second is that this ethnically leased cultural diversity and heterogeneity have been systematically sustained through the values, attitudes, and behavioural patterns of the ethnic groups. The third is that the family has been the basic mediating agent in the process of maintaining ethnic identity, but in a context of dynamic adaptibility. The fourth is that religion as a major element in ethnic culture may also play a key role in perpetuating ethnic identity. These assumptions have a bearing on sociological theory and also on cultural policy. In brief, we reject a sociology of cultural hegemony, dominance, and dependence. From this rejection derives our overall policy recommendation—that multiculturalism is the right policy for Canada because Canada is a multicultural, multiethnic society.

NOTES

1. Gerhard Lenski, ed., *The Religious Factor: A Sociological Study of Religious Impact on Politics, Economics and Family Life* (Garden City, New York: Doubleday and Company, 1961).
2. George Murdock, *Ethnographic Atlas* (Pittsburgh: University of Pittsburgh Press, 1967).
3. Abdul A. Said and Luis R. Simmons, eds., *Ethnicity in an International Context* (New Brunswick, N.Y.: Transactions Press, 1967), p. 10.
4. Martin L. Leisler and B. Guy Peters, *The Implications of Scarcity for the Peaceful Management of Group Conflict*, University of Maryland, Mimeographed, March 1971.

5. Talcott Parsons' paper, "Some Theoretical Considerations on the Nature and Trends of Change of Ethnicity," in Nathan Glazer and Daniel P. Moynihan, eds., *Theory and Experience* (Cambridge, Mass.: Harvard University Press, 1975), pp. 56-71.
6. Walker Connor, "The Politics of Ethninationalism," *Journal of International Affairs*, Vol. 27, No. 1, pp. 1-21.
7. *The Annals* of the American Academy of Political and Social Science, Philadelphia, Penn., 1972.
8. John C. Calhoun, *A Disquisition on Government* (Indianapolis: The Bobbs-Merrill Co., 1953).
9. Dictionary of the 1971 Census terms, Statistics Canada.
10. Gordon Milton, *Assimilation in American Life* (Toronto: Oxford University Press, 1964).
11. 1971 Census of Canada, Bulletin 1.5-11.
12. Royal Commission on Bilingualism and Biculturalism, 1967, pp. XXXVII-XXXVIII.
13. Stanley Liberson, *Language and Ethnic Relations in Canada* (New York: John Wiley, 1970); J. Reitz, "Language and Ethnic Community Survival," *The Canadian Review of Sociology and Anthropology* (Toronto: University of Toronto Press, August 1974).
14. E. P. Patterson, *The Canadian Indians: A History Since 1500* (Don Mills: Collier-Macmillan, 1972).
15. "The Socio-Political Dynamics of the October Events," *The Canadian Review of Sociology and Anthropology*, 91, 1972, pp. 33-56.
16. Royal Commission, the Work World, Vol. 4.
17. Raymond Breton, "Institutional Completeness and Ethnic Communities and Personal Relations to Immigrants," A.J.S., 70, 1964, pp. 193-205.
18. Charles Hobart and C. S. Brant, "Eskimo Education, Danish and Canadian," *Canadian Review of Sociology and Anthropology*, 3, No. 2, 1966, pp. 47-66
19. Leo Driedger and Glenn Church, "Residential Segregation and Institutional Completeness," *Canadian Review of Sociology and Anthropology*, 11, 1974, pp. 30-52
20. Royal Commission, 1969, Vol. 4, p. 150.
21. Royal Commission, 1969, Vol. 4.
22. Royal Commission, 1969, Vol. 4, pp. 172-177.
23. John Porter, *The Vertical Mosaic* (Toronto: University of Toronto Press, 1965).
24. Jacques Brazeau, "Language Differences and Occupational Experiences," *Canadian Journal of Economic and Political Science*, 49, 1958, p. 536.
25. Helen C. Abell, "Adaptation of the Rural Family to Change," in Parvez Wakil, ed., *Marriage, Family and Society* (Toronto: Butterworth & Co., 1975); Arthur W. Calhoun, *A Social History of the American Family*, 3 vols. (Glendale: A. H. Clark & Co., 1917).
26. Ernest Burgess, "The Family in a Changing Society," A.J.S., 53, May 1948, pp. 417-422.
27. Ralph Linton, "The National History of Family," in Ruth N. Anthen, ed., *The Family: Its Functions and Destiny* (New York: Harper, 1959), pp. 30-52.
28. Talcott Parsons et al., eds., *Theories of Society* (New York: Free Press, 1961); Kenneth E. Beck, "Evolution, Function and Change," *American Sociological Review*, 28, 1963, pp. 229-233; Herbert R. Barringer, George I. Blanksten, and Raymond W. Mack, *Social Change in a Developing Area: A Reinterpretation of Evolutionary Theory*, 1, Cambridge: Schenkman, 1966.
30. Frederick Engels, *The Origin of the Family, Private Property, and the State* (Chicago: Kerr, 1902).

31. Leo Driedger, ed., *The Canadian Ethnic Mosaic* (Toronto: McClelland and Stewart, 1978).

32. Nathan Glazer and Daniel P. Moynihan, *Beyond the Melting Pot*, 2d ed. (Cambridge: M.I.T. Press, 1970).

33. F. Elkin, *The Family in Canada*, the Vanier Institute of the Family, Ottawa, 1970; Stewart Queen and Robert W. Habenstein, *The Family in Various Cultures* (Philadelphia: Lippincott, 1974).

34. Government of Canada, *First Annual Report of the Canadian Consultative Council on Multiculturalism*, Minister responsible for Multiculturalism, December 1975, pp. iv-v.

35. M. C. Henderson, "The Ethnicity Factor in Anglo-American Folkloristics," *Canadian Ethnic Studies*, Vol. II, No. 2, 1975.

36. Gabriel Almond and Sidney Verba, *The Civic Culture* (Princeton: Princeton University Press, 1963).

37. John Porter, "Ethnic Pluralism," in *Vertical Mosaic*, pp. 267-304.

38. *Ibid.*, pp. 293-294

39. *Ibid.*, pp. 267-304.

II

ETHNIC FAMILIES AND
SOCIO-CULTURAL SYSTEMS

INTRODUCTION

The general objective of this section is to provide systematic and descriptive accounts of the structural aspects, the behavioural patterns, and key problems relating to the families of the major ethnic communities in the multicultural Canadian society. The ethnic groups chosen include the Greek, the Polish, the Dutch, the Japanese, the Southern Italian, the French, and the Chinese immigrants in Canada. While the analyses of the non-French Canadian family systems share a common framework of concerns and interests, both theoretical and problematic, the two studies on the French Canadian family employ a slightly different kind of frame and focus. The difference derives from the fact that the non-French Canadian studies are more historically oriented and that they explicitly invoke immigrant context of the ethnic families concerned. The two French Canadian studies concentrate more on the contemporary and functioning realities of the ethnic family.

The studies on the non-French Canadian ethnic families presented here are all concerned with the immigrant framework of the ethnic family. This concern results in a common emphasis on certain basic features and problems of the family system. Firstly, they all undertake a brief historical exercise in tracing the ethnic family system back in time and space to the original home country and society. In other words, they build into their study systematically the home society, its institutional patterns, and its value system. Secondly, and precisely because of the above concern, they focus at considerable length on the process of socio-cultural adaptation to an alien socio-cultural as well as geographical environment. The record of the different ethnic family systems with regard to their ability to become integrated into the host system seems to be different.

The adaptation or acculturation patterns that emerge from these studies constitute a veritable spectrum of sociological structuration. At one extreme we have Henry Radecki's account of the Polish family, which presents a case of substantial assimilation into the Canadian host system. At the other end of the spectrum we have Peter Chimbo's presentation of the Greek Canadian model in which the original pre-immigration patterns are strongly preserved. In between we have the case of Southern Italians presented by Franc Sturino, which involves a structural balancing of the home and host elements. In this case, as Sturino demonstrates, the home elements become the basic resources for adaptation and survival in the new environment. The model of the Canadian Japanese family presented by Minako Maykovich is by far the most complex, as it focuses on a differentiation of pattern rooted in inter-generational differences. Thirdly, all these studies focus on the current problems faced by the ethnic families concerned. All these problems relate in one way or other to the process of assimilation, adaptation, and integration. More precisely formulated, these problems are different manifestations of the tension between the initially brought immigrant socio-cultural equipment and the demands of the new environment. In the context of this tension, which appears to be a continuing tension for ethnic communities in Canada, two opposed patterns have emerged. On the one hand, the home elements have been utilized as a resource, as, for instance, in the case of the religious identity and ideology. On the other hand, they have been significantly modified after having been perceived as dysfunctional to the process of survival. Lastly, all these studies imply, even when they do not explicitly state, the problem of a potential political conflict of interests between the new ethnic groups and the two dominant groups.

The two French Canadian studies cannot be fitted into the above framework of perspectives and problems. Michel Verdon's study examines a central theme in French Canadian sociology, that of the Quebec stem family. In his analysis of the historical and current situation, Verdon separates science from ideology, and, in the process, explodes the myth of an authoritarian and patriarchal stem family. The reality he presents is a good deal more complicated since what one encounters is a complex structure of contradiction—contradiction between nuclear families striving to assert their autonomy and identity within the superficial framework of economically motivated co-residence. Philippe Garigue's study discusses the nature of the kinship structure of the French Canadian community in the specific setting of urban life. While noting some weakening in the system of kinship exchange in recent times, Garigue argues that it will continue to be functional to the French Canadian community.

Within the general theoretical framework, sketched above, we shall present brief and introductory comments on the individual papers in this section. This would make it possible to see the theoretical links between the separate papers.

Peter Chimbos suggests that the Greek Canadian family continues to function as a considerably persistent structure as it continues to provide individual members of the family at least three crucial inputs—security, identity, and community. In this function, the community religion plays an important role. Through the institutional devices of intrafamily socialization and ethnic endogamy, the Greek Canadian family helps strengthen the Greek linguistic cultural identity. The family performs the dual function of preparing the Greek Canadians to adapt themselves to the Canadian socio-cultural and economic realities, and of strengthening the community identity. As a consequence, the Greek family in Canada acquires the quality of being structurally transitional—transitional in relation to the dominant Anglo-Saxon family system about which we know next to nothing. The study ends with the hope that the shift will not become so sharp as to weaken the more worthwhile communitarian values of the old Greek family culture.

Radecki's account of the Polish Canadian family begins with an historical survey of the different phases of Polish emigration to Canada, and this process is conceptualized as a "chain movement." According to him, immigration took place not on the basis of large groups but on the basis of individual families and even single people, and this process set up a further chain movement for others related or associated with the persons involved in the process. As a result, community concentration on ethnic basis was difficult and rare. This also implied a somewhat consistent effort to preserve ethnic socio-cultural identity. In his brief account of the original family in Poland, he draws attention to a clear-cut pattern of authority distribution within the family and an implied set of norms and values. The pre-1956 immigrants apparently found it more difficult to maintain the original pattern. Up until 1931, the Polish Canadians, however, were more rural in their settlement patterns, and hence they found it relatively easier to preserve a strong linguistic identity. Subsequently, the linguistic cultural identity weakened as the group underwent greater urbanization.

Radecki devotes some attention to the conflict between the old world values and the new environment. In this connection he mentions patriarchalism, but notes that the result has been a renegotiated and readjusted pattern. His empirical data relates to Metropolitan Toronto. Further, he notes that while the patriarchal norms may be consciously subscribed to, the pressure of the situation prevents its full acceptance in practice. The traditional evaluation of the marital status as desirable seems to continue, but the statistical data suggest that the proportion (41.5% for the Polish group as against the overall Canadian figure of 44.0%). The original Polish wedding ceremony—very colourful, expensive, elaborate, and time-consuming—has disappeared, leaving in its place a modest, urban middle-class ceremony. In demographic terms, the average rate of children for a married couple has been much less than in Poland, and, in fact, up to 1961, has been less than the overall Canadian figure. In the area of kinship, the traditional Polish solidarity has weakened, especially in the last decade or so. The social stratification of the Polish Canadians conforms to the overall Canadian pattern, with the result that the middle class values and lifestyle seem to prevail.

Paradoxically the Polish Canadian middle class also is the group most seriously and consistently preoccupied with the problem of preserving the Polish socio-cultural and linguistic identity. In contrast to the working class, it is more involved in emigré politics. On the whole, the class situation is complicated by criss-crossing variables. The Polish family life in Canada is characterized by a significant degree of stability, anchored in traditional norms and values. But the situation itself may be changing. By and large, the historical process of immigration and adaptation has achieved a precarious balance between the traditional old world values and the new socio-ecological forces.

Maykovich's study of the Canadian Japanese family focuses on a comparative analysis of acculturation and familism among three generations, which she designates as *Issei*, *Nisei* and *Sansei*. Each generation is age-specific and is characterized by a distinctive subculture. The Issei had more direct experience of the feudal Japan of their childhood, and thus had roots in the traditional culture based on Confucianism and Buddhism. This tended to emphasize a more collectivistic norm, demanding the subordination of the individual to the family and the nation. It implied a hierarchical, obedience-oriented system. In Canada, the Issei (immigrants) managed to maintain their traditional values and identity. After World War II, the Nisei, the children of immigrants, experienced a substantial improvement in their socio-economic position. They also appeared to have been successfully absorbed into the mainstream Canadian social system. The Sansei, the children of Nisei, have begun to express serious doubts and reservations about the White Canadian values. An element of ethnic revivalism seems to characterize their behaviour.

Using historical backdrop, Maykovich examines empirically a Toronto sample. As a result of it, she concludes that (1) the Issei continue to turn their back on the overall Canadian system, but they do not influence the Nisei who are significantly acculturated; (2) the Nisei are caught up in a conflicting situation, subject to the contrary impact of their adopted values and their traditional norms; and (3) the Sansei are also under the double pressure of the White Canadian society and the values of that society's youth subculture, and their behaviour is characterized by adherence to familistic norms on the one hand, and, on the other, the values of the rebellious White Canadian youth.

Sturino examines the factor of family and kin solidarity as displayed in the life of southern Italian immigrants of the post-World War II period. The Old World socio-cultural system of the immigrants has proved to be more a resource than a handicap in the process of acculturation in Canada. The operationally more adaptable original system of rights and obligations governing the kin relations has become a basis for survival in the new environment. The consequential co-operative structures of behaviour have strengthened solidarity at three levels— the nuclear family, the family circle, and the kin group as a whole. This solidarity is characterized by mutually interdependent roles within the nuclear family, the emergence of work teams within the family circle, and the solidarity-affirming rites of passage, practised by the kin group. Insofar as the patterns observable in this group congrue with those of the dominant post-World War II Italian immigrants in general in Canada, it may be justified to extend the findings of this study to the Italian immigrants as a whole.

Verdon's study questions systematically the myth of the authoritarian Quebec family, and the further claim that this generated a clerical or theocratic-oriented intelligentsia. The historical evidence collected by contemporary Quebec historians, however, demonstrates that the intelligentsia, in fact, was aggressively opposed to clericalism. Verdon is concerned to show the untenability of the authoritarian family thesis. The stem family, the term accorded to the authoritarian family model, was authoritarian not so much because of structural properties inherent in it, as because of internally destabilizing factors. In the new version, the head of the stem family is not so much a legitimized authoritarian as a desperately pragmatic despot, out to neutralize the legitimate claims of the members under his control. The family system was, as a result, a structural compromise—a co-residential system of opposed nuclear families united for purely economic purposes. What discipline and obedience it generated was not structural but purely situational.

Verdon's close attention to behavioural data shows that the stem family was not structurally an authoritarian system. He attributes ideological motivations to the authoritarian interpretations of the stem family. In particular, he points to the Protestant prejudice as behind such images of the stem family. Making a more economic analysis of the situation, he is able to counter the authoritarian thesis. In conclusion, Verdon pleads for a sociology purified of ideological obsessions, and this would call for a radical revision of the currently dominant interpretations of the Quebec stem family.

Garigue's French Canadian study explores the inter-relationship between kinship and urbanism. The thesis of the paper is, briefly, that kinship solidarity and cohesiveness decline relatively as a result of changes in cultural value than as a result of increasing urbanization. Based on a study of a sample of French Canadian households of Montreal in 1955, he found that kinship relations rested on a combination of obligation and personal choice. In the maintenance of kinship solidarity, family socialization, and ethnic identity play an important role. Garigue does not find any shift in the French Canadian kinship pattern towards a more circumscribed and selective model observable in the United States. This is because kinship and urbanism are functionally inter-related among French Canadians. But the system is flexible and capable of adaptation to a variety of contingencies. The flexibility derives from the notion of "priority" kin.

Garigue also finds that the current pattern has a historical continuity with the period of New France. In fact, this continuity should be seen as a result of the flexibility and elasticity of the system. Underpinning this system lies a normative system extolling the values and ideals of the family life. In a concluding theoretical part, Garigue refers to the relevant literature. He shows the bias in this literature on urbanization arising out of an exclusive research focus on the experience of the United States.

The paper on the Chinese Canadian family uses the official Census data and immigration statistics to examine the issue of nuclearization in the context of modernization. The authors attempt to analyze a variety of data—economic, social, educational, occupational, and demographic—to test the proposition that the Chinese family system tends to become nuclearized in response to the environmental pressures of the host country. They demonstrate empirically that the immigrant Chinese family in Canada does undergo nuclearization as part of its adaptive strategy. But they also suggest that, in fact, the Chinese family becomes relatively more nuclearized than the average ethnic family in Canada. Their study offers a complex explanatory model, which includes not only the historical specificity of the home country but also the minority status of the Chinese immigrants in the overall Canadian system. In short, the Chinese case points to the need for analyzing the family structure in terms of what may be designated as the process of over-adaptation. It also shows that the issue of cultural continuity and change has significant political overtones.

As the foregoing analysis implies, the process of interaction between the host environment and the immigrant family system takes many forms, depending on the historical background and the contemporary nature of the immigrant groups, their institutional arrangements, their status within the power-structure of the host system, and contingent variables difficult to predict. These studies, taken as a whole, raise certain theoretical issues, only partly resolved by the data and interpretation they offer. One issue is whether we can arrive at a general theory of immigrant modernization. The family seems to perform a dual role. On the one hand, it functions as an institutional mechanism to promote socio-cultural continuity. On the other hand, it also seems to function as a mechanism for renovating the traditional system. These two functions may be subsumed under the single process of adaptation and selective modernization.

2. The Greek Canadian Family: Tradition and Change*

PETER D. CHIMBOS

This paper examines some aspects of family life among Greek Canadians. The need for such a task arises from the fact that in a multicultural society, it is in the family that the distinctiveness of the ethnic group is or is not transmitted from one generation to the next. Family life in Greece, reflecting the Old World's values and institutions, shall be analyzed, and the demographic and social characteristics of the family in Canadian society shall be presented.

THE FAMILY IN GREECE

The family in contemporary Greece has been shaped by religious traditions, the rural nature of the country, and the continuous political instability after the revolution of 1821 against the Turkish conquerors. Probably the greatest influence on the Greek family has been the Greek Orthodox Church. This is mainly due to the fact that Greece was occupied by Turkey from 1453 to 1821. During those four centuries of occupation the institution that managed not only to survive, but also to keep alive the Greek language and culture, was the church. This explains why Greek Orthodoxy and Greek nationalism are almost inseparable.

The domination of contemporary Greece by a conservative and authoritarian church, especially in rural communities where the church has been a major source of social control, accounts for some of the features of the Greek family. For example, divorce and remarriage have been strongly discouraged by Greek Orthodoxy, and marriage is ex-

---

* This paper is part of a larger study on Greek Canadians commissioned by the Multicultural Program, Department of the Secretary of State, Ottawa.

pected and even required by law to be a sacrament rather than simply a legal contract.

Historically, the strength of the Greek church has been its ability to reach the masses, especially the peasantry, and identify itself with them. The influence of the Greek church on family structure and relationships has been described by Campbell:

> The family is also a religious community with its own "sacra" icons, and other objects. In the popular mind it is an earthly reflection of the Heavenly Family of God the Father, the Mother of God and Christ. Relations between members of a family ought to be modelled on the attitudes which, it is imagined, inspired the relations of the Heavenly archetype family and its members. A father ought to have wisdom and foresight, a mother compassion, a son courage and respect, a daughter virginity and so on.[1]

The agricultural economy of the country has maintained certain characteristics of the extended family system. It was not common, especially in the rural areas of Greece, to find extended families where aged parents were living with married children and their families. This kind of family structure was suited to agricultural communities where the population mainly consisted of farmers or shepherds or both, who needed the labour supplied by both children and grandparents. Although social change has affected family structure considerably, the care of the aged parents still remains a moral obligation for Greek children, regardless of their socio-economic background and geographical (rural or urban) residences. Children who have emigrated to Canada or other countries also provide their parents who were left behind with financial support.

One of the most important features of the Greek family has been its patriarchal and authoritarian nature. Generally, the women had a low status, marriages were arranged, and the dowry system was dominant. The tradition of a male-dominated family structure is slowly disappearing among educated classes of Greek society, but still predominates among those with little formal education and especially the peasants.[2]

Other important aspects of the Greek family and kinship were moral obligations based on family solidarity. For example, sibling solidarity and the obligation of caring for parents were important expectations. Campbell, in his study of Greek family life in rural communities, found that "in the elementary family, the principles of sibling solidarity and parental obligations are complementary, and together guide its members in their duties and exclusive affections."[3] The solidarity within the kinship structure is reflected in the socio-psychological and economic support that kinsmen provided for each other when in need. Brothers are responsible for providing their sisters with dowry; aged parents are cared for by their adult children; and moral obligations are extended to relatives by marriage.

A prevalent value which influenced familial relationships in Greece was family honour. According to Campbell, "the intrinsic principles of honour refer to two sex-linked qualities that distinguish the ideal moral character of men and women: these are the manliness (andrismos) of men and the sexual shame (entropi) for women."[4] Members of the kinship structure were expected to show a strong commitment to family honour and defend it through physical violence if necessary. Campbell, in his study of a rural community in North Central Greece, has observed that men must not fail to defend their family honour. He writes:

> Objectively . . . honour is an aspect of the integrity and social worth of the family as this is judged by the community; subjectively it represents the moral solidarity of the family, an ideal circle that must be defended against violation by outsiders.[5]

The above-mentioned family relationships and moral obligations were most pronounced and valued in Greek rural communities. However, the traditional features of the family are gradually decreasing under the influence of urbanization, technology, and American and European contacts. The greatest changes have occurred in large urban communities such as Athens and Thesalonika.

The feminist movement which received an impetus during the 1940s has helped in the gradual modernization of the Greek family. As a result of this and other social and political movements, "the Greek woman is slowly but surely gaining her intellectual and spiritual freedom."[6] In 1975 the Greek Parliament adopted a constitution that gave the two sexes equal rights and obligations. The charter allowed the parliament seven years to implement this clause. In 1976 a commission headed by Professor Andreas Gazis was appointed to draft new legislation which would eliminate sex discrimination and provide women with more equal status. According to proposed legislation:[7]

a) Men will be legally responsible for helping with house work and child care, particularly if their wives are working.
b) Women will be responsible for contributing to the family's financial support.
c) Laws that discriminate on the question of work, pay, and pensions will be eliminated.
d) There will be equal educational opportunities for both sexes at a higher level.

Equal opportunities for higher education in Greece have been improved in the 1970s. In 1976, for example, women accounted for about 50% of the students entering Greek universities. This compares with about 25% in the early 1960s. Changes towards equal status for the sexes will, however, continue to be slow as long as Greece is dominated by conservative politico-economic institutions.

THE GREEK FAMILY IN CANADA

When the Greek immigrant came to Canada, he carried with him the customs and traditional beliefs of family life that he had learned in the home society. Upon his arrival he discovered that such cherished ways of thought as respect for elders, obedience to parents and teachers, and male dominance were not observed by many Canadians, especially those from Anglo-Saxon background. Greek Canadians have shown a relatively low degree of social integration into Canadian culture, partly because their family life remains influenced by the home society's values and historical experiences. But as any immigrant participates in the socio-economic life of the host society, his traditional ways of thinking cannot remain unaffected. Acculturation is a continuous social process and the immigrant slowly acquires the roles, values, and lifestyles of his new society. In the following pages we discuss some demographic aspects and other features of the Greek family in contemporary Canada.

SIZE OF FAMILY

One might expect the immigrants who come from a traditional family system (characterized by an extended family structure with many children) to have large families. However, the size of the Greek family in Canada is smaller than the average in the general Canadian population. In 1971 only 18% of the Greek families in Canada consisted of 5 persons or more, compared with 27% of families in the general Canadian population. (See Table 1.)

TABLE 1
FAMILIES WITH HEAD OF GREEK ETHNIC ORIGIN COMPARED TO
FAMILIES OF THE GENERAL CANADIAN POPULATION, BY SIZE OF
FAMILY, 1971

No. of Persons in Family	Greek Ethnic Group		General Canadian Population	
	Number	Percent	Number	Percent
2	6985	23.2%	1 591 600	31.4%
3	7840	26.0	1 046 375	20.6
4	9815	32.6	1 056 925	20.8
5	4135	13.5	662 855	13.1
6	995	3.3	358 845	7.1
7 or more	435	1.4	354 290	7.0
TOTAL FAMILIES	30 135	100.0	5 070 685	100.0

Source: 1971 Census of Canada, Cat. 93-714, Vol. II (part 11), June 1973. Information for Greeks was specially processed for this study by Statistics Canada, August 1974.

The fact that there are fewer children in Greek families may be due to the improvement of the Greek immigrants' economic status in Canada, since upwardly mobile couples tend to perceive children as economic liabilities. It could also be due to the fact that a large proportion of Greek Canadian married couples are relatively young and thus their families are incomplete.[8]

FAMILY DISSOLUTION

Leaders and clergymen of Greek Canadian communities, especially in smaller ones where most of the families are known to community leaders, report very few divorces and separations. According to Statistics Canada (see Table 2), the divorce rate amongst Greek Canadians is lower than that for the general population, though the difference is not statistically significant. (The lower percentage of widowed is probably due to the relatively younger married Greek Canadian population.) No information is available on the rate of marital dissolution due to separation (non-legal and contractual) which have not culminated in formal divorce.

Divorce rates, of course, are not a precise index of serious marital conflict. Such conflict occurs in Greek marriages, but spouses who have been influenced by the old country's mores feel that divorce is a disgrace, and thus are more likely to put up with conflict than to seek a divorce. Relatives at times may find it proper and necessary to intervene and advise in their children's, siblings', or even cousins' marital conflicts: intervention seems to be a moral imperative, and indicates, perhaps, the persistence of family obligations among Greek Canadians. However, it can have negative consequences upon kinship relationships: intervention by relatives in marital conflicts can at times prevent reconciliation and lead to more serious family crises.

TABLE 2
PERCENTAGES OF MARITAL DISSOLUTION OF THE TOTAL GREEK AND
CANADIAN MARRIED POPULATION, 1971

Marital Dissolution	Greek Ethnic Origin	General Canadian Population
Widowed	5.2	8.8
Divorced	1.3	1.7

Source: *Marital Status by Ethnic Group, 1971 Census of Canada, Cat. 92-734, Vol. 1 (part 4), February, 1974.*

KINSHIP IN THE HOST SOCIETY

In the home society the kindred[9] played an important role in the socio-economic survival of the Greek family. Kinsmen aided each other during family crises such as illness, loss of crops, or death, negotiations of "match-making," the cultivation of farms, and the facing of a hostile environment during the Nazi occupation and the civil war of 1946-49. In the new society the kindred are still considered important, as they provide each other with moral and socio-economic support in making adjustment to the new cultural setting. Established relatives who sponsored new immigrants in the 1950s and 1960s helped them to find homes and jobs, and reduced culture shock by providing a familial setting.

In business matters, too, the immigrant has looked to his relatives for economic assistance and co-operation. When the Greek immigrant needed a loan or a partner to open a restaurant, he would turn to his relatives. In many Canadian cities it is not uncommon to find restaurants owned and managed by Greeks who are related to each other. Even the employees could be members of the immediate families or outside kinsmen, such as cousins and inlaws. This kind of interfamily co-operation is in the successful establishment of small businesses, and spurs the upward social mobility of many Greek immigrants in Canada.

Economic support can also be extended to relatives in Greece. The Greek immigrants came to Canada not only to improve their own lives, but also to help relatives they left behind. Many immigrants, as soon as they acquire their first "fortune" in Canada, send clothing, food, and financial aid to relatives back home. The money may be used to purchase a farm, start a business, remodel a house, or pay for the education of children.[10] Economic aid of this kind has always been welcomed, but was especially appreciated during the late 1940s and the 1950s, when Greece was recovering from the economic catastrophes of World War II and the subsequent civil war. The economic support by Canadian and American Greek immigrants to their relatives at home, especially after World War II, has been an important factor in the improvement of the standard of living of many Greeks. Such improvement may have functioned as an insulator against potential political upheavals and communist appeals. Similarly, the success of relatives in Canada and the vacation visits may encourage indigenous Greeks to model their political and economic structures on the democracies, as opposed to socialist and communist countries.

The solidarity among kinsmen can also be expressed in social events where related families participate. The celebration of baptisms and namedays, for example, are occasions where exchange of personal wishes strengthen and renew kinship solidarity. To what extent social networks are extended to non-related families is not known, but immigrants who cannot speak the English language mainly associate with relatives or at least with other Greeks. Earlier inquiries in Toronto[11] and a city in northern Ontario[12] have shown that friendship and leisure time activities of Greek families rarely extend to non-Greeks. A more recent survey has also shown a high rate of ethnocultural homogeneity of friendship networks among Greeks, similar to that existing among Italian and Portuguese immigrants.[13]

Greek familism, with its emphasis on solidarity, mutual support, and moral obligations, inevitably creates some conflict between kinsmen. Such conflicts, usually centred on family matters and business transactions, rarely result in permanent estrangements. According to the Greek custom, blood relationships are mutual and, at least symbolically, are never broken. The idea that your kinsmen respond to your needs even after bitter conflicts is expressed in the proverb "the blood never becomes water, and even if it will, it won't become muddied."

Spiritual relationships are also an important aspect of the Greek family's social network. They refer to those reciprocal relationships between individuals or families based on important religious sacraments, such as baptism and weddings. In a wedding, two previously unrelated persons (the bridegroom and the wedding sponsor) are drawn into a spiritual relationship in which "their mutual esteem and respect are profoundly committed."[14] A relationship of this kind involves moral obligations and responsibilities between the concerned persons and thus enhances family solidarity. In other words, it is an institutionalized relationship and does not end with the wedding ceremony. According to Greek custom, the wedding sponsor usually becomes the godfather (nounos) of the first child. The child's godparent is chosen by the parents from family friends, co-workers, and other non-related persons of the Greek Orthodox faith.[15] Symbolically speaking, then, the godfather (or godmother) becomes the spiritual parent of the child. The godchild addresses his spiritual father as godfather (nouno), while the natural father and the spiritual father address one another as "Koumbaro," or in more formal terms, as "synteknos" (co-parent).[16]

An essential characteristic of the spiritual kinship system is that it provides spiritual kinsmen with socio-economic support and co-operation when the need arises. During the earlier periods of immigration, many immigrants who came to Canada were sponsored by the spiritual kinsmen who had already established themselves in Canada. When these immigrants first arrived in Canada, spiritual relatives would help them to find a job and an apartment or a house to rent. Like the kindred, spiritual relatives are also involved in business transactions. When kindred are unavailable, the Greek who needs a business partner may turn to his spiritual kinsmen. This is why Greeks may often attempt to find spiritual relatives (kourmbari) whose monetary resources and social position will aid them economically.

SELECTING A MATE

The Greeks of Canada are predominantly endogamous. According to a recent inquiry, the Greeks, like the Portuguese, are concerned that spouses be similar on the three factors of birthplace, mother tongue, and religion.[17] Previous inquiries in Toronto[18] and in Thunder Bay,

Ontario,[19] also indicated strong preference for endogamous marriages among Greek Canadians. In Thunder Bay, when Greek parents were asked if they would favour their child's marriage with someone outside their nationality, 73% were definitely opposed to such a marriage. This compared with 52% of the Slovaks and 11% of the Dutch immigrants in the sample. More extensive exploratory inquiries are needed, however, in order to make meaningful comparisons of inter-ethnic marriages of first and second generation Greeks, and to find out how inter-ethnic marriages are related to such variables as sex, age at immigration, and educational achievement.

Greek Canadian immigrants seem to be more concerned about the ethnic than the religious background of their child's prospective spouse. In the study carried out in Thunder Bay, the respondents were asked if they would approve their son's or daughter's marriage with someone who was outside their ethnic group but of the same religion. Greek immigrants were less likely than Dutch and Slovak immigrants to accept religious endogamy without ethnic endogamy. The most common reasons Greek immigrants in Thunder Bay gave for objecting to inter-ethnic marriages were desire to maintain Greek culture and religion, belief that marriages can be happier if spouses have the same values, and belief that people from their nationality make better husbands and wives.[20] The same reasons for objecting to inter-ethnic marriages were also given to the writer during informal discussions with many Greek parents in the cities of Calgary, Montreal, and Toronto. These observations are similar to parental attitudes among Greeks in the United States. Greek American parents have emphasized the advantages of having a spouse of the same faith, and warned their children of mixed marriages and the loss of Greek identity.[21]

The strong resistance to inter-ethnic marriages creates anxiety among Greek immigrant parents. In Greek families, when children reach the dating age, the parents become disturbed lest their children date or marry non-Greeks.[22] Many parents realize that, for the most part, the traditional parental choosing of mates is inappropriate in Canada, but they do not approve of Canadian courtship patterns or of exogamous marriages. A long period of disappointment and grief is commonly observed among parents whose children defied their wishes and married an outsider (xeno). These parents see their son or daughter who marries a non-Greek as one who is "lost" (hathike). The term "lost" in the Greek context means that the person who practises exogamy will inevitably maintain social distance from his family and ethnic community and his children will not learn Greek language and ways of life. In many instances, eventually the parents are reconciled with the child who has married out, and the spouse is accepted into the family and the ethnic community.

Parental pressures on children to marry within the ethnic group will continue to be strong and thus slow down the assimilation process.

Even in the mid-1970s "match-making" of endogamous marriages among Greek Canadians can be observed. The "go-betweens," who are usually relatives or friends, may talk over the marriage prospect with the parents, and if they agree, then the boy and the girl are encouraged to meet and perhaps cautiously date each other. If they are mutually interested, the courtship continues and the engagement follows. On the other hand, pressure for ethnic endogamy is expected to be less strong among second and third generation Greek Canadian families whose values and social patterns are more similar to those of the host society.[23] However, ethnic exogamy among second generation Greeks may be less than among certain other second generation immigrants in Canadian society.

HUSBANDS AND WIVES

As indicated earlier, the majority of Greek immigrants come from agricultural and traditional communities of Greece, in which the husband was the head of the household and the family's representative in the community. His authority over the wife was absolute, and the wife was expected to be modest and submissive.[24] This type of relationship between sex roles was carried over from Greece to Canada by many immigrants. However, the influence of Canadian values and institutions has modified such familial structures, and wives are beginning to enjoy higher status and greater intellectual freedom. Along with these changes, the Greek Canadian wife is also enjoying more economic independence and technological conveniences, such as electric appliances.

The Greek wives in Canada now play an important role in the discipline and socialization of children, and assist their husbands in business, making domestic decisions and contributing substantially to the family's economic welfare through hard work in the factory or restaurant. The argument presented by Kourvetaris regarding husband-wife roles among Greek immigrants in the United States can also be applied in Canada. He writes:

> To an immigrant husband who left his parents at a young age, his wife was more than the sociological sex-role partner. She was the wife, the adviser, the partner, companion and homemaker. She also assisted her husband in his business and the family decision making. Wives/mothers usually exercised their influence in the family decision making indirectly through the process of socialization of the children because the Greek father had to work incredibly long hours away from home.[25]

Although andrismos (manliness) and the demand for paternal leadership are still persistent social attributes among Greek male immigrants, systematic studies of sex-role differentiation would probably indicate that more equalitarian relations between spouses are becoming prevalent. It can also be argued that the power relationship in marriage varies with the spouses' academic achievement, length of residence in Canada, and age at the time of immigration. In inter-ethnic marriages, where the husband is a Greek immigrant and the wife a Canadian born non-Greek reared in a more equalitarian family structure, traditional marital relationships may also be expected to be met with disapproval from the wife.

Power relations in Greek immigrant families have been slowly shifting from traditional male dominance to companionship and co-operation between husbands and wives. What effect such changes have upon the "traditionally directed" Greek husbands is not known. Nor do we know under what conditions or circumstances Greek husbands may take the authority back and prevent their spouses from doing what they want.

PARENTS AND CHILDREN

The relationship between Greek immigrant parents and their children seems to be somewhat different from that of most Canadian Anglo-Saxon families. The manner of rearing children is usually identified by parents as one of the chief differences between Greek and Canadian family life. The Greeks maintain that the majority of Canadian children enjoy unnecessary freedom and do not have sufficient respect for their parents, elders, teachers, and other officials. There is a conflict of the old world's traditional values with those of the new society, especially those of individualism and personal freedom.

Parental demands and familial control over children seem to be important factors for the relatively low incidence of juvenile delinquency in various Greek communities throughout Canada.[26] The ethnic group's controls, including gossip about the deviant children and children's active participation in the ethnic community's life, are also effective methods for the prevention of delinquency in small Greek communities. The immigrants' anxious striving for respectability and acceptance within the ethnic community and in Canadian society in general seem to account for the concern over their children's behaviour. However, familial and other group controls seem less effective in large cities like Montreal and Toronto than in smaller centres. More deviant subcultures are found in a metropolis, and the ethnic group's "conformity pressure" over its members is decreased where intra-ethnic relationships are more impersonal.

Parent-child conflict is observed in many families of Greek immigrants. Much disagreement arises between parents and adolescent children, especially concerning dating, courtship, and inter-ethnic marriages. Disagreement on such matters between parents and children is occasionally strong but unlikely to result in serious consequences for the majority of the families.

Some observers (notably teachers and social workers) of Greek communities have described parent-child relationships as problematic and the Greek family milieu as unfavourable to the child's social and academic development.[27] Such generalizations should be considered with extreme caution, as they are based on a few individual cases and not supported by systematic inquiries. It may be argued that attachment to Greek values and institutions provides the child with more psychological security and social control, and, therefore, he/she is less likely to become involved in deviant behaviour, such as delinquency and drug use. It may also be argued that apparent adverse effects of ethnic background on the child's academic achievement are in fact related to the variable of social class.[28]

The intimate social and physical contacts of the child's early life are also an important aspect of socialization in the Greek family. Campbell, in his study of family life in contemporary Greece, observed that "Greek children from the day of their birth are the centre of attention and interest in the family. The needs of the infant take priority over all others."[29] This kind of family interaction is also commonly observed in Greek Canadian families. The child's early life involves a high degree of interaction with parents, grandparents, and relatives. It would appear that by the age of six, the average second generation Greek child receives much hugging, kissing, touching, and playing from his parents, siblings, and relatives. Such emotional and physical contact extends even in adult life, as it is not unusual for adult friends and relatives of the same sex to greet each other with hugs, kisses, and tears.

PROSPECTS FOR FUTURE RESEARCH

Extensive sociological studies are needed in order to show more precisely the changes occurring within the Greek family and its adjustment to Canadian culture. The longer an immigrant has been in Canada, the more likely he is to accept the familial roles of his new society. However, the age at which the immigrant arrives in Canada is a more important variable than the length of his or her residence here. The younger the age at which an immigrant enters Canada, the more likely he or she is to internalize Canadian values and thus to accept the familial roles of Canadian society.

Further research may be enhanced by the inclusion of more sophisticated criteria to measure power in the family, and by comparing the findings with those based on other ethnic family systems in Canadian communities. The family power structure may be measured in terms of certain decisions, such as buying a house or business, disciplining children, buying home furniture, handling bank accounts, and the dating patterns of adolescent children. Especially valuable to ethnic family studies would be a comparative analysis of family dissolution rates between marriages of pure ethnic descent (spouses both Greek) and mixed marriages (only one spouse Greek), while controlling the variables of educational achievement, religious background, and parental approval.

The Greek family's involvement in external social relationships (formal and informal networks)[30] is also expected to vary with socio-economic status. We would expect that the higher the family's social class position, the more numerous its members' connections to formal social networks within the Greek community and the outside Canadian social structure. On the other hand, in an ethnic group such as the Greeks, where there is a strong sense of familism and ethnic identity, we might not be able to find a significant relationship between class position and informal social networks, especially with related families. Familial obligations and socio-economic co-operation for survival in a foreign land increase the Greek family's contacts with relatives and families from their own background.

The Greek family in Canada, then, can be viewed as a relatively stable unit which provides its members with security, identity, and community. Familial solidarity and socio-economic co-operation is extended to kindred and spiritual relatives from the Greek ethno-religious background, including those still residing in Greece. As a primary group, the Greek family plays an important role in maintaining the vitality of the Greek language and culture in the new land, through the socialization of the young and the demand for ethnic endogamy. As a social control agency it seems to be effective in directing children to conform to the accepted standards of Canadian society while maintaining an admirable equilibrium between the Canadian and Greek culture. Although the Greek family still possesses many of its traditional attributes, it is in transition from a traditionally oriented unit to one in which the size, roles, and relationships resemble those of the English Canadian and French Canadian family systems.

NOTES

1. J. K. Campbell, *Honour, Family and Patronage* (Oxford: Clarendon Press, 1964), p. 37. This and other quotations by J. K. Campbell in this chapter are used by permission of Oxford University Press, and are copyrighted © Oxford University Press 1964.
2. Constantina Safilios-Rothschild, "A Comparison of Power Structure and Marital Satisfaction in Urban Greek and French Families," *The Journal of Marriage and the Family* 29 (May 1967), p. 349.
3. J. K. Campbell, *op. cit.*, p. 54.
4. *Ibid.*, p. 269.
5. *Ibid.*, p. 193.
6. Athina Tatsoulis, "Greek Women Poets of Today," *Hellenia* 23 (July-September 1953), p. 11. For a more detailed analysis of family change in contemporary Greece, see Panos D. Bardis, "The Changing Family in Modern Greece," *Sociology and Social Research* 40 (September 1955), pp. 19-23.
7. See the *Globe and Mail*, November 4, 1976, p. F2.
8. According to 1971 Census data, 18.6% of the Greek Families had 3 or more children. This compares to 27.7% of the families in the general Canadian population.

9. "Kindred" refers to cognate relatives whose blood ties can be linked through the father's or mother's side as far as the degree of second or even third cousins.

10. It should be noted that other important contributions to the Greek economy by Greek immigrants include vacation visits and investments of Canadian dollars in small businesses.

11. Judith A. Nagata, "Adaptation and Integration of Greek Working Class Immigrants in the City of Toronto, Canada: A Situational Approach," *International Migration Review*, Vol. IV (Fall 1969), pp. 44-67.

12. Peter D. Chimbos, "A Comparison of the Social Adaptation of Dutch, Greek and Slovak Immigrants in a Canadian Community," *International Migration Review*, Vol. 6 (Fall 1972), pp. 230-244.

13. Paul Larocque et al., "Operationalization of Social Indicators of Multiculturalism." Paper presented to the Fourth Departmental Seminar on Social Indicators: The Department of the Secretary of State, Ottawa (November 1974), p. 55.

14. J. K. Campbell, *op. cit.*, p. 222.

15. Occasionally godparents may be chosen from relatives such as cousins, aunts, and uncles.

16. For a detailed analysis of wedding sponsor or godparent relationships, see Stanley E. Aschenbrenner, "A Study of Sponsorship in a Greek Village," Ph. D. dissertation (Minneapolis: University of Minesota, 1971).

17. Paul Larocque et al., *op. cit.*, p. 54.

18. C. A. Price, "Report on the Greek Community in Toronto," M.A. thesis (Toronto: York University, 1958).

19. Peter D. Chimbos, "Immigrants' Attitudes Towards Their Children's Interethnic Marriages in a Canadian Community," International Migration Review, Vol. 5 (Spring 1971), pp. 5-16.

20. *Ibid.*, p. 9.

21. Theodore Saloutos, *The Greeks in the United States* (Cambridge, Mass.: Harvard University Press, 1964), pp. 313-314.

22. Greek parents do not object to the ethnicity of their children's friends in childhood or pre-adolescence. The nationality of the Greek child's friends becomes of greater parent concern when the son or daughter is approaching the age for dating or marriage. See Louesa Economopoulou, "Assimilation and Sources of Culture Tension of Second Generation Greek Pre-Adolescents in Toronto," M.A. thesis (Toronto: Ontario Institute for Studies in Education, 1976).

23. The study of Tavuchis indicates that in the second Greek generation American family, "there is a trend toward a less patriarchal structuring, a high incidence of exogamy, and the development of patterns consistent with those exhibited by the dominant society." See Nicholas Tavuchis, *Family and Mobility Among Second Generation Greek Americans* (Athens: National Centre of Social Research, 1972), p. 33.

24. J. K. Campbell, *op. cit.*, pp. 150-154.

25. George A. Kourvetaris, "The Greek Family in America," in Charles H. Mindel and Robert W. Haberstein, eds., *Ethnic Families in America* (New York: Elsevier, 1976), p. 176.

26. This observation is based on interviews with leaders of the Greek community and probation officers in the large cities of Edmonton, Ottawa, and Thunder Bay.

27. This refers, for example, to certain papers presented to the Greek Intercultural Seminar on March 29, 1974, at St. Barnabas Anglican Church in Toronto.

28. Earlier studies in the United States have shown how achievement motiva-

tion of second generation Greeks has its origin in early parent-child interactions which enhance the child's chance of upward mobility. Rosen, for example, found that Greek children had higher academic aspirations and thus were more upwardly mobile than children of other ethnic groups, such as Italian and French Canadian. This, according to Rosen, is due to standards of excellence emphasized in the home by parents, and the fact that academic achievement by children received the approbation of the entire Greek community. See Bernard C. Rosen, "Race Ethnicity and the Achievement Syndrome," *American Sociological Review*, 24 (February 1959), p. 52. See also Peter D. Chimbos, "The Hellenes of Missoula Montana: Social Adjustment," unpublished M.A. thesis (Missoula, Montana: University of Montana, 1963), pp. 44-48.

29. J. K. Campbell, *op. cit.*, p. 154.

30. "Formal networks" refer to the family's social relationships with the school, church, and other public institutions and voluntary associations. "Informal networks" are the patterns of social relationships with and among relatives, friends, and neighbours. See Elizabeth Bott, *Family and Social Network* (London: Tovistock, 1957).

3. The Polish-Canadian Family: A Study in Historical and Contemporary Perspectives*

HENRY RADECKI

OUTLINE

The aim of this article is to consider various dimensions of the Polish family in Canada.[1] The scope of the inquiry includes phases and patterns of immigration, background of family customs, traditions, and values in Poland, adjustment, and changes in the Polish family in Canada. In this last area, the article discusses problems encountered by the Polish immigrant family and their resolution. It also considers changes in structures and patterns of family relationships among the rural and the urban settlers. The discussion includes selected demographic data, and a partial analysis of the Polish family drawing on the 1971 Canadian census and other information.

PHASES OF IMMIGRATION

Polish settlers in Canada were noted since 1752, but in the next 150 years only individuals and small groups chose Canada rather than the United States for permanent settlement. The migratory movement of people in search of land, opportunity, political or religious freedoms began around 1895 and continues on a small scale to the present. Over the past decades their numbers grew through further immigration and natural increases, and at present they constitute one of the larger ethnic groups in Canada, representing 1.5% of the total Canadian population. According to the 1971 census, there were 316,425 individuals belonging to this group, domiciled in all provinces and territories.

* I wish to thank K. Ishwaran for helpful comments on this article.

41

TABLE 1
POLISH GROUP, 1971

Canadian Born	210 920	66.0%	
Foreign Born	105 505	33.0	
TOTAL	316 425	100.0	
			Canada Percentage for Comparison
Urban	254 695	80.4%	76.2%
Rural Non-Farm	33 860	10.8	17.3
Farm	27 875	8.8	6.5

Source: 1971 Census of Canada, Cat. 92-723, 1973.

Polish settlement in Canada can be divided into five phases: individuals and small groups of families to 1895; the mass movement of peasants, farm workers, and labourers in the years 1895-1914; the resumption of this movement, but on a smaller scale, in the years 1920-1939; the post-World War II influx of refugees and political exiles in the years 1946-1956; the final, ongoing but numerically smaller migratory movement directly from Poland and elsewhere.[2]

The first numerically small phase consisted on one hand of individual males who adapted quickly, intermarried, and became assimilated often beyond the point of recognition of their ethnicity. On the other hand, some original small groups, consisting of complete families, maintained ethnic identity and Polish family traditions and values over generations. One example are those who settled around Barry's Bay and Wilno in North Eastern Ontario.[3]

Polish immigrants began to come to Canada in much larger numbers after 1895, following Canadian Government's desire to settle and exploit the newly opened prairie lands. The advertising campaigns for settlers and workers attracted primarily landless peasants and farm workers, but there were also petty tradesmen and urban proletariat. In this phase, over 100,000 Poles were registered at the Canadian ports of entry,[4] but well over three-quarters of them moved to the United States or returned to Poland. Despite the numbers, this was not an organized or planned movement. There was rarely more than one family leaving their community at the same time; more often fathers went alone and brought their wives and children at some later date. Other relatives and friends followed, encouraged by the news of free land and plentiful job opportunities. There is no information to tell us what proportion of this, and the next phase, was composed of males, married or single, but the mobility pattern and rates or returnees suggest that the male-female ratio was at least 3:1 in favour of males.[5]

These newcomers differed sharply on a number of cultural attributes from their hosts: Polish language has no affinity with either English or French; family values were past-oriented; dress and behaviour—sheepskin coats or traditional dress, lengthy deliberation prior to decision-making, dietary habits, and standards of hygiene—all were seen by the established Canadians as very strange, even threatening to their own customs and values.[6] Traditional familistic values and distinct cultural ethos posed problems of adjustment for those working in towns and cities. Their culture was misunderstood or derided, and some public opinion questioned the Polish immigrants as suitable additions to the Canadian society. A variety of derogatory stereotypes were especially problematic for the younger people in the context of schools and peer-group interaction, posing questions of culture or ethnic identity and allegiance to one or another frame of reference. That is, in public situations youngsters attempted to escape stereotypes by "blending-in" and becoming "Canadians," while in family settings they were expected to retain part of the traditional heritage. Those who settled on farms occasionally established Polish "colonies" but more frequently settled among other European immigrants, especially the Ukrainians who shared similar values and traditions. For the rural settlers the period of transition was slower and less problematic and Polish family customs and values were maintained over time.

The next numerically smaller phase of migration from Poland to Canada took place between 1920 and 1939, and over 50,000 came in that period.[7] The socio-economic character and family values of those arrivals were similar to those of their predecessors of the second phase. By the 1920s most of the homesteading land was taken and the immigrants settled in towns and cities but often moved from one area to another in search of work in mines, steel mills, factories, forests, farm work, or general labour. The Great Depression, which began in 1929, affected these people severely. Permanent work was difficult or impossible to obtain and families remained separated for many years, with husbands and fathers in Canada, wives and children in Poland. Reunification was not possible for many years because of World War II and later political divisions in Europe.

The post-World War II phase began with the recruitment of over 4,000 Polish Army male personnel in Italy and Great Britain for a two-year contractual farm labour. In the years 1947-1952, Polish people in European refugee camps were recruited for industrial and service work on one-year contracts. Thousands of refugees and political exiles were admitted to Canada under special immigration laws. Between 1946 and 1956, over 63,000 Poles settled in Canada.[8] Unlike their predecessors, immigrants in this phase reflected the overall structure of pre-war Poland on occupational and educational criteria, and types of community of origin.

The most outstanding characteristic of this phase was the strong national or patriotic ethos, the result of individual's participation in the struggles for Poland's freedom, and the rejection of the Communist socio-political system imposed on Poland by the Soviet Union in 1944. These were people who would not have necessarily emigrated from Poland under normal conditions, but now preferred exile to life under an alien or undesirable system. Unlike the earlier Polish immigrants, the exiles and refugees strongly emphasized their cultural and traditional heritage in relationships with others, stressing the maintenance of cultural distinctiveness for younger generations raised or born in Canada. They possessed greater educational resources and organizational know-how to achieve their aims. At the same time they were hampered by various problems of adjustment to the new society and instability of family life.

Complete families were in a minority. War-time disruption scattered people across Europe and elsewhere, and many perished through war, disease, or starvation. Reunification of families was slow and for some has not yet been achieved. Among the complete Polish families coming to Canada at that time was a proportion of mixed marriages, where Polish military personnel or veterans selected non-Polish mates in the areas they found themselves in.[9] In time a more even sex-ratio balance was achieved in the arrival of single females from European refugee camps and directly from Poland after 1956.

Political changes in Poland in 1956 relaxed previously rigid laws on emigration. From that year on family reunification was possible, single females came to marry Poles in Canada, and whole families were occasionally allowed to emigrate. Since 1956, over 36,000 Polish immigrants arrived in Canada but in the last decade the numbers decreased to about 1,000 annually. This group represents a variety of occupations, levels of educations, and family ties. Today's Poland is a modern, industrialized society and these immigrants are less subject to "culture shock" but continue to face problems of language, work, and occupational qualifications.

In summary, Polish immigration to Canada took a form of phases characterized by a "chain movement." This was a pattern where emigration of larger groups from one community was rare. Rather, individual families and single people, including husbands, went ahead, to be joined later by wives, relatives, and neighbours. During all phases, Polish people experienced problems in reunifying their families in Canada. Husband-wife separation, often lasting many years, was common and the grandparents generally remained in Poland. There were only a few communities established by the Polish rural settlers and those in towns and cities never formed a Polish ghetto. There were rural and urban concentrations but they represented families and individuals from diverse parts of Poland, and as such, they were not transplanted Polish communities. These conditions strongly effected the preservation and maintenance of Polish family values, customs, and traditions in Canada.

BACKGROUND OF POLAND

With the exception of those who came after 1956, Polish immigrants to Canada shared a common background in family customs, traditions, and values. This "cultural baggage," brought over from Poland, continued to serve as a basis of family life for shorter or longer periods.

Until 1945, when the new Polish regime introduced family laws similar to those then present in the Soviet Union, assuring total equality in family and in society for both sexes, Polish society and family were basically rural and traditional, characterized by stable, patriarchal family relations.[10] A three-generation, bi-lateral family system was the typical norm and "the influence of grandparents on the conduct of family affairs was strong, even if the grandparents were not living with their married children."[11] Social class differences in family life were related to their economic bases. For a peasant or a farm worker, family life was dictated by the farm-work cycle and the criterion of land ownership.[12] For the small entrepreneur family, life revolved around his enterprise. The middle- and upper-classes saw family as a means of maintaining their socially high status and power. It has been noted that "traditional and past-oriented social relations were strongly evident among all social and economic groups,"[13] and common to all families were the dominant position of a patriarch, pervasive influence of religion and priests on family life, and strong bonds of affection or obligation between family members.[14] There was a basic harmony between mores and value orientation of the society and authority structure and other family customs, assuring continuity of such family models over generations. The ideal, shared by all, emphasized belongingness to a family group, common effort in obtaining family objectives, and mutual aid in time of need. In this, care of aging parents was among the highest family values.

Well into this century, selection of marriage partners was based on economic considerations or physical attributes for peasants, and on suitable socio-economic criteria for the middle- and upper-classes. Being in love was not a prerequisite for marriage, but parental choice or approval was crucial since without it, land and dowry or legitimation and thus social position could be denied. The desirable attributes in mate selection did not emphasize age or personal appearance but more pragmatic considerations, such as a wife who could do the washing two hours before giving birth and feed livestock two days later, and a husband who owned land, livestock, and farm implements.[15] Among the rural population and the working classes in cities, the wife was often regarded more as "the mother of children than as companion or a sex mate."[16] Spinsterhood was socially stigmatized, widows and widowers were expected to remarry. The peasant marriages were usually arranged, as were those of upper classes, according to customs and economic or social considerations. Wedding ceremonies were lavish affairs, lasting two or three days.

As a rule, Polish families were large. The Church admonished the couple to be fruitful and multiply, but community values also played their part. To sire many children was to demonstrate health, strength, virility, and ability to provide for large numbers.[17] Also, many hands were necessary, especially on land, to provide the required pool of labour, and a better potential for security and comfort for the old age. Women who could not have children were pitied and men were ridiculed. For as long as he maintained legal possession of property, the patriarch or the father was the head of the family in all social classes. This authority included final decision on the disposition of property, approval or selection of marriage partners, and selection of occupations for his sons. Among nobility and peasants this authority frequently bordered on despotism.[18] Obedience to the rules and parental expectations was emphasized for all children and physical punishment meted out for infractions. "The discipline exerted by the father was strict and harsh, especially among the peasant and worker families."[19] It was a common belief that parental strictness, especially as maintained by the father, would toughen the child and prepare it for the later struggles in life.

In relationships with his wife, the man regarded himself her superior, and through tradition and custom the wife was expected to acknowledge this position in public by deferring to his opinions and decisions. This was another societal standard which saw "a good family where the father was the head and conducted himself accordingly."[20] As in other societies, wife-dominated families existed, but as abberations, they were the subject of scorn, derision, or pity from the kin, friends, and community.

The sharp division of authority was accompanied by an equally strong and traditional division of family and household tasks in what was termed, in a different context, "men's work" and "women's work."[21] Family tasks and responsibilities were adhered to strictly among the peasants and working class families. In this scheme, it was seen as a severe loss of prestige and status for the male if his wife was to engage in paying work outside her home. Common belief was that the only proper place for the wife and mother was at home with the children.

In summary, well into the late 1950s, families in Poland were characterized by adherence to a clear division of authority in family relationships. Polish immigrants coming to Canada prior to 1956 also shared these norms and values but conditions and situations related to migration affected Polish families almost immediately in the new environment, and continued to undermine its traditional bases to the present. Stable, traditional patterns, values, and practices were not easy to maintain within the less formalized environment in Canada.

ADJUSTMENT

It has been generally acknowledged that in Canada pressures for total assimilation of the newcomers were never strong, but socio-economic and cultural standards, to which all immigrants were expected to adjust, existed at all times. A period of necessary adjustment can be problematic and prolonged for those coming from a society differing sharply from their hosts in lifestyles, values, and traditions.[22] It has been argued that "the family can play a major role in the capacity of its members either to integrate quickly or to persist in customs and mores alien to the society of the receiving country."[23] In the first case, rapid integration may require modifications or changes in patterns of family organization, values, and traditions, seldom an easy if at all possible task for people imbued with centuries-long sets of distinct values. On the other hand, maintenance of cultural distinctiveness will inevitably create problems for the generations raised or born in the new society, and exposed to the influences and values of this environment. This problematic situation has been documented among the earlier immigrants to the United States, where the consequences resulted frequently in family disorganization.[24] Similar problems faced the Polish family in Canada.

It is likely that the most significant factors in adjustment were related to the migratory structure, and patterns of settlement in Canada. The available information[25] tells us that, as a rule, complete families did not emigrate from Poland. A typical pattern, until 1939, was of single individuals undertaking this step, and of fathers who came ahead, joined by their families when sufficient money was saved for their passage.[26] The basic reason was economic in that there was not sufficient money to pay for the passage over for all family members at once.

TABLE 2
SEX RATIO, POLISH GROUP IN CANADA, MALES PER 100 FEMALES

Year	Polish Males	Canadian Average
1911	158	102
1921	125	101
1931	129	102
1941	116	102
1951	117	101
1961	112	101
1971	101	101

Source: R. K. Kogler, "A Demographic Profile of the Polish Community in Canada," in T. W. Krychowski, ed., Polish Canadians; Profile and Image, (Toronto: The Polish Alliance Press, 1969).

The separation often extended over years as these unskilled and uneducated or undereducated people were subject to seasonal layoffs, lowest remuneration, and lack of protection from sickness or injury.[27] Necessary savings for passage money was slow and such enforced separation inevitably weakened family bonds. In addition, it was rare that more than one or two individuals (or families) emigrated from the same village at the same time, thus retarding easy or quick re-establishment of traditional extended kin or community norms and relationships in Canada.

Even when a complete family emigrated, the financial costs of the passage precluded taking grandparents or other relatives along. In effect, when families were reunited or new ones were established, they were nuclear and isolated and this was characteristic among both rural and urban settlers. There were a few cases noted where Polish families were totally isolated from other Poles,[28] but on the other hand Polish immigrants rarely established rural colonies or communities and never formed an urban ghetto. In the prairie provinces, where most were directed until the 1930s, they were scattered among other groups and even where concentrations were present, these were seldom if ever composed of people from the same villages or communities in Poland.[29]

In effect, the shared norms and values, maintained by the close-knit communities in Poland, were absent for them in Canada. The pattern of settlement on homesteads—relative physical isolation of households as contrasted with the densely built-up village in Poland—detracted from establishing and maintaining cohesive family and community life. Praying, observing, and gossiping, important means of assuring adherence to the norms, customs, and traditions, were not possible under these circumstances. That is, the re-establishment of the physical and cultural boundaries was not possible for the vast majority of Polish immigrants. Also, families settling on homesteads did not have funds to purchase farm equipment or livestock, and fathers were forced to seek work wherever it was available to earn the necessary cash. This resulted in absences from their families which stretched over months, further weakening traditional family relations.[30] Despite these conditions, Polish family values and traditions changed slowly. While families were isolated and generally nuclear, there were few pressures for change, and other European settlers, sharing similar values and conditions, provided additional reinforcement to traditionalism. Under these conditions, Polish families resisted changes over time. Unlike the massive migration to the United States in the 1890-1914 period which led to the growth of large concentrations of Polish people in such cities as New York, Buffalo, Detroit, Chicago, and Milwaukee, to name a few, the movement to Canada was comparatively small. The immigrants settled or worked primarily on land, but a minority searched for earnings in cities and towns. Until 1930 they were directed by the immigration officials to the prairie provinces, but many drifted, in search of better and more remunerative working conditions, to other parts of Canada.

The urban pattern of settlement was somewhat different in that Polish families and single individuals tended to live in certain districts: Queen and Bathurst area in Toronto, St. Charles and Frontenac districts in Montreal, and the "North End" in Winnipeg, which was the largest urban Polish concentration until 1940, but even there they were always numerical minorities. It is illustrative that the greatest urban concentration of Polish people at present in Toronto's High Park-Parkdale districts, known as "Little Poland," represents just over 25% of Polish people in two census tracts.[31] These concentrations were not permanent. Polish males, characterized in the past by inadequate education and inappropriate skills or training, were subject to economic fluctuations and were frequently forced to move to another location or city in search of work or better conditions. "Poles were more mobile than the rest of the population."[32] The inability to establish roots contributed to the weakening of traditional patterns, retarding the establishment of communal and extended kin relations. Still, for as long as mother remained at home, she could maintain a role of a guardian of traditional family customs and values. This changed significantly during the period of the Great Depression (1929-1939), where Polish mothers could get some work while the fathers remained jobless for months or years.

Other conditions and situations forced adjustments and changes in the Polish family in Canada. These were: the influences exerted by the outside society on the generations born or raised in the new setting, weak or inadequate reinforcement of the traditional norms and values provided by Polish Canadian institutions and organizations, and the urbanization trends of the previously rural settlers.

Unlike their parents, the children of immigrants were quickly exposed to the influences of the host society, especially through public schools which aimed at making them "good Canadians,"[33] and peer group pressure advocating different norms and values. There were few direct demands for changes in Polish family norms and values, but there were strong expectations to adopt Canadian practices which were considered superior to all other. Combined with the necessity to escape perjorative stereotypes, young people were susceptible to change, learning to define their parents' customs and traditions as less comprehensible or meaningful or even strange, foreign, and undesirable. Maintenance of ethnic distinctiveness, including family customs and traditions, was, and continues to be, closely related to the willingness and the ability of the family to socialize its Canadian-born members into its cultural heritage. For the young children this takes place at home, but voluntary organizations and institutions need to be mobilized to aid in this process. Ethnic parishes and congregations provide the first such contexts, while ethnic schools are the most important agencies, designed to aid the family in inculcating a broader range of ethnic culture.[34] Later, youth organizations may contribute further to the processes begun at home.

There is evidence that Polish parents wished to socialize their Canadian-born children into the cultural heritage of their forefathers by stressing Polish language and traditions at home, and enrolling them in Polish youth organizations.[35] Yet, preoccupation with economic survival and geographical mobility were not conducive to such designs. The necessary reinforcing agencies—Polish schools and other institutions—had to be established and maintained, and even when this was achieved, lack of expertise, human and material resources were generally missing or were inadequate to meet parental expectations.[36] The pervasive and overriding influence of the outside society neutralized any such efforts as demonstrated by at least one indicator, Polish language maintenance. While in 1931, 81.4% of the total group had Polish as their mother tongue, the proportion fell to 76.8% in 1941, to 55.8% in 1951, decreased further to 50.0% in 1961, and only 38.4% of the total group gave Polish as their mother tongue in 1971.[37]

The figures above note that until 1931, Polish language (and other aspects of culture) were maintained by a majority of Polish families in Canada, but significant decreases were observed in the succeeding decades. The loss of Polish as mother tongue and other family changes corresponded to the increasing urbanization of the Polish group. According to the 1931 census, only 46.6% were urban dwellers, but urbanization was accelerated during the Great Depression when thousands of farm workers and farmers sought better economic conditions in towns and cities and, as a result, this proportion increased to 54.3% in 1941. The urbanization trend continued during World War II as Poles were attracted to regular jobs in war-time industries and post-war economic demands. The Polish urban segment represented 61.6% of the total Polish population in Canada in 1951, and this category rose to 69.6% in 1961. By 1971 just over 80.0% of all Polish people in Canada were urban residents, while only 8.8% remained on farms. It has been argued elsewhere[38] that the rural environment allowed the survival of customs and traditions over generations while city life quickly undermined them, forcing changes on Polish family. This process became accentuated from the 1930s to the present, as was suggested by a Toronto area study which will be discussed later.

OLD COUNTRY TRADITIONS IN THE NEW SETTING: PATRIARCHALISM

The new conditions and situations facing the Polish family in Canada challenged the authority and power of husbands and fathers, and in time traditional and patriarchal customs and practices were renegotiated, questioned, or abandoned. The initial separation of fathers and their frequent absences in search of work necessitated the wives to assume greater power in running their households, in decision-making, and in disciplining the children.

While the Polish ideal stressed that the mother should remain at home, increasingly greater numbers of them entered or were forced, as during the Great Depression, into the labour market. During this period many mothers were the sole family supporters,[39] and in this role were creating a need for a re-evaluation of the previously subordinate role to the father who remained unemployed. World War II put additional demands on women's participation in the labour market and Polish women also joined the war effort.[40] They continued to work for wages in the post-war years, and by 1971, 45.2% of all Polish females 15 years old or over were in the labour market.

TABLE 3
SELECTED OCCUPATIONS
POLISH FEMALE LABOUR FORCE, 1971

	Number	%
All Occupations	52 510	100.0
Managerial	750	1.4
Professional	1 230	2.3
Teaching and Related	2 585	4.9
Medicine and Health	3 555	6.8
Clerical and Related	14 905	28.4
Sales	4 010	7.6
Service Occupations	10 385	19.8
Agriculture	3 185	6.1
Manufacturing	4 890	9.3
Other and Not Stated	7 015	13.4

Source: Modified from H. Radecki, "Ethnic Organizational Dynamics," op. cit., 1975, Table 2.9, p. 81.

The subordinate status of the mother has changed as was found in the Toronto study.[41] Of the 60 Polish families studied in 1970, 72.2% of fathers shared all important decisions (purchase of a house or automobile, changing his job) with their wives and the remaining 27.8% involved the whole family in such decisions. Fathers are no longer solely responsible for deciding on their children's education. In 58.3% of cases both parents decided, while in 35.0% of instances the children were given the responsibility for this decision. In the remaining 6.7% of cases, the decision was reached through a mutual agreement between parents and children.

While the Toronto study suggests that father's authority and power in family relations has been redistributed, the relative hierarchy of visible or public status of the sexes remains to the present. Among both the immigrant population and to a lesser extent the Canadian-born generations, there are strong residues of traditional respect and gallantry shown to the females. Among the white collar and professional people, females are seen as gentle, fragile, helpless, and to be protected, and are shown deference or respect but are also incapable of taking charge or assuming responsibility and giving orders. This was clearly demonstrated in a study of Polish voluntary organizations which found no females heading larger units, but well represented as ordinary members or on "ladies' auxiliaries."[42] A similar situation was discovered among the Poles in Boston, Massachusetts, where "the outside representation of the family as well as the (Polish) community remains a male's prerogative. For example, when it comes to the election of community members to represent the group in public, men 'naturally' come first."[43]

It may be suggested that in the context of private family interaction, previously patriarchal husband-wife relations have been replaced by the prevailing urban Canadian more equalitarian norms. At the same time a significant proportion of male immigrants and their Canadian-born sons adhere to the "ideal" where the female's place is at home, dependent on and subordinate to her husband. In the Toronto study, the majority of male respondents rationalized their wives' working on such grounds as prevailing norms of society or a need for greater economic security, but not a desirable situation.[44] The residues of patriarchalism clearly remain in the public sphere, creating an ambiguous reality for Polish women even at present.

In relationship with his children, father's power and authority quickly became subject to the norms prevailing in rural and urban environments at any time. Obedience to parental authority among families living on farms survived longer as is suggested by the fact that some marriages were arranged by parents until 1920.[45] In the earlier period of settlement (1895-1914), the father maintained control through possession of land and finances, but the all-pervasive paternal dominance, exercised in Poland, was no longer possible in Canada, especially over boys. Economic opportunities were soon discovered and sons no longer needed to await their inheritance. Daughters remained under strong parental control and influence, but a degree of independence in selection of marriage mate, for example, was available to them as well. In time, obedience from children came to depend more on respect for, and influence exercised by the father, rather than on financial or economic considerations.

In towns and cities the Polish family was exposed more to the outside influences and differing models of decision-making, patterns of family interaction, and different lifestyles. In the case of urban settlers, the old blueprint for family relationships, characterized by strict obedience and harsh punishment for infractions of the rules, was rejected by the mother and children and the Canadian born or raised generations adopted the prevailing urban Canadian practices at their maturity.[46]

According to the available research, Polish adults continue to believe that children should respect and obey their parents, but admitted that this was not always shown them. In the Toronto study, 48.7% of parents stated that their children were disrespectful or rebellious and another 35.0% claimed that they did not have "a proper understanding" with their adolescent children.[47] Similar findings were noted in the Boston study with "too much independence, occasional arrogance, and lack of respect towards the parents on the part of the young, second- and third-generation American Poles."[48]

MATE SELECTION AND MARRIAGE

Until the last decade or two, young Polish people in Canada experienced problems with finding or selecting a Polish mate. During the period of settlement on homesteads (1895-1914), the factor of isolation meant that young people had little opportunity to meet. Parents solved the problem by a marriage arrangement, but unlike the carefully considered selection in Poland, the arrangement was "blind," that is, there were no considerations for previously important criteria of wealth, possessions, or capabilities.[49] This practice was no longer observed among the Polish people after World War I, but other problems remained.

For decades, the sex ratio was heavily in favour of males (see Table 2), and single men did not always have an opportunity to establish a family with a Polish mate. In addition, males from other ethnic groups were competing for the eligible Polish females, accentuating the uneven sex ratio further. It was noted[50] that as one solution, sweethearts or prospective brides were encouraged to come to Canada from Poland. Because of these drawbacks some never married, while a growing proportion sought wives from among other ethnic groups.

Since the 1920s, the previous strict control exercised by parents in selection of mates was replaced by influence or advice and love became an important criterion. The choice was no longer limited to Polish people since increasing members were marrying Ukrainians and other Slavs but "less than four percent of married Poles had wives of British origin."[51]

Since 1929, Polish single men were subject to chronic unemployment, and lack of funds precluded bringing over sweethearts or fiances from Poland. From 1939 to 1956, access to Poland or exits from Poland were closed by World War II and by the "Iron Curtain." This period corresponded to high rates of exogamous marriages. In 1941, 49.0% of Polish people married non-Poles.[52] The rates were slightly lower in 1951, and at that time 44.3% of Polish males and 43.3% of Polish females entered exogamous marriages. By 1961 there was another increase where 51.0% of males and 46.9% of females married non-Poles.[53] More recent information on the rates of exogamy for the Polish group is not yet available, but it is possible that the rates will decrease because of two factors: firstly, since 1956 Poland relaxed its previously rigid emigration laws and it is now possible for individuals to find a Polish mate through visits to Poland, through mail contacts and sponsorship for immigration to Canada, or through advertisements for a suitable mate in the Polish language press in Canada. Secondly, since 1971, sex ratio for the Polish group is nearly balanced, thus the pool of eligible female marriage partners is greater.

TABLE 4
POLISH GROUP BY MARITAL STATUS, 1971
WITH TOTAL CANADA PERCENTAGES FOR COMPARISON

	Number	%	Canadian Total %
Polish Single	140 625	44.4	49.4
Polish Married	156 790	49.5	45.2
Polish Widowed	15 215	4.8	4.5
Polish Divorced	3 795	1.2	0.9

Source: *1971 Census of Canada, Cat. 92-734, 1974.*

In general, a larger percentage of Polish people than the average are married, and this would suggest that they see marriage as a desirable status, retaining the traditional view that everyone should marry, or that no alternatives are possible or desirable. On closer examination of "Polish Married" by age groups,[54] it can be noted that, in fact, a somewhat smaller proportion of both males and females in the 20 to 24, and 25 to 34 age categories are married than the Canadian average (41.5% for the Polish and 44.0% for total Canada in the first category, and 80.0% for the Polish and 81.8% for total Canada in the second category.) A slightly higher percentage of Poles in the 45-54 age category are married than the Canadian average (86.0% and 85.8% respectively), but it is primarily the 65-years-or-over group that contrasts by a higher rate of "Married" status from the Canadian average (58.0% for the Polish and 53.1% for total Canada). Without the 65-and-over age category, a proportion of "Polish Married" would be somewhat lower than the Canadian average, suggesting that Polish young people are postponing marriage, or are opting out for alternatives such as living together or remaining single. The Census data note also that both males and females in the 20 to 34 age categories are marrying later in life than the Canadian average, and for the males, a significant proportion never marry.

POLISH WEDDINGS

A word should be said about Polish weddings. In the major family transitions (birth, christening, funeral), wedding was the most festive and elaborate ceremony. In rural areas the feast was often celebrated for two or three days (and nights) with plentiful food, refreshments, and dancing. Inevitably, the period of transition following migration curtailed some of these practices, although one source[55] refers to a very elaborate and lengthy Polish wedding in 1939, and another[56] noted specific Polish customs—the bride's veil being thrown to the bridesmaids, gifts in the form of cash for the young couple, elaborate and plentiful food and refreshments—all being maintained in Canada. Only a few specifically Polish wedding customs and traditions survive to the present, and the Polish couples conform generally to the urban, middle-class practices.

FAMILY SIZE

The number of children in Polish families in Canada were never as large as in Poland. A demographic analysis established that the "fertility rate of Polish women in Canada up to 1961 has consistently been lower than that of Canadian women in general."[57] This may be explained in part by the frequent absences of husbands in search of work, and the economic insecurity facing immigrants during their initial years in a new society. The Toronto study[58] found that while 63.2% of respondents came from families with five or more children, in Canada only 6.7% had 5 or more children. Of the total (N=60), 55.0% had only one or two children and did not plan to have further additions. In general, the number of children in the Polish group is below the Canadian average.

TABLE 5
AGE GROUPS

	Polish Group Totals		Canada Percentage
Under 15	76 475	24.2	29.6
15-44	133 335	42.1	43.7
45-64	77 965	24.6	18.7
Over 65	28 655	9.1	8.1

Source: 1971 Census of Canada, Cat. 92-734, 1974.

At present, the Polish group is "older" than the Canadian average, and this is accentuated by under-representation in the under 15 age category. The data suggest that in the next two decades the Polish group will experience a further shift in its age structure, becoming heavily over-represented in the over-65-years-of-age category, and under-represented in the 35-44 age group. The majority of the present aged population, and those in the 45-64 categories, are Polish-born.

Kinship Ties

There is little information to document the extent that family cohesion or familism were present among Polish immigrants in Canada. Immigrant memoirs and other sources[59] suggest that, once family structures and relationships were re-established and followed by a process of stabilization, strong family bonds re-emerged and were maintained in the new society. Interestingly, family ties with relatives left in Poland were also maintained. Prior to 1956, ties and contacts were maintained through very infrequent visits and by mail. More importantly, there is evidence that material aid—food and clothing parcels and money representing many millions of dollars—were dispatched to relatives in Poland, especially in the years following the two World Wars,[60] but continuing on a less intensive scale to the present. In fact, a number of trading companies have been established with the aim of facilitating dispatch of goods, medicine, and funds to relatives in Poland.[61] Since

1956, visits to Poland have become more frequent because of the relative economic well-being of the Polish group and the advent of charter flights. The Canadian Polish-language press notes that over 10,000 Polish Canadians visited Poland in 1974 and their numbers increase each year, commenting further that visits to Poland are made primarily by immigrants to their relatives, but there is a small proportion of Canadian-born visiting their kin as well.

Kinship ties in Canada involve primarily three generations of one family; that is, if a patriarch or a matriarch is alive, the children and grandchildren are expected to gather for family celebrations and other occasions. Two traditional-religious dates remain very important for Polish families—the Christmas Eve Supper, called *Wigilia*, and the Easter Day celebration. In the Toronto study,[62] it was found that 93.2% of the families celebrate these occasions and do so with the presence of some extended kin. These occasions reinforce extended family ties and obligations through exchange of gifts, reunite, if briefly, scattered members, and reintroduce Polish family customs and traditions. The extent of kinship ties and commitment to kin among Polish families in Canada has not been a subject of research but it is likely that close contacts, both expressive and instrumental, are maintained between parents and their married children involving affection, advice, companionship, and material aid.[63]

In the last decade another significant change is taking place, in that the Polish family no longer accepts full responsibility for looking after their aged parents. Polish family values emphasize as a matter of great importance, even of family honour, the care for its aged parents, but since the 1960s increasing numbers of the aged are persuaded, or are forced, as claimed by many oldsters, to enter senior citizens' homes. More significantly, by 1977 there were *Polish* senior citizens' homes in Vancouver, Edmonton, Winnipeg, and Montreal, and two are being built in Toronto. According to the Polish couples interviewed in the Toronto study,[64] the changing attitudes and values on the elderly remaining within a family are related primarily to the factors of working wives, and thus the inability to provide adequate care for the elderly. Other reasons given for placing the aged parents in senior citizens' or nursing homes were inadequate space, generation conflicts, especially a communication gap with the grandchildren, and better facilities in institutions. A relative broad awareness of the Polish group in Canada allows this writer to claim that the elderly members of the family continue to receive much respect from their children and grandchildren, and this resolution is not seen as desirable but justified under the circumstance.

The pattern of households among Poles in Canada was where the initial periods of settlement, in all phases, was characterized by two-generation households, since grandparents usually remained in Poland. In time, three-generation families became a norm with the birth of new generations in Canada, and the general custom of aged parents living with one of their children. It is probable that the newly emerging pattern is once again of two-generation or nuclear families or an "empty nest" household. As among the Canadian urban population, Polish young couples favour neo-local residence, aged parents are economically more secure and perhaps themselves favour independence in a separate household or even in a senior citizens' home.

STRATIFICATION

Until 1939, Polish immigration to Canada represented almost exclusively occupational categories of farmers, farm workers, and unskilled labourers.[65] Socio-economic mobility for the group was slow. Prior to 1939, the middle-classes consisted of the more prosperous farmers, petty entrepreneurs, clergy, and a small number of professional and white collar workers. Before 1930, over 50.0% of the male labour force were engaged in agriculture, while other major occupations represented primary industries, especially mining and logging, and labourers. Factors related to the low occupational status of Polish families was the initial lack of education, English language facilities, material resources, the low "entrance status,"[66] and the absence of appreciation for higher education as a means of higher occupational mobility, dictated perhaps by the necessity to assure economic security through earnings or labour of children. At the same time, formal education for rural families in Poland was not considered important and this attitude survived for a time among them in Canada.

The realization of the advantages offered through higher education followed the urbanization trend which began in the 1930s, and the demands made by the war-time Canadian industry. The Canadian-born generation became, in turn, more concerned with higher education as means of occupational mobility for their children. An additional factor was the arrival of about 700 Polish engineers and technicians in 1941, followed by the larger influx of exiles and refugees (1946-1956), representing a variety of occupations, trades, and skills. These new arrivals provided the missing middle class models for family relations, values, and aspirations.

In 1941, 37.4% of the Polish male labour force was employed in agriculture, 7.1% in primary industries, and 12.7% were labourers. At the same time, only 0.1% were in the professional, and 1.6% in clerical occupational categories. By 1971, the occupational structure of the Polish male labour force clearly reflected a significant upward mobility. In that year, only 9.1% were in agriculture, 2.5% in primary industries, and under 5.0% were labourers. At the same time, the proportion of the professional categories rose to 9.2% and that of clerical to 6.5%.[67]

The data clearly note that the Polish group experienced a significant socio-economic "upgrading" if occupations are accepted as a measure. Both numerically and proportionally all "low status" occupations have declined sharply over the past three decades, while there is a corresponding rise in the "high status"[68] occupations.

It is extremely difficult to elaborate on class differences among Polish families in Canada at present. It is most likely that differences reflect those of the Canadian society, that is, the Polish middle-class families adhere to the values, norms, and lifestyles observable among the middle-class families generally, and a similar comparison would also apply to the working or lower class families. Polish people have been in Canada for a number of generations, experiencing assimilation or acculturation to the dominant cultural models. At the same time a few observations can be made regarding visible distinctions between the Polish middle, and the lower or working class families in Canada.

On the whole, Polish middle class families are more concerned with maintaining cultural distinctiveness involving language, history, literature, and other aspects of Polish cultural heritage among their Canadian-born children than the lower or working class families. This is demonstrated in the enrollment in the Polish part-time schools and other youth organizations such as Polish Scouts in Canada, membership of which is heavily over-represented by the middle-class families. Also, the middle-class parents are more involved and active in emigre politics and are more concerned with the Polish government in exile in London, England, while maintaining a strongly opposed position to the "Soviet imposed government" in Poland.[69] Emigre politics are less important to the lower or working class families.

The lower or working classes tend to maintain a double standard of education for their children based on sex, that is, aspirations for a higher education for girls are not encouraged, or are even discouraged, while the middle class families encourage educational aspirations for both sexes.[70]

The Toronto study[71] found that the middle-class families attend church services less frequently than the lower or working class families, and the middle class tended to disregard the teachings of the church on such matters as artificial birth control or divorce more often than the lower or working class individuals.

Social class differences among Polish families in Canada do not seem to be sufficiently grounded for bases in face-to-face relationships in situations where they meet, primarily in the contexts of parishes and voluntary associations, and do not serve to promote severe status competition or conflict within the group at large. Rather, there are many similarities reflecting residues of Polish family traditions and values such as role and status division, concern for the aged parents, kinship ties, and emphasis on celebrating special occasions in the context of extended family.

FAMILY PROBLEMS

No reliable information is available to tell us if the Polish immigrant families experienced severe problems in intra-family relationships but, "there is little to suggest family disintegration, moral turpitude, juvenile delinquency, or prostitution" above the average Canadian rates.[72] It is more likely that the rates were lower, as suggested by a study which found that the rate of convictions for the Canadian-born individuals in the 1951-1954 period was 86.6% for 10,000 males in the 15-49 age categories, while the corresponding figure for the Polish-born was 42.7%.[73] A review study on recent transition in premarital sex relations found that "most conservative about premarital sex are: devout students, Catholics, those with French or Polish ancestry."[74] It may be suggested that once re-established, the Polish family in Canada was sufficiently strong and influential to imbue into its younger members desirable moral and societal values. Since the mid-1960s, the Polish family, as other families in Canada, are confronted with a host of alternative family values and different models of relationships. The youth became strongly influenced by mass media and peer group pressure, rebelling against or rejecting all vestiges of patriarchal values, customs, and patterns or relationships. It is most likely that this change affected the Polish family in Canada as well.

Only a slightly higher proportion of Polish spouses than the Canadian average are widowed, but no explanation or analysis can be offered on this difference at this time. On the other hand, the equally small but higher than the Canadian average proportion of "Polish divorced" is interesting, given the fact that 70.9% of the Polish group in Canada were Roman Catholics in 1971, and the Church maintains a clear prohibition of divorce. It is possible to offer two tentative hypotheses to explain the "Polish divorced." One is related to the post-war marriages, which were often undertaken hastily without a face-to-face courtship period.

It has been previously noted that single Polish males sought wives by visits to Poland, through mail, or advertising in the Polish-language press in Canada. While no figures are available, letters to the editors, newspaper articles or reports, and interviews conducted by this writer, all refer to cases of difficult adjustment to life in Canada for these Polish brides, and disappointments in appearance, age, and character for both mates. In addition, some husbands believed that their mates entered marriage as a pretext to leave Poland and to receive a landed immigrant status on marrying a Canadian citizen. The other hypothesis is related to the loss of influence of the Church on matters of divorce. In the Toronto study,[75] 60.9% of regular church goers considered divorce permissible under certain circumstances. It is likely that these two sets of factors can account for the "Polish divorced" category.

CHANGE AND CONTINUITY

Initially most Polish families experienced fragmentation through separation of family heads from their wives and children, isolation from the extended kin and from community. The re-established families in Canada were nuclear, but the cultural background carried over from Poland, modified and adapted to the new environment, continued for a time to have important structural and behavioural consequences. Especially during the period of transition and adjustment, family became a refuge from the strange world, drawing on each member for comfort and security, maintaining the only known orientations and values.

In general, extended family structures and relationships were re-established in time, but the authoritative, patriarchal norms and values could not survive for long under circumstances facing Polish families in Canada, especially in urban settings. It is generally true that the rural settlers experienced fewer pressures for change. Except for the influences exerted through public schools, there were few direct pressures for change and conformity to the "Canadian norm." While at times it was subject to sharp criticisms, cultural diversity was tolerated in the past and survives to the present as suggested by such groups as the Hutterites, the Mennonites, the Dutch, and many others.[76]

Polish rural families were also able to maintain some of their past traditional values and customs over generations, and these remain, albeit in a modified form, to the present. One community where these can be observed is Wilno, Ontario.[77] But this segment is a small minority within the total Polish group in Canada.

On the other hand, changes in family values, traditions, and practices were more rapid for those who settled in cities and towns. Where Polish organizations, associations, and institutions were established, the process was retarded but not reversed. Polish families were subject to influences and pressures from the market place, work environment, and mass media, and for the children, from public school and peer groups. The Canadian-born generations became quickly concerned with attaining full status in their new society, and if this demanded abandonment of "strange" customs or values it was done. Subsequent generations born in Canada further shed family values and traditions brought over from Poland by their forefathers. But the Canadian-born were not the only groups subject to change. The Toronto study[78] documents that the post-war Polish immigrants have largely abandoned the traditional patterns of authority within family relationships, and by 1970 were characterized by equalitarian family values and relationships, new orientations and attitudes towards economic achievements, status mobility, and higher education.

The Polish group in Canada contains several generations of Canadian-born who adopted the dominant society's family norms and values in their immediate environments. In fact, their claim to ethnic and cultural distinctiveness rests largely on their ethnic surnames and on a broad awareness of the place of origin of their forefathers. In general, they could not be distinguished in their views, values, family structures, and relationships from other Canadians.

In "transitory" generations, those born of immigrant parents, are aware of Polish family values and traditions still maintained by their parents, but as products of the new society they have two models to draw on, and the host society's values and customs are adopted as more desirable and suitable for family life in Canada. Partial information[79] suggests that they differ little from other urban Canadians in family planning, and on the number of children desirable. In fact, they are just as likely to postpone having children while both mates are working and saving for a specific goal as are other Canadians. In relationships with their kin, close contacts and ties are maintained with their parents, but there is a changed attitude towards having their elderly parents live with them. In effect, the Canadian-born Polish families do not now represent a distinct ethnic type outside of maintaining a few traditional customs and practices.

The immigrant Polish families, while continuing to adhere to some patriarchal values and traditions, are experiencing change through acculturation to the new environment, its norms and expectations. Among the most affected is the unequal husband-wife status and power hierarchy. The necessity, or preference of the wife to work for gain, the absence of customs reinforcing kin and community, and the practices prevailing in Canada led to renegotiation of power in family context. Here, the relationships between parents, and parents and children, are based more on the equalitarian model where decision making is no longer the exclusive prerogative of the father. At the same time, inequality of the sexes retains its traditional expression in the public sphere, in situations where other Polish people are present, and this is not likely to change, despite the appeal of the feminist movement and differing norms of the outside society. The fact is that, by and large, Polish women agree with and approve of such "public" inequality.

Polish immigrant parents tend to retain, as an ideal, the traditional expectations of children's obedience and respect and care for the aged in the family setting. They are connected with and maintain various contacts with extended kin in Poland and in Canada. Strong emphasis is given to celebration of family and religious-cultural anniversaries with their children and other relatives. In summary, immigrant families maintain some traditional values and customs but, at the same time, they are adapting to the new society, a process where traditionalism is shed, displaced, or rejected.

A more detailed discussion and analysis of Polish family in Canada is not possible without further research, but it may be concluded that the whole represents a broad variety of family types, structures, relationships, and corresponding lifestyles. With the exception of the most recent immigrants from Poland and a small proportion of rural residents, the Polish family in Canada is fast becoming indistinguishable from the urban Canadian model. Polish family experienced initial fragmentation, separation, and isolation from the extended kin, faced problems of adjustment to the new society, new demands, and new expectations. There does not seem to be any evidence of large-scale family dissolution related to the process of adjustment, and all indicators suggest that Polish family has coped successfully with new situations, conditions, and demands. Polish family serves as an example of the resilience of this societal organization not only for the Polish group, but for other immigrant families as well.

NOTES

1. Reliable and consistent data on family life of the Polish group in Canada is almost non-existent. To the best knowledge of this writer, the total consists of a chapter in the history of Poles in Canada; Henry Radecki with Benedykt Heydenkorn, *A Member of a Distinguished Family; the Polish Group in Canada* (Toronto: McClelland and Stewart, 1976); one well-researched novel, Melchior Wankowicz, *Three Generations* (transl. by Krystyna Cekalska), (Toronto: Canadian Polish Research Institute, 1973); immigrant memoirs which provide many personal insights, *Pamietniki Emigrantow: KANADA* (Warsaw: Ksiazka i Wiedza, 1971); selected demographic data, R. K. Kogler, "A Demographic Profile of the Polish Community in Canada," in T. W. Krychowski, ed., *Polish Canadians: Profile and Image* (Toronto: The Polish Alliance Press, 1969); a field study of one Toronto area, Henry Radecki, "Polish-Canadian, Canadian-Polish, or Canadian?" (Toronto: York University, Mimeograph, 1970); and a few sketchy references found in the earlier Canadian writings, such as the account of a Polish wedding in James S. Woodsworth, *My Neighbour* (Toronto: The Missionary Society of the Methodist Church, 1911). The following overview draws on the available sources but relies heavily on this writer's familiarity with Polish family in Canada derived from interviews and personal knowledge.
2. H. Radecki with B. Heydenkorn, *op. cit.*, 1976. Discuss the phases and immigrant's characteristics in some detail.
3. S. K. Gleborzecki, "Kanadyjskie Wilno," *Zwiazkowiec*, Toronto, Nos. 23, 25, 27, 1957. Brenda B. Lee-Whiting, "First Polish Settlement in Canada," *Canadian Geographical Journal*, LXXV (1976), 108-112; J. L. Perkowski, "Folkways of the Canadian Kashubs," in Cornelius J. Jaenen, *Slavs in Canada*, Vol. III (Toronto: Ukrainian Echo Pub., 1971).
4. Report of the Royal Commission on Bilingualism and Biculturalism, *The Cultural Contribution of the Other Ethnic Groups*, Book IV (Ottawa: Queen's Printer, 1970), Table A-1, pp. 230-245.
5. H. Radecki with B. Heydenkorn, *op. cit.*, 1976. See also W. Turek, *Poles in Manitoba* (Toronto: The Polish Alliance Press, 1967).
6. Rev. W. Bridgeman, *Breaking Prairie Sod* (Toronto: Musson, 1920), and James S. Woodsworth, *Strangers Within Our Gates*, N. P. Frederick Clarke Stephenson, 1909.
7. Report of the Royal Commission, *op. cit.*, 1970.
8. *Ibid.*
9. H. Radecki, "Cultural Mosaic: A Micro View," in B. Heydenkorn, ed., *Topics on Poles in Canada* (Toronto: Canadian Polish Research Institute, 1976), pp. 127-140.
10. For historical background on Polish family see C. R. Barnett, *Poland*, HRAF Press, 1958; Jadwiga Komorowska, ed., *Przemiany Rodziny Polskiej* (Warsaw: Instytut Wydawniczy CRZZ, 1975); Jan Szczepanski, *Polish Society* (New York: Random House, 1970). On more recent changes see Franciszek Adamski, *Modele Malzenstwa: Rodziny a Kultura Masowa* (Warsaw: Panstwowe Wydawnictwo Naukowe, 1970) and A. Dudzik-Litynska, D. Markowska *Wspolczesna Rodzina w Polsce* (Warsaw: Ksiazka i Wiedza, 1975).
11. J. Szczepanski, *op. cit.*, 1970, p. 182.

12. Wladyslaw S. Reymont, *Chlopi*, 4 Vols. (Warsaw: Panstwowy Instytut Wydawniczy, 1970).

13. Zygmunt Bauman, "Economic Growth, Social Structure, Elite Formation: The Case of Poland," *International Social Science Journal*, 16 (1964), pp. 203-216.

14. C. R. Barnett, *op. cit.*, 1958.

15. M. Wankowicz, *op. cit.*, 1973, p. 279.

16. C. R. Barnett, *op. cit.*, 1958, p. 348.

17. For similar attitudes towards procreation, see Oscar Lewis, *Five Families* (New York: Basic Books, 1959).

18. Wincenty Witos, *Jedna Wies* (Chicago: Polskie Stronnictwo Ludowe, 1955).

19. C. R. Barnett, *op. cit.*, 1958, p. 348.

20. H. Radecki with B. Heydenkorn, *op. cit.*, 1976, p. 127.

21. K. Ishwaran, *Family Life in the Netherlands*, The Hague, Uitgeverij van Keulen N. V.

22. This subject received some attention in the United States. See, for example, Charles H. Mendel and Robert W. Habenstein, eds., *Ethnic Families in America: Patterns and Variations* (New York: Elsevier, 1976). In Canada ethnic families are the subject of K. Ishwaran, ed., *The Canadian Family* (Toronto: Holt, Rinehart and Winston, 1976), and S. Parvez Wakil, *Marriage, Family and Society: Canadian Perspectives* (Toronto: Butterworth, 1975).

23. W. O. Borrie, *The Cultural Integration of Immigrants*, Unesco, 1959, p. 293.

24. W. I. Thomas and F. Znaniecki, *The Polish Peasant in Europe and America*, 2 Vols. (New York: Dover, 1958).

25. Jozef Okolowicz, *Kanada: Garstka Windomosci dla Wychodzcow* (Krakow: Polskie Towarzystwo Emigracyjne, 1913); W. Turek, *Poles in Manitoba, op. cit.*, 1967; and Helena Znaniecki Lopata, "The Polish American Family," in C. H. Mendel and R. W. Habenstein, *op. cit.*, 1976, pp. 15-40.

26. This is not unique for Polish families, as was documented in the case of Portuguese immigrants to Canada. Grace M. Anderson, *Networks of Contact: The Portuguese and Toronto* (Waterloo: Wilfrid Laurier University, 1974).

27. *Pamietniki, op. cit.*, 1971.

28. Jozef Lubicz, *Kanada—Kraj i Ludnosc* (Toledo, Ohio: A. A. Paryski, 1929).

29. W. Turek, *op. cit.*, 1967.

30. *Pamietniki, op. cit.*, 1971, and M. Wankowicz, *op. cit.*, 1973.

31. These are tracts Nos. 48 and 52. H. Radecki, "Ethnic Organizational Dynamics: A Study of the Polish Group in Canada," unpublished Ph.D. Thesis, York University, 1975.

32. R. K. Kogler, *op. cit.*, 1969, p. 16.

33. J. T. M. Anderson, *The Education of the New Canadians* (Toronto: J. M. Dent and Sons, 1918) and Robert England, *The Central European Immigrant in Canada* (Toronto: Macmillan, 1929).

34. Report of the Royal Commission, *op. cit.*, 1970, p. 106.

35. *Ksiega Pamiatkowa Zwiazku Polakow w Kanadzie, 1906-1946* (Toronto: Polish Alliance Press, 1946).

36. Problems facing Polish part-time schools are discussed in H. Radecki, "How Relevant Are the Polish Part-Time Schools?" in B. Heydenkorn, ed., *Past and Present* (Toronto: Canadian Polish Research Institute, 1974), pp. 61-72.

37. H. Radecki with B. Heydenkorn, *op. cit.*, 1976.

38. *Ibid.*

39. *Pamietniki, op. cit.*, 1971.

40. Ksiega Pamiatkowa, *op. cit.*, 1946.

41. H. Radecki, "Polish-Canadian," *op. cit.*, 1970.

42. H. Radecki, "Ethnic Organizational Dynamics," *op. cit.* 1975.

43. Ewa Teresa Morawska, "The Maintenance of Ethnicity: Case Study of the Polish-American Community in Greater Boston," Ph.D. thesis, Boston University, 1976, p. 141.
44. H. Radecki, Interview data, 1970.
45. Howard Palmer, *Land of the Second Chance: A History of Ethnic Groups in Southern Alberta* (Lethbridge: The Lethbridge Herald, 1972), p. 246.
46. H. Radecki, Interview data with six individuals 65 years old or over, Toronto, 1974.
47. H. Radecki, "Polish-Canadian," *op. cit.*, 1970.
48. E. T. Morawska, *op. cit.*, 1976, p. 137.
49. M. Wankowicz, *op. cit.*, 1973, illustrates one such example.
50. Pamietniki, *op. cit.*, 1971.
51. W. Burton Hurd, "The Case for a Quota," *Queen's Quarterly*, XXXVI, 1929, pp. 145-159.
52. Report of the Royal Commission, *op. cit.*, 1970, Table A-75, p. 300.
53. *Ibid*, Tables A-61, A-62, p. 291.
54. This information is available in the 1971 Census of Canada, Cat. 92-734, 1974.
55. M. Wankowicz, *op. cit.*, 1973.
56. J. S. Woodsworth, *My Neighbour*, *op. cit.*, 1911, pp. 139-144.
57. R. K. Kogler, *op. cit.*, 1969, p. 28.
58. H. Radecki, "Polish-Canadian," *op. cit.*, 1970.
59. Pamietniki, *op. cit.*, 1971; M .Wankowicz, *op. cit.*, 1973.
60. B. Heydenkorn, "Polonia Kanadyjska," *Kultura*, 144, 1959, pp. 85-107, and Ksiega Pamiatkowa, *op. cit.*, 1946.
61. Branches of PEKAO.
62. H. Radecki, "Polish-Canadian," *op. cit.*, 1970.
63. Interview data with 21 Polish Community Leaders in Toronto. H. Radecki, "Leaders and Influentials: Polish Ethnic Group in Toronto," in B. Heydenkorn, ed., *From Prairies to Cities* (Toronto: Canadian Polish Research Institute, 1975), pp. 43-59.
64. H. Radecki, "Polish-Canadian," *op. cit.*, 1970.
65. H. Radecki with B. Heydenkorn, *op. cit.*, 1976, p. 169.
66. Concepts provided by J. Porter, *The Vertical Mosaic* (Toronto: University of Toronto Press, 1965).
67. Data for 1941, modified from H. Radecki with B. Heydenkorn, *op. cit.*, 1976, Table 13, p. 179, and for 1971, modified from H. Radecki, "Ethnic Organizational Dynamics," *op. cit.*, 1975, Table 2.9, p. 81.
68. Bernard R. Blishen and Hugh A. McRoberts, "A Revised Socioeconomic Index for Occupations in Canada," *The Canadian Review of Sociology and Anthropology* 13:1 (1976) 71-79.
69. H. Radecki, "Ethnic Organizational Dynamics," *op. cit.*, 1975.
70. E. T. Morawska, *op. cit.*, 1976, p. 138.
71. H. Radecki, "Polish-Canadian," *op. cit.*, 1970.
72. H. Radecki with B. Heydenkorn, *op. cit.*, 1976.
73. P. J. Giffen, "Rates of Crime and Delinquency," in W. T. McGrath, ed., *Crime and Its Treatment in Canada* (Toronto: Macmillan, 1965).
74. D. Perleman, quoted in *Chatelaine*, June 1973.
75. H. Radecki, "Polish-Canadians," *op. cit.*, 1970.
76. K. Ishwaran, *op. cit.*, 1976; K. Ishwaran, *Family Kinship Community* (Toronto: McGraw-Hill, 1977; M. Davis and J. F. Krauter, *The Other Canadians* (Toronto: Methuen, 1971).
77. J. L. Perkowski, *op. cit.*
78. H. Radecki, "Polish-Canadian," *op. cit.*, 1970.
79. H. Radecki, interview data, 1974.

4. Acculturation Versus Familism in Three Generations of Japanese Canadians

MINAKO K. MAYKOVICH

This paper compares the extent of acculturation and familism among the three generations of Japanese Canadians. The paper begins with an historical background, followed by the results of empirical research on Japanese Canadians in Toronto.

The words Issei, Nisei, and Sansei are unique expressions used to describe generations of Japanese immigrants to Canada. They are unique because each generation is age-distinct and has developed its own subculture. The bulk of the Japanese immigration took place between 1890 and 1920. It succeeded the prohibition of the Chinese immigration and lasted until various restrictions were placed on Japanese immigration (Maykovich: 1975).

In the Japanese language, the word "Issei" literally means "first generation," but in practice refers to immigrants from Japan. During the early period of 1890 through 1910, the migration consisted primarily of adult males. It was not until the Gentlemen's Agreement of 1907, when restrictions were placed on male immigration, that female immigrants as picture brides increased (Young: 1938). Immigrants from Japan numbered 4738 at the time of the census of 1901 and settled in British Columbia. Before World War II, there was little geographical movement by the 95% concentrated in British Columbia by the 1941 census (Yearbook: 1970-1971). The Issei by now had reached the old ages of 80 to 100 years, consisting of 1.6% of the total Japanese population in Canada according to the 1971 census (Census: 1971, 1.4-3, Table 4).

The children of the Issei, called Nisei, were generally born between 1910 and 1945. They attended Canadian schools and are currently in their middle age. The children of the Nisei are called Sansei, and are found in the school-age population.

After World War II, the Japanese moved toward the East and by now British Columbia had only 36% of Canada's Japanese (Census: 1961, 1.2-5, Table 35). Others were located in Ontario (41%), Alberta (13%), Quebec (5%), and Manitoba (4%). The heaviest concentrations were seen in two cities, Toronto (15%) and Vancouver (11%).

By 1971 there were 37,260 persons of Japanese descent in Canada, which amounts to 2.1% of the total Canadian population. Forty-two per cent of them report Japanese as their mother tongue against 55% for English. However, the language most frequently spoken at home is English in 74% of the cases and Japanese in 25% (Census: 1971, 1.4-8, Table 21). Approximately half the Japanese descendents believe in Christianity, while 32% believe in other religions (likely to be Buddhism), and 17% in no religion (Census: 1971, 1.4-7, Table 18). The profile of marital status among the Japanese is quite similar to that of the total Canadian population. Forty-eight per cent are single, 47% are married, 4% are widowed, and .6% divorced (Census: 1971, 1.4-6, Table 14).

Thus, the overall picture of the Japanese in Canada is that of a well-acculturated group. Yet the Japanese as a group are far from homogeneous. Many internal differences are found among Issei, Nisei, and Sansei. Because of the chronological distance from Japan and the age factor, each generation has developed and maintained its own unique sub-cultures, which are neither Japanese nor Canadian in the strict sense. This paper compares the extent to which each generation retains the traditional Japanese cultural heritage, particularly the family ideals.

1. TRADITIONAL FAMILY VALUES

Through their parents and grandparents, the Issei had experienced direct contact in their childhood with the feudal culture of the Tokugawa era (1603-1867). The long duration of the Tokugawa era allowed a very firm consolidation of cultural patterns. The Meiji era (1868-1911) that followed it saw many great changes, but in many ways allowed the continuation of the old social order. It is in Tokugawa culture that we find the sources for the identities of the Issei (Bellah: 1957; Moore: 1967; Tsunoda: 1958).

In order to consolidate their power, the Tokugawa Shogunate made use of the deeply ingrained ethical and religious systems of Confucianism (Yutang: 1938) and Buddhism (Jacobson: 1965). Both Confucianism and Buddhism stressed the importance of collectivity, such as the family and the nation above the individuals. The state was perceived as an extension of the family. Each individual was assigned a definite position in a hierarchical scale which bound him to others in a network of moral duties and rules for proper conduct. The individual had to be sure not to bring shame to the family (Kawashima: 1968; Tamaki: 1953; Nakane: 1970).

The individual's relations with superiors, such as diety, rulers, and parents as benevolent super-ordinates were governed by the theory on on. The superior being in some form dispensed blessing (on) and it was the obligation of the recipient to repay these blessings. The blessings the individual received were so much greater than his ability to repay them that he could only return an infinitesimal amount. This was the basis for the concept of filial piety. Children were indebted to their parents for the simple fact that the latter gave birth to the former and took care of them while they were young. For these blessings (on), children were expected to sacrifice their own needs and conveniences in order to give utmost comforts to their parents.

Confucianism rationalized hierarchical relations between the ruler and the ruled—the patriarch and his family members because of the assumed superior attributes possessed by the former. The authority of the father as household head was enormous, and absolute obedience of children was expected. Children were taught never to question the wisdom of their parents. The hierarchical structure of the traditional family placed the conjugal relation secondary to the parent-child relationship. The primary responsibility and loyalty of a married son was to his parents rather than to his wife.

Although suppressed by the power of collectivities such as family and nation, the individual was also encouraged to work hard and achieve success for his family and his nation. Self-cultivation was interpreted as a means of repaying the blessings the individual had received from his family and his nation (Maykovich: 1972a).

Unification of Japanese society during the Tokugawa and the Meiji eras cultivated strong nationalism. The Japanese were proud of their race and culture and enjoyed a sense of superiority over others. Thus, before crossing the Pacific, the Issei were equipped with values such as familism, social conformity, achievement orientation, and above all, pride in their cultural heritage.

2. THE DEVELOPMENT OF GENERATION CULTURES

A. Issei

Upon arrival in Canada, Japanese immigrants inherited the Chinese legacy as the yellow peril. The Issei were classified as non-assimilable aliens with a different cultural heritage and with inferior and subservient characteristics. They were prejudiced and were discriminated against legally, economically, and socially (Maykovich: 1975; Wynne: 1963; Andracki: 1958; Davis: 1971).

The pride in their cultural heritage and perseverance sustained this generation and developed a unique Issei culture. The Issei culture was based on their strategy of accommodation to given situations (Kitano: 1969). The Issei did not protest against discriminatory treatment but tried to rise above outrage and to take a positive stand in the face of adversity. This special ability has been explained in terms of Japanese cultural values: self-control, familism, and conformity to social order. These cultural values were implemented by social control exercised by the Issei themselves. Anyone who did not live up to the standards set by the cultural values was made to feel that he had disgraced the whole Japanese Canadian community, as well as Japan as a nation.

Insulated from the economic, political, and social institutions of white society, the Issei developed various multi-functional organizations of their own in their segregated community (Young: 1938; Miyamoto: 1939; Wangenheim: 1956). Particularly important was the economic mutual aid system which pooled resources to help small businesses get started. Many Issei entered into small businesses such as grocery stores, laundry shops, etc., catering mostly to the Japanese. As such, they were identified as members of the Issei community to which they were not to bring shame. In such a community it was possible to retain many aspects of the Japanese lifestyles. Most Issei did not learn English beyond the minimum necessary.

Given the insularity, the low acculturation of the Issei, and their original intention of returning to Japan, the Issei tried to inculcate in their offspring, the Nisei, essentially the same values the Issei had learned in Japan, especially the continued importance of the family ideal. The Nisei children were sent to Japanese language schools, which frequently incorporated within the curriculum the stern moral lessons or ethics courses of the Japanese educational systems. Some Nisei children were sent to Japan to obtain Japanese high school and college educations.

Prejudice and discrimination culminated to the internment of the Japanese in relocation centres during World War II (LaViolette: 1948). The Issei were uprooted from the ghetto-like Japanese-Canadian communities and were sent to desert camps. This experience shattered the Issei culture symbolically and institutionally.

Their pride and loyalty to Japan became the target of attacks. Most cultural activities of the Issei were dissolved because they were construed as symbolic affiliation with Japan and were suspected of being a conspiracy against Canada.

Another force which contributed to the weakening of the Issei culture was the rise of the Nisei during camp life. Parental authority over Nisei children was undermined through the semi-communal lifestyle of the camp. For instance, prior to camp life, the family dinner served as a time and place of socialization in which parents inculcated traditional values in their children. In the camp mess hall, however, seating arrangements by age group rather than by family group developed, wherein children occupied tables away from parents and their supervision. Also, the Nisei youth were gaining power since they, as Canadian citizens, were given more responsible positions in the camp than were their parents, who were at that time denied Canadian citizenship because of their birth in Japan. It was during the camp experience that the Nisei began to be emancipated from parental influence.

By the time the Issei returned from the camps, pre-war Issei communities and institutions had disappeared. Instead, the Nisei who were reaching adulthood began to take the lead in developing a new Japanese Canadian culture, the Nisei culture.

After the war, the Issei had recovered some of the institutions and activities of pre-war time, but they no longer functioned as survival resources for the Issei. Rather, they served as a psychological linkage among Issei senior citizens who liked to reminisce about the old days.

B. Nisei

The Nisei culture was a product of power relations as well as the mixture of two cultures. Being Japanese descendents and possessing Japanese attributes placed the Nisei at a disadvantage. Consciously or unconsciously, the Nisei developed a self-hatred. They did not want to identify themselves with the Issei culture, which appeared to them as the source of their powerless minority status. They wanted to be accepted as Canadians but were excluded from white society. Being squeezed out of the two groups, the Nisei developed their own subgroup and sub-culture.

During the pre-war days the Nisei group acted as a buffer for Nisei school children being bullied by other children. Because they looked different and because their parents did not speak English, Nisei children were ridiculed while in grade school. In their high school days they were alienated from white peers, being considered unsuitable for dating and courtship by the whites.

The Nisei culture also helped to define the role ascribed to the Nisei, which was ill-defined in terms of their expectations of society. At school they were taught to believe in the Canadian doctrine of equality and freedom of opportunity. Yet in reality, the colour of their skin counted more than their abilities. At the time of World War II, their citizenship did not save the Nisei from being sent to the relocation centres. The problems the Nisei suffered were not well understood by the Issei parents whose identification was with Japan. Only the Nisei culture could interpret the marginal role for the Nisei and provide their reaction patterns against other groups.

Precisely because of their marginal status, the Nisei group was threatened by various forces. If the individual Nisei became too involved in personal friendship cliques, their collectivity identity would be lost. Should individuals move into the world of the non-Japanese, the Nisei identity again would lose its force. Accordingly, the Nisei had to be watchful of their own behaviour as well as of the behaviours of others, lest someone leave the Nisei group or become too egocentric and forget about the group identity (Lyman: 1971).

Another characteristic of the Nisei culture was their compulsive work ethic. One way that Nisei resisted the marginal role was to prove to the world that they were worthier than the role given them. Their motto became "Work hard and make yourself such a fine citizen of Canada that you will be respected everywhere." They knew that the key to success was education. The median school years completed was higher for the Asiatics (Japanese and Chinese combined) than for the whites in 1950. By 1960 the percentage of Asiatics occupying professional or technical positions was greater than that of the whites. By 1970 the Nisei occupied as high, if not higher, status in education, occupation, and income, than did the dominant whites in Canada (Maykovich: 1975).

From the findings of occupational mobility, one writer (Varon: 1967) has concluded that the Japanese Canadians no longer constitute a minority, since, by Louis Wirth's (1945) definition, minority status carries with it the exclusion from full participation in the life of the society.

Various studies of acculturation of Japanese have indicated that they have been broadly integrated into the larger society. However, there remains a subtle difference. Until the mid-1960s, mass media, school textbooks, and public opinion paid little attention to Japanese Canadians. When they did, they patronizingly depicted the Japanese as submissive and somewhat different (Maykovich: 1972b). Also, some Nisei have not yet broken away from the psychology of marginality—they seek recognition and acceptance by whites.

C. Sansei

It was in this milieu that the Sansei began to question the Nisei attitudes concerning racial issues. Around 1965, starting in California, the efforts and achievements of the Nisei began to be openly challenged by the Sansei. Sansei called Nisei "banana"—white inside and yellow outside—to criticize the Nisei's overconformity to white values, despite their obvious inability to change the colour of their skin. In defiance of the banana image, some Sansei began to seek a new identity through the Yellow Power movement. They no longer seek for white acceptance but find pride in belonging to the yellow race. This movement was active in California where (1) anti-Oriental sentiment culminated in the war-time internment; (2) Japanese are still heavily concentrated; and (3) many other civil rights movements originated.

Several factors may be behind this rising activism. First, there is more awareness of prejudice and discrimination against the Japanese. The traditionally held idea that Japanese are well accepted has been highly and accurately criticized. Second, the recent black and Chicano movements have had a great impact on their situation. In the 1960s blacks changed their tactics from peaceful integrationist to violent separatism. Their black power movement instigated many Sansei activists. Third, there is a generation gap. The Sansei cannot accept parental values of conformity and passivity and are looking for new values and identity. Finally, the rise of activism owes much to the relative material affluence in which the Sansei live. Unlike Issei and Nisei, Sansei now have more free time to examine critically their social environment without worrying as much about their daily bread (Maykovich: 1972a).

Unlike Issei and Nisei, however, the Sansei have become heterogeneous as a group. Not every Sansei is a member of a Yellow Power movement. In fact, four types of Sansei culture were identified in California during the emergence of activism: the conformists, the anomic, the liberated, and the militants (Maykovich: 1972a).

The conformists, who were the majority, accepted traditions of diligence and social conformity and were not involved in social issues. They came predominantly from upper middle class families with conservative parents. The anomic rejected traditional values, but were not ready to take action in changing the present society. Their working-class fathers were reported to feel powerless, to be conservative, and to be authoritarian to their children.

Both the liberated and the militants were political activists. While the former wanted to bring about social change within the existing social structure, the latter preferred a revolutionary change by rejecting the traditional values. As shown later in the Toronto study, the Canadian Sansei tend to be more conservative. They are likely to fall into the conformist category, if we use the above classification.

As Gordon (1964) stated, acculturation or assimilation is a blanket term encompassing various dimensions and directions. The process of acculturation is not necessarily unilinear in that the adoption of new culture is accompanied by the abandonment of old culture. On the level of adoption of the Canadian lifestyle, the Japanese Canadians have progressed linearly from Issei to Nisei to Sansei. While the Issei insulated themselves in Japanese communities, the Nisei moved into the white middle-class neighbourhoods. The Sansei are participants of various non-Japanese activities formally and informally.

On the level of retention of the Japanese cultural heritage, however, the pendant seems to have swung between generations from one extreme to another. The Issei, as proud Japanese, cherished the traditional Japanese culture and tried to transmit it to the Nisei. The Nisei, born and raised among whites, were anxious to merge into white society. The Nisei were plagued with ambivalence between love and hatred of their Japanese heritage, which hindered their assimilation into Canadian society. Sansei, particularly the activists, began to seek for new identity as the Japanese descendents. They respect the Issei for maintaining the Japanese spirit, while condemning the Nisei for losing their Japanese identity.

The relationship between the adoption of a new culture and the retention of an old culture is a complex one. Some scholars have proposed (Caudill and De Vos: 1956) a value compatibility hypothesis that Japanese acculturation was due to the fact that their original values of achievement orientation was compatible with those of white middle class. It is true that the Nisei have achieved considerably more educational and occupational mobility than the Issei, presumably because they had very high achievement orientations. However, some Canadian middle class values, particularly those concerning kinship relations, such as the inclinations toward a nuclear family and romantic love, differ radically from traditional Japanese practice and norms.

Many previous studies indicate the retention of certain characteristics of the traditional Japanese family values among the Japanese, despite their adoption of American or Canadian cultural values. For instance, otherwise acculturated Japanese still indicate linear kinship relations (Kurokawa: 1968), collectivity orientations (Connor: 1974), and emotional interdependence (Osako: 1976), rather than individualistic nuclear family relations.

The following section presents the findings of a survey in order to elucidate the extent to which traditional Japanese values of familism are retained in each generation.

3. ACCULTURATION VERSUS FAMILISM: RESEARCH FINDINGS

Familism is defined as the value orientation in which the welfare of the family is considered more important than that of the individual. Typically, familism is characterized by a family collectivity orientation, age-stratified relations, and endogamy.

The samples of this study, conducted in 1974, consist of Japanese Canadians in Toronto (48 Issei, 100 Nisei, 102 Sansei) and 103 Caucasians who are approximately of the same age and education levels as the Sansei.

The Japanese Canadians were selected randomly and separately from the Directories of Japanese Canadians compiled by Japanese Canadian newspapers. The response rate was 42%. The caucasians were chosen by the quota sample, matching sex, age, and education with those of the Sansei sample.

The questionnaire was developed to measure the extent of (1) acculturation on the behavioural and psychological levels, and (2) traditional Japanese familism. For the sake of comparability and reliability, some items were adopted from previous studies in this field, such as the Ethnic Identity Questionnaire (Matsumoto et al.: 1970) and the study by Connor (1974). The items were scored on a 5-point scale (5: strongly agree; 4: agree; 3: undecided; 2: disagree; 1: strongly disagree). Questionnaires were mailed out or distributed by hand. The Nisei, Sansei, and Caucasians received an English version while the Issei received a Japanese version.

A. Issei

Acculturation   On the behavioural level the Issei are far from acculturated. Not a single Issei respondent showed fluency in English. They have developed their own language system which is a combination of Japanese and English. For instance, they call a car *"mishin,"* because they think of a car as a machine, just as the Japanese in Japan call a sewing machine "*mishin*." "*Mishin*" is their way of pronouncing the word "machine," which title they give to many technical instruments. Such a language is comprehensible only to those Japanese Canadians who have lived in the Japanese Canadian communities.

A large percentage of the Issei use Japanese mass media, such as newspapers (52%), TV programs (70%), and movies (43%). The percentages could have been larger if the Issei were not handicapped by old age. Their opportunities to subscribe to a Japanese paper, to turn on a Japanese TV program, or to be driven to a Japanese movie theatre are contingent upon the conveniences of their family members and friends.

Their friends are predominantly other Issei. They come to prefectural association meetings; attend Buddhist church ceremonies and activities; come to the Japanese Canadian picnics and bazaars. Here again, because of old age, the Issei have to depend on others for transportation to various activities.

On the psychological level the Issei still identify themselves as Japanese. The mean score for the Issei is low for the statement, "I always think of myself as a Canadian first and as a Japanese second."(#1) They tend to believe that "once a Japanese always a Japanese"(#2) (see Table 1).

TABLE 1
SOCIO-PSYCHOLOGICAL ACCULTURATION BY GENERATION
(MEAN SCORES)

Item	N:	Issei 48	Nisei 100	Sansei 102
1. I always think of myself as a Canadian first and as a Japanese second.		1.50	3.42	3.49
2. Once a Japanese always a Japanese.		3.94	2.71	2.80
3. Japanese Canadians who enter into new places without any expectations of discrimination from Caucasians are naive.		2.71	3.42	2.90
4. Japanese Canadians should not disagree among themselves if there are Caucasians around.		3.90	3.78	2.32
5. It would be more comfortable to live in a neighbourhood which has at least a few Japanese Canadians than in one which has none.		4.03	3.51	2.02

Scores: 5: Strongly agree; 4: Agree; 3: Undecided; 2: Disagree; 1: Strongly disagree.

Sources: *Items 1 through 5 were adopted from Matsumoto, Meredith, and Masuda, 1970, "Ethnic Identification: Honolulu and Seattle Japanese Americans,"* Journal of Cross-Cultural Psychology 1:63-76.

Their insularity is shown in their preference to live in a Japanese Canadian neighbourhood (#5), and their perceived need for ethnic solidarity to shield them from anticipated discrimination (#3). They think that the Japanese Canadians should stick together and should not disagree among themselves when there are Caucasians present (#4).

Familism　A large number of the Issei live very close to their children: 38% share the same household; 15% reside in the same flat or apartment; and 11% have their children in the immediate neighbourhood. All except two others have at least one child in the metropolitan Toronto area. Thus we have a picture of old Japanese parents physically or geographically very close. Although only half of the sampled Issei actually live under the same roof as their children, they are within a short distance, which would enable them to have daily contact. The rest-home concept is quite objectionable to the majority of the Japanese.

The preservation of family ideals by the Issei is seen in Table 2. The Issei score high on all the items. The family collectivity orientation is held by the Issei, who state that "a man can never let himself down without letting his family down at the same time" (#6). The Issei gains the greatest satisfaction from being with his family (#7). In times of need the Issei thinks it best to rely on his own family for assistance rather than to seek help from others or to depend entirely upon himself (#8).

TABLE 2
FAMILISM BY GENERATION AND RACE (MEAN SCORES)

Item	N:	Issei 48	Nisei 100	Sansei 102	Caucasian 103
6. A man can never let himself down without letting his family down at the same time.		3.87	3.96	3.32	2.77
7. In the long run the greatest satisfaction comes from being with one's family.		4.34	4.39	3.70	3.49
8. In times of need it is best to rely on your own family for assistance rather than to seek help from others or to depend entirely upon yourself.		3.99	3.58	3.04	2.87
9. Parents can never be repaid for what they have done for their children.		3.88	3.26	2.89	2.54
10. The best way to train children is to train them to be quiet and obedient.		3.95	2.71	2.01	1.85
11. Children should support their parents in old age.		3.83	2.63	2.22	1.85
12. It is necessary for Japanese Canadian parents to make it a duty to promote the preservation of Japanese cultural heritage in their children.		4.13	3.00	2.06	3.11

13. Although children may not appreciate Japanese schools at the time, they will later when they grow up.	4.17	3.56	3.01	3.49
14. It is better that Japanese Canadians date only Japanese Canadians.	3.38	2.11	1.80	1.50
15. Interracial marriage between Japanese Canadians and Caucasians should be discouraged.	2.50	1.98	1.72	1.20

Scores: 5: Strongly agree; 4: Agree; 3: Undecided; 2: Disagree; 1: Strongly disagree.

Sources: *Items 6 through 10 were adopted from John W. Connor, 1974, "Acculturation and Family Continuities in Three Generations of Japanese Americans,"* Journal of Marriage and the Family 36:159-165. *Items 12 through 14 were adopted from Matsumoto, Ibid.*

A hierarchical relation between parents and children is expressed by the Issei stating that "parents can never be repaid for what they have done for their children" (#9) and that "the best way to train children is to train them to be quiet and obedient" (#10). They also agree with the statement that "children should support their aged parents" (#11). Thus, Confucius' ideology of filial piety is well maintained in the minds of the Issei as general family values.

The Issei consider it a duty for Japanese Canadian parents to promote the preservation of the Japanese cultural heritage in their children (#12). They think that "although children may not appreciate Japanese schools at the time, they will later when they grow up" (#13)

The Issei are reluctant to see their offspring drifting away from the Japanese Canadian group. They think that "it is better that Japanese Canadians date only Japanese Canadians" (#14) and that "interracial marriage between Japanese Canadians and Caucasians should be discouraged" (#15).

Even if the Japanese Canadians wish to fulfill the filial responsibility and various other demands derived from traditional familism, they are likely to experience conflict with other roles generated by modern, urban, and industrialized Canadian society—as a worker, spouse, and consumer.

Modern occupational life, with frequent geographical mobility demands, does not favour family solidarity. The Issei's answers are indeterminate concerning the view that "an adult child should move thousands of miles away from his (her) aged parents for a special opportunity such as a job offer, job promotion, marriage, etc." (#16).

As a person becomes more acculturated into Canadian society, he is likely to accept the importance of conjugal relations. The traditional precedence of intergenerational ties over the conjugal relationship causes great friction when a person has to choose between the two. It is interesting to note that even among the Issei, as many as two-thirds

TABLE 3
ROLE CONFLICTS BY GENERATION AND RACE (IN PERCENTAGE)

Item	N:	Issei 48 %	Nisei 100 %	Sansei 102 %	Caucasian 103 %
16. An adult child should move thousands of miles away from his aged parents for a special opportunity, such as a job offer, job promotion, marriage.	Agree	19	28	52	57
	Undecided	65	43	23	21
	Disagree	16	29	25	22
17. A person should side with his (her) spouse rather than with his (her) parents if he (she) thinks that his (her) spouse is right.	Agree	69	70	85	88
	Undecided	20	14	11	10
	Disagree	11	11	4	2
18. An adult child should willingly help his (her) parents financially even at the expense of reducing his (her) own children's educational expense.	Agree	15	39	42	44
	Undecided	68	41	12	13
	Disagree	17	20	46	43
19. An adult child should willingly help his (her) parents financially even at the expense of foregoing luxury items and activities.	Agree	54	56	45	42
	Undecided	27	14	13	15
	Disagree	19	30	42	43

Sources: Items 18 and 19 were adopted from M. Osako, 1976, "Intergenerational Relations as an Aspect of Assimilation: The Care of the Japanese Americans," Sociological Inquiry 46:67-72.

of the sample agreed with the statement that "a person should side with his (her) spouse rather than with his (her) parents if he (she) thinks his (her) spouse is right" (#17). It can be interpreted as the result of the great extent of the Issei's acculturation into Canadian values or the sense of loss of power by the Issei.

As the middle class consumer who "must keep up with the Joneses," the Nisei or Sansei will experience role strain in helping their aged parents if it involves considerable financial sacrifice. Two-thirds of the Issei cannot decide their position relative to the statement "an adult child should willingly help his (her) parents financially even at the expense of reducing his (her) own children's educational expense" (#18). Over a quarter of the elderly Issei are not sure if they have a right to request help from their children, who then must "forego luxury items" (#19).

On the general level the Issei have retained the traditional values of familism. However, in concrete situations they do not seem to consider it right to force hierarchical family values upon their offspring.

B. Nisei

Acculturation After World War II, the Nisei broke away from the control of their Japanese community and began to participate in the activities of the larger society. They speak English fluently, although half of the Nisei respondents (52%) have a Japanese accent. As for the Japanese language, one quarter (24%) of them speak fairly well, although with some accent. One-fifth (21%) speak practically none, and one-half (55%) of them speak some Japanese. Most of them (89%) were sent to Japanese language schools while young, but many of them did not have enough interest to master or to retain the language.

Concerning the mass media, the majority of the Nisei subscribe to Japanese newspapers for their Issei parents but seldom read them themselves. They turn on Japanese TV programs mainly for the Issei parents, and only occasionally do they view the programs. As for Japanese movies some Nisei (18%) have developed a taste for Samurai pictures, but others simply provide their parents with transportation to the theatre. The Nisei are active in both Japanese and Canadian organizations. Some are active members of Buddhist churches, while others attend Christian churches. Some of the organizations, such as the Japanese Canadian citizens league, Japanese Canadian Chambers of Commerce, and country clubs, have been established by the Nisei with membership including both Japanese and Canadians. However, on an informal level away from formal organizations and occupational associations, the Nisei are likely to choose other Nisei (83%) as close friends. They seem to be more able to relax with other Nisei than with Caucasians.

It is interesting to note that the Nisei are more inclined to expect discrimination than the Issei (#3). The Nisei's insularity is evidenced by their efforts not to disagree among themselves (#4) in the presence of Caucasians and their preference of a Japanese Canadian neighbourhood (#5). It may be due to the marginality of the Nisei generation. The Issei could tolerate discrimination because their identification was with Japan rather than with Canada. The Sansei, who hardly know Japan, are less sensitive to prejudice against themselves. It is the Nisei who went through the wartime internment in spite of their citizenship and who therefore would usually be hypersensitive about their position as Japanese Canadians (Table 1).

Their psychological identification is that of Japanese Canadians. They are less likely than the Issei to agree with a statement such as "once a Japanese always a Japanese" (#2), and are also less likely to disagree with the statement: "I always think of myself as a Canadian first and as a Japanese second" (#1). What is not obvious from their answers to these items is that in their minds ethnic identification is not a dichotomous but rather a trichotomous issue. They do not perceive themselves either as Japanese or Canadians, but as Japanese Canadians who have shared the unique experience of marginality.

Familism   The majority of the Nisei (83%) report that the family was stressed by their parents when they were young. Also two-thirds of the Nisei respondents say that as children they were told that it was very important not to bring shame to the Japanese community. For instance, when a Nisei child received a low grade, he was scolded by his parents and told that he brought shame to his family as well as to the Japanese Canadian community as a whole.

The retention of family ideas inculcated by the Issei parents can be seen in the Nisei responses (Table 2). As for the collectivity orientation of a family unit, the scores are not much different between the Issei and the Nisei. The Nisei are as likely as the Issei to agree with the importance of the family, that a man must not bring shame to his family (#6), that he gains the greatest satisfaction from his family (#7), and that he can rely on family members (#8).

As for parent-child relations the Nisei are less likely than the Issei to uphold the traditional filial piety ideals. Even so, they are much more traditional in comparison to the Sansei and the Caucasian respondents. The Nisei still tend to agree that children are indebted to parents (#9), that they should be trained to be quiet and obedient (#10), and that they should support their parents in old age (#11).

As transmitters of cultural heritage, the Nisei are less serious than the Issei. The Nisei are less likely to consider that the preservation of the family ideals is a parental duty. Also they are more likely than the Issei to encourage inter-racial dating and marriage.

Caught between occupational and filial role requirements, 28% of the Nisei agree that an adult child should choose an occupational role over a filial role, while the other 29% disagrees, and 43% are undecided (Table 3).

Blind obedience to parental demands is not accepted by the Nisei. When they think that their spouses are correct, they do not hesitate to oppose their own parents. Note, however, that the majority of the Issei respondents take the same attitude.

Dilemma between devotion to parents and children is resolved by the Nisei's placing priority on parents (39%), rather than on children (20%). However, a large percentage of the Nisei (40%) are uncertain whether or not they should help their parents financially at the expense of reducing their children's educational outlay. Half of the Nisei respondents (56%) are willing to give up their own luxury and comforts to help their parents financially. This percentage is about the same as among the Issei. A difference is found in that a greater percentage (30%) of Nisei than Issei (19%) disagree with personal sacrifice for their parents.

C. Sansei

Acculturation   The Sansei who are of college age now speak English fluently without an accent (87%) but practically no Japanese. Less than one-third (30%) speak some Japanese, and only 9% speak fairly well. This small percentage of the Sansei turn out to be the college students specializing in Japanese culture. These same people read the Japanese newspapers (8%), watch Japanese TV (9%), and go to see Japanese movies (8%) frequently. Others show little interest in Japanese mass media.

The majority of Sansei participate widely in college extracurricular activities, such as being actively involved in school offices and school athletics. At the same time they have their own Sansei groups, such as Japanese Canadian Christian or Buddhist churches and Sansei bowling clubs. The proportion of Japanese-Canadian versus Canadian activities engaged in by the Sansei is on the average three to seven. Furthermore, the majority of the Sansei have more non-Japanese (62%) than Japanese friends (38%).

They tend to express their identity as Canadians first and as Japanese second (#1). The mean score among the Sansei in supporting the statement, "once a Japanese always a Japanese" (#2), is not significantly different from the score for the Nisei. An analysis of an open-ended question reveals the underlying reason for this result, namely that the Sansei do not perceive themselves as Japanese, hence do not consider the above statement as applicable to them. In their eyes only the Issei and the Nisei are Japanese (Table 1).

The Sansei are slowly emerging from their shell into the larger society, although still protected by the Sansei subculture. They are less likely than the Nisei to anticipate discrimination, or to feel the necessity of sticking together against the Caucasians, and to prefer a Japanese Canadian neighbourhood.

Familism In comparison with the Issei and Nisei, the Sansei score low on the scale of family collectivity orientation. Even so, the Sansei are much more likely than the Caucasian youth in the same age category to consider the family as a psychological and financial haven and to be careful not to disgrace it (#6, 7, 8). Most Sansei are still living at home with the Nisei parents, who seem to have considerable influence. They are more likely than the Caucasians to think that they can never pay back for what their parents have done and therefore it is their duty to support their parents in old age (#11). Also, they agree more frequently than the Caucasians with the need for parental disciplining of children to be quiet and obedient (#10) (Table 2).

As for the preservation of cultural heritage, it is interesting to note that the Caucasians are more anxious than the Sansei that Japanese Canadian parents make special efforts to transmit Japanese culture to their children (#12, 13). However, this does not mean that Caucasians are trying to remain distant from Japanese Canadians. In fact, they are more likely than the Sansei to support interracial dating and marriage (#14, 15).

When familism comes in conflict with other roles, the Sansei and the Caucasian youth tend to react in a similar way, which deviates from traditional familism sustained by the Issei and Nisei. Half of the Sansei and the Caucasian respondents agree that they should grasp opportunities to improve their own lives even if it means departure from their elderly parents (#16). The traditional idea of occupational success for the sake of the family collectivity is being replaced by the individualistic success model among the younger generation, whether Japanese or non-Japanese (Table 3).

Blind acceptance of parental ideas which oppose their own and their spouses (#17) is hardly evident in the Sansei (4%) and the Caucasians (2%). Disagreements are found in many areas, such as the selection of dating partners, the ways to spend money, the style of dressing, the expression of respect for the elderly, etc.

The Sansei, while acknowledging the idea of the child's indebtedness to the parents, take practical attitudes when filial piety demands sacrifice. Over 40% of the Sansei and the Caucasians are not willing to help their parents financially at the expense of reducing their own children's educational outlay (#18) or foregoing luxury items and activities (#19). Note, however, that there is still a substantial percentage of the Sansei and the Caucasians who are ready to sacrific their own needs for their parents.

Unlike the Sansei in California, most Sansei in this study in Toronto are relatively conservative. The majority of them fall into the category of conformists. They are not militantly against their parental values of social conformity and acculturation into white society. Their complaints about the Nisei parents are concentrated on the latter's restrictiveness and lack of appreciation of the youth culture. Generation conflict between Sansei and Nisei are usually not racial or ethnic, but seem to reveal differences in the lifestyles of the two age groups.

The Sansei conservatism in Toronto reflects the general racial climate of Toronto. Unlike the United States, Toronto does not suffer from an acute black versus white racial conflict, but rather enjoys multiethnic pluralism. The Sansei in Toronto do not seem to feel the necessity to militantly assert their rights.

4. CONCLUSION

The Japanese immigrants came to Canada around the turn of this century. Since the majority of them arrived within a certain period of time, their descendent generations represent distinct age groups. Thus the degrees of retention of traditional family ideals must be examined in terms of two factors: (1) distance from Japan in time, as measured by generation, and (2) social roles played by age groups. The Issei are most anxious to adhere to the traditional Japanese values, but are not provided with authoritarian positions as parents and grandparents. Because of old age and lack of acculturation, the Issei are not in a position to exert control over the middle-aged Nisei who are quite successful socially and economically. The Nisei are currently caught in conflicting role demands and some of them are drawn toward non-filial roles. The Sansei are under the influence of the central values of Canadian society as well as sub-cultural values of Caucasian youth, which includes rebellion against the older generation. They have retained traditional familistic values in abstraction, but in concrete situations involving role conflicts their attitudes do not differ much from those of Caucasian youth.

Gordon's theory that acculturation is a multi-phasic process is supported in that the Japanese Canadians show different degrees of acculturation, whether measured by the adoption of Canadian values or by the retention of Japanese familism. Also, the model of non-lineality of acculturation is supported in that the adoption of Canadian values does not mean replacement of Japanese values.

REFERENCES

Andracki, Stanislaw
  1958 "The Immigration of Orientals into Canada with Special Reference to Chinese." Ph.D. thesis, McGill University.

Bellah, Robert N.
  1957 Tokugawa Religion. Glencoe: Free Press.

Canadian Yearbook
  1970-1971 Ottawa: Dominion Bureau of Statistics.

Caudill, William and George De Vos
  1956 "Achievement, Culture, and Personality: The Case of Japanese Americans." American Anthropologist 58:1102-1126.

Census of Canada
  1961, 1971 Ottawa: Dominion Bureau of Statistics.

Connor, John W.
  1974 "Acculturation and Family Continuities in Three Generations of Japanese Americans." Journal of Marriage and the Family 36:159-165.

Davis, Morris, and J. F. Krauter
  1971 The Other Canadians. Toronto: Methuen.

Gordon, Milton
  1964 Assimilation in American life. New York: Oxford University Press.

Jacobson, Nolan Pliny
  1965 Buddhism. New York: Humanities Press.

Kawashima, Takeyoshi
  1968 Nihon Shakai no Kazokuteki Kosei (Familial Structure of Japanese Society). Tokyo: Nihon Hyoron-sha.

Kitano, Harry H. L.
  1969 Japanese Americans. Englewood Cliffs: Prentice-Hall.

Kurokawa, Minako
  1968 "Lineal Orientation in Child-rearing Among Japanese." Journal of Marriage and the Family 30:129-136.

LaViolette, F. E.
1948   Canadian Japanese and World War II. Toronto: University of Toronto
       Press.

Luman, Stanford
1971   The Asians in the West. Reno: Desert Research Institute, University of
       Nevada System.

Matsumoto, Gary M., Gerald M. Meredith, and Minoru Masuda
1970   "Ethnic Identification: Honolulu and Seattle Japanese Americans."
       Journal of Cross-Cultural Psychology 1:63-76.

Maykovich, Minako K.
1975   "Japanese and Chinese in the United States and Canada." In Politics
       of Race, edited by Donald G. Baker. Westmead, England: Saxon
       House, pp. 95-120.

Maykovich, Minako K.
1972a Japanese American Identity Dilemma. Tokyo: Waseda University
       Press.
1972b "Reciprocity in Racial Stereotypes." American Journal of Sociology
       72:876-897.

Miyamoto, Shotaro F.
1939   "Social Solidarity Among the Japanese in Seattle." University of
       Washington Publications in the Social Science 11:57-130.

Moore, Charles A., ed.
1967   The Japanese Mind. Honolulu: University of Hawaii Press.

Nakane, Chie
1970   Japanese Society. Berkeley: University of California Press.

Osako, Masako M.
1976   "Intergenerational Relations as an Aspect of Assimilation: the Case of
       Japanese Americans." Sociological Inquiry 46:67-72.

Tamaki, Hajime
1953   Nihon Kazoku Seido-ron (A Theory on the Japanese Family System).
       Kyoto: Horitsu Bunka-sha.

Tsunoda, Tyusaku, et al., eds.
1958   Sources of Japanese Tradition. New York: Columbia University
       Press.

Varon, B. F.
1967   "The Japanese Americans: Comparative Occupational Status, 1960
       and 1950." Demography 4:809-819.

Wangenheim, Elizabeth D.
1956   "The Social Organization of the Japanese Community in Toronto."
       M. A. thesis, University of Toronto

Wirth, Louis
1945   "The Problems of Minority Groups." In The Science of Man in World

Crisis, edited by Ralph Linton. New York: Columbia University Press, pp. 354-363.

Wynne, R. R.
  1963   "Popular Reaction to Oriental Immigration in the States of Washington and in British Columbia." Ph.D. thesis, University of Washington.

Young, Charles H., and H. Reid
  1938   The Japanese Canadians. Toronto: University of Toronto Press.

Yutang, Lin
  1938   The Wisdom of Confucius. New York: Modern Library.

5. Family and Kin Cohesion Among Southern Italian Immigrants in Toronto*

FRANC STURINO

INTRODUCTION

It is the purpose of this paper to explore some of the ways that Italians who immigrated to Toronto after World War II through kinship chains have been able to preserve family and kindred cohesiveness in the face of a New World environment while at the same time adjusting to it.

The argument presented herein was derived from material collected as part of a wider study on the social history of South Italian immigration to Canada from the turn of the century to 1967. In this endeavour a case study approach was used, the focus being on a number of villages located in the west-central part of the province of Cosenza. The province lies within the region of Calabria, the southernmost part of the Italian peninsula. In this study, in addition to utilizing standard historical sources, such as archival and governmental material, recorded oral interviews were employed as a source of information. It is primarily from these interviews that the following analysis is derived.

My account draws specifically from information presented by 92 immigrants, who for the most part had been former peasants, primarily from villages composing one of the larger communes in west-central Cosenza. In both 1951 and 1961, the commune had a population of 12,000.[1] By 1967 its immigrants numbered roughly 5,000 amongst Metropolitan Toronto's Italian element of 200,000, an element that formed about 9% of the Metropolitan population of almost 1,900,000.[2]

Forty-seven of the villages contacted were interviewed in depth over

* I wish to express my thanks to the Canada Council, whose kind support made the original research upon which this paper is based possible.

a number of days. About half these individuals were recorded on tape and half were recorded through written accounts of the interviews drawn up from notes taken during the conversations. The remaining immigrants were interviewed less extensively and for a shorter period. Ten of these were recorded on tape; the others through written accounts. Although an attempt was made to tape-record the interviews, taping often proved unsuitable. It was found that where the tape-recorder made the participant uncomfortable, it was advisable to omit its use so that the conversation could proceed as freely as possible. Furthermore, on many occasions the interviews took place in a social setting (a dinner, for example), where tape-recording would have been inappropriate, if not actually offensive.[3]

A number of these conversations were held while I was involved in the Italian community in a "participant observer" position. This involvement took place on two levels. I worked within the wider Italian community, though mostly with southern Italians, in the capacity of a community worker during the summers of 1973 and 1974. More particularly, I attempted through various contacts between 1974 and 1976 to involve myself as much as possible in the social life of the immigrant community from Cosenza. In addition, I had visited western Cosenza during the summer of 1971.

Because of its nature as a qualitative case study of kin-linked migration, the wider thesis from which this paper is derived made no attempt to collect data that would lend itself to a discussion of the *statistical* representativeness of the population at hand and likewise no attempt to argue along such lines will be made here. However, there are a number of points that should be borne in mind.

First, the majority, or nearly 60% of the 250,000 Italian immigrants that settled in Canada between 1946 and 1961 (the height of the inflow occurred between 1951 and 1960), were from Southern Italy.[4] And of all the Italian regions, Calabria (alongside Abruzzi-Molise) contributed more immigrants to Canada than any other, or about 20%.[5] Further, Cosenza was a major province of origin of these immigrants.[6]

Second, it should be noted that the Italian immigrant, especially if he was from the South, was more likely than not to be a former peasant. Hence, in the mid-fifties about three-quarters of the Italian immigrants fourteen years of age or over who had been gainfully employed in Italy came from the agricultural sector, essentially from the peasantry.[7]

Third, the great majority of Italian immigrants, especially Southerners, entered Canada through kinship ties. That is to say, of the 409,414 Italian immigrants between 1946 and 1967, around 90% were sponsored.[8] The Canadian White Paper on Immigration Policy in 1966 correctly connected this sponsorship with the family and peasant background of the immigrants:

The majority of the sponsored have been drawn from Southern Europe, primarily as a result of the influx of immigrants from the under-developed, rural parts of this region in the early post-war years, the strong family relationships in those areas, and the economic pressures to emigrate from them.[9]

The point is, then, that the following discussion is based on the experience of immigrants who conformed to the major characteristics of post-World War II Italian immigration to Canada. As such, their experience is not only illustrative of that of similar fellow villagers, but moreover, as Southern peasants who immigrated to Canada via kinship chains, the general outline of their experience may be indicative of the experience of a great number of Italian immigrants.

SOUTHERN ITALIAN BACKGROUND

As a number of social scientists have noted, peasant society is a part-society; that is, it exists and is defined in relation to the larger society of which it is a part, while at the same time manifesting itself as a unique local entity. This linkage is all-encompassing and occurs on the political, economic, cultural, and social planes.[10]

In concrete terms this means that the Southern Italian peasant immigrant does not come from a background of traditional, isolated villages as some social scientists indicate.[11] Rather, his background is one of continual contact with a modern industrial state. He is familiar with urban (albeit often pre-industrial) trades and ways, he has been conscripted into a national army, he has been integrated for generations into a national, and even international, economy. It is not surprising, then, that upon immigrating to Canada, the Southern Italian is much more prepared to confront his new environment than a simplistic view of his peasant background would lead us to believe.

It is the fact that he comes from a part-society that largely explains why the Southern Italian immigrant is able to first confront Canadian society and then evolve an Italo-Canadian synthesis, that is to say, adjust, rather than succumb to disintegrative pressures and consequent assimilation.

Related to this question regarding the nature of the southern Italian background, much has been written on the quality of social relations which have alternatively been viewed as competitive and malicious on one hand, and co-operative and well adjusted on the other.[12] Characterizing Southern Italy as motivated by "amoral familism"—the unrelenting drive to maximize "the material, short-run advantage of the nuclear family"—Banfield sees social relations marked by selfishness and distrust.[13] Two recent studies on the south by Brögger and Davis, however, take issue with this interpretation. Both stress the coherence of the kindred, the importance of friends and neighbours, the practice of work parties, and the intricate system of rights and obligations binding individuals to one another.[14]

Similarly, these two perspectives are reflected in writings regarding

Southern Italian immigrants in the New World. Cronin, for example, in her study of Sicilian immigrants in Australia, concurs with the familism presented by Banfield, whereas Boissevain, in his study of the primarily Southern Italian community in Montreal, shows how commitment to kindred, friends, and neighbours binds the community together.[15]

My own evidence substantiates the "co-operative" perspective. This is not, of course, to say that competitive friction does not exist, for as Boissevain notes, it does.[16] Further, as an excellent paper by Blaxter has argued, by the very nature of peasant society, competitiveness and co-operation are by no means mutually exclusive.[17]

Nevertheless, my study gives predominance to co-operativeness rather than competitiveness. For not only did the immigrants themselves stress cohesion over friction, but also the very process of kin-linked chain migration by which the immigrants came to the New World would have been impossible had the strict familism and competitiveness expounded by Banfield been predominant.

ELASTICITY OF KINSHIP[18]

Chain migration along kinship lines and the adjustment of the kindred once they reached Toronto was facilitated by two interrelated types of flexibility: the elasticity of southern Italian kinship per se, and the elasticity of interpersonal relationships between kin.

There are two aspects regarding the elasticity of kinship per se. First, although one is born into his kin group and behaviour within this group is prescribed—the closer the kin, the more binding the prescription—still, there is a significant degree of elasticity or personal choice in determining whom to affiliate with and the exact content the prescribed behaviour (doing favours, for example) will take. Where these kin or ascribed relationships have remained latent (as in the case of broken migration chains), there is personal choice in whether or not to make these manifest.[19]

To understand the second aspect of this elasticity, we must distinguish between various levels of Southern Italian kinship. The unit claiming the individual's primary loyalty is the nuclear family consisting of the father, mother, and their children. The word famiglia is used to refer both to this grouping and to the Southern Italian grouping of familiari or "family circle." Familiari include kindred up to (but excluding) the degree of cousin and their spouses. But not all kindred who are genealogically familiari are in fact so. Only those who live relatively near one another and interact closely as a unit are familiari. The members of such a family circle perceive themselves as a bounded group in distinction to other kin. Henceforth, familiari will refer to this family circle, whereas "wider familiari" will refer to the genealogical field of members.[20]

The third level of kin consists of all remaining relatives up to second cousin. Up to this kin boundary one cannot intermarry, and substantial rights and obligations exist. The last level of kinship extends to cousins up to the fourth degree, whom one is expected to "recognize," but with whom the commitment of reciprocal rights and obligations is much weaker. Inter-marriage with these third and fourth cousins is permissible.

The point is that though the kinship field is large, meaningful relationships are only entered into with some of the kin. And though the strength of rights and obligations binding the kin largely correlates with the levels of kinship outlined above, the boundaries are flexible so that though one may be genealogically outside the *familiari* grouping, for example, functionally he may be within it, just as the reverse is true.

The second type of flexibility concerns interpersonal relationships between kin. In general, kin and non-kin alike relate to each other in a multi-stranded way, that is to say, on several levels—social, economic, religious, and political. At any one time, however, one or another level may become primary, depending on the need.[21]

Similarly, co-operative forms (such as work parties) bind kinsmen together on several levels, though any one may predominate. These co-operative forms are made operative through a system of reciprocal rights and obligations, the content of which may change, depending on subjective and objective determinants. Rights and obligations permeate all relationships between kinsmen and these reciprocal ties vary in intensity directly with the closeness of the kinship tie. Since the *de facto* closeness of kinship is flexible, the intensity of rights and obligations can change.

In short, just as the kinship tie *per se* is flexible, so are the interpersonal relationships between them due to their multi-stranded nature and the flexibility of rights and obligations. Keeping this elasticity of kinship in mind, we will now turn briefly to the Toronto immigrant experience of kinsmen from Cosenza and then deal at length with the major forms that bound them to one another.

THE KINDRED COLONY

After the settlement of the first immigrants from Cosenza in North America at the turn of the century, government restrictions, the Great Depression, and World War II suspended the process of chain migration that had been set in motion. From 1927 until 1947, the village kindred remained in a state of suspended animation, as it were, waiting for the day they could join the small colony already established in the New World.[22] When Canada resumed immigration from Italy in 1947, prospective immigrants looked to their Toronto kin for a linkage with the New World. The elasticity of kinship meant that the prospective immigrant could readily establish contact with North American kinsmen he had had little to do with for over two decades and whom he sometimes did not know. Once contact was made and the kin relationship was made manifest, a new cycle of reciprocal rights and obligations was set in motion. At the same time, the bestowing of aid on the part of the North American kin was also a continuation of the system of rights and obligations that years of havoc had interrupted. Aid given to a village nephew, for example, was often repayment of debts between brothers that had been delayed.

The migration process would frequently throw together several kin to make migration possible for any one individual. While an uncle in Toronto might act as "sponsor," dealing with bureaucrats in order to prepare the necessary documents, a second uncle in Chicago would loan the nephew the passage money, while a third in the village would check with Toronto in-laws to see if a job could be made available. If the migrant was married, financial constraints would usually force him to leave his family behind for a year or two until he could send for them. In this case the immigrant's wife and children would be maintained by the male members of his family, the younger, unmarried brothers assuming responsibility for their protection. Female members were instrumental in giving emotional as well as domestic support to his wife and children.[23]

The migrant would search out kin who were leaving for Toronto at the same time so that they could support each other during the migration. Likewise, when his wife was able to rejoin him, it was imperative that a male kinsman accompany her. It was often difficult to locate such companions within one's usual circle of kin, and so more distant kin or even fellow villagers (paesani) were sought to play such a role. It was not unusual for migrants to emerge from their common experiences on the journey, and often from mutual support in their initial settlement, as familiari if they had been cousins or as kindred if they had been paesani.

The immigrant would usually be met at the train station by a group of close kin led by his sponsor. Generally, it was the immigrant's closest kin, usually a member of the wider familiari, who acted as sponsor and provided the immigrant with housing during the initial adjustment period.

Toronto kinsmen were also responsible for helping the new arrival find a job and generally orient the immigrant to his new environment. They would point out the neighbourhood stores where Italian could be spoken and Italian food products could be bought; they would introduce the new arrival to the parishes where Italian masses could be heard; and they would refer him to doctors, lawyers, and other professionals he would have need of.[24]

The system of rights and obligations determined that in return for the pre-War kinsman's provision of sponsorship, loans, housing, employment, contacts, and advice, the immigrant would reciprocate with visiting, presents, respect, and favours.

The emerging colony of kin and *paesani* would often locate near the core of pre-War settlers who had been the initiators of the migration chain. It was these kin centres inter-lacing numerous parts of the city, and not Toronto's stereotyped "Little Italy," that served as the immigrant receiving areas for the new settlers.[25] In the early years, these mainly male kindred, who in the village had been scattered, were bound together in mutual aid and support. As the process of chain migration unfolded and separated, *familiari* groupings were reunited, the initial close association amongst the more distant kindred was weakened. At the same time, however, these relationships did not come to an end for, as we shall see later, contacts were maintained and frequently reinforced at the many social gatherings of the kindred.

Within the growing immigrant colony of kin and *paesani*, the groups of *familiari* that eventually emerged amongst the kindred did not include all the potential members, but rather, as in the village, only those who interacted frequently and intimately. Moreover, these family circles were not identical in membership to those in the village. In part this resulted because some chose, and others were forced, to remain in the village. Essentially, however, the new family circles were determined by differential rates of social mobility among the wider *familiari*. Stated another way, people chose to coalesce with *familiari* of the same social status.

Social mobility amongst the wider *familiari* and kinsmen opened up new avenues through which the imported system of rights and obligations could be enacted. The elasticity of this reciprocity meant that it could take on new content within the Canadian context. As kinsmen, often children of the pre-War settlers, emerged with new urban skills as lawyers, caterers, real estate and insurance agents, they supplied necessary services within a framework of trust, and sometimes reduced rates, while their kin clients reciprocated with favours, referrals, and public support.

THE FAMILY

It was noted earlier that kinsmen are bound together by co-operative forms made operative by a system of rights and obligations. The flexibility of this system made possible the survival of traditional co-operative forms upon migration to Canada. At this point I wish to consider some of the major manifestations of these co-operative forms between kinsmen as expressed in the immigrant generation. It should be borne in mind, however, that my evidence suggests that in general these forms persist until the third generation, while, of course, undergoing considerable modification in each generation.

At its most basic level, the nuclear family in both southern Italy and Toronto can be considered a co-operative form united through reciprocal rights and obligations. This reciprocal relationship, however, should be understood as pervasive and implicit, rather than definite and explicit. As Campbell puts it:

Because of their very diffuseness it would not normally occur to an individual to balance his rights and privileges against those of another member of the family. There is no conscious accountancy of this solidarity. In general terms everybody has the right to expect material, moral and affective support from the family. . . .[26]

Nevertheless, for the sake of conceptual clarity, we will speak of rights and obligations between family members as if they were explicit.

FAMILY ROLES IN ITALY

In Southern Italy, the father was, above all, the family's "provider." It was his ability to maintain or improve the economic position of his family through holding and working land that was the main index of his social status. However, the family's wealth was not seen as a matter of individual ownership, but rather as held in trust by him for the benefit of his family. A father who squandered the wealth of his family was held in disrepute. Essentially, the Southern Italian family, with the father as head, was a corporate group in which property and status was seen to be held in common.

In return for his material support, the husband held exclusive rights to his wife's sexual services.[27] It was necessary for the wife to observe this obligation in order to uphold the family's honour and cohesion. She was responsible for the upbringing of children, the household, and the tending of farm animals. Though it was unacceptable for her to work in her own right, she had considerable power over the family purse, since it was her duty to buy the family's daily necessities.[28]

The children were expected to obey and respect their parents. They were incorporated from the age of three or four into the economic life of the family by being given simple agricultural or household tasks to do in imitation of their parents. Single young men were generally expected to contribute directly to the family wealth either by working the land or earning a salary. They were also responsible for the good reputation of their sisters and family honour.[29] Unmarried female children were expected to contribute to the family upkeep by unhesitatingly undertaking the many household and domestic tasks required by the family. Like her mother, a young woman was expected to protect her own, and hence her family's, honour.

FAMILY ROLES IN CANADA

It was the father's desire to improve the family's social and economic status, or at least to maintain it; that was the raison d'être for his migration to Toronto. In Toronto, he still regarded himself as primarily a provider of his family, though he now did so indirectly in an urban context rather than directly by working the land. With the exception of family businesses, it was impossible to keep intact the family as an economic unit, and hence the loss of the father's position as economic overseer of the family enterprise somewhat diluted his dominance. Nevertheless, through homeownership, he was able to regain and then improve his propertied status, as well as provide a focus for his family's social unity.[30]

For the immigrant wife, her primary sphere of influence remained her home and children. Though she frequently entered the marketplace as a wage earner, the nature of her economic role was such that it did not seriously conflict with family values. She often did home work for textile or needle firms, frequently in company of other female *familiari*. In this way, she was able to integrate her work with her domestic responsibilities. As this work became less abundant over the years, she turned to work in textile or food processing factories; but in any case, she would travel to and from work with groups of female fellow villagers, thus keeping intact her reputation.

Since her work was in low-paying, unstable sectors of the economy, her earning power never seriously threatened the male's role as provider and chief authority. Indeed, her wage was often seen as an extension of her role as the family's shopper and it was considered as akin to an allowance or as mere spending money for the purchase of accessories. It was rarely referred to as a necessity.[31]

In Toronto, as in the village, parents judged the success of their lives primarily in terms of their offspring: the support they provided them with as children, the extent to which they were able to set them up at marriage, the honour they maintained intact and augmented in order to bequeath to them. These obligations were pervasive and primary, and of necessity, individual pursuits and comforts were subordinated to them. Though greater economic security and affluence was experienced by all upon immigrating, the parents still felt deep responsibility for their children. The father still experienced wealth in its corporate sense as a holding in trust, and both parents put aside newly possible individualistic pursuits in the way of entertainment, vacations, and personal assets in favour of contributing to the betterment of their children. It is in this sense that parents spoke of having "sacrificed" for their children.[32]

For their part, children were to show gratitude for the sacrifice of their parents primarily through a pervasive attitude of respect. This quality was to be manifested in numerous ways, depending on the stage of the child's life cycle. It ranged from mere obedience in childhood to supporting aged parents in adulthood. Indeed, the "obligations" that children owed their parents could just as easily be spoken of in terms of manifesting respect. As young adults, children were expected to contribute to the family's wealth and status. For a male, and especially one who immigrated as a young man, this took the form of working and turning over a portion of his salary (though smaller than village standards) to his parents. If the male had immigrated at a young age and showed academic promise, he was encouraged to further his education, though, at the same time, he usually took on a part-time job and contributed at least some of his earnings to his family.

His education was not seen as a vehicle for "individual fulfillment," but rather as an investment which should contribute to the furtherance of the family's material and social status. The son was expected to reciprocate the "sacrifice" the parents had made in his education by adding concretely to the good standing of the family.[33] Hence, whereas a son was encouraged to pursue professional and technical training, he was not encouraged to pursue liberal and artistic fields, which, moreover, because of their amorphous nature, were difficult for the parents to comprehend.

A son had the responsibility to contribute to his family's good name, not only through hard work, but also through overseeing the behaviour of his sister. Though the parameters of acceptable behaviour widened vis-à-vis village standards and minor infractions would be blinked at, a brother was expected to protect the sexual reputation of his sister.

A daughter was generally discouraged from pursuing post-secondary education, for not only would her virginity, and hence the collective honour of the family, be threatened, but also her future was thought of in terms of wife and mother. Because of this expectation, a daughter's domestic role was stressed within the immigrant family. The girl's good reputation and later success as wife and mother added to the family's honour, whereas female careerism was distrusted (again because of the greater likelihood for sexual compromise).

Most young women, however, entered the work world at lower white collar levels temporarily, if not permanently. A young woman would undertake part-time employment after school hours, or "temporary" employment after graduation as a salesgirl, bank teller, or secretary. But this was done within the acceptable context of contributing to her family's wealth or, what was often the same thing, her trousseau, in anticipation of marriage and fulfillment of her traditional roles.

SISTEMAZIONE

We pointed out earlier that the nuclear family in the village was corporate in nature, owning property in common. The main function of this common wealth was to enable the parents to provide their children with the means by which they could establish themselves as independent adults. This process of *sistemazione* involved both the successful marrying off of children and their adequate material provision to ensure independence, ideally within a separate household.[34] The partition of family wealth at the time of marriage was not as much a claiming of individual rights as the redeployment of resources from one corporate family to a new one, which, in part, was sprung from it. The bilateral kinship system of Southern Italy, by which descent was traced through both parents and by which daughters as well as sons had claim to the family's wealth, meant that this common wealth could not be contained within the framework of a single corporate body with continuity through time, that is to say, within a single lineage.[35] Such corporate continuity would have required a tradition of unilineal descent.

For a son, *sistemazione* essentially meant the endowment of land, and for a daughter, a dowry and trousseau of linen. A house or cash could be supplied to either. The endowment of land and the dowry were decided upon by the father. The mother was responsible for the trousseau, in which she often invested considerable money and labour.[36]

Upon immigrating, the parents' concern for the *sistemazione* of their children remained, although it took on a different content. For the male, land was generally replaced by a substantial cash "gift," and for the female the dowry was updated to include electrical appliances and other modern conveniences, while the trousseau was bought ready-made from commercial firms rather than being embroidered and finished at home. Parents supplied both sexes with major furniture items and appliances. They also gave assistance in their children's acquisition of their own homes. As in the village, the assets contributed to the family wealth by the children, and held in trust by the father, were often returned in this process of establishing a new conjugal unit. This frequently took the form of the immigrant parents turning over to their children bank accounts or insurance policies which they had kept for them. Such funds could also be used to pay for the wedding itself or turned over when the child reached the age of majority.

An important part of the *sistemazione* of children involved setting them up in their own household. In the few cases where the parents were sufficiently wealthy, one set of parents, or both together, could simply buy the new couple's house for them as their wedding "present" and thus meet their obligation in that manner. However, two more modest types of assistance were more frequent. First, the parents could give or lend money to the new couple to allow them to negotiate a reasonable mortgage. Second, the newlyweds could live temporarily with the parents best able to accommodate them until they were able to save sufficient money for their own home.

Furthermore, as an alternative to establishing a separate household, the new couple could enter into a permanent arrangement with one pair of parents, whereby both families would share the same dwelling.[37]

Although both the temporary and permanent extended household arrangements allowed the saving of costs, these arrangements were not solely the result of financial considerations. Rather, they were sometimes a chosen preference, reflecting a past in which extended households were frequently found. Indeed, in living arrangements where nuclear families could be separately accommodated, as in homes with separate entrances or duplexes, the situation was more akin to living "near" one another—a familial ideal of the *paesani*—rather than living "with" one another. In addition, where the permanent arrangement was also a joint ownership of the house, it reflected the immigrants' corporate past.

For most immigrants, however, and especially with the addition of grandchildren, the village ideal of establishing separate households prevailed, and extended family arrangements were temporary with this view in mind. Invariably, though, the new household was within walking distance of at least one set of parents.[38]

RENDERING RESPECT

In reciprocity for their *sistemazione* and earlier upbringing, the children were above all to show respect towards their parents. As had been the case in the village, this quality was to be manifested in various ways, such as visiting and doing favours. It was manifested most saliently, however, in two main ways.

First, the son was expected to name his first child after his father or mother. It was acceptable that the parent's name be anglicized upon being bestowed to the grandchild, for by this time the parents themselves were often known by such anglicized forms, rather than their original Italian names. It was rarely acceptable, however, to give the grandchild the parent's name as a middle name, for not only was the practice unknown in the village, but more important, such a designation would not be used, and as such, implied in some sense that the son was ashamed of his father or mother.

The second major manifestation of respect involved caring for the parents in old age. This involved supplying both material support if need be, and emotional support through living nearby and frequent contact. The children were expected to take the parents into their own home if this was required or desired, and to take in a single parent upon widowhood so that he or she would not have to live alone.

Reflecting the bilateral kinship system of the village, a married couple was responsible for both pairs of parents. Amongst siblings, all contributed to the support of the parents, although responsibility of accommodation generally fell on the one most able to care for them. It was the childless sister or the better-housed brother that was expected to take the parents in.

To care for aged parents was not only an obligation but a moral duty keenly felt by the children. Through sacrificing some of their own individual pursuits and comforts, children reciprocated, at least partially, the sacrificing of their parents and thus reaffirmed the cohesiveness of the family.[39]

THE FAMILIARI

It was said above that the rights and obligations in the nuclear family are both implicit and diffuse. There is no separation between the context in which these rights and obligations occur and the nuclear family itself. On the other hand, with respect to *familiari*, rights and obligations take on a more definite character and occur within concrete circumstances. In other words, a man "lives" rights and obligations—like he breathes the air, so to speak—within his nuclear family, but he does not do so with *familiari*. Rather, there is a more conscious recognition among *familiari* of rights and obligations.

Due to their definiteness, reciprocal rights and obligations between *familiari* are best examined within the concrete circumstances in which they occur rather than solely as repertoires of behaviour between individual members. It would be beyond the scope of this paper, and also unnecessary, to delineate all the concrete circumstances under which rights and obligations between *familiari* occur. It will suffice to consider this reciprocal relationship as it occurs within the context of the work party—the most important of co-operative forms binding the *familiari* as a group.

WORK PARTIES IN ITALY

In the village, various work parties formed around critical junctures in the agricultural cycle. The paradigm of these work parties occurred during the June grain harvest in which *familiari*, as well as some cousins and friends who also lived in the neighbourhood, were brought together. This work party varied in size, depending on the total amount of grain to be harvested and the availability of kindred, but usually it consisted of fifteen to twenty adults. Through a process of reciprocity, this group would work each member's field until, within the space of a couple of weeks, all the members' grain had been harvested. Similar work parties based on reciprocal rights and obligations formed for the grape harvest and wine making in October and the hog slaughter and meat processing in January.[40]

During these events, the host family was obliged to provide food and drink for the workers. Often the family's best preserved meats and wine were saved for these occasions. Not only did this reciprocate for the work being rendered, but it also "cut a good figure," thus winning respect from the others.

Though these work parties had a definite economic function, they also acted as social excursions. They were particularly looked forward to by young single men and women who took advantage of these situations to court eligible members of the opposite sex.

At all these agricultural junctures there were objective economic conditions that facilitated co-operation. In each case, for example, the task had to be accomplished within a short period of time lest spoilage set in, and each task was labour intensive, requiring more hands than could be supplied by the nuclear family.[41] Nevertheless, as was true in Toronto, it was the *paesani's* kinship system and the system of rights and obligations that shaped the nature of the co-operation.

WORK PARTIES IN CANADA

Obviously the harvests and hog slaughter ended with immigration to Toronto. But groups of *familiari* still formed for the annual making of wine and preserved meats. These tasks, which usually involved the pressing of grapes and processing of carcasses, still required a co-operative effort amongst *familiari*, though the work parties that formed were often smaller than in the village. Often these items were bought in bulk by *familiari*, thus saving both time and money by eliminating individual purchases. Although the grapes came from California, the carcasses were frequently acquired from a kin or *paesano* farmer on the city's outskirts.

Where joint purchases were made and the product was commonly worked and distributed, no obligations remained. In this case, as in the village, reciprocity between *familiari* took the form of a matched exchange of labour, that is, labour of the same kind. But the system of rights and obligations was flexible and reciprocity often took other forms. A man might buy part of the product, but not be able to work it, in which case he might reciprocate the other's labour by doing favours when the need arose. Or a man might contribute labour without having any ownership in the grapes or carcasses and be reciprocated by a "sample" or "gift" of the finished product. In any case, although cash was abundantly available compared to village standards, it rarely passed hands among *familiari* in such work parties. The payment of obligations in cash would have removed the service rendered out of the social-moral realm and out of its co-operative context, placing it unabashedly in the economic and individualistic realms in which labour was a mere commodity to be exchanged, thus debasing the kin relationship that bound *familiari* together.[42]

As in the village, the host family's women provided the workers with preserved meats and wine. The serving of these specific items, which were co-operatively made by the *familiari*, acted as a symbol of gratitude both for the co-operative effort at hand and for past work parties that contributed to the very meats and wine being served. The host family's head presided over the work being done, although often a recognized expert in the task at hand within the work party would take *de facto* charge of the operations. Both males and females participated in the work parties, although each divided their tasks in the traditional manner, the men being responsible for the more arduous ones.[43]

The economic necessity in the village for work parties, whereby they contributed to a yearly food supply, was eliminated in Toronto. Now it was the kindred's cultural preference for traditional village foods and the opportunity that work parties provided for a social get-together that accounted for their survival in Canada. For their part, the young no longer saw work parties as a potential forum for romance, since the greater freedom allowed them in Canada opened up alternative avenues for courting; and moreover, the smaller size of work parties in

Toronto virtually eliminated eligible partners. Many youths participated, however, both because of the joviality of such occasions and in order to acquire the desirable victual skills their parents would some day no longer be able to perform.

The importance of homeownership in Toronto as a form of property ownership brought into prominence a variation of the work party that had had relatively less importance in the village. This was the building work party. First as homeowners in the older sections of the city and then in newly built subdivisions, kinsmen were continually improving, finishing, or adding to their homes. Some, who were in the building trades, built their own. The home rather than the land became the major focus of property ownership.[44] And just as work parties concerned with the land were of prime importance in the village, so now work parties concerned with the home became such.

The fact that building often required special skills that, unlike agricultural skills, were not widely distributed amongst the kindred, often made the exchange of matched labour difficult. Where the aid consisted of little else but a strong back, the obligation could easily be repaid in kind. But, if the aid consisted of a plumbing job or electrical wiring, for example, a man frequently chose to reciprocate through some special skill or position he held, rather than through simple labour. If he were a barber, he might reciprocate through rendering his skill for a period of time; or if he were a grocer, he might give a "present" of foodstuffs.[45]

In the village, labour contributed within the context of work parties was usually reciprocated by matched labour. A man had the right to receive help from *familiari* in cutting his wheat and was obligated to help them in the same way. In Toronto, however, it was often not possible to reciprocate with matched labour the aid contributed within work parties. The flexibility of the system of rights and obligations made possible the development of alternate and suitable arrangements.[46] In this manner, the co-operative form of the work party was kept intact while the interpersonal dynamics that bound its members was adjusted to the Canadian context.

KINDRED COHESION

Reciprocity amongst *familiari* united through work parties was part of a wider, comprehensive network of explicit rights and obligations that bound the kindred as a whole. In this network, kinsmen were bound by dyadic relationships of mutual exchange of goods and services. There was constant exchange between individuals and families of complimentary specialized services, of matched aid, of "samples" of domestically made products, and of visiting and gifts. But at the same time, there were specific occasions when members of the kindred as a whole came together as a group. The most important of these occasions were the rites of passage.

The rites of baptism at birth, confirmation at maturity, and marriage at the assumption of full adult status marked major watersheds in one's life cycle and were given due recognition by the kindred.

MARRIAGE IN ITALY

Of the rites of passgae, marriage was socially most important (baptism being more critical religiously). One did not truly gain independence from one's parents, one did not truly contribute to the polity of the community until one was married.[47] In making men providers of their own family and women mothers, marriage, in the kindred's eyes, bestowed upon the participants the primary criterion of adulthood. In the village, the importance of marriage was attested to by the fact that not one, but four celebrations surrounded the rite.

The engagement and posting of the banns were occasions for celebration, bringing together up to fifty *familiari* and near kin. On the day of marriage itself, twice this number would be invited to the festivities. On all these occasions, gifts of a useful domestic nature were brought by the kindred; although at the wedding, cash gifts were commonly given in lieu of goods, especially by the more distant kin. In return, the hosts supplied food, wine, and music for their guests.

On the Tuesday following the marriage, the "Tuesday of Presents," the newlyweds would be visited by their wedding guests and brought various gifts of food and spirits to stock up the bridal pantry. This was a day of informal sociability and the new couple was not expected to reciprocate with meals and music, but with a modest array of sweets and drink.

The costs of these ceremonies was borne by the spouses' parents, sometimes being partially offset by the kindred's gifts. These gifts outweighed the costs incurred, and the difference was the kindred's contribution to the *sistemazione* of the bridal couple. In turn, the hosts were expected to reciprocate the kindred in the same way in upcoming marriages.

The gifts of goods helped furnish the new couple's home and the cash gifts gave them a liquid reserve when it was most needed. It was in this manner that the kindred formed a co-operative unit during the celebration of marriage to contribute to the setting up of a new independent family amongst them.[48]

MARRIAGE IN CANADA

In Toronto, these occasions surrounding marriage underwent much change. The "Tuesday of Presents" was eliminated altogether, since new-found affluence made the giving of food to newlyweds seem quaint, to say the least. And since this affluence made possible the adoption of the honeymoon, which in the village had been practised only by the elite, the new couple would, in any event, be unavailable for its celebration. The posting of the banns, by which fellow villagers were officially asked to bear witness to the engaged couple's intention to marry, became inconsequential in the context of a large populous city in which the *paesani* were scattered and belonged to various parishes. The celebration surrounding this event was, therefore, also discarded. The engagement party was operative in the early immigrant years on a scale similar to that of the village. Its later continuation, however, became a matter of individual discretion, increasing in importance for some, while being eliminated altogether by others.

On the other hand, the Canadian practice of giving a "shower" for the engaged woman was generally adopted and adapted as the social form by which the earlier gift-giving function of the engagement and posting of the banns celebrations was continued. Invariably, the Italo-Canadian shower was a larger and more formal event than its Canadian counterpart, replete with multi-course meals and sometimes rented halls. The guests consisted principally of kin, both the bride's peers and their mothers. As in the village, the kindred's gifts were both substantial and utilitarian, marking, in part, the closer kindred's contribution to the *sistemazione* of the new family.

The wedding itself underwent much expansion in Toronto so that it became the single, most important event binding the kindred as a whole. Weddings of 400 people became commonplace, and more distant kinsmen who would not have been brought together for a single social function in the *paese* now interacted perhaps half a dozen times in any one year at such affairs.

Both the increased size and the content of the wedding reflected the kindred's increased standard of living. In the village, the reception was held at the bride's parents' home; the meal, though abundant, rarely included little meat; music was modestly provided by *paesani*; and if the bridal couple had a car at all to get to and fro, it was rented. In Toronto, on the other hand, spacious halls were rented; the meal included prime steaks and roasts; music was provided by professional bands; and the automobile was taken for granted by all.[49]

Once initiated, the system of rights and obligations ensured the continuation of these large kin reunions, for the invitation, *per se*, to a kinsman obligated him to reciprocate by inviting the hosts at the earliest opportunity. The wedding acted to broaden the network of reciprocity already existing amongst the kindred, since it added matrimonial gift-exchanges to the existing repertoire of rights and obligations. To the extent that these gifts contributed to the *sistemazione* of the new couple, the village wedding, which had bound only closer kin through the system of rights and obligations surrounding this setting up process, was substantially widened to include more distant kin.

In contrast to the village, the kinsmen almost exclusively gave cash gifts to the bridal couple, since increased prosperity ensured that all their domestic needs would be taken care of by presents forthcoming either at the shower or from the spouses' families. Generally, the extent to which one was expected to contribute to the *sistemazione* of the new family was determined by the closeness of the kinship tie.[50] At the very minimum, the most distant guests were obliged to offset their cost "per plate" of the reception, and at the other end the *familiari* were expected to contribute the most generously, three times this amount being a standard starting point.

COMPARAGGIO

A similar expansion took place around the celebration of baptism. In the *paese* the festivities seldom included more than two dozen *familiari*. In Toronto, although some chose to limit the guests to *familiari*, the numbers invited were invariably expanded and many opened the ceremonies up to the more distant kindred, gatherings of 100 to 200 people being common. Further, confirmation, which was seldom celebrated beyond the family scale in the village, became the occasion for at least a house party of *familiari*, and often it approached the scale of baptismal festivities.[51]

Common to all these rites of passage was the institution of *comparaggio*, or ritual kinship. Through *comparaggio*, one adult conferred upon another the honour of godparenthood at baptism, sponsorship at confirmation, or witness at marriage, though in each case the individuals involved referred to each other as *compare*. A *compare* could be chosen from kin and non-kin alike, the former usually being preferred.[52]

The institution of *comparaggio* was, most commonly, a means by which a *de facto* close relationship could be made *de jure*: it was a means by which close non-kin were given kinship status and distant kin were given the status of *familiari*.[53] Since the migration process necessitated the working out of a new equilibrium within the kinship field, this salient feature of *comparaggio* was utilized relatively more often in Toronto than had been the case in the village. Such utilization of *comparaggio* was especially pronounced in the formation over time of new circles of *familiari*, which corresponded with the individuals' status and personal preferences.[54]

Not only did marriage and the other rites of passage expand upon migration to Toronto to include within their reciprocal systems a greater number of distant kin than had been possible in the village, but also, through the institution of *comparaggio* at these rites, the formal status of *familiari* was often conferred to formerly distant kin. Through the systems of rights and obligations that were both initiated and validated at these occasions, the cohesiveness of the kindred as a whole was reconfirmed.

CONCLUSION

The experience of post-World War II Southern Italian immigrants in Toronto who entered Canada via migration chains illustrates a process of adjustment by which the Old World cohesiveness of the family and kindred survived the Atlantic crossing. The experience of these immigrants was neither one of disintegration nor one of wholesale transplantation of Old World patterns.[55] Rather, both the form and content of family and kindred life were necessarily adapted to, and merged with, the New World environment to form a unique synthesis.[56] At the three kinship levels of nuclear family, family circle, and kindred, elements from a peasant past were merged with an urban present. The kinship patterns that emerged can neither be referred to as Canadian nor as Italian, but as uniquely "Italo-Canadian." Evidence suggests that this emergent entity is sufficiently consonant with the culture of the host society that it will prove to be tenacious, though only with time and the birth of new generations will its durability be confirmed.

NOTES

1. Instituto Centrale di Statistica, *IX Censimento Generale Della Popolozione 4 Novembre 1951* (Rome, 1956), 1, Fascicolo 79, p. 26; *10° Censimento Generale Della Popolozione 15 Ottobre 1961* (Rome, 1966) 3, Fascicolo 78, p. 28.

2. The number of immigrants from the commune in Toronto is based on the estimate given in interviews. Anthony H. Richmond, *Immigrants and Ethnic Groups in Metropolitan Toronto* (Toronto, 1967), p. 25.

3. See also Andrei Simić, *The Peasant Urbanities: A Study of Rural-Urban Mobility in Serbia* (New York: Academic Press, 1973), pp. 21-27.

4. Samuel Sidlofsky, *Post-War Immigrants in the Changing Metropolis with Special Reference to Toronto's Italian Population*, Ph.D. thesis, University of Toronto, 1969, pp. 97, 110.

5. Derived from Istituto Centrale di Statistica, *Annuario Statistico Italiano 1956* (Rome, 1956), p 48; *Annuario Statistico Italiano 1960* (Rome, 1960), p. 55; Sidlofsky, *op. cit., p. 111*.

6. Sidlofsky, *op. cit., p. 112.*

7. Derived from *Annuario Statistico Italiano 1951* (Rome, 1951), p. 54; *Annuario Statistico Italiano 1955* (Rome, 1955), p. 61; *Annuario Statistico Italiano 1956* (Rome, 1956), p. 51.

8. Derived from Freda Hawkins, *Canada and Immigration: Public Policy and Public Concern* (Montreal: McGill-Queen's University Press, 1972), pp. 47-48, 54. Boissevain quotes an estimate giving 91% of all Italian immigrants as sponsored by relatives, a figure confirming my calculations. Jeremy Boissevain, *The Italians of Montreal: Social Adjustment in a Plural Society* (Ottawa, Studies of the Royal Commission on Bilingualism and Biculturalism, 1970), p. 10.

9. White Paper, *Canadian Immigration Policy* (Ottawa, Canada, 1966), quoted in Hawkins, *op. cit.*, pp. 9-10.

10. Stanley H. Brandes, *Migration, Kinship and Community: Tradition and Transition in a Spanish Village* (New York: Academic Press, 1975), pp. 1-5; Simić, *op. cit.*, pp. 10-21.

11. For example, see Leonard W. Moss and Stephen C. Cappannari, "Patterns of Kinship, Comparaggio and Community in a South Italian Village," *Anthropological Quarterly*, 33 (1960), pp. 24-25.

12. George M. Foster, "Interpersonal Relations in Peasant Society," *Human Organization*, 19 (1960-61), pp. 174-180.

13. Edward C. Banfield, *The Moral Basis of a Backward Society* (New York: Free Press, 1958), p. 83ff.

14. Jan Brögger, *Montevarese: A Study of Peasant Society and Culture in Southern Italy* (Oslo: Scandinavian University Press, 1971), pp. 41-52, 82-86, 117-123; J. Davis, *Land and Family in Pisticci* (London: London School of Economics, 1973), chaps. 4, 6.

15. Constance Cronin, *The Sting of Change: Sicilians in Sicily and Australia* (Chicago: University of Chicago Press, 1970), pp. 184-202; Boissevain, *op. cit.*, pp. 9-13.

16. Boissevain, *op. cit.*, pp. 27-28.

17. Lorraine Blaxter, "Rendre Service and Jalousie," in *Gifts and Poison: The Politics of Reputation*, ed. F. G. Bailey (Oxford: Basil Blackwell, 1971), pp. 119-138.

18. Commencing with this section on elasticity, the argument flows from the interviews conducted with the villagers under study, although reference will be made to studies which have contributed to the analysis or which expand on the issue at hand.

19. Davis, *op.cit.*, pp. 64-65; Simić, *op.cit.*, pp. 109-111; Philippe Garigue, "French-Canadian Kinship and Urban Life," in *The Canadian Family: A Book of Readings*, ed. K. Ishwaran (Toronto: Holt, Rinehart and Winston, 1971), p. 429.

20. Davis, *op. cit.*, pp. 59-61; Moss and Cappannari, *op. cit.*, p. 29.

21. Brandes, *op. cit.*, p. 8.

22. Canadian as well as Italian authorities acted in 1927 to virtually close Italian immigration, and it was not until 1947, when Italians were removed from Canada's enemy aliens category, that the movement was resumed. Sidflosky, *op. cit.*, pp. 53-54, 100-101.

23. Simić, *op. cit.*, pp. 82-85.

24. Franc Sturino, "A Case of a South Italian Family in Toronto, 1935-1960," *Urban History Review*, No. 2-78 (1978), pp. 42-57. Harvey M. Choldin, "Kinship Networks in the Migration Process," *International Migration Review* 7 (1973), pp. 163-175; Simić, *op. cit.*, pp. 101-107.

25. Sturino, *op. cit.*, p. 57; Humbert S. Nelli, *The Italians in Chicago, 1880-1930: A Study in Ethnic Mobility* (New York: Oxford University Press, 1970), pp. 53-54.

26. J. K. Campbell, *Honour, Family and Patronage: A Study of Institutions and Moral Values in a Greek Mountain Community* (Oxford: Oxford University Press, 1964), p. 190.

27. *Ibid.*, p. 189; Davis, *op. cit.*, pp. 43-49.

28. A. L. Maraspini, *The Study of an Italian Village* (Paris: Mouton, 1968), p. 183.

29. Leonard Covello, *The Social Background of the Italo-American School Child: A Study of the Southern Italian Family Mores and Their Effect on the School Situation in Italy and America* (Leiden, Netherlands: E. J. Brill, 1967), pp. 196-198, 233-234; Brögger, *op. cit.*, pp. 50-52.

30. Boissevain, *op. cit.*, pp. 9, 13-14.

31. Virginia Yans McLaughlin, "Patterns of Work and Family Organization: Buffalo's Italians," in *The Family in History: Interdisciplinary Essays*, eds. Theodore K. Rabb and Robert I. Rotberg (New York: Harper and Row, 1973); Maraspini, *op. cit.*, pp. 173-174.

32. Davis, *op. cit.*, p. 50.

33. *Ibid.*, pp. 51, 53.

34. Maraspini, *op. cit.*, pp. 158-159.

35. *Ibid.*, p. 142; Campbell, *op. cit.*, p. 189.

36. Maraspini, *op. cit.*, pp. 158-159; Davis, *op. cit.*, pp. 34-36.

37. Davis, *op. cit.*, pp. 44-45.

38. Sturino, *op. cit.*, p. 47.

39. Covello, *op. cit.*, pp. 195.
40. Brögger, *op. cit.*, pp. 41-49; Davis, *op. cit.*, pp. 101-102; Brandes, *op. cit.*, pp. 82-87; J. A. Pitt-Rivers, *The People of the Sierra* (Chicago: University of Chicago Press, 1961), pp. 85-86.
41. Brögger, *op. cit.*, pp. 43-44, 48-49; Brandes, *op. cit.*, pp. 82-86.
42. Blaxter, *op. cit.*, pp. 128-132; Brandes, *op. cit.*, pp. 82-83.
43. Pitt-Rivers, *op. cit.*, pp. 85; Davis, *op. cit.*, p. 102.
44. Boissevain, *op. cit.*, pp. 16-17.
45. Blaxter, *op. cit.*, pp. 125-127.
46. Simić, *op. cit.*, pp. 109-110.
47. Davis, *op. cit.*, pp. 22-25.
48. *Ibid.*, pp. 32, 37, 39.
49. Boissevain, *op. cit.*, pp. 11-12.
50. Davis, *op. cit.*, pp. 38-39.
51. Boissevain, *op. cit.*, pp. 11-12.
52. Moss and Cappannari, *op. cit.*, pp. 30-31.
53. Davis, *op. cit.*, p. 61
54. Simić, *op. cit.*, pp. 140-142.
55. See Oscar Handlin, *The Uprooted* (New York: Grosset and Dunlap, 1951); Rudolph J. Vecoli, "*Contadini* in Chicago: A Critique of *The Uprooted*," *Journal of American History*, 51 (1964), pp. 404-417.
56. See Robert F. Harney, "Ambiente and Social Class in North American Little Italies," *Canadian Review of Studies in Nationalism 2 (1975), pp. 208-224.*

6. The Quebec Stem Family Revisited

MICHEL VERDON

DEFINITION AND METHOD

In one way, one could say that Quebec sociology started with the stem family. Quebec's first sociologist, Léon Gérin, spent his life trying to establish a typology of French Canadian families, pivotal to which was the stem family as the traditional French Canadian type.[1] There is no room in this paper for a review of the literature, but such a review would show that much of the debate in early Quebec sociology was centred on family sociology and generated by some of Gérin's generalizations. To my knowledge, the stem family in itself was not seriously restudied, although Gérin had based all his work on one single case. The type was taken over directly from Gérin, with the characteristics that he had found in it. Miner's study of a French Canadian parish devoted one chapter to the family, in which the "type" was not altered.[2] Much of the subsequent debate in Quebec family sociology then boiled down to finding out how much the urban family, or the "modernized" family of rural areas, diverged from the "traditional type" as described by the forefather. In more than one way, Gérin's work was to set the tone of much of the sociological enquiry about Quebec.

The gist of Gérin's thinking and conceptual legacy about the stem family is that of a very authoritarian, patriarchal group, where the *paterfamilias* rules over an estate which he tries to consolidate into a self-sufficient domain in order to bequeath it undivided to one of his sons. The two critical features of Gérin's stem family were thus the absolute authority of the father-owner (and concomitant subordination of heir and children), and the impartible inheritance. The two features were intimately linked in that only the unquestioned authority of a *paterfamilias* could maintain such a seemingly unfair system of inheritance.

Gérin's legacy, from my point of view, was double: (1) a popular sociological image of the traditional "Québécois" as being submissive to parental authority, a conception which led other sociologists to view it as utterly consonant with submission to the clerical authority; (2) a tradition of confusion about one of the key institutions of rural Quebec, the stem family.

The present paper aims at clarifying these two issues by focusing especially on stem families in a pioneer village of Lac St. Jean, what some refer to as "a frontier parish." Some will argue that I have not proved the homogeneity of the institution throughout Quebec or French Canada. They are right. But it will be noticed that the key features of the institution as studied date back to the origins of the community, in the 1880s. In that respect, they are somewhat "traditional." Moreover, the pioneers shared with the settlers of older regions the conviction of the agricultural vocation of Quebec. As such, they cannot be argued away as a fringe group.

To dispel some of the confusion which has marred family sociology from a deeper understanding of an institution like the stem family, I introduce two distinctions: (1) that family and residence are two different things. In my terminology, a family is simply the group composed of parents and offspring. Family members may live in different residential groups, as they do in some parts of Africa or Melanesia. If the family happens to reside in one single dwelling-place, the two concepts must nevertheless be distinguished in the analysis. Strictly speaking, I should be writing about the "stem residential group" and not the "stem family"; I retain the latter concept simply because it is so widespread in the literature; (2) that, in the study of residence, it is not the notion of structure that is important. At one point in time, two residential groups may display the same structure: father, mother, married son, daughter-in-law, and young grandchildren. In one case, the married son and his family will move out as soon as they have enough money to build; in the other case, they will stay permanently. These two phenomena are obviously different, but how will we conceptualize the difference? One possible solution, and the one I have adopted here, is to study residential groups as groups over time. One should thus analyze their process of growth to determine the type of structure beyond which they never evolve. This type is then conceived as a "structural limit," and it is the phenomenon to be explained.

With this in mind, let me now define what I understand by "stem family." If a family consists of parents and offsprings, a widow or widower with her or his children do not form a family and nor do divorcees with their children. Following the above distinction, the stem family is thus *a residential group which contains only two families* with one overlapping member: a parental family and the family of only one of their sons (or daughters if there are no sons to inherit).

Should the parents build a cottage or a separate annex and move to re-side in it, the result will *not* be a stem family.

This residential group (the stem family) will normally form one do-mestic group, at least with respect to food consumption. It need not form one group of production, although it will not be part of a greater group. Above all, in this residential group, father and son form *one group of ownership*. In other words, the two families are united through ownership of the raw material and equipment involved in the process of production, although only one of the families (usually the heir's) may be actively involved in production. The co-residing son is the heir and the only heir of the land on which the buildings are built, of the buildings themselves and of the adjoining chattel. This is known as impartible inheritance. The father may help other sons to establish themselves on lands in the neighbourhood, but the main part of the estate where the chattel is located is not divided. *Imparti-ble inheritance is a necessary but not a sufficient condition to create a stem family.* The rule of impartible inheritance exists in many places (England, Wales, France) without being accompanied by the institu-tion of the stem family. Many authors have confused the two (impart-ible inheritance and stem family), including Léon Gérin. This is where the notion of "structural limit" is important. The stem family must be analyzed as a "structural limit"; if the heir in a given society (like Wales) never gets married before one of his parents dies (and only one needs to die), then no two families ever co-reside and there is not a stem family but a different type of residential group.

Furthermore, a stem family does not contain any more than two families expected to co-reside permanently until one of the two is disrupted by death. Other families or other individuals may be tempo-rarily attached. Individuals, insofar as they do not form families, may even be permanently attached (uncle, aunt, nephew, niece, brother-in-law, any kin or affine) and the residential group will still be classified as a stem family. *It is the presence of families and the mode of their linkage which is critical.* As a result, it must be proved that the *nor-mal* growth of the residential group in a given society can include the two families of the owner and heir before one can classify the group as a stem family. If it cannot be proved that the heir got married while both parents were still alive and that the two families co-resided, it is unwarranted to treat the group as a stem family.

The presence of ownership added to the fact of residence also led me to link residence to production. Insofar as the community studied included groups involved in different processes of production, I have found it useful to account for the existence of particular residential, familial, and matrimonial practises in terms of differences in the modes of production.

In other words, I suppose that the involvement in the process(es) of production provides a useful framework to understand the institutions of the village and their evolution, with a particular emphasis on problems related to family, kinship, and marriage. This particular orientation raises three major problems: (1) to identify the processes of production in the community at its beginning; (2) to derive most of the organizational features of the community from the properties of these processes of production; and (3) to demonstrate how the changes in these organizational features can be interpreted as resulting from changes in the processes of production themselves.

I. THE COMMUNITY AT ITS BEGINNING

The village studied, which I call Dequen, was originally settled around 1885 in the southern part of Lac St. Jean, an area of Quebec which was not generally settled before the 1880s. The settlement followed a general wave of colonization of forest lands far from the St. Lawrence valley by French Canadians who were urged to do so by a clergy who wanted to root the survival of French Canadian ethnicity in the land.

From 1885 to 1900, Dequen was not yet an independent community, but simply a group of settlers at the periphery of the inhabited area. How the community suddenly became autonomous, or how gradual it was, is impossible to ascertain. All I know is that by 1900, the community was fully grown. It was demographically mature, having reached a level which was not to vary greatly for the rest of its history (approximately 500 inhabitants). From a Mission of a neighbouring parish, it became a full-fledged parish in 1903, with its own resident parish priest. The status of municipality soon followed and Dequen was able to elect its own mayor. In the same years, Dequen opened its first primary schools, cheese factories, and even a saw-mill which, built in 1905, burned down in the same year and was never rebuilt. At the demographic, political, religious, educational, and economic levels, it seemed fairly autonomous and independent around 1900 to 1905.

But already during that period one could detect the major divergences which were to scar the community up to this day. By 1900, the people of Dequen were involved in two different processes of production: agriculture and lumber industry. These differences were simultaneously echoed in the settlement pattern, the mode of inheritance, and the family system.

II. PRODUCTION AND SOCIAL STRUCTURE

A. Mixed Farming

Some of the conditions of pioneer immigration and settlement must be reviewed in order to understand the outcome. The movement of colonization, directing people towards the most distant land, was immediately marked by its *geographical isolation*. Settlers migrated in conjugal families and the lands they occupied around the lake were heavily forested. The presence of forests simply intensified the isolation, making communication more difficult, but it also attracted English-Canadian capitalists who invested in the lumber industry. To them, the settlers represented a handy source of manpower. The land on which migrants settled was already divided into long and narrow strips of land of 104 acres each. The settlers would build their house at one end, where a road would link the habitations. Although houses sometimes faced one another, the closest neighbour on one's own side could be as far as half a mile away. The line of contiguous strips of lands (called "lots") thus settled was called a *rang*, a pattern of settlement peculiar to Quebec, with very scattered houses in the pioneer areas. Finally, the Lac St. Jean area is equally notorious, as is northern Quebec, for its long and severe winters. The winter aggravated the communication problem and rendered acute problems of production and consumption. No agricultural production was then possible. The farmers were freed from agricultural production during the winter, but they still faced the problem of feeding themselves. The problem of winter consumption could only be solved in a limited number of ways: through hunting or, better still, through mixed farming. The latter solution was adopted.

The great isolation and the adoption of mixed farming as a solution to winter food shortages created the conditions for an economy of quasi self-subsistence, a domestic economy at the least, where the products are not marketed, but mostly consumed by the producers themselves. The animal population thus served two related needs: food consumption in the winter and raw material for self-subsistence: wool, hide, and so on. In order to satisfy those needs, the animal population had to be composite, consisting of cows, swine, sheep, poultry, and horses.

The keeping of an animal population (mixed farming) in the context of a domestic economy generated, in turn, a certain number of constraints, as the animal population itself had to be fed during the winter. Food thus had to be stored to feed the animals during the winter, a necessity which created formidable demands on agricultural production. As a result, most if not all of the field crops were given to the animals, and human consumption needs were essentially catered for through animal production and horticulture. All this was complicated by the fact that forested land only yielded mediocre arable land. Finally, all agricultural production was based on muscular energy: the horse and the human population. Being the key-pin to agricultural production, the horse had to be fed more than the other animals, and the best food. I believe these constraints to be the main causal factors in explaining the particular settlement pattern and the ecological ceiling to growth.

The Settlement Pattern The settlers did not decide the shape of their lands. They were given to them in "lots" of fixed geometrical shapes. The houses were built at the extremity of the lot, but the good arable land might not be there; worse still, it might not be all in one place. The cultivated part of the land was, in fact, sometimes divided into two or three separate locations and distinct from the pasture area. The men, who were in charge of the agricultural production (most of it), spent most of their days in the fields, away from the house. But only cows and sheep had to graze; the chickens and pigs could not be left to roam around and could not be under the men's care. Consequently, the pigsty and the hen-house were built near the house and were the wife's responsibility. The stable and the pen for the sheep were also built near the house, since the animals had to be sheltered at night and during the winter. So the house and its adjacent buildings for animals and farm machinery and food storage formed a very complex whole, occupying a fairly large area. And the cultivated lands were not always close to the buildings, nor were they all of one piece.

The Ecological Ceiling   In this system of production, there is room for some increase in the agricultural and animal production, but not indefinitely so. In other words, the human and animal populations can support one another up to a certain size, but this ceiling is fairly low, since all the production is directly consumed by the producer to replace his energy loss. Any increase in the production effort would have to be matched by an increase in the consumption input. Production would only rise to satisfy increased consumption needs; there would be no room for the creation of a surplus. Where agricultural and animal production are directly geared towards consumption by the group of production itself, and where production is based on muscular energy, there is a built-in limit to the potential of growth and this limit is low.

A first implication of the above is that both settlement pattern and the low potential of growth help explain why the estate cannot be divided:

1. the complex of buildings cannot be split up, it can only be duplicated. The road crosses the lot at one of its ends, and the lot is too narrow to accommodate more than one such arrangement. To divide the animal population is tantamount to rearranging the whole of agricultural production, which is split on different parcels of land scattered through the lot; it is next to impossible and it is ecologically aberrant. There is one other possibility: all sons but one could simply build their dwelling places near the central area where the animals are kept. In this way, all sons could be equally heirs, form one single group of ownership, one group of production, but separate residential groups containing only one family. Or they could all live in the central living quarters, forming one single residential group. The latter situation requires that one son be designated as trustee to the estate; after the father's death, this son would act as the head of the group. This is how extended families operate. But why should brothers put up with such inequality when they all have the opportunity to clear the land next door and be masters on their own land? This arrangement would not make sense in a situation where every able-bodied man can own his land, and a vast

area of it. Subdivision of holdings or corporate ownership are both quite impractical in this particular situation.

2. the low potential of growth generates similar constraints. A pioneer family arrived on a forest land with a minimum animal population. After years of hard work and as their family grew, agricultural and animal production increased, but so did the consumption needs of the growing family with new young adults until production reached a maximum per capita. Beyond that level, the output can only decrease, as sons leave or bring in brides and create new families. There is only a limited number of solutions: (a) if all grown up children leave as they get married, the old couple cannot manage the production and it falls drastically; (b) if all grown up sons stay, bring their wives and have children, the group of production would quickly outgrow its maximum size and per capita output would decrease. Moreover, the settlement pattern does not allow sons to stay or division of the estate and chattel. But these solutions are nevertheless plausible. Solution (a) would require greater incentives in leaving than inheriting, either because there are better sources of employment elsewhere or that living with the parents is an intolerable burden. Solution (b) might appear if there were strictly no alternative source of employment to farming. People would then be compelled to accommodate their settlement pattern and their consumption needs to this new situation, especially if there was a land shortage. But in Lac St. Jean, land was abundant and available free to everybody; moreover, there was always an alternative source of employment (lumber industry). Consequently, the most logical solution appeared to be the impartible inheritance (or rather, devolution) to a single heir.

It is thus the ecological aspects of the process of production, and not land pressure or shortage, which led to impartible inheritance. But it must be immediately emphasized that *impartible inheritance is not stem family*, although a condition for it. We still have to understand why, unlike the Welsh solution, the French Canadian owner's wife tolerated her daughter-in-law in the same house, or why the son would not forego his right to marry during his parents' lifetime. In order to answer this critical question, we will have to look more closely at the way the stem family operated in this pioneer phase.

The pioneers were deeply religious people, following the clergy's exhortation to colonize. They were also deeply committed to the perpetuation of agriculture in French Canada and were quite suspicious of life in the city, a life deemed devilish. These pioneer families would spend years clearing the forest and cultivating the land with their children. There was no rule about who would inherit the land; the father would not commit himself as long as he could. Some of the sons would stay with the father, but, fed up with the uncertainty about their own fate, would get married. Their wife would hardly tolerate living with her in-laws unless the husband was the designated heir. Such pressures from marrying sons would force the old man to designate one of his sons. The other sons would then only stay with their parents until they had accumulated enough money to buy their own plot, build their own house in the village, or move to the city. Their part of the inheritance (movable property and cash) would not necessarily be transmitted on the day of their marriage. All married sons would thus be likely to stay with their parents for a few years. The children, married or not, were not paid while working for their father; their part of the inheritance was thus conceived as post-dated wages for their part in the production.

Most of the sons could not bear the uncertainty about devolution and left the father to become lumbermen. Eventually a son would be designated or would stay on, and it would be assumed that he was the heir. In this pioneer phase, the elders remember bitterly, commitments about inheritance were only verbal commitments. Sometimes wills were not even made and the transmission of property was not achieved during the lifetime of the owner. Most owners recall stories of parents left destitute on public charity after bequeathing the estate to their heir during their lifetime. In order to avoid this kind of treatment, the old people would literally use economic blackmail to ensure the obedience of the son's family. This is clearly stated by the eldest citizens. The father-owner would sometimes resort to threatening his heir that he could disinherit him and give the farm to another son who was farming near by, or a labourer in the village or in town. The owners thus used economic blackmail in order to maintain the subordination of the heir and his family and to keep control of the farm. The old man would make the key financial decisions until his death, older people say. Such a state of conflict (where blackmail was resorted to) did not exist in all families, but this latter fact is then explainable by the very submission and obedience of the son. Where conflicts arose due to the son's more independent character, blackmail would be the weapon. In both cases, the result is the same: the relationship between adjacent generations was predicated on the complete subordination of the younger generations, but it was always threatened and rarely achieved. This subordination extended to all descending generations. Grandfathers tried to control their grandchildren in the same way that they tried to impose themselves on their children.

Blackmail and conflict were always associated with the person of the daughter-in-law. She was seen as the main protagonist in this family drama of the son being pitted against his own father, as the main manipulator trying to pull the rope to her side. This she was capable of because the husband was, in fact, supposed to side with his wife. *It is because the son-heir felt a greater loyalty towards his wife than his parents that co-residence was so difficult and led to such extreme measures.* To summarize, the owner in the pioneer phase refused to transmit property *inter vivos*, and sometimes resorted to economic blackmail because he was afraid of being literally pushed out of his own domicile should the heir take control. Ownership of the estate clearly meant control over the people residing on it. Ownership could not be devolved without losing authority.

The blackmail can only be read as a sign of insecurity on the part of the father-owner. Paradoxically enough, the reason for this insecurity seems to be of his own making, since he accepted a daughter-in-law in the house. Should he refuse the marriage of his heir during his lifetime, none of these problems would arise. If the father did not do it, it must be assumed that he could not do it. In this case, the son must be regarded as having some kind of bargaining power that enabled him to bring a wife in, despite the threat that this action represented to his parents.

The sons' position was in fact a complex one. The sons knew that the old man would *not* part with his property until his death. Not knowing when death would occur, this was a substantial risk. Worse still, even the heir could not be certain of ever inheriting the land; he might wait for years and a capricious old man would withdraw it from him and give it to another brother. This was known to have happened, as family fortunes are known to fluctuate. With this built-in uncertainty, why should a son not marry to find himself deprived of his inheritance and a bachelor? Conclusion: if the father does not want to devolve the property until his death and will not commit himself to his son, why should the son commit himself to bachelorhood? The father had grounds not to commit himself irrevocably to one son. He wanted to be sure that the heir was dedicated to agriculture. The land was important for the pioneers, as the main symbol of the agricultural mission of the French-Canadian people. Most pioneer farmers did not want to see the land they cleared turn back to forest. And it takes a long time to test a son's committal to agriculture, as the same old folk stories will tell: so and so's son inherited the land, sold not long after, and squandered the money in town. Time is the surest way to try a son, especially with the knowledge that this son is eventually going to marry. Many a wife has been accused of luring her husband out of farming to enjoy the facility of city life. By controlling the daughter-in-law, the father had a way of ensuring his own son's engagement to perpetuate the estate.

But the son also had direct bargaining power; without it, the whole struggle for subordination would hardly make sense. The heir could and did very often threaten the old man to leave him alone, to desert farming. This would have left the father in a begging position; he would then have had to accept the conditions laid out by another son before finding a replacement. The heir could use blackmail in his turn as he truly had the opportunity to leave and work outside, either in the lumber industry or anywhere in a town or city. The existence of alternative sources of employment was thus a key factor in maintaining the balance between paternal and filial blackmailing and threats, and helps to account for the particular features of the French-Canadian pioneer family. Above all, it helps to account for the existence of the stem family in this pioneer situation. By resorting to blackmail, the father was showing that he did not have the authority that he wanted to have. And the son's own bargaining power was further strengthened by another feature of the pioneer and to some extent of the French Canadian rural economy: the lack of agricultural labourers. This fact is almost tautological in the context of a domestic economy operating in the midst of an abundance of land and better opportunities to earn cash outside of farming. Why would a man work for others when he could be his own master on his own land? And how could a farmer have paid labourers when his production was only marginally marketed?

The process of production within the general context of the economy thus provides the essential set of co-ordinates to understand the main features of the residential structure. And the same process also helps to account for much of the family behaviour: (a) husband and wife were integrated in the same process of production and their relationship was based on collaboration; (b) because of the mutual blackmail rendered possible by an alternative source of employment, the relationship between generations within the same residential group was highly strained and the older generations were striving to maintain a rigid pattern of superordination-subordination; mother-in-law/daughter-in-law relationships were especially tense, especially in the first years of marriage; (c) because of the strain on family relationships brought about by the presence of a daughter-in-law in the same residential group as her affines and married to the heir, consanguineous kin were sought as spouses for the heir. This is strongly supported by the data; of all marriages up to 1920, 17% were with consanguineous kin (up to the fourth degree of collaterality as defined by the Roman Catholic Church in Quebec), and more than 90% of them involved heirs. The search for a consanguineal spouse is best understood by the fact that a niece is going to be more respectful of her mother-in-law who is her own aunt. The niece is also a safe "investment" as far as her moral character is concerned, since her background is well known; (d) finally, land, animals, and tools for agricultural and animal production were easily available to many people; they were within everybody's reach. The knowledge involved in the same production was also available to everybody. Consequently, all groups of production were structurally equivalent, none renting or leasing land. Their only differences were in the structure of the residential groups (two or three generations) and in their wealth. Despite the wealth differences, small according to any standard, no family controlled any other family, although some families would exert more political influence because of their education.

B. The Lumber Industry
In a similar fashion, the conditions of the lumber industry at its beginning will help us to understand some of its critical features. Unlike

mixed farming, the timber industry was a purely capitalist one. The capital almost exclusively belonged to English Canadian investors who hired local labour. The industry was divided in two sectors: the primary, represented by the logging camps, and the secondary, essentially limited to the saw-mills. The mills processed the wood to produce timber for construction. Pine was the main species which fed the industry, and it was found in the immediate surroundings of Lac St. Jean (a belt of approximately forty miles), which are composed of mixed forest. The population of Dequen was mainly involved in the logging camps. Investment in a saw-mill was not excessively expensive, but the only one ever built in Dequen burned down the very year of its construction. Because of the clash with settlers, logging camps could not be located too close to the human settlements. Moreover, logging and transportation out of the forest were also based on muscular energy. The basic problem was how to produce and transport at reasonable costs. There were only two solutions: the utilization of snow and waterways, both of which were used. The logging camps operated near rivers and were only open during the winter. Logs were pulled to the river by horses and left there on the ice. With the spring thaw, the logs would be carried downriver and the mills were built at the mouth of rivers.

A man could be hired in the camps as soon as he was big enough to fell a tree. Father and son could thus work in the same logging camps and be paid equivalent wages. The camps being away from the settlements, the men used to leave for up to six months every year, and would not come back for most of the logging season. As a consequence, the group of production was totally separate from the residential group and was directly involved in the market economy. The men had no rights of ownership over the product of their labour. They were simply paid in cash for their labour. Apart from their tools, fairly inexpensive equipment, the men did not own any special machinery, nor did they practise agriculture or animal husbandry. They only owned small parcels of land in the village on which their houses were built. There was no estate to transmit, no special inheritance, except the little movable property they owned. No special heir was thus designated, but all inherited equally. As a result, although sons would stay with their parents a few years after their marriage until they were rich enough to be residentially independent, there were no stem families. Residential groups amongst the lumbermen only temporarily included married children; this was their greatest extension, their structural limit.

Within the family, even the behaviour was different. As a result of the separation of the group of production from the residential group and the male residence in logging camps over long periods, the husband-wife relationships were strained. From their exclusive residence in common during the winter, the men would learn to loaf around in groups when back in the village, while the women would stay at home, thus deepening the cleavage between spouses. Moreover, since both father and son were equal in the group of production (as lumbermen), the father lost much of the authority he claimed in the other type of process and the relationship became much more egalitarian. Consanguineous unions were much rarer, if not totally absent, amongst the lumbermen. Within their group of production, the only structural difference between villagers was introduced through the ownership of technology. Those who owned horses (very often farmers themselves) were known as "jobbers," whereas those who fell the trees were simply lumbermen. This difference was nevertheless only in wealth and not in structural position, since both jobbers and lumbermen were employees of the same industry and none had control over the work of the others.

As a result of these features, there was structural homogeneity of the residential groups within their respective processes of production at the community level. Moreover, the processes were separate, although individuals could combine both. Structurally, no socio-economic group dominated the other. The only differences were differences in the wealth of families.

In answer to the three problems raised in this second section, it can already be seen that an analysis of the process of production has helped to understand the mode of inheritance, residential structure, family behaviour, marriage patterns, stratification, and, as we shall see in the following part, village and regional politics.

III. EVOLUTION OF THE COMMUNITY

A. 1885-1920: Atomization and Symbiosis

What happened before 1900? It is quite likely that many of the pioneers were not pioneers at all. Many probably were "timber thiefs," as mentioned in the literature. Some of them cleared their lot of the best trees on it, and turned to the timber industry. After the opening of the logging camps, they probably sold parcels of their lots to others who wanted to join in the lumber industry. These eventually formed the nucleated settlement now known as the village (as distinct from the rangs). This was the first generation of pioneers and sons of pioneers who migrated with their fathers.

There is nevertheless something very problematic about this community. Its lack of geographical unity, coupled with divergences in the settlement pattern, the economic activities, the type of residential group could hardly help to create a feeling of unity. As a parish, the parish priest gave it some sort of cement, but one man could not keep the community together, as later events were to prove. In fact, I conjecture that this unity was only possible because *the ecological cycles of the two processes of production were complementary, a complementarity which favoured some kind of economic symbiosis.* During the summer, the lumbermen were free to help with agricultural production; during the winter, the farmers or their older sons were free to work in the logging camps where they often served as jobbers with their horses. Consequently, the lumbermen could work for kinsmen who were farmers during the summer and would receive products in exchange. The farmers, on the other hand, could sell part of their products to the logging camps during the winter, work for cash with their horses in the same camps, and also sell products to the lumbermen during the summer. The farmers were thus using logging camps as a source of cash and a market for their products; apart from that, there were many reciprocal, non-lucrative exchanges of services for products or products for cash on the basis of kinship links within the community. This economic symbiosis at the village level allowed for some kind of autonomy. Villagers depended on the lumber camps for their supply of cash, but depended very little on other villages, except for the occasional visit to the general store.

At the regional level, this resulted into some kind of atomization. Regional politics were very parochial, a reflection of village politics itself. Towns were built as service centres for the villages, for agriculture, and for lumber industry. Men identified primarily with their village, and the conflicts of interest were of one village against another.

B. 1920-1950: Agricultural Specialization and Political Fission

Around 1915, new factors came to change this picture of the pioneering days. The pulp and paper companies were opening their first mills on the St. Maurice River (100 miles south of Lac St. Jean), and later elsewhere in the Lac St. Jean area itself. There was a massive emigration towards La Tuque and other centres near those mills. The pulp and paper industry depended on spruce, not on pine. There was no typical coniferous forest in the immediate vicinity of the lake, only beyond the belt of mixed forest. Logging camps were thus opened farther away from the original settlement areas around the lake. With the movement of camps away from the agricultural belt, the farm lost its main market and source of cash.

During the same period, agricultural prices fell rapidly, for reasons beyond the scope of this article. This slump did not stop until 1935. As the logging camps were moving away, so was the population. New towns were created and some of the older centres on the lake shore swelled with the incoming wave of immigrant lumbermen. On the whole, the farmers were losing their main market and source of cash, they were getting less and less for their products, and the towns on the border of the lake were now swelling (period 1920 to 1930). The farmers now had to get their cash from outside, from those new towns and cities. In order to market outside, they had to specialize. There were very few avenues open. There were no textile industries for the farmers' sheep and meat (pigs and poultry), and eggs could not be stored or refrigerated. But cheese factories existed in almost any rang, near the place of production in most cases; the milk could thus be stored for a long time in the form of cheese. The farmer thus had only one alternative: to become a lumberman and migrate or to specialize in dairy production.

In the 1911 census, 86 farmers were reported for Dequen; in 1921, their number had dwindled to 51. Whether they migrated to the village or outside the community is impossible to ascertain; I would surmise that they departed from the community. Despite this mass migration of farmers, the area in field crops did not change significantly, a suggestion that the land abandoned was acquired to consolidate larger holdings. The census also reveals a major shift in agricultural practices: mixed grains had almost disappeared in 1921, and the acreage of cultivated hay had doubled in 1931. This change can only be interpreted as a beginning of specialization in dairy production. This shift nevertheless meant *specialization without the context of a domestic economy* and not yet full-scale production for the market. Swine, sheep, and poultry were indeed kept in significant numbers, not much less than in previous years (I can only establish this on country averages).

This beginning of specialization was to have serious implications for the farmers. From this point on, they depended more and more on the outside towns in order to find their cash. Although their closest rapport was with the local cheese factory, they had to sell outside part of their products to establish rapports with customers, suppliers, auctioners, and other farmers.

In the other sector of the population (the lumbermen), two new factors helped to transform their lives. By 1920, the second generation (born in Dequen) was already reaching maturity and before the end of that period, third and fourth generations were already born. Upon reaching maturity these sons did not see lumbering as the only alternative to farming, as had their pioneer fathers and siblings. They saw the prospects of new trades in the growing towns and many turned to these new occupations: carpentry, plumbing, and later electrical, mechanical work, and so on. The successful ones migrated immediately upon finding a reliable job in the city. The other ones, incapable of finding permanent employment outside the community, vacillated between lumbering and their own trade and remained in the community. They would practise their trade in the summer and leave for the logging camps in the winter. The non-farmers in Dequen were then not only lumbermen; they were rather labourers, looking for jobs either in the city or the forest, wherever they could find it, *but henceforth working as labourers all year long, and not only for one season.*

The second major factor was the introduction of the automobile in the lumberman's life. The automobile was less attractive to the farmer, who essentially had to carry milk or transport animals. But the labourers needed the automobile in the summer to go to the construction sites, and sometimes in the winter to go to the more distant logging camps. Because of their dual occupation and the increasing distance of the logging camps, labourers depended more and more on motorized transportation.

The first automobile was bought in Dequen in 1919. In 1931, there were 1,075 cars in the Lac St. Jean area, 398 of which only belonged to farmers' families. As there were 3,922 families of farmers, approximately one-tenth of the farmers' families had cars. There were thus 677 cars left for less than 4,000 families of labourers; one-sixth of the labourers' families thus had cars. Since labourers lived in nucleated settlements surrounded by kinsmen, and as more than one person could travel in a car, I would venture to say that more than one-third of the labourers' population had direct or indirect access to a car already by 1930. One can easily imagine the situation fifteen years later. This had serious implications for the labourers: (1) it replaced the horse for transportation and facilitated the contacts with the outside; it literally opened the community to the outside; (2) the car depended on fuel, not foodstuff like the horses. Car and fuel had to be obtained from outside, whereas foodstuff and horses could be obtained from the farmers; (3) horses and foodstuff could formerly be paid for with services; car and fuel only with cash. Consequently, the labourers depended increasingly on cash, and this at a geometric rate.

During the same census years (1931), only 54 farms had trucks in Lac St. Jean as a whole or one-sixtieth of all farming families. By 1941, this number had only doubled and left 3.3% of the farming families with a truck—a hardly significant number.

The shift in agricultural production towards greater specialization in the framework of a semi-domestic, semi-market oriented production left the structure of the residential group untouched, but affected the other sectors. The father-son relationship in the farming group was the first one altered. Because of the new trades, the new industries opening in the area and the slump in agricultural prices, sons were more interested in emigrating than staying on the farm, although inheriting a large holding was still an interesting prospect. The threat of losing all one's sons to the city or the lumber camps was too great this time to allow any autocratic method. Whereas, to the lesser threats of the earlier period, the father-owner could respond with attempts to force subordination on the descending generations co-residing with him, the strains of this period could not allow him to establish this type of semi-autocratic relationship. Had he done so, no heir would have stayed on the farm. Moreover, contacts with the outside forced the fathers to give the heir a greater say in the direction of the operations. Heirs would not accept to stay home while the father transacted alone in the neighbouring auctions or markets. The owners had to relinquish more and more control, and this was not without consequences on the mode of inheritance. Sons would not accept the uncertainty any more. The heir had to be designated much earlier, and the heirship formalized through a will at the notary's Heirship was thus a much more secure position and actual control of the farm was passed on to the heir during the lifetime of the owner, although actual ownership was not devolved until the death of the owner. The father-son relationship in the younger families became one of association instead of strained subordination. With the more unsettled conditions of agriculture, the father had lost much of his bargaining power.

As a result of this change, father and son were brought closer together, and a first serious wedge was driven between husband and wife. Insofar as dairy production now entailed more frequent contacts with the outside, with the market, these contacts were an exclusively male sphere. Women were not to leave the house. They still took an active part in animal and agricultural production but were not allowed to take part in the dealings with the outside, the "public" sector of social life. The distinction between the "public," the male sphere, and the "private," the female domain, was greatly accentuated. The woman's role was to remain domestic in an agricultural economy which was slowly absorbed by the outside market.

These major changes in family behaviour had an effect on the matrimonial system: the incoming daughter-in-law was less of a threat, because the heir was much closer to the owner. In fact, to the mother a daughter-in-law became an accomplice against the men. With the threat to authority lifted, co-operation was made easier and consaguineous unions between 1920 and 1950 dropped to 2% of all marriages (from 17% in the previous period).

Amongst the labourers, these transformations only accentuated trends which were already present. But the emergence of dual occupation in the younger generations had a different effect, when added to the specialization in dairy production amongst the farmers. With the logging camps farther away and the necessity to look after their cattle (milking) during the winter, the farmers had much less opportunity to work in the forest. And by working in their trade during the summer, the labourers were withdrawn from their involvement in farming. Labourers spent most of their time, and also their money, outside the community. This parallel movement disrupted the ecological complementarity upon which the former symbiosis was built:

(1) through the purchase of cars and the practise of new trades, the labourers spent the summer away and completely cut their links with the farmers. They stopped buying the farmers' products and working on his land during the summer;

(2) the farmer was also turning outside, more and more involved in a market economy. His own relationships, formerly directed towards his kinsmen in the community, were now directed towards suppliers, customers, and auctioneers.

Relationships formerly based on some form of reciprocity were now commercialized. Farmers and labourers were no more exchanging as kinsmen within the community. They were both dealing with outsiders. The disruption of the earlier symbiosis and the dependency on the outside led to an increased socio-economic awareness, which first emerged amongst the farmers and eventually led to forms of group action based on purely socio-economic realities.

At *the village level*, these cleavages were politically institutionalized by a split. The individuals' interests were no more identified with the community at large, but only with the section of the community which was involved in the same process of production and members of other communities which were also sharing the same involvement. In 1947, the move was initiated by the farmers, and the rangs separated themselves to form a distinct municipality.

At *the regional level*, this increasing separation was echoed in the birth of trade unionism. As with political fission at the municipal level, the farmers were the first to organize, because of the greater homogeneity of their economic involvement. The labourers were engaged in different groups of production during summer and winter, and from one summer or winter to the next. It was more difficult for them, granted the seasonality of operations, the fact that some individuals were not working twice in the same group of production, to organize as swiftly. But the prospects were so dismal in agriculture that the clergy itself took the initiative, in order to save this very agriculture which they perceived as the key to French Canadian survival. In 1930 the U.C.C. was founded, the first farmers' trade union.

C. 1950-1970: Mechanization and Monoproduction

In 1951, the farmer was faced with the following situation: using horses which were not gaining in value, but were eating agricultural products which had doubled in price. By getting rid of his horse before their price fell drastically, the farmer could still get enough money to deposit as a first instalment on a tractor. But above all, by getting rid of his horse, the farmer would free his best agricultural products from consumption and could give them to the cows. Animal scientists have calculated that a sudden improvement in the diet of milch cows can increase their milk production over a one-year period by 80% to 100% (that is, by 14.1 kL to 18.8 kL a year). By consuming the foodstuff formerly given to the horses, cows would double their dairy production; dairy prices had themselves doubled in the previous decade. This situation helped to persuade the farmers to sell their horses in order to mechanize.

The introduction of the tractor had a certain number of important consequences: (1) It had to be operated on fuel; formerly, both horses and food for the horses were produced by the farmer himself. (2) The tractor, fuel, and repair parts had to be *bought* from *outside* and paid for in *cash*. The tractor thus increased the farmers' need for cash and their dependency on the outside. The result was to deepen their market involvement, which pushed them exclusively into dairy production and completely out of the domestic economy. This monoproduction, sustained by the constant need for more sophisticated technology once the producer is engaged in a competitive market, eventually extended to the whole of Lac St. Jean and Quebec to a large extent. The government intervened and set limits to production, limits which did not allow small farmers to make a profit. The result was unequivocal. By 1966, there were only 28 farmers left in Dequen, and only ten of them declared their operations as being "commercial," that is, earning them more than $2,500 a year. Most farmers did not survive.

At this stage, transformations in agriculture were far-reaching enough to change the developmental cycle of the residential group, and consequently its structural limit. With the complete specialization, the new technology, the new contacts with the outside, the new administrative problems created by a budding "enterprise," the sons who accepted heirship in this period were playing a key role in the operations because of their greater literacy and readiness to understand and accept new methods. In these last years, with the decline in agricultural prosperity following the trend towards monoproduction, no son wants to remain on the paternal land. Farmers almost have to lure one of their sons into taking over. Moreover, with the institution of old-age pensions, the old fear of deprivation by the heir's family has vanished. Old days are now safe by governmental decree. For this last generation of heirs, the mode of inheritance itself has changed; fathers now create corporations with their heir or sell their estate to the heir in exchange for an annual allowance until their death and that of their spouse. No more in control and financially secure, the last farmers to devolve their farms have not started building their own separate house on an adjacent piece of land. This heralds the disappearance of the stem family. Although close neighbours, *the father's and the heir's families now form separate residential groups*. The developmental cycle and structural limit of the residential group has completely changed. Father-son relationships and mother-in-law/daughter-in-law relationships are now as positive as they can be. From stern disciplinarians towards their grandchildren, grandparents have now changed into the sweet, affectionate figures known to members of urban nuclear families. But women have paid the price of these transformations. With mechanization and the exclusive concentration on dairy production, women have been withdrawn from active participation in agricultural and animal production. They are more and more secluded and confined to the domestic sphere, separated from their husband's work. The husband-wife relationship in the *rangs* is gradually resembling that found amongst the labourers.

Without following in detail the evolution of the pulp and paper industry, it could be shown how it has influenced village and regional politics by creating widespread unemployment during the winter. With the introduction of new machinery, the winter logging almost disappeared and the labourers faced the dilemma of joining lumber camps or construction sites in the summer. In the winter, all faced the same predicament: unemployment. At a certain stage, both labourers and farmers realized their fate as a developing proletariat against the swelling and prosperous industrial cities developing around the lake.

As a consequence, their interests merged again and the village was reunited politically in 1969. The Social Credit movement emerged on the regional scene, trying to revive the values of a threatened agricultural society.

CONCLUSION: THE STEM FAMILY IN QUEBEC'S SOCIOLOGICAL IMAGE

As we saw in the introduction, Gérin was the first in Quebec sociology to link the stem family to a very strong authority structure. Once the family was demonstrated to be the bulwark of the strongest type of authoritarianism, the parallel was immediately established with the clerical or theocratic orientation of the ruling intelligentsia. Micro- and macro-structure were thus shown to fit perfectly. Thus originated the myth of the "authoritarian" Quebec social organization, still prevalent in English-speaking sociological circles.

The new generation of Quebec historians has done much to prove that Quebec's ruling intelligentsia was, in fact, fiercely anti-clerical until the advent of Mgr Bourget in the 1870s. This piece of ethnography aims at disproving the second part of the equation, that of an authoritarian, traditional family structure. The stem family, this presumed archetype of the Quebec patriarchal family, only seemed authoritarian because it was internally threatened. In fact, the head of the stem family has nothing "patriarchal" about him; he rather gives the impression of a powerless despot ready to resort to any devious means to keep his subjects. This suggests that the subjects had specific rights, and the power to move away.

The Quebec stem family, as it emerged in the pioneer areas, could rather be presented as being based on a compromise: it was the reluctant covenant of two nuclear families, with opposed interests, to co-reside for purely economic reasons. The two nuclear families united in this co-residence were not necessarily co-operating amicably; they were as often ridden with conflicts of the bitterest kind. Where co-operation existed, as in Gérin's stem family, it could be attributed more to the psychological proclivity of father and son rather than to structural reasons.

From a structural point of view, none of the mentioned features of the pioneer stem family, like its mode of devolution, the type of family relationships, or even the explanations that the actors themselves give of their institution, would accord with the reality of the stem family as an authoritarian and patriarchal family. A patriarchal society would not allow a son to side with his wife against his own father, nor would it resort to economic blackmail to keep one son at home. The features of the stem family as studied in Lac St. Jean rather suggest the reality of nuclear families striving to be autonomous and independent, but co-residing under specific economic pressures.

This ethnographic study helps to understand the strong ideological biases which have bedevilled the interpretation of Quebec social structure. From the image of absolute paternal authority inherited from one family in Gérin's sociology, sociologists were quick to label a whole society as "authoritarian" and "patriarchal." The image fitted well the prejudices of a prevalent Protestant ethnics ... Inserted in its proper context, the analysis of family structure reveals a completely different picture, rooted in economics and not in psychology: that the authority of the father was perhaps never so much questioned and threatened than in the Quebec family, as was the authority of the clergy questioned and threatened by the intelligentsia, throughout much of Quebec's history. What has been labelled "traditional," like the clericalism or a male chauvinist sexual division of labour are, in fact, the outcome of recent changes and trends. The "traditional" Quebec wife was as much involved in productive activities as was her husband; it is only recently that the wives had been more and more confined to the domestic domain.

The popular sociological image of Quebec social structure thus needs complete revision. The same kind of ideological sociology, this time reversing the roles, could equally well present the image of a patriarchal and clerical, sedate and conservative English Canadian society, in contrast to the dynamic and democratic Quebec ... But such types of ideological biases must be eradicated from Canadian sociology, since they simply serve as the vehicles of ethnic discrimination.

NOTES

1. L. Gérin, *L'habitant de St-Justin*, 1898, reprinted in J.C. Falardeau et P. Garigue, *Léon Gérin et l'habitant de St-Justin* (Montreal: Les Presses de l'Université de Montréal, 1968). Also by Gérin, *Le type économique et social des Canadiens*, originally published in 1937 and reprinted by Fides in 1948.
2. H. Miner, *St. Denis: a French-Canadian Paris* (Chicago: University of Chicago Press, 1939).

7. French-Canadian Kinship and Urban Life*

PHILIPPE GARIGUE

The present study is aimed at describing the importance and character of kinship among French Canadians of Montreal. It is directed at the problem raised by Wirth[1] and numerous other sociologists, who have assumed that kin ties lose significance in an urban setting. The data were collected between September 1954 and February 1955, from 52 persons in 43 households. As the study was specifically directed at assessing the influence of urbanism on kinship, only informants of urban background were selected, though some households included persons who were born outside Montreal. No significant difference seems to appear between those households whose members were all born in Montreal, and those with members born elsewhere. Thirty genealogical tables were collected from persons whose background was urban from birth. We believe it can safely be assumed that the sample conforms to the dominant urban behaviour among French Canadians, even though the extensiveness of interviews and the consequent restriction on the number of people who could be visited in the five months of the fieldwork prevented the taking of random sample.

All interviews were conducted in French, and took place in the homes of the informants. The informants are mostly of medium income; only three were of high income, and five of definitely low income. The study is not intended as an analysis of the total effect of urban life on the kinship system of all Montreal French Canadians—for instance, no attempt was made to study the "pathology" of urban life—

* Reproduced by permission of the American Anthropological Association from The American Anthropologist 58:1090-1101, 1956.

but enough data were collected to answer the more limited question as to the general influence of urbanism upon kinship.

The urban French-Canadian kinship system is a variant of that generally reported for Western Societies. It is a patronymic bilateral structure, with two major dimensions of lateral range and generation depth. While awareness of descent and pride in the history of a family name is shown by the majority of informants, frequency of contact is highest between members of the same generation, and cuts across consanguineal and affinal ties. These lateral and generation dimensions involve different patterns of behaviour: a formal pattern of expected obligations operates between the generations; a more informal choice according to personality preference operates between members of the same generation. The nuclei of the kinship system are the parent-child and sibling relationships of the domestic family, which is held to be an autonomous unit. The expected roles of the members of the broader kin group vary according to their position in the formal and informal patterns, and their closeness to Ego's domestic family. These roles separate the total kin into a number of subgroups having special functions. The total kin group is expected to come into action only for very formal occasions, such as a funeral; in most situations, only the subgroups are involved. Women are more active within the kinship system than men, and this fact, combined with their primary role as wives and mothers, gives them a great deal of influence and supplies the continuity of the kin group. While all informants showed a high degree of conformity to kinship obligations, they also reported factors which they believed were causing segmentation. The most important of these were said to be social mobility and cultural differentiation, which resulted in a decrease or even loss of contact between members of a kin group.

THE STRUCTURE OF KINSHIP KNOWLEDGE

Thirty of the 52 informants were asked for the range of their genealogical knowledge. The maximum limit of this range was determined by knowledge of the sex of a person, in addition to his family name. For instance, children of lateral kin were included if the informant was aware of their sex in addition to their proper genealogical link. The mean of such knowledge is a range of 215 persons. The smallest range was 75; the ten with least knowledge ranged from this to 120. The next ten ranged from 126 to 243; the highest ten from 252 to a maximum of 484 known kin. These known kin were distributed in a wide lateral range rather than extensive depth of generations. Including Ego's generation, one informant reported three generations, ten informants reported a range of four generations, thirteen informants reported five generations, and six informants claimed knowledge of six generations. The three cases with the lowest range of knowledge can be regarded as abnormal. In one instance, the mother's line was not known, and in two more the true bilateralism was distorted by ignorance of the second ascending generation.

The most extensive knowledge of kin was usually concentrated into the generations of Ego and his parents, which together included from one-half to two-thirds of the total persons known. Knowledge of the second ascending generation was often reduced to from one to eight known ancestors. In the third and fourth ascending generations, knowledge was restricted in most instances to a single ancestor. Variations in the lateral range, total size, depth of generations, etc., were linked to the age, sex, and marital status of the informants.

The age of the informants varied from 19 to 72, with an average of 30.5 years. There was a definite tendency for depth and breadth of range to increase with age. The controlling factor in the ratio of increase seems to be the size of the informant's kin group during adolescence. Among informants up to about 40 years of age, their own and their first ascending generation were most important. Among older informants, descending generations became increasingly important. The largest kin knowledge was reported by married persons.

The sex of the informants seemed to be an important factor in kin recognition; only two of the informants who reported the fifteen largest kin groups (186 to 484) were men. All of the ten largest kin groups were reported by women. Sex is also a major factor in determining the stress placed by the informant on the father's or the mother's line. Just over half of the men had a greater knowledge of their father's line; women knew more of their mother's line than their father's by a ratio of three to one. If knowledge of Christian names is taken as a sign of greater kinship awareness, a second and more limited range can be distinguished, which runs from a minimum of 54 to a maximum of 288. The proportion of kin whose Christian names are also known, to those known only by family name and sex, varied from one-half to nine-tenths. These ratios do not correlate with the extremes of the first range, and there was only a slight increase in the largest ranges. Ignorance of Christian names was always greatest in the descending generations of the domestic families with which there was little contact.

If kinship ties are graded in order of their importance as foci of activities, the first among them is the sibling tie. This seems to relate to the size of the sibling groups, and to the maintenance of sibling unity after marriage. The average size of the informant's sibling groups was 5, with one instance of an informant who was one of 16 siblings. There is an over-all correlation between total knowledge of kin and the size of the sibling groups closest to the informant: his own, his father's, and his mother's. The larger the number of persons in these groups, the greater the total kinship range. Moreover, the scope of lateral kin is increased through marriage of siblings, since these in-law ties tend to be rather firm. Thus, the "core" of the kinship system is formed by domestic families linked by sibling and parent-child ties, and by lateral ties arising through the marriage of siblings. Recognition outside that core operates according to lines of descent. In this instance, only some of the members of the sibling groups involved will be known. Some qualification must be introduced between the recognition arising from membership in the core, and through descent. Because of the frequency of cousin marriages among French Canadians, both modes of recognition can operate at the same time. While it is not possible to say whether the importance given to affinal ties through sibling marriages may not be due to the frequency of cousin marriages, there is no doubt that many kinship ties created through the marriage of a sibling are as important as those of cousinship.

Another characteristic of the urban French Canadians is the wide geographical scattering of their kin groups. While all had kin within Montreal, proportions running as high as three-fourths were reported scattered not only within the province of Quebec, but further afield in Canada and in the United States.

IMPORTANT ASPECTS OF KINSHIP BEHAVIOUR

Urban French Canadian men and women not only give different stress to kinship, but also have different roles. Men, for instance, reported that they usually thought of their kin group in terms of their male relatives; their knowledge of their female relatives was more restricted. In all instances, however, their attitudes towards their mothers, wives, or sisters, gave these female relatives great influence not only over household matters, but also in many outside affairs. Women seemed to have a greater awareness of the kin group as composed of both sexes. Not only was their knowledge of the total kin group greater so that in a number of instances wives knew more of their husbands' kin than the husbands themselves did, but they also had a much greater knowledge of the affairs of the kin group. While men reported their kin contacts as being largely for leisure-time activities, the women reported their reasons for contact as mostly "family affairs" such as children, births, marriages, or illness. A marriage or a funeral was the occasion for intense activity by the women, and it was they who took the initiative in organizing the gathering of relatives, who suggested visits to each other's homes, and who wrote letters or telephoned news to relatives. They also spent more time with their kin than did the majority of men.

While there are individual variations in behaviour, this sex diferentiation was a formalized expectation. A number of wives reported that while they were intimate with only a limited number of kin in their husband's line, they were expected by most to keep them informed of family affairs by letters or telephone calls. The wife, not the husband, would have been blamed for failure to do this. All informants, male and female, stressed the fact that it was the women who acted as links between the various households of the kin group.

It is beyond the scope of this paper to explore the reasons for this sex differentiation. It may have a close relationship to the fact that, as domestic families are generally large and servants beyond the means of most French Canadians, the women are essentially housewives and only work outside before having children, or because of great economic necessity. It would be wrong, however, to take this predominantly domestic role of women as a sign of their inferior status in the kin group. On the contrary, the continuity of the kinship system over time may be attributed to their dominant position in it. This influence of the women in the kin group is distinct from the authority role of men within each domestic family. The domestic family is headed by the husband, in whom the Civil Code of the province of Quebec vests a great deal of authority; it is an autonomous unit, with a sole legal representative. Within each household, however, the exercise of this authority is qualified by consultation with one's wife, and outside the domestic family by consultation with one's mother or sisters. But even then, the use of authority is held to be a male prerogative. Within a sibling group it may also happen that the eldest brother, especially at the death of the father, will acquire a position of authority over all the other siblings. Similarly, a grandfather has a great deal of authority. The pattern of authority, even apart from the legal definitions given to it by the Civil Code of Quebec, is therefore male, and relates to age and descent.

The equalitarian relationship between father and children or between persons of a different age, reported for the United States, is not present among the French Canadians. While a father allows his children a certain latitude of behaviour, it is not marked by any feeling of emotional closeness. Emotional ties are more usually directed toward the mother or the wife, or located within the sibling group. Thus, while a woman's legal status is subordinate, her roles as a mother or wife or sister make her the focus of most of the emotional life of the kin group. While the men determine the status position of their domestic families or of the whole kin group, the women are the "integrators" of the kin group, and as such its effective leaders. This female leadership role is different from the role of older men, who act as symbols of kinship continuity, but who are not the active agents of the life of the group. The foci of kin links are thus the women, and particular women can actually be regarded as leaders of the kin group. In the case of a grandmother of one of the informants, this leadership role had become a benign dictatorship, and practically all formal kin activities took place at her home.

For both men and women, the frequency of contact with relatives was the result of a number of factors. For instance, while only 16 of the 43 households reported relatives in the same parish, all informants reported their highest frequency of contact with their fathers and mothers and with their siblings, even if these lived in distant parishes of Montreal. Only when the degree of kinship was more remote did informants remark that geographical distance influenced contacts. Besides degree of kinship and geographical location, personal preference was an important factor in contact. Personal preference for kin was reported as a factor outside Ego's family of orientation and, if married, his household and his spouse's family of orientation. We may distinguish formal recognition from personal preference in kin relationships. While overlap between these two was reported, the formal dimension operates predominantly between generations, especially upward, while personal preference was especially strong in the selection of contacts with affinals or cousins.

This can best be illustrated by describing the frequency of contact reported by a married man, aged 34, who was a skilled worker in a Montreal factory. He has been chosen as an example because he is about average in the range of kinship recognition, with a total of 233 kin, 203 of whom were alive at the time of the survey. Of these, 93 lived in Montreal, scattered in a number of parishes; 72 were reported living in various parts of the province of Quebec; and 38 more were reported in Ontario and in the United States. During each week the informant frequently met members of his two brothers' households, who also lived in Montreal. Contacts with one of these households were more frequent, as they lived in the same parish. There were few weekends in which the brothers did not meet. He also visited his wife's parents some weekends, but his wife went more often, taking along their three children. He was very friendly with his wife's brothers, and the husband of one of his wife's sisters; he sometimes went out with either his brothers or his wife's brothers, or with his wife's sister's husband. It was rare, however, that they all came together as a group. Several times a month he met various uncles and cousins who also lived in Montreal, either through a chance meeting or because they were visiting the same household. He saw members of the household of one of his uncles more frequently, as they owned a grocery store where the family sometimes shopped. He reported that he met an average of 40 to 45 relatives each month, including those of generations older and younger than himself. He met far more of them in certain seasons of the year such as Christmas, and during Christmas 1954 he thinks that he must have seen nearly all of the 93 relatives who live in Montreal. He also went regularly, about once a month, to see his own parents who lived a few miles outside Montreal. He usually went with one of his brothers who owned a car, and they took their families with them. During the summer his wife and children generally went there for about a fortnight. Each time he visited his parents he usually met one of his married sisters who lived near their parents' home. He would also meet members of another sister's household when they came from the Eastern Townships to Montreal. About every other year, another of his brothers would come up from the United States where he lived with his family, and they would gather for a family reunion, either in Montreal or at their parents' home. The relatives he did not meet he heard about, either through letters, or through conversations. Altogether, he had seen 115 of his relatives during 1954, and had heard from another 57. He admitted that he wasn't always as interested in family affairs as he should be, and that his wife knew more of his own relatives than he did. By way of an excuse, he said that he was a junior executive in his local trade union branch, and had very little time to spare between his work and his union duties.

What seems interesting in this informant's report about his frequency of contact, which was quite different from that of his wife, was that he recognized a strict obligation to see only a certain number of relatives. Outside of this range, frequency of contact and the sense of formal obligation were much less important. However, because all his siblings were married, the range of formal obligation comprised the core of the kinship system and totalled over 50 persons. Yet, since some of these persons were located outside Montreal and were seen less often, the informant reported himself as lax in his kin duties. Informants also made a distinction between obligations to meet relatives who were very close and obligations to meet kin of ascending generations. They reported that while they were expected by older relatives, other than their father and mother, to fulfil certain kinship obligations, this expectation was satisfied by a low frequency of contact, usually limited to visits at Christmas or the gathering for a family reunion. The frequency of these reunions varied, and most informants reported them as taking place about once a year. They had no fixed dates and usually took place at the home of one of the relatives who acted as a focal point for the activities of the kin group. A very good excuse had to be given for not going, but most informants stated that they went willingly. Sometimes as many as 40 or more persons would get together, depending on the size of the home or the economic resources of the persons involved.

The highest frequency of contact took place between relatives of the same generation and, apart from sibling contact, were mostly based on personal preference. This personal preference was recognized as the major factor in the contact, and informants verbalized it in the statement that such meetings were the result of "just liking to get together." It can thus be suggested that all the various modes of kinship recognition which have been described operate according to different criteria. Certain kin, such as Ego's parents, siblings, spouse's parents, or siblings' spouses, are held to have special claims and are given priority over all others. Recognition of these claims keeps the legally defined autonomy of the domestic family, as well as its life as a unit, at a low threshold, since its members will readily adjust their own lives to the needs of such kin. With other persons, a formal recognition will exist but this recognition can be satisfied by more limited actions, such as attendance at a funeral or a wedding, or by letter-writing, so that the autonomy of the domestic family with regard to them is much greater.

The criteria which give rise to these different modes of recognition, and which govern frequency of contact, cannot be presented as clear-cut categories. Involved in the idea of kinship recognition are factors which informants characterize as differences in "family spirit," or "family unity," so that there are extensive variations as to who is included in those having "priority," or just a "formal" recognition. Many informants, for example, held that cousins were persons who involved some formal recognition, while others would regard close affines as more important to them than cousins. Difficulties in trying to determine the range of each category were often linked to the frequency of cousin marriages. Cousin marriages among the 30 informants who gave their genealogical knowledge varied from one instance of a second-cousin marriage, to two first-cousin and four second-cousin marriages in one kinship group. Altogether, 11 of the 30 informants reported such marriages. In another case, three brothers had married three sisters, and the two kin groups, which had not been previously related, had developed multiple ties which cross-cut the various dimensions of the kin group.

Closely related to the frequency of contact is the frequency of services between relatives. It could be offered as an unverified generalization that those kin who are held by close kinship links, and who see each other most frequently, help each other most frequently. These services included the loan of needed objects, baby-sitting, shopping, taking care of the household during the mother's illness, gift giving, the making of extensive loans, or the giving of general economic help. A young mother reported that she was receiving help from her mother, sisters, and female cousins. Less frequently, she would also turn to her husband's female relatives.

The pattern of services revealed even more clearly than did the frequency of contact that the kin group of birth is preferred to the kin group of marriage. Not only would there be a preference for one's own line, but also a preference for help from members of one's own sex, within each kin group. However, occasions were reported in which the distinction between the lines was blurred. All the adult females of a kin group, consanguineal and affinal, would help in preparing the family reunion. The buying, preparing and serving of the food, as well as the clearing up, would be the joint task of all the women who came. Another instance of overlap was given by a lawyer, who reported that his relatives, both consanguineal and affinal, came to him for legal advice, for which he charged a fee according to the economic status of the relative. Relatives in the medical profession are also reported as having their services requested by kin. Persons who sell things required by relatives, such as groceries and household utensils, were reported to have their kin as customers. This does not mean that all goods and services were obtained through relatives, but there is a certain degree of economic reciprocity holding the kin group together. Moral problems as well as economic were referred to relatives, especially to those in Holy Orders. Twenty-six of the 30 informants reported relatives in Holy Orders. One informant had 11 such relatives, both priests and nuns. One of these, a priest who was met during one interview, said that he was usually asked to officiate at the baptisms, weddings, and funerals of his relatives. Occasionally, they also came to him for advice. The only religious service he did not wish to perform for them was to act as their confessor.

All informants reported that they had received important services from relatives at some time during their lives. One stated that she would not think of going to a place where she had no relatives. Another informant reported that the problem of childrearing in a city was minimized if a mother could have the help of female relatives. One male informant stated that life in Montreal would have been impossible for him and his own domestic family during the depression of the 1930s if his relatives had not helped him. He not only received loans and other economic help, but went to live with his inlaws, and was able to find work through cousins. Of the 43 households visited, nine either comprised three generations or included other relatives outside the consanguineal unit. Working for a relative was frequently reported, and most informants stated that they knew of kin who were in this position. Certain economic enterprises are operated by persons who are related to each other in various degrees. Instances of this were given for a garage, a hotel, a grocery store, and a small industrial plant. Services are sometimes also requested of relatives who are marginal to the frequency of contact. Distant kin who, because of their status and general social position, can give important recommendations or introductions, are sometimes asked to exert their influence. If these relatives are also political figures, their politics will be supported as well as their help sought. The kinship system of urban French Canadians is an important mechanism for manipulating the social environment, and what might be called nepotism, but is referred to by French Canadians as "family solidarity," is a daily practice.

One of the marked characteristics of French Canadian urban kinship is its high degree of elasticity. Outside the range of "priority" claims, narrow formal recognition is balanced by selective contact according to personality preference, and the resulting kin group is as much linked to personality preference as to institutionalized formal recognition. This elasticity also permits it to adapt itself to the elements which operate against its continuity in time. Among such elements is the process of social differentiation caused by social mobility. There is, in fact, a close correlation between social status and frequency of contact, and informants who were upwardly mobile were those who reported the greatest loss of contact with their lateral kin. Social mobility therefore tends to dislocate the lateral range in which personal preference is so important, but it does not seem to separate a person completely from the kin group. Certain formal ties are still recognized, and informants reported instances of a person helping his entire sibling group to move upward. Furthermore, a new kin group forms rapidly at the higher level. Social mobility does not seem to imply a complete loss of the recognition of kin obligations, but merely the movement from a kin group at one level to another kin group at a different level. Cases were quoted in which the acceptance of a spouse into the kin group at the higher social level was conditioned by the possibility of having to accept a number of the spouse's relatives. If the spouse was rejected, there would be a gradual loss of contact with the person who had married "beneath" him. In this instance, there would be a regrouping with the kin at the lower social level.

Segmentation of the kin group is caused not only by social mobility, but also by the development of cultural differences. Informants quoted instances of relatives who had "gone English," and with whom little contact was maintained. Cultural differentiation usually arose through marriage with a non-French Canadian. While the majority of marriages reported in the informants' kin groups were with French Canadians, each informant could also list marriages outside, but never more than three for a single kin group. They were to be found at all social levels. Informants stressed that such marriages usually meant a loss of contact unless the spouse was a Catholic, spoke French, and accepted the assigned kin role. Again, the lateral kin ties were more vulnerable in such situations; the "priority" relatives generally kept their association. While parents and siblings usually came to accept these marriages, it was the more distant relatives, with whom personal choice was most important, who showed disapproval and dropped the couple, so that their children grew up with a restricted kin knowledge.

CONCLUSIONS

The collected evidence indicates no trend toward transformation of the present French-Canadian urban kinship system into the more restricted system reported for the United States. While difficulties were reported in maintaining a united domestic family or an integrated kin group, there is no reason to suppose that these difficulties were caused primarily by urban living. Moreover, many cases were reported where the kin group re-formed after a period of disunity. There are many reasons for believing that the present system will continue. Far from being incompatible, kinship and urbanism among French Canadians seem to have become functionally related. Each urban domestic family, each household, each person, is normally part of a system of obligations arising from the recognition of kinship ties.

The present system is elastic, and can readily adapt itself to different situations. This is due largely to the limitations placed upon kinship recognition by French Canadians. The "priority" kin are limited in number compared to the total recognition. The formal extension between generations is satisfied by a low frequency of contact. The wide lateral range offers the greatest freedom of choice through the operation of personal preference. Lastly, because the "priority" claims are related to a small number of large sibling groups, kinship contact and awareness of kinship obligations must always be multiple. The fact that a French Canadian is normally socialized in a large household conditions him at an early age to multiple kinship obligations. The socialization is carried out in a kinship world in which authority is male and narrowly defined, and emotional needs are satisfied through sibling, cousin, mother-child, grandmother, and aunt relationships. The pattern is continued in adult life, but with a greater freedom since each person can have a wide range of personal preference. The fact that personal preference will bring together persons of roughly the same age, status, and background, makes for a great deal of unity in these subgroups. These peer groups not only serve as leisure-activity groups, but after marriage are often the kinship group into which the children of a new couple will become socialized.

It is beyond the scope of this paper to go into the psychological implications of this type of socialization, and the possibility of avoiding the constraint usually attributed to extensive formal kin obligations by manipulating them to suit personal preference. While the whole kinship range cannot be thus manipulated, and a "priority" core remains unchanged to give continuity, enough elasticity is obtained to suit a wide range of situations. Furthermore, because the women are most active in kinship affairs, and yet not identified with the legal formal authority structure, kinship is not conceived of as a pattern of strict, "patriarchal" obligations, but as a reciprocal relationship from which much pride, pleasure, and security can be derived. Lastly, as sibling groups are large, selection according to personal preference does not unduly decrease the size of the kin group, but allows emotional ties to unite a large number of kin according to the emphasis placed on emotional preference. The resulting personality type seems to be that of an individual who, while he recognizes many kinds of kinship obligations, actually satisfies these obligations by selecting kin with whom he has the best relationships.

These characteristics of urban French Canadian kinship are no new development, but seem to have been in existence since the period of New France.[2] It can be suggested that one of the reasons for this continuity is its elasticity, already referred to. All informants agreed that there was a French-Canadian family ideal. While not aware of all its implications, they would verbalize about it and criticize variations from this ideal on the basis that to cease to behave like a French Canadian was to become "English." These ideals about family and kinship were not isolated but were part of a cultural complex which included the French language as spoken in Quebec, a specific system of education, membership in the Catholic Church, and various political theories about the status of French Canadians in Canada. To be a member of a French-Canadian kinship group implied attitudes and beliefs about some or all of these.

In conclusion, some of the theoretical implications of the research can be pointed out. One of these is the relationship between the size of sibling groups and kinship behaviour. The hypothesis is offered that socialization in a family of many full siblings results in special perceptions of kinship obligations. It was found that the size of sibling groups tends to run in families, and that children raised in large families accepted as normal the fact of having many children and the implications of multiple kinship recognition. French Canadians, one of the most prolific groups in the Western world, have made the tradition of a large sibling group one of the ideals of family life. This raises the problem of assessing the influence of urbanism on French-Canadian kinship. One of the most widely accepted generalizations about kinship is the proposition that the greater the urbanization, the smaller the kinship range, and that this apparent result of city life is everywhere the same. A number of writers believe that the invariable result of urbanization is to reduce the kinship range to the domestic family. Wirth[3] gave this statement its classical formulation, and it has been reiterated by more recent authors such as Burgess and Locke,[4] Cavan,[5] and Kirkpatrick.[6] While it is to be accepted that there will be a difference in birth-rate between rural and urban areas, this does not necessarily imply that urban kinship is doomed to universal disappearance.

Against this hypothesis of universal similarity, recent studies carried out in London[7] have shown that kinship recognition is compatible with urban life. While there may be a world trend toward urbanization and industrialization, there is little evidence for the disappearance of kinship awareness. The cluster of social characteristics by which urbanism is usually defined, such as population density, specialized functions, and a distinct pattern of social relationship, may exist in a variety of cultures. There is apparently a basic cultural difference in the description of kinship as reported in London and in the United States.[8] Perhaps this difference does not arise from fundamental variations in urbanization but from variations in concepts about the family and kinship.

One recent study[9] suggested a great deal of uniformity between the rural and urban kinship systems in the United States. While some societies are undoubtedly more urbanized than others, it seems that the critical factors in diminishing kinship recognition are the cultural values of the society, not its degree of urbanization. For instance, French Canadians share what might be called the techniques of the American way of life. Yet the kinship system of the French Canadians of Montreal seems to be fundamentally different from that reported for the United States. These differences, furthermore, are not due to more extensive rural survivals among the French Canadians, or to longer urban conditioning in the United States, but in each instance seem to be part of the established urban way of life with its cultural values.

Many writers seem to have identified the effects of urbanization as a world-wide process with the effects of the cultural values to be found in the United States. This is understandable, since most studies of urbanization have been carried out in the United States. However, this study of the French Canadians suggests that the relative influences of urbanization and cultural values on kinship must be seen as distinct.

NOTES

1. Louis Wirth, "Urbanism as a Way of Life," *American Journal of Sociology*, XLIV, 1 (1938), pp. 1-24.
2. See Philippe Garigue, "The French-Canadian Family," in Mason Wade, ed., *Canadian Dualism—La dualité canadienne* (Toronto: University of Toronto Press; Québec: Les Presses Universitaires Laval, 1960), pp. 181-200.
3. Op. cit.
4. E. W. Burgess and H. J. Locke, *The Family* (New York: American Book Company, 2d edition, 1953).
5. R. S. Cavan, *The American Family* (New York: Crowell, 1953).
6. Clifford Kirkpatrick, *The Family* (New York: Ronald, 1955).
7. R. F. Firth, "Studies of Kinship in London" (M.S., to be published by the London School of Economics); Michael Young, "Kinship and the Family in East London," *Man*, LIV, 210 (1954), pp. 137-39; L. A. Shaw, "Impression of Family Life in a London Suburb," *The Sociological Review*, II, 2 (1954), pp. 179-94; Peter Townsend, "The Family Life of Old People," *The Sociological Review*, III, 2 (1955), pp. 179-195.
8. Helen Codere, "A Genealogical Study of Kinship in the United States," *Psychiatry*, XVIII (1955), pp. 65-79.
9. D. M. Schneider and G. C. Homans, "Kinship Terminology and the American Kinship System," *American Anthropologist*, LVII (1955), pp. 1194-1208.

8. The Chinese-Canadian Family: A Socio-Economic Profile*

RAVI VERMA, KWOK B. CHAN, AND LARRY LAM

INTRODUCTION

The 1975 Canada Year Book reports a total of 118,815 Chinese in Canada in 1971, with major concentrations in Vancouver and Toronto. Although the Chinese represent a small percentage of the entire population of Canada (0.3% in 1961, and 0.5% in 1971), their history of settlement in Canada is unique and merits analysis in its own right.

This paper examines the social, economic, and demographic characteristics of Chinese immigrants in Canada by using the census data and 1966-1975 immigration statistics. Specifically, the paper will address itself to two questions: First, to what extent and in what ways do the Chinese families as defined by the Census conform to the average Canadian pattern with respect to such demographic and socio-economic variables as language spoken at home, family size, median earnings, educational attainment, labour force participation, and occupational distributions? Second, do the Chinese in Canada still maintain a cultural continuity between their traditional "extended family types" and the more isolated "nuclear family types" that, according to Parsons (1943, 1955), are predominant in modern industrial society? The paper then seeks to probe the extent of the universal and historical inevitability of the "nuclearization" of the Chinese families in Canada today.

The census data do not classify families as "nuclear" or "extended." Instead, family membership is defined in terms of "census family" and

*We are indebted to Professors K. Ishwaran, Dorothy Haccoun, Anthony Richmond, and Fred Elkin for their kindness in having read and made useful comments on the draft version of the paper.

"economic family,"[1] which, unfortunately, do not correspond to the dichotomy of "nuclear family" and "extended family." A "census family" consists of a husband and wife living in the same dwelling with children (adopted children and stepchildren having the same status as own children) who are not married. An "economic family" consists of two or more "census families" and/or persons who are not related to the head of the household, either by blood or marriage. For the purpose of this paper, recognizing the limitations of definitions, we shall match "census family" and "economic family" with "nuclear family" and "extended family" respectively. One further problem in analyzing census data and immigration statistics arises from the place of birth of Chinese. For instance, Hong Kong, a British Colony, is not part of China, but the Census invariably assumes as such. As a result, we cannot trace the actual place of birth of many of the Chinese immigrants.

CHINESE IMMIGRATION TO CANADA

The first wave of Chinese immigration began in the late 1850s in response to the gold rush in Frazer River at Barkerville, B.C. The immigrants were mostly poor young peasants from the southern provinces of China, and were later followed by similar young peasants in the 1870s and 1880s. Upon prompt and frustrative discovery that there were no more "goldmines" for them to "dig," a Chinese expression indicating their motivation to come to Canada at that time in terms of striving to save and accumulate enough money on their retiring back to homeland, they, together with the contracted labour brought in by various other contractors, laboured under appalling conditions to build the CPR. This large pool of cheap and hard labour contributed significantly to the realization of building a Canada from sea to sea. Upon the completion of the CPR, Chinese immigrants and labourers migrated to other parts of the country, such as Calgary, Edmonton, and Toronto, and began to establish their communities to counteract the various discriminatory practices and policies instituted by the governments, labour unions, and private industries (Krauter and Davis: 1978, 61-64).

The historical pattern of eastward internal migration of the Chinese within Canada can be seen in the light of a direct response to the shortage of labour demand in the West on the one hand, and to the unfair competition practices implemented by institutions in the receiving society on the other hand. The Canadian government, yielding to public pressure, instituted the head tax, which increased from $50 per head in 1885 to $100 in 1900 and to $500 in 1903 (Lee: 1967). The Chinese Immigration Act in 1923 effectively excluded the entry of Chinese to Canada. Only 44 Chinese were allowed to land in Canada between 1923 and 1947 (Kung: 1962). The restrictive measures virtually stopped the formation of Chinese "families" in Canada by stipulating explicitly that "the only Chinese allowed to enter until 1952 were those whose immediate family members were Canadian citizens or residents"

(Krauter and Davis: 1978; 81). By and large, the Chinese immigrants have always been, and still are, labelled as "middleman minorities" (Blalock: 1967; Loewen: 1971; Bonacich: 1973) or "sojourners" (Lopreato: 1967; Mangin: 1970). As such, they were considered to be incapable of full-scale assimilation into the mainstream of the Canadian society, and would then have to be excluded entirely (Ferguson: 1975).

However, with the changes implemented by the Immigration Act in 1962, Chinese immigrants came to Canada in increasingly larger numbers. A total of 8,883 Chinese immigrants were allowed to land in Canada between 1962 and 1965; the corresponding figures for 1966 to 1970 and 1971 to 1975 were 32,534 and 51,218. Most of the immigrants' intended destination was either British Columbia or Ontario (Vancouver and Toronto).[2] Vancouver, historically the most significant Chinese community assuming a dominant position for the larger Chinese population of Canada, was by the first decade of the twentieth century the largest Chinese community in Canada (Sedgewich: 1973). However, the eastward internal migration of the Chinese spelled a cross-country shift, with Toronto gradually assuming the centre of gravity in recent years. Between 1962 and 1965, as many as 2,865 Chinese immigrants chose Ontario as their intended destination, while British Columbia was chosen by only 2,723. The corresponding figures for 1966-1971 and 1971-1975 were 12,098 vs. 11,133 and 21,807 vs. 15,415 respectively.

Johnson (1977) has argued that the early restrictive measures of the immigration policy imposed upon the Chinese immigrants made the family formation impossible:

"... From the beginning legal disability made it impossible for Chinese migrants to even contemplate commitment to a society that so categorically rejected them from full membership. When we looked to Chinese-Canadian family structure, it is determined partly by the cultural characteristics of China but largely by Canadian law which severely constrained the kinds of family structures that could emerge. For much of Chinese-Canadian history it was simply impossible for most Chinese-Canadians to form families in Canada."

The census data indicated a decline of 11,982 Chinese in Canada between 1931 and 1947, while the sex ratio in 1941 was 10:1 (Lee: 1967, 420). This unbalanced sex ratio resulted not only in a "bachelor society" consisting primarily of a population of male migrants who, regardless of their actual marital status, were deprived of normal family relationships, but also in the Chinese males' over-indulgence in activities like gambling, opium-smoking, and prostitution (Davidson: 1952). In their analysis of the 1971 Census data, Richmond and Kalbach (1979) uncovered some fragmentary evidence of the detrimental consequences of the bachelor society. They reported relatively low median earnings of the older generations of the Chinese immigrants in Canada. Though these elderly immigrants, because of old age, tended to earn less than those in the younger age cohorts, the underlying explanation for the case of Chinese migrants has to be constructed in a different context. The elderly Chinese migrants who came to Canada in the earlier decades were not allowed to bring their family members with them. They worked, and hoped to go back to their homeland when they had accumulated sufficient wealth. However, for one reason or another, many of them failed to fulfill that aspiration. Meanwhile, they either sent their earnings back home to support their family, or, for those who were single, spent their earnings in activities that were characteristic of a "bachelor society." As they became older, their earning ability declined because they were no longer physically capable of gaining employment in industries. They had never been able to accumulate enough capital to start their own businesses, and, as often, they failed to possess the minimum educational and occupational credentials to meet the requirements of an industrialized society like Canada. The relatively low median earnings of the Chinese immigrants reflected in the 1971 census data must then be explained in terms of the aftermath of the restrictive measures of the immigration policy in Canada. In other words, our argument is that if they were allowed to bring their family members to Canada, they would not have spent their earnings needlessly and might have accumulated enough capital to start businesses on their own.

However, things have been changing. First of all, the eastward movement of the Chinese immigrants witnessed a range of changes in the types of economic activities pursued, which seemed to be disproportionately concentrated in Toronto. The Chinese found their way into a few business areas such as groceries, laundries, and restaurants, where competition with members of the host society was less intense. The restaurant business in particular sprang up in the 1950s due to the gradual upsurge of the entrepreneur aspirations of some China-born Canadians, sons of Canadian missionaries who brought nothing back but a fondness for Chinese cuisine (*Maclean's Magazine*: 1955). With the concomitant relaxation of the immigration regulations, more Chinese migrants were allowed to come to Canada, a phenomenon not only contributing to important changes in the traditional occupational structure of the Chinese in terms of a numerical increase of the Chinese entry into professional fields such as medicine, natural sciences, and financial managements, but also stabilizing the restaurant business and groceries enterprises by creating, expanding, and sustaining an "ethnic market."

Furthermore, one also witnessed important changes in patterns of formation of Chinese families as a result of changes in the immigration regulations. Up to 1962, the working ideology and principle of the Canadian immigration policy was preoccupied with the "preferred vs.

non-preferred" categories (Richmond: 1977). The preferred categories which originally included the citizens of Great Britain, the United States, and France, were extended to residents of other Western countries in 1956, but not to the Asians (Lai: 1971, p. 123). It is only after the implementation of the "point system" in 1962, when the trends of Chinese immigration to Canada took some fundamental changes, especially in terms of the large influx of Chinese women who were instrumental in the growth of the emergent second and third generations and who effectively utilized increasing educational and occupational opportunities provided by the host country, that they, in turn, contributed immediately to the enormous growth of the Chinese professional class (Porter: 1965, pp. 88-89). Corresponding changes can also be identified within the Chinese families since the era during which "family reunions" were made possible by legislative changes. In fact, the changes in the Immigration Act in 1962 and its subsequent changes in 1967 made it possible for the Chinese immigrants who were already in Canada to bring their family members to Canada to reconstitute "a family," and also for those who have met the requirements for admission as immigrants to emigrate to Canada as "family units" in the late 1960s. Data from the reports of the Department of Manpower and Immigration have demonstrated, at least implicitly, that family formation of Chinese immigrants in Canada is a recent phenomenon. During the period of immigration, 1962 to 1965, there were more females allowed to come to Canada than males, 5,400 vs. 3,443. The corresponding figures for the period between 1966 and 1970 were 17,377 vs. 15,157 respectively. These figures included those under the age of 15 and over 55, which might indicate that either they came with their parents as family units, or came to join their sons and daughters who were already in Canada. In an attempt to interpret the data indicating the recent, massive importation of Chinese women into the country, one might suggest that they came primarily to join their husbands, to get married, or to fulfill earlier marriage arrangements. Excluding those who were under the age of 20 and those who were over 50, the data have shown that between 1962

TABLE 1
A SUMMARY TABLE OF THE DEMOGRAPHIC AND SOCIO-ECONOMIC CHARACTERISTICS OF THE CHINESE-CANADIANS (NUCLEAR AND EXTENDED FAMILIES) AND TOTAL CANADIANS

Variables*	Chinese Canadians vs.	Total Canadians	Chinese-Canadians Nuclear vs.	Extended
Age				
median (years)	25.3	26.3	23.8	29.1
0-14	31.0%	30.0%	35.8%	10.7%
15-64	62.0%	62.0%	58.9%	72.6%
65 and over	7.0%	8.0%	5.3%	16.7%
Sex-ratio	109	100.3	109.1	108.9

Dependency Ratio	63	60	70	38
Young	51	47	61	15
Old	12	13	9	23
Marital Status:				
Single	53.0%	28.0%	53.2%	53.8%
Married	41.0%	62.0%	43.8%	27.8%
Widowed, divorced and separated	6.0%	10.0%	3.1%	18.4%
Children Per Family	2.6	2.7	2.6	2.8
Official Languages				
English	77.0%	67.0%	79.0%	69.0%
French	0.4%	18.0%	0.2%	1.3%
Both	3.0%	3.0%	3.6%	1.7%
Neither	19.0%	2.0%	17.0%	28.0%
Holding Canadian Citizenship (foreign-born only)	52.0%	60.2%	58.2%	31.2%
Language at Home (ie., English)	36.6%	22.0%	39.0%	26.0%
Level of Schooling				
Elementary	55.0%	37.2%	56.3%	47.9%
Secondary	30.0%	52.9%	28.7%	35.5%
University	15.3%	9.9%	15.0%	16.7%
Labour Force Participation Rate				
Female	52.0%	40.0%	54.5%	46.0%
Male	76.1%	76.4%	81.6%	58.7%
Class of Workers				
Wage earners	83.0%	88.0%	81.0%	93.0%
Unpaid family workers	7.0%	3.0%	7.0%	4.0%
Self-employed	12.0%	9.0%	14.0%	4.0%
Occupation (male				
Service	35.0%	10.0%	—	—
Sales	11.0%	10.0%	—	—
Natural Sciences	10.0%	4.0%	—	—
Clerical	6.0%	8.3%	—	—
Medical & health	5.0%	1.7%	—	—
Occupation (female)				
Clerical	22.0%	34.5%	—	—
Service	18.3%	17.3%	—	—
Processing & machining	11.0%	8.7%	—	—
Sales	8.3%	9.4%	—	—
Medical & health	5.8%	8.8%	—	—
Income (mean earning)				
Male	$4 715	$6 538	$5 408	$2 523
Female	$1 829	$2 883	$1 928	$1 529

Source: 1971 Census of Canada, 1% public use sample tapes, individual file (excludes P.E.I., Yukon and N.W.T.).

* For detailed description of the variables, see Dictionary of the 1971 Census Terms, Statistics Canada, Ottawa.

and 1965, there were 2,836 female immigrants vs. 1,553 male immigrants; and between 1966 and 1970, the figures were 9,234 vs. 8,580 respectively. It is reasonable to conclude, perhaps not definitively, that the changes in the immigration regulations reflect an attempt on the part of the government to allow "bachelors" already in Canada to bring their spouses in and to reconstitute a "family." Thus, the unbalanced sex-ratio, a distinctive feature of Chinese immigrants in the earlier decades, has gradually levelled off.

SOME GENERAL DEMOGRAPHIC CHARACTERISTICS

The 1971 census of Canada registered a total of 124,600 persons under the category of the Chinese ethnic group,[3] which altogether represented about half of 1% of the total Canadian population. About 81% of the Chinese-Canadians were identified as living in the nuclear or "census" families which included the head of the household, wife, and unmarried children. The extended or "economic" families, consisting of either three generations or relatives and non-relative members of the household accounted for only 19%.

Forty-three per cent of the Chinese population in Canada were born in China and/or Hong Kong. The Canada-born Chinese accounted for another 38%. Four per cent were born in India and the West Indies (2% each), with about half of one per cent in Africa and 11% in other countries. Among families defined as nuclear, 41.4% were Canadian-born, and 59.2% were foreign-born. Among families defined as extended, 20.9% were Canada-born, and 79.1% were foreign-born. Among the Canada-born Chinese, 89.5% were living in nuclear families, and 10.5% in extended families; the corresponding figures for the foreign-born Chinese were 76% and 24% respectively. Thus, there were more extended families in the foreign-born Chinese cohort than in the Canada-born cohort.

The formation of Chinese families in Canada is a recent development. While 6% of the Chinese population came to Canada before 1946, 19% came in 1946 to 1960, 8% in 1961 to 1966, and 29% in 1966 to 1971. Of particular interest is the type of families that prevailed in Canada by years of immigration. In 1946 to 1960, 90.9% were defined as nuclear families (probably the majority of them were bachelors), while the percentage declined to 81.7% in 1961 to 1965, and to 67.2% in 1966 to 1971. On the other hand, the proportion of extended families increased from 9.1% in 1946 to 1960 to 18.3% in 1961 to 1965, and to 32.8% in 1966 to 1971. Among the foreign-born Chinese families, 17.1% of the extended type arrived in Canada in 1961 to 1965. The large number of extended families admitted to land in Canada indicates the changes in the immigration policy over the years which made possible the formation of families.

A large majority of the parents of the Canada-born Chinese were born outside Canada. The percentage of both parents born outside Canada was 84% in 1971. Only 9% of the Canada-born Chinese had both parents who were native-born. About 7% of the Canada-born Chinese had either mother or father born in Canada.

While the median age of the total Canadian population, according to the 1971 census data, was 26.3 years, it was 25.3 for the Chinese Canadians (Table 1). However, substantial differences can be found between the Chinese nuclear and the extended families. The Chinese-Canadians in the nuclear families had a lower median age (23.8 years) than those living in the extended families (29.1 years). The relatively higher median age of Chinese-Canadians in the extended families indicate that they have taken opportunities made possible by changes in the immigration policy to sponsor their older parents and/or other relatives to join them in Canada. The changes in the immigration policy are also reflected in the distribution of sex-ratio. The excess of males over females is one of the historical demographic characteristics of the Canadian population. In 1971, the sex-ratio (male to female) for the total Canadian population was 100.3, and the Chinese-Canadians, with a ratio of 109 males per 100 females, did not depart from this pattern. This observation does not vary between the nuclear and extended Chinese families.

In comparison to the nuclear ones, the extended Chinese-Canadian families had fewer young people. For the nuclear families, there were 35.8% in the 0-14 years of age group, while only 5.3% were in the 65-plus years of age; the corresponding figures for the extended families were 10.7% and 16.7% respectively.

MARITAL STATUS

The distribution of the Chinese-Canadians by marital status is considerably different from that of the total Canadian population. About 53% of the Chinese-Canadians in 1971 were single in comparison with only 28% for the total Canadian population. While 41% of the Chinese-Canadians in 1971 were married, the percentage for the total Canadian population was 62%. However, the proportion of widowed, separated, and divorced was lower for the Chinese-Canadians than for the Canadians in general: 6% as compared to 10%. The distribution of the Chinese-Canadians in marital status is affected by family type. Among the Chinese-Canadians in the nuclear families, 3.1% were identified as widowed, separated, and divorced, while the corresponding figure for those in the extended families was 18.4%. We also found more married people in the nuclear families than in the extended families: 43.8% vs. 27.8% respectively. Correspondingly, a slightly higher percentage of single persons were found in extended (53.8%) than in nuclear families (53.2%). The relatively higher proportion of unmarried, single Chinese-Canadians in extended families is probably an artifact of census definition and classification, according to which the extended families include not only immediate family members but also distant relatives and non-relatives who happened to be temporary boarders in the household. An alternative explanation might be that many of the Chinese immigrants who were single, particularly those who came to Canada in the pre-War decades as bachelors, remained single because of various aversive conditions imposed on them. Perhaps many of these Chinese-Canadian singles, in spite of their intentions to get married, were having difficulties in getting eligible partners simply because they were too old by then. As such, they lived together with other relatives or non-relatives, and were accordingly enumerated as single in the census.

FAMILY SIZE

The myth that Chinese have large families has no empirical support in the Canadian context. In fact, the census data indicate that the Chinese-Canadians have consistently raised families of relatively small size, a pattern conforming to the Canadian norm. The fertility rate of the Chinese-Canadian females was slightly lower than that of their Canadian counterpart. The number of children ever born to married women aged 15 years and over in 1971 was 2.6 for the Chinese-Canadian females and 2.7 for the Canadian.

LANGUAGE AND CITIZENSHIP

The 1971 census indicates that the majority of the Chinese-Canadians were fluent in English. The distribution of Chinese-Canadians by official languages spoken were: 77% English only, 0.4% French only, 3% both English and French, and 19% neither English nor French. In comparison with the total Canadian population, the Chinese-Canadians had higher representation in the "English only" and "neither English nor French" categories, and fewer in the "French only" category. Yet, proportionately speaking, there were as many Chinese-Canadians who were proficient in both English and French as the total population. The percentage distributions of the total Canadian population by official languages were: 67% English only, 18% French only, 3% both English and French, and 2% neither English nor French. The percentage distributions of the Chinese-Canadians by official language, particularly in the categories of English only and neither English nor French, plus the small percentage distribution in the French only category, may partially explain the heavy concentration of the Chinese-Canadians in English speaking Toronto and Vancouver.

The distribution of language proficiency of the Chinese-Canadians also varies by family type. There was a higher representation of neither English nor French speaking Chinese-Canadians in the extended families (28%) than in the nuclear families (17%). There were more Chinese-Canadians who had knowledge of English only as the official language in the nuclear (79%) than in the extended families (69%).

It is a widely accepted view in the literature of immigrant studies that having knowledge of at least one official language in Canada enhances the chances of an immigrant in coping with the demands of the Canadian society at large. If taking up citizenship is regarded as an index of degree of acculturation or adaptation, the Chinese-Canadians on the whole, excluding those who were Canada-born, would be expected to have done relatively well in this process. In 1971, among the total foreign-born population in Canada (3.3 millions), 60.2% had taken up Canadian citizenship. Among the total foreign-born Chinese-Canadians, 52% had taken up Canadian citizenship. About 18% of them claimed United Kingdom citizenship,[4] 21% retained Chinese citizenship,[5] and 8.5% had citizenship from other countries.

The proportion of the Chinese-Canadians in the nuclear families having Canadian citizenship was 58.2% compared with 31.2% for those who were members of the extended families. In contrast, the latter group contained a still greater number of the Chinese-Canadians who had allegiance to China and the United Kingdom. More than one-third of the members of the Chinese-Canadian families owed allegiance to China, with 17% of them to the United Kingdom. This compares to only 20% of the Chinese-Canadians in the nuclear families who claimed allegiance to the United Kingdom and China. That members of the Chinese-Canadian extended families were fewer in taking up Canadian citizenship, and conversely, were more inclined to retain Chinese citizenship is probably due to the fact that a substantial proportion of the older immigrants perceived no apparent benefits or advantages in taking Canadian citizenship after a lengthy life of struggle under aversive conditions. And there were still those recent immigrants who recently came to the country to rejoin their family and had yet to fulfill the residence requirements.

The 1971 census data also reveal a gap between the proportion of Chinese-Canadians having knowledge of English as one of the two official languages and the proportion of English being spoken at home. A total of 36.6% of the Chinese-Canadians had English as their spoken language at home; the other 63% spoke "all other languages," including Cantonese, Mandarin, or other dialects of the Chinese language. It is important to note that the percentage of the Chinese-Canadians taking English as the language of the home was substantially higher than the total foreign-born population in Canada: 36.6% vs. 22%. Furthermore, the proportion retaining mother tongues as languages of the home (for example, German, Italian, Netherlands, Polish) was about 74% for the total foreign-born population, but only 63% for the Chinese-Canadians. The differential is probably due to the considerable representation of Chinese immigrants from Hong Kong who had already possessed some proficiency in the use of the English language.

In relating family types to languages spoken at home, we have found that there were more members of the extended Chinese families using their mother tongue as the spoken language at home (72%) than those of the nuclear families (60%). On the other hand, more of the latter group used English as their spoken language at home (39%) than those of the former group (26%).

EDUCATION

According to the 1971 census, as many as 64.8% of the Chinese-Canadians aged five years and over were not attending school; 3.7% attended school part-time and 31.5% attended school full-time. The difference in proportion of members of the nuclear families and extended families not attending school was not substantial, 63.6% vs. 69.7%. The proportional difference in attending school part-time by family type was 3.5% vs. 4.7%. The higher proportion of the Chinese-Canadians in nuclear families attending school full-time (32.9%) than those in the extended families (25.6%) was probably due to the fact that there were more young people in the former group.

The data are more revealing in regard to the level of schooling attained by the Chinese-Canadians. The overall pattern of distributions was quite different from that of the total Canadian population. About 55% of the Chinese-Canadians finished elementary schooling (up to Grade 8), 30% had secondary education (from Grade 9 to Grade 13), and 15.3% received at least some university training (with or without degree). The percentage distributions for the total Canadian population were: 37.2% with elementary schooling, 52.9% with secondary education, and 9.9% with university training. The data clearly indicate that a greater proportion of the Chinese-Canadians than the total Canadian population had university education. Considering the fact that education, even at the elementary level, was not compulsory in Hong Kong and China,[6] the data seem to suggest a higher level of educational aspirations among the Chinese in general.

The data also indicate that the educational attainment of the Chinese-Canadians varies by family type. Among the nuclear families, there were 56.3% with elementary or no schooling, 28.7% with secondary education, and 15.0% with university training. The corresponding distributions for the extended families were 47.9%, 35.5%, and 16.7% respectively.

Meanwhile, it has been posited in the literature that immigrants or native-born Canadians with foreign-born parent(s) are better motivated than others to seize the educational opportunities available in Canada. This general premise seems to receive partial support from the data on the educational attainment of the Chinese-Canadian. About 57% of them received their highest grade of education in Canada, whereas the other 34% obtained theirs from outside Canada. Only 8.7% of the Chinese-Canadians reported no schooling. The small percentage reporting no schooling may probably reflect the differential impact of the immigration selection process which places considerable weight on education in the "points system."[7] The data also indicate that about 32% of members of the nuclear families had taken their highest grade/degree outside Canada, most likely at their last place of permanent residence. The percentage of members of the extended families who had taken their highest grade/degree from outside Canada was 44%. The proportion of the Chinese-Canadians reporting no schooling was higher among those from the extended families (17.5%) than those from the nuclear families (6.7%). The higher proportion of members of the extended families having taken their highest grade/degree outside Canada may be due to the fact that many of them were labelled as "independent applicants" and were allowed to come to Canada on the basis of their own qualifications. Likewise, the higher proportion of members of nuclear families having obtained highest grade/degree in Canada may reflect the consequences of changes in the immigration policy under which many of them might have come as family units and have their children or even themselves educated here.

With respect to vocational training which is aimed at improving occupational qualifications through apprenticeship or enrolment in either full-time or part-time courses in arts and craft, literacy and language, investment, homemaking, and music, there were proportionately lesser representations of the Chinese-Canadians than the total Canadian population: 5% vs. 7%. Slightly more of the Chinese-Canadians from the extended families (7.3%) than from the nuclear families (5%) took up the option of vocational training. In general, both the Chinese-Canadians as well as Canadians at large were less oriented toward vocational than formal training.

LABOUR FORCE PARTICIPATION

The census identify persons who are fifteen years of age and over either as "in labour force" or "not in labour force." For the total Canadian male population, the labour force participation rate was 76% in 1971. The rate for the Chinese-Canadian males was exactly the same, 76%. However, considerable difference in rate of labour force participation was found between the total Canadian female population and the Chinese-Canadian females, 40% vs. 52%. This may indicate that either more immigrant women were working in the labour force, or many Chinese-Canadian families were "two-career families," or a combination of both. The high percentage of the Chinese-Canadian females in the labour force does indicate that they are no longer merely housewives as they were in the traditional Chinese family.

The labour force participation rates were further affected by family type. As many as 41.3% of the males in the Chinese extended families, as compared to only 18.4% of the males in the nuclear families counterparts, were not in the labour force. The higher proportion of males in extended families not in labour force is not surprising, since this type of family is more likely to include the in-laws or other relatives who are too old to work.

In comparison with the total Canadian female population, the Chinese-Canadian females from both types of families had a higher labour force participation rate. The difference in labour force participation rates of females between the two types of families is not so dramatic as in the case of the Chinese-Canadian males. About 55% of the Chinese females from nuclear families and 46% from extended families were in the labour force.

CLASS OF WORKER

The 1971 census of Canada classified the experienced labour force into three main groups: wage earners who worked for someone else for salaries, commissions, and/or wages; unpaid family workers who helped without pay in a family farm or family business; and self-employed workers, either in private professional services or in contractual basis as free lancers.

Most Chinese-Canadians (83%) were employed as wage earners, a proportion slightly lower than the total Canadian population (88%). There were more unpaid family workers among the Chinese-Canadians than the total Canadian population, 7% vs. 3%. For the self-employed category, a difference of 3% was found, 12% for Chinese-Canadians, and 9% for Canadians at large. The high representation of unpaid family workers and the self-employed among the Chinese-Canadians is probably due to the recent proliferation of the so-called family business enterprises, such as grocery stores, laundries, restaurants, or "take-out-order" Chinese restaurants in large shopping plazas, which hire family members as part-time or full-time employees without actually having them on the payroll.

Members of the Chinese nuclear families were more likely than those of the Chinese extended families to be self-employed: 14% vs. 4%. In the category of wage earners, the proportions for nuclear families and extended families were 81% and 93% respectively. About 7% in nuclear families were unpaid family workers, whereas for extended families, the proportion was only 4%. The relatively higher proportion of unpaid family workers and self-employed workers in the Chinese nuclear families may possibly indicate that family business enterprises were more likely to be established by nuclear families than by extended families. The higher proportion of wage earners in the extended families perhaps suggests the need to take up employment either within the ethnic community or in society at large in order to maintain a large household.

OCCUPATION

Although the Chinese-Canadians enjoyed wide distribution in the occupational system, some significant concentrations were obvious. In general, those who were members of the labour force aged 15 years and over were concentrated in natural sciences, medical and health services, and service occupations, and were relatively underrepresented in such occupations as managerial and administrative, clerical and related jobs, machining, construction, and transportation. The heavy concentration of the Chinese-Canadians in white-collar occupations is apparent. This pattern does not vary between members of the nuclear and extended Chinese families.

A more detailed inspection of the internal distribution of the Chinese-Canadians by type of occupation reveals the following: 28% in service, 11% in clerical and related jobs, 10% in sales, 7.2% in natural sciences, engineering, and mathematics, and 5.5% in medical and health services.

The distribution of the male Chinese-Canadians by occupation shows a similar pattern: about 35% in service occupations, 11% in sales, 10% in natural sciences, 6% in clerical and related jobs, and 5% in medical and health services. The distribution of the total Canadian males aged 15 years and above in these occupations, however, varies: about 10% in the service occupations, 10% in sales, 4% in natural sciences, 8.3% in clerical and related jobs, and 1.7% in medical and health services. The total Canadian males, instead, tended to concentrate in other occupational divisions: 13.4% in machining and 10.5% in construction; the corresponding figures for Chinese-Canadian males were only 5% and 1%. Also, the Chinese-Canadian males, in comparison with their total Canadian counterparts, were underrepresented in the managerial and administrative categories: 1.2% vs. 5.7%.

Differences are found in type of occupational representations between the Chinese-Canadian females and the total Canadian females at large. For the Chinese-Canadian females, the distribution was: 22% in the clerical and related jobs, 18.3% in service occupations, 11% in product fabrication (garment industry), 8.3% in sales, and 5.8% in medical and health services. For the Canadian females, the percentage distributions were: 34.5% in clerical and related jobs, 17.3% in service occupations, 9.4% in sales, and 8.8% in medical and health services. It seems that the Chinese-Canadian females, compared with their male counterparts, were more inclined to take after the general Canadian females in their occupations in spite of some minor variations here and there.

INCOME

The Chinese-Canadians earned less than the Canadians in mean income in spite of earlier data indicating that they, in comparison with the total Canadian population, were higher in labour force participation, level of schooling, and education attainment.

Among the total Canadian population who were members of the labour force in 1970, the mean earnings for males and females were

$6,538 and $2,883 respectively. In comparison, the Chinese-Canadians were considerably lower in their earnings: $4,715 for the males and $1,829 for the females. Members of the Chinese nuclear families earned more than members of the Chinese extended families: $3,784 vs. $2,048. The Chinese-Canadian males in the nuclear families reported higher earnings than those in the extended families, with a difference of almost $3,000 ($5,408 vs. $2,523). For the females, the difference was about $400 ($1,928 vs. $1,529).

DISCUSSION AND INTERPRETATION

The disproportionately high representation of single (as a result of involuntary separation) and never-married Chinese-Canadian males in Canada unmistakenly reflects the long-lasting, historical impact of the Canadian immigration policy, which functioned to create a "bachelor's society" among the older Chinese males. As a result of a constellation of historical and circumstantial factors, including persistent poverty and over-extended periods of physical separation, these never-married, Chinese-Canadian singles were never able either to bring in their spouses from their homeland to complete family formation, or simply to contemplate the idea of remarriage because of severe lack of financial means and resources. As this segment of the Chinese-Canadian population becomes older, the prospect of marriage becomes grimmer and the legacy of the impact of historically discriminatory Canadian immigration statuses spells out its detrimental consequences.

Shifting our attention from the prevalent marital status of the Canadian-Chinese to their present socio-economic status in terms of education, occupation, and income, some positive and encouraging visions seem to have emerged. In comparison with the total Canadian population, the Chinese-Canadians have more university graduates, are more inclined to pursue formal, academic training in the universities rather than vocational training in the community colleges, and are more diversely represented in various occupational divisions. However, this general trend of socio-economic emergence of the Chinese-Canadians in general parallels an apparent contradiction which stems from the discriminatory socio-political structure of the Canadian society: the Chinese-Canadians, like other ethnic minorities, have less earnings in spite of higher level of educational attainment.

That our data show the Chinese-Canadians possessing a relatively high level of proficiency in the English language and speaking English more often within the households than expected cast doubt on the old, persistent societal stereotypes of the Chinese in Canada being unassimilable sojourners who have their national and emotional allegiances elsewhere. The majority of the Chinese-Canadians, according to the 1971 census data, are very much ready to speak English, and, to a lesser extent, French. It seems that it is only among the never-married Chinese single males where old Chinese citizenships are retained, and where Chinese is still invariably spoken on a wide range of occasions of social discourse within and without the households. It is this same segment of the Chinese-Canadian population which has never been able to arise out of poverty, and is, therefore, heavily reliant on the ethnic networks within the enclaves of the Chinatowns where Chinese is spoken in both business and social dealings.

Again, contrary to most stereotyped impressions held by both the laymen and government policy-makers, the average Chinese-Canadians, compared with the total Canadians, have smaller family size, lower rate of fertility, and fewer children born to ever-married women. Seen in this perspective, the typical Chinese-Canadian family as a demographic and socio-economic type is converging towards the average Canadian norm.

While the Chinese-Canadian males do not differ from the total Canadian counterparts in overall rates of labour force participation, there are more Chinese-Canadian than total Canadian females in the work force. Our suggestion, based on the 1971 census data, that there is a relatively higher incidence of "two-career" families proportionately among the Chinese-Canadians than the total Canadians might have dispelled another set of myths and stereotypes seeing the typical Chinese woman in the Canadian society as non-working mother and housewife only.

The 1971 census data also indicate that the Chinese-Canadian extended families accommodate a significantly large number of the single, the never-married, the widowed, the separated and divorced. This suggests that the extended families act as vital private institutions providing socio-emotional, economic, and psychological support to the marginal and deprived segment of the Chinese population. The extended families thus function as "ethnic refuges," where various kinds of resources are accessible to the needy persons who otherwise could have become a burden and a liability to the social welfare and social service system.

How, then, do the Chinese-Canadian nuclear families compare with the extended families in terms of extent of convergence toward, or divergence from, the average Canadian norms? Our data suggests that the nuclear families are smaller in size, have less children born to ever-married women, and have a lower fertility rate; however, in terms of total number of years of schooling, incidence of labour force participation, and level of median earnings, the Chinese-Canadians in the nuclear families are, in general, doing much better than those of the extended families.

Moreover, it is also the Chinese-Canadians in the nuclear rather than extended families who are more proficient in English and French, speak English more often at home, and have more often taken up or are eager to take up Canadian citizenship. One might want to argue, on the basis of these few demographic characteristics, that it is the Chinese-Canadians in the nuclear families who are more readily enthused with

the idea of assimilation and who are more keen in behaviourally prac-
tising it.

We have already documented a comparatively higher representation
of the Chinese-Canadian population in the nuclear than the extended
families. One might suspect a parallel incidence of disintegration of
old, extended families to newly formed nuclear families as younger
generations of Chinese-Canadians choose to have their own separate
residential units. The data, then, seem to point to a gradual overall
trend of nuclearization of the Chinese-Canadian families. However, we
would also like to hypothesize that in spite of this universal process of
nuclearization, the extended families, or, more accurately, the "modified" extended families, will stay to perform their vital and strategic
functions for the elderly and the marginal for a few more decades
among the Chinese-Canadians.

The more immediate sociological concern in future studies of the
Chinese-Canadians should then be centred upon the extent of both
their historical convergence toward and their divergence from the
Canadian norms of familial patterns in view of their struggle as a minority group to preserve socio-cultural tradition and to effect changes
in the process of adaptation and coping. With the aid of socio-psychological and survey data from specifically designed studies, we hope to
achieve a more comprehensive understanding of the dynamic interplay
between tradition and change among the Chinese-Canadians.

NOTES

1. For official definitions of the "census" and "economic" families, see *Dictionary of the 1971 Census Terms*, Statistics Canada, Ottawa, pp. 6-8. Economic
families may be a temporary arrangement for the initial adjustment of newly arrived immigrants to life in Canada.
2. Immigration statistics do not specify the cities of immigrants' destination. It
is assumed that most immigrants would settle in urban centres rather than in
rural areas.
3. This refers to ethnic or cultural background traced through father's side.
Language spoken by the person or by his paternal ancestor on first coming to
Canada was a guide to the classification of ethnic groups.
4. Chinese born in Hong Kong are said to be United Kingdom citizens, since it
is still a British colony.
5. This probably includes refugees from mainland China who came to Hong
Kong after the 1949 Communist revolution, residents holding Hong Kong Cer-
tificate of Identity, and those holding passports from Taiwan. In fact, Chinese
citizenship does not necessarily indicate allegiance to either mainland China,
Hong Kong, or Taiwan.
6. In Hong Kong, primary education (Grade 1 to Grade 6) was made compulsory only in the late 1960s.
7. "Points system" enables the selection of immigrants, regardless of colour,
race, nationalities, and religions. Up to 20 assessment units could be awarded
on the basis of one unit for each successful year of formal schooling.

REFERENCES

Blalock, H.
1967   Toward a Theory of Minority Group Relations. New York: Wiley.

Bonacich, E.
1973   "A Theory of Middleman Minorities." American Sociological Review
        38 (5):583-594.

Davidson, A. M.
1952   An Analysis of the Significant Factors in the Patterns of Toronto
        Chinese Family Life as a Result of Recent Changes in Immigration
        Laws. Unpublished M.S.W. thesis, University of Toronto.

Department of Manpower and Immigration.
1974   The Immigration Programme. Ottawa: Manpower and Immigration;
        Three Years in Canada. Ottawa: Manpower and Immigration, 1974.

Ferguson, T.
1975   A White Man's Country, Toronto.

Freedman, M.
Winter 1961-62 "The Family in China, Past and Present." Pacific Affairs
        31 (4):334.

Johnson, G. E.
1977   "Immigration and Organizational Change in Canadian Chinese Com-
        munities Since 1974." In Multiculturalism in Canada: Third World
        Perspective, edited by G. Paul. Toronto: Prentice-Hall.

Krauter, J. F. and M. Davis
1978   Minority Canadians: Ethnic Groups. Toronto: Methuen.

Kung, S. W.
Winter 1962 "Chinese Immigration into North America." Queen's Quar-
        terly 68:4, pp. 612-616.

Lai, V.
1971   "The New Chinese Immigrants in Toronto." In Immigrant Groups,
        edited by Jean L. Elliot. Toronto: Prentice-Hall, pp. 120-140.

Lee, David T. H.
1967   A History of Chinese in Canada. Taiwan: Hai Tin Printing Co. (text in
        Chinese).

Lee, S. C.
1953   "China's Traditional Family: Its Characteristics and Disintegration."
        American Sociological Review 18 (1953), pp. 272-280.

Loewen, J. W.
1971   The Mississippi Chinese. Cambridge, Mass.: Harvard University
        Press.

Lopreato, J.
1967   "Emigration and Social Change in Southern Italy." In The Sociology
        of Community, edited by C. Bell. London: Cass., pp. 84-96.

Mangin, H. B.
   1970   Peasants in Cities: Readings in Anthropology of Urbanization, Cambridge, Boston.

Marr, W.
   1976   Labour Market and Other Implications of Immigration Policy for Ontario. Working paper No. 1/76, Ontario Economic Council.

Parsons, Talcott
   Jan.-March, 1943   "The Kinship System of the Contemporary United States." American Anthropologist 45:22-38.

Parsons, Talcott and Robert F. Bales
   1965   Family Socialization and Interaction Process. Glencoe, Ill.: The Free Press.

Porter, J.
   1955   The Vertical Mosaic. Toronto: University of Toronto Press.

Richmond, A.
   1977   "Factors Associated with Commitment to and Identification with Canada." In Identities, edited by W. Jsajiw. Peter Martin Associates Ltd.

Richmond, A., and G. L. Rao
   1976   "Recent Development in Immigration to Canada and Australia: A Comparative Analysis." International Journal of Comparative Sociology XVII, 3-4:183-205

Richmond, A., and W. Kalbach
   1979   Immigrants in Canada. Forthcoming, Statistics Canada, Ottawa.

Sedgewick, C. P.
   1973   The Context of Economic Change and Continuity in an Urban Overseas Chinese Community. Unpublished M.A. thesis, University of British Columbia, Canada.

III

ETHNIC FAMILIES AND SOCIO-RELIGIOUS SYSTEMS

INTRODUCTION

While the cases examined in this section may be accommodated within the general framework of adaptation and innovative change, they involve a significant departure from the cases in the preceding section to the extent that they involve groups less receptive to the pressures for change and innovation. The groups examined—the Mennonites, the Doukhobors, and the Hutterites—are not merely ethnic minorities in relation to the two dominant ethnic communities in Canada, but they are also marginal groups in relation to the rest of the society. This marginality arises not from some "primitive" isolation from the overall Canadian situation, but from their being ideologically and consciously opposed to the mainstream society. In the case of the ethnic groups analyzed in the preceding section, the tension between the original home system and the host system derives from an objective conflict between two sets of values, which, in principle, are not totally irreconcilable. In a sense, the problem in their case is a conflict between peasant-rooted, community-oriented family systems and the industrial society—a process not basically unlike the one out of which the industrial society arose both on the European continent and its North American colonies. This process is a continuation of the process of the emergence of a standard Euro-American family model. To be sure, it presented problems arising from ethnicity, but these were not insurmountable. Even the Japanese family, though they depart in some respects from this paradigm, can be fitted into the framework.

But the family systems in this section cannot be fitted into this framework. They each have a consciously elaborated community structure and culture, supported by explicit ideologies which reject the mainstream Canadian system. As the studies in this section show, these communities have emerged in a context of explicit rejection of the mainstream values. From a sociological perspective, their significance derives from the empirically observable fact that they have been fighting a losing battle against the mainstream impact. At the same time, the changing socio-cultural configurations within the mainstream system, as it has done in the case of the Japanese Sansei, may work to the advantage of the marginal ethnic groups' efforts to resist acculturation.

Alan Anderson and Leo Driedger focus on the Mennonite family in rural Saskatchewan. They designed their research work on the explicit assumption that the ethnic community and the family provided structural barriers to assimilation into the mainstream system—the demographic-ecological factor of concentration of community settlement and the family to resist acculturation. The pattern of segregated bloc settlements is not exceptional to the Mennonites, since other ethnic communities share a similar ecological pattern. The authors found that an overwhelming majority of the community consciously opposed assimilation and managed successfully to continue their community structure—institutional system and value system. The community identity was encapsulated in religion, language, and customs. Yet, they point out that the situation is undergoing a change, and the ethnic identity is involved in this process.

The increasing physical and social mobility experienced by the group has begun to undermine the community identity, but not to the extent of significantly endangering the identity. In the process of preserving this identity, family solidarity and family stability have been of critical relevance. In other words, while there are changes to be observed, these have not upset substantially the ethnic self-identity. Such changes include a shift from the large, kin-oriented network system to the nuclear family system, a shift to a more liberal role for the woman in the family system, and a shift more favourable to ethnic and religious intermarriages. Urbanization and industrial impact are making some dent in the traditional ethnic structure, but this process has, to date, failed to dislodge seriously the strong ethnic identity.

The Doukhobors, who left Russia for political reasons at the close of the nineteenth century, are, like the Mennonites, a marginal community with a strongly knit ideological and institutional solidarity. Their original institutional system and ideology developed later after arrival in Canada, as expressed in their religious identity. Their subsequent history in Canada has been one of political conflict with the federal and provincial governments in Canada. Their whole historical background was tailor-made for the development of a strong community identity. This sense of identity, solidarity, and cohesiveness is exemplified in the community rites associated with marriage and death. In particular, the religious rite of the Sobranie is significant as an occasion for reinforcing community solidarity. The Doukhobor ideology, however, does not emphasize birth as a major passage of life, since it upholds a conception of the individual as a developing person, imbibing systematically over a period of time the basic Doukhobor religious tenets and values.

Examining the marriage system, the study records that in Russia and Canada the community showed a change in pattern—from one based on parental control to one away from it. This process in Russia was motivated by the need for material security, while in Canada it was essentially a response to the Anglo-Canadian environment. While this aspect points to a dynamism, the other ritual practices point to the opposite aspect of cultural survival. The study makes a detailed analysis of the death observance as a complex and elaborate ritual which brings together within the compass of a single event the realities of family solidarity, community coherence and identity, and ideological commitment. The Doukhobor religious ideology is a progressive one, as it emphasizes the possibility of progress from "worse to better" for the individual but within a community context, both in the sacred and secular spheres. As a result, the process of change at the level of the individual person becomes structurally built into the more secure and stable community culture through the complex system of the rites. This means that the changes are evaluated in relation to the more basic demands for community identity.

Using a complicated conceptual model in which social time and space are systematically related to the family structure, Ishwaran and Chan provide an insight into the changing pattern of family relationships in a rural Dutch community in Ontario. Basing their interpretation on an intensive study of twenty-five households, they show that a community's notions of time and space are interdependent on its institutional components. They further point out that the family relationships among the rural Dutch involve specific notions of space and time, and that they are dynamically involved in a process of modernization taking place within the family structure. Their study thus focuses attention on the ideological dimensions of immigrant adaptation and acculturation.

Karl Peter, in his paper on the Hutterite family in the wider setting of its community culture, shifts his focus of attention from the more familiar issue of the survival of what he calls a *Gemeinschaft*—culture amidst an industrial society to the question of the behavioural aspects of the situation. The community's own claim to being a blissful, perfectly harmonious system comes under critical scrutiny. Peter points out that the community is involved in a process of cultural self-determination and social independence, but not without facing the problems arising from dependence on a hostile environment. Over the years they have evolved a discriminatory principle of acculturation, but this has created the problem of community destabilization. The fact that the

Hutterites have chosen to isolate themselves from the environment makes it difficult for the collection of sociological data, which should not be accepted at their face value. Claiming to penetrate beyond this initial obstacle, the author makes an empirical-historical study combining the methods of participant observation and individual biography. The author notes that the community socialization process is very rigid and authoritarian, including the "lash."

The Hutterite world-view is a dualistic one in which the animal aspect is controlled by physical coercion in the interest of a non-animal, rational, and hence superior part. This is rooted in the notion of the Fall and the original sin. But the Hutterite conception of rationality has been historically bypassed by the European Enlightenment with its individualistic emphasis, and goes back to the period of the Protestant Reformation. Their religious ideology is an adaptation of Anabaptism to community life, and it is this context which defines rationality. This enables the members of the community to adopt a "situational normative" approach to behaviour, and makes for great flexibility in operation, leading to problems of inconsistency. The inconsistency problem gets resolved only by intense interaction within community life. What is rational, therefore, becomes simply codified in the situational norms. The latter not only operate as guides to behaviour in contingent situations, but they also constitute the basis of the educational socialization processes under the auspices of the community supervision. This process involves such institutions as the common meal.

A community life demanding constant interpretation and reinterpretation of historically changing norms presupposes a high degree of religious scholarship. The author draws attention to a decline in this scholarship. In fact, most of the serious interpretative literature goes back to before 1665. This makes the process of adaptation in the light of religious reinterpretation impossible. As a result, since the seventeenth century there has emerged a rigid traditionalism with authoritarian overtones. Traditionalism, as distinct from a living tradition, is inimical to adaptation. A pragmatic solution was historically evolved by which both the survival of the tradition and the acceptance of modernization were subject to an opportunistic pattern of behaviour.

We find that the Hutterite society today presents the case of a social system which adopts an authoritarian pattern of socialization and social control. This leaves very little room for the individual to adapt himself to the pressures from the external but sufficiently immediate environment. The individual member finds himself faced with a rigid choice of alternatives—either he does not change within the traditional system or he can change only by rejecting totally the traditional order. In other words, the Hutterites have yet to resolve the problem of modernization.

9. The Mennonite Family: Culture and Kin in Rural Saskatchewan*

ALAN ANDERSON AND LEO DRIEDGER

INTRODUCTION

In this paper we assume that both the ethnic community and the ethnic family act as mini-social structures which form boundaries to maintain specific cultural values and ethnic families. The traditional rural ethnic community, often isolated ecologically, institutionally, and socially, provides opportunities to limit outside contacts so that the ethnic family, through generations, can be perpetuated. The ethnic community acts as a small social system which maintains boundaries and controls linkages with other ethnic communities or the larger social system. As the rural traditional community and/or the ethnic or religious enclave is invaded by industrialization and urbanization, the subsystem is increasingly exposed to outside influences which change the family structure and interactional patterns. The task, then, is to select an isolated traditional rural community to examine the extent to which ethnic families are changing.

This study focuses on the Mennonite family and culture in rural Saskatchewan. In the first part of this paper we will describe the ecological setting and demographic characteristics of Mennonites. Ethnic groups established a mosaic pattern of bloc settlements in prairie regions, such as in north-central Saskatchewan, with at least eighteen such settlements, including one large and a smaller Mennonite settlement (where our research was conducted). In the second part we will compare Mennonite cultural identity with that of their rural French, German Catho-

* We wish to thank G. N. Ramu for a critical reading of this paper and for his helpful comments.

lic, Ukrainian, Polish, Hutterite, Russian Doukhobor, and Scandinavian neighbours. To what extent is cultural identity preserved by religious attendance, ethnic language use, and practice of distinct customs? The third part will deal specifically with the Mennonite family, taking into account the family structure, such as family size, sex roles, mobility, and patterns of interaction, including attitudes toward ethnic and religious intermarriage and extent of intermarriage.

I. ECOLOGICAL AND DEMOGRAPHIC CHARACTERISTICS

To better understand the setting in which Mennonite culture and the Mennonite family survive, we shall sketch some of the relevant historical, ecological, and demographic factors. A short review of Mennonite history shows how they got to Saskatchewan; ecologically they comprise but one of many rural ethnic enclaves in the region; and demographically they represent a small, but fairly dense, population.

Historical Background of the Mennonite Settlements in Saskatchewan

Mennonites date their origin back to the spread of Anabaptism from Switzerland and the Netherlands during the sixteenth century under the leadership of Menno Simons. Faced with persecution, they began to migrate into northern Germany, particularly into west and east Prussia. Later, invited by the Russian crown, lured by military and taxation exemptions, and granted permission to found their own schools and local governments, numerous Mennonites migrated into Russia, settling in numerous colonies in south Russia between 1789 and 1889. However, by 1874 a large-scale emigration of Mennonites from these Russian settlements to Canada had commenced, due to the further revocation of privileges (Epp: 1962).

Mennonite immigrants from south Russia established the East and West Reserves in Manitoba in 1874 (Francis: 1955). Later, many of these Manitoba Mennonites, together with their co-religionists direct from Russia and Prussia or from the United States, established a variety of settlements in the neighbouring province of Saskatchewan. The large bloc settlement centred on Rosthern-Hague-Osler developed in several stages between 1891 and 1918 (Epp: 1974). The initial nucleus of this settlement came into existence in 1891-94 with the settling of the immediate area around Rosthern by immigrants of the *Rosenort Gemeinde* (later General Conference Mennonites) from west Prussia, Russia, and Manitoba. Next, a compact reserve consisting of as many as twenty villages was then established south of Rosthern, between Hague and Osler, by Old Colony Mennonites from Manitoba in 1895-1905 (Driedger: 1955, 1977). These adjoining Mennonite settlements then expanded into a single vast settlement (50 km in diameter), with the establishment of additional communities and congregations by Mennonite Brethren from the American Midwest (particularly Minnesota, Nebraska, Kansas, and Oklahoma), directly from Russia or via Manitoba in 1898-1918; by Krimmer Mennonite Brethren from Kansas and Nebraska in 1899-1901; by Sommerfelder or Bergthaler Mennonites from Manitoba in 1902; by General Conference Mennonites largely from the Midwest (Kansas, Oklahoma, Minnesota), but also directly from Russia or via Manitoba in 1910-12; and by Bruderthaler or Evangelical Mennonite Brethren from Minnesota in 1912 (Anderson: 1977b).

A second large Mennonite settlement similarly emerged in the Swift Current region in southern Saskatchewan between 1900 and 1914. In the meantime other smaller Mennonite settlements had developed elsewhere in the province. Finally, between 1923 and 1926, approximately fifteen thousand *Russlaender* Mennonites emigrated from Russia to Ontario, Manitoba, and Saskatchewan (Epp: 1962). In the latter province this immigration resulted in the formation of many new concentrations of Mennonites, such as in the Hanley-Dundurn, Glenbush-Rabbit Lake (the Meeting Lake settlement), and Herschel-Fiske areas, as well as resulting in the augmentation of the Mennonite population in the Rosthern-Hague-Osler settlement.

Ecological Setting
The Mennonites in the Rosthern-Hague-Osler settlement were in the midst of a series of rural bloc settlements established by a variety of ethnic groups including French, German Catholics, Scandinavians, Ukrainians and Poles, Hutterites, and Russian Doukhobors. Much of rural Saskatchewan, particularly the north-central region, was a mosaic of ethnic bloc settlements. Each settlement was an ethnic territorial enclave, within which the particular group established its institutions and sought to maintain its distinctive ethnic identity and culture. Most of the ethnic groups were segregated from each other, so that there was minimal contact in the early days. Improved transportation and communications, making for increased mobility and urbanization, have changed the exclusive ethnic solidarity somewhat, but most of these groups still perpetuate their identity (Anderson: 1972, 1977a; Driedger: 1977).

Demographic Characteristics
In 1971, the 168,150 Mennonites were a small ethno-religious group in Canada, representing only 0.8% of the total Canadian population (Census of Canada, 1971). Three-quarters of these Mennonites are located in the four western provinces, 59,555 (35.4%) in Manitoba, 26,315 (15.6%) in Saskatchewan, 14,645 (8.7%) in Alberta, 26,520 (15.7%) in British Columbia, compared to 40,115 (23.9%) in Ontario, and only 0.7% in other provinces. Before 1971 the Mennonites were the only religious group, of the twenty largest in Canada, who were still more rural than urban (52.6% rural in 1971). The Saskatchewan Men-

nonites are more rural (60.5%) than the national Mennonite average, but many are beginning to move especially into smaller towns and the city of Saskatoon (which had 5,695 Mennonites by 1971). In 1971 about 11,000 Mennonites lived in the rural bloc settlement between Saskatoon and Rosthern, and perhaps some 900 in the Meeting Lake settlement, the two settlements from which our data have been obtained.

The conservative Old Colony Mennonites who settled in villages in the Hague-Osler area sought to live a simple, segregated lifestyle, teaching their children in their own village German schools, and worshipping in traditional churches (Driedger: 1955). Other more liberal Mennonites, including General Conference Mennonites and Mennonite Brethren, had moved into the area by the 1920s, when some Old Colony Mennonites moved to Mexico because of encroaching urbanization and industrialization (Epp: 1962; Driedger: 1973). There were also several schisms within traditional Mennonite groups. The Bergthaler sect split because they wished changes in the church services; the Rudnerweide sect separated to emphasize a more evangelical version of Christianity; recently a new Chortitzer Mennonite church was built in Osler, whose members desired greater change. There has been a great deal of mobility in and out of the conservative community. Thus, the Mennonites presently living in the bloc settlement are very diverse, ranging in their adherence to traditionalism from conservative, Old Colony Mennonites to more liberal, urbanized, General Conference Mennonites. Given this variation in Mennonite sub-groups, the Mennonites on the whole are not nearly as conservative as the Hutterites in the Prairies. In fact, in many respects even the conservative Old Colony Mennonites in Saskatchewan are not as traditionalistic as Old Order Mennonites and Amish in Ontario. On the other hand, research has indicated clearly that, in general, Saskatchewan Mennonites have not been as prone to change as the German Catholics who formed their own large bloc settlements (Anderson: 1972, 1977a).

II. MENNONITE CULTURE

We have already discussed the ecological and demographic context in which the rural Mennonites of Saskatchewan are located. Let us now examine to what extent Mennonites favour identification with their culture; whether they attend religious services regularly; what their language preferences are; and to what extent they participate in the ethnic customs of their ingroup. To enrich the discussion and control our conclusions about Mennonites, we shall compare rural Mennonites with eight other ethno-religious groups who also settled in neighbouring blocs in Saskatchewan.[1]

We will explore the cultural factors related to boundary maintenance of ethnic enclaves. The bloc settlement facilitates the maintenance of ethnic cultural features. Kurt Lewin (1948) proposed that the individual needs to achieve a firm, clear sense of identification with the heritage and culture of the ingroup in order to find a secure "ground" for a sense of well being. Farber (1964) maintains that the family must be understood in terms of its culture. We suggest that favourable attitudes to future marriage partners and the perpetuation of the Mennonite family will depend greatly on the extent to which Mennonites maintain an enclavic culture within which such loyalties can be groomed (Driedger and Church: 1974; Driedger: 1975).

Institutional Completeness of Ethnic Communities

In addition to territorial and cultural means of boundary maintenance, several Canadian sociologists have suggested that the institutional completeness of ethnic communities is important. The rationale for institutional completeness is that when a minority can develop a social system of its own with control over its institutions, then the social interaction patterns of the group will take place largely within the system; such patterns will lead to the creation and maintenance of boundaries and control over systemic linkage (Breton: 1964; Driedger and Church: 1974). Ethnic identity is likely to persist if (a) the members of an ethnic group successfully resist structural assimilation, defined by Gordon (1964) as large-scale entrance into the institutions of the host society; (b) there is a high degree of organizational or institutional dependence within the institutional framework of an ethnic community; (c) certain institutional foci within an ethnic community tend to be multi-functional (e.g., an ethnic-oriented congregation or parish involved in ethnic-oriented voluntary associations, schools, etc.); (d) the local ethnic community has a church (or equivalent religious establishment) specifically oriented toward the maintenance of ethnic consciousness; (e) the ethnic group controls the education (at as many levels as possible) of its members, and more generally controls the institutions responsible for the socialization of group members into an awareness of group identity; (f) a wide variety of ethnic-oriented voluntary associations are available to the members of an ethnic group; and the members participate as regularly as possible in these associations (Anderson: 1975; Driedger: 1975).

Thus, the struggle of the Mennonites in Saskatchewan for preservation of their ethno-religious identity, for cultural survival against assimilatory tendencies and forces, has depended on maintaining a sufficient degree of ethnic enclosure or ethnic exclusiveness and of institutional completeness. In other words, they had to remain distinctly Mennonite rather than integrating into the general society to the extent that their unique identity would cease to exist; they had to preserve a uniquely Mennonite way of life; and the institutional structure of the local community had to be sufficiently oriented toward the minority culture rather than toward the general society. Doubtless the capability of Mennonites to control local institutions in the settlements under discussion is greatly enhanced by the fact that in the Rosthern-Hague-Osler settlement, all but three communities sampled had Mennonite proportions of over 90% (and these three exemptions had proportions of over two-thirds). In the Meeting Lake settlement this was less apparent, although Mennonites constituted a clear majority or plurality in three of the four communities where interviews were conducted.

Attitudes Toward Identity Preservation

Three-fourths (75.4%) of the Mennonites (N=244) in Anderson's study (1972) favoured preservation of their Mennonite identity (Table 1). A greater proportion of Hutterities, Ukrainians, Poles, and Doukhobors interviewed (total sample N=1000) favoured identity preservation than the Mennonites, but respondents in other ethnic groups (particularly German Catholics) indicated less favourable attitudes.

TABLE 1
PROPORTION OF RESPONDENTS IN EACH GENERATION (BY ETHNIC GROUPS) FAVOURING IDENTITY PRESERVATION

Group	Favour Identity Preservation %	N	By Generation First	Second	Third
Hutterite	100.0	(6)	—	100.	100.
Polish Catholic	92.3	(14)	100.	88.9	—
Doukhobor	85.0	(17)	100.	90.0	60.0
Ukrainian Catholic	81.8	(126)	100.	82.1	55.5
Ukrainian Orthodox	79.5	(66)	100.	73.0	68.4
Mennonite	75.4	(184)	95.3	81.7	64.2
Scandinavian	74.4	(64)	100.	79.4	61.9
French	70.3	(142)	87.5	80.4	47.2
German Catholic	32.6	(62)	73.0	34.6	10.5
Sample Total	68.1	(681)	—	—	—

By generation, Anderson (1972, 1977a) found that almost all of the first generation Mennonites (95.3%) favoured identity preservation. This declined moderately to 81.7% in the second generation, then more emphatically to two-thirds (64.2%) of the third generation who wished to preserve their identity. Except for the Hutterites (100%), the desire to preserve ethnic culture declined for all of the groups from the first to the third generation. The decline, however, varied by ethnic group. The decline for the German Catholics (73.0 to 10.5%), and the French (87.5 to 47.2%) was very sharp, while there was no Hutterite decline. The Mennonite decline was less pronounced than that of many of the other groups, although it was considerable. We would expect that the younger respondents in the third generation might become somewhat more favourable toward preservation of their identity when they grow older, but we do not know.

Extent of Church Attendance

The Mennonites are a religious group which, through the centuries, have maintained ethnic characteristics (although many General Conference Mennonites today prefer to stress their Mennonite identity in *religious* rather than *ethnic* terms). This is also the case for most ethnic groups in western Canada. Religion has long been stressed by sociologists as an important cultural factor to consider in defining ethnicity.

TABLE 2

PROPORTION OF RESPONDENTS IN EACH GENERATION (BY ETHNIC GROUPS) ATTENDING CHURCH SERVICES REGULARLY

Groups	Attend Church Regularly %	N	By Generation First	Second	Third
Hutterites	100.0	(6)	—	100.0	100.0
German Catholic	93.7	(78)	94.6	97.4	89.3
French	91.1	(185)	100.0	94.6	81.4
Scandinavian	87.2	(75)	69.2	82.4	97.4
Mennonite	86.1	(210)	97.6	86.6	81.7
Ukrainian Catholic	81.8	(126)	94.7	84.3	55.6
Ukrainian Orthodox	69.9	(58)	96.4	57.1	78.9
Doukhobour	55.0	(11)	60.0	80.0	0.0
Polish Catholic	53.3	(8)	100.0	22.2	—
Total Sample	85.7	(857)			

Using church attendance as one indicator of religious activity, Anderson (1972, 1977a) found that the Mennonites again ranked in the middle compared to other ethnic groups: 86.1% of the Mennonites interviewed attended church services regularly, compared to a higher proportion of Hutterites (100%), German Catholics (93.7%), French Catholics (91.1%), and Scandinavian Lutherans (87.2%); but a lower proportion of Ukrainian Catholics (81.8%), Ukrainian Orthodox (69.9%), Russian Doukhobors (55.0%), and Polish Catholics (53.3%). Almost all Mennonites of the first generation (97.6%) attended church regularly, and most of the third generation (81.7%) continued to do so. The high church attendance of Mennonites of all generations would suggest that religion is an important part of their culture and identity. The high degree of church attendance of most groups may be a feature of rural ethnic life, where most of the people consider religion important.

Language Preference in Home and Community

Apart from religion, another of the distinctive features of most ethnic identities is language. Traditionally the Mennonites spoke Low German at home and in their bloc community, and High German in the church.

TABLE 3
LANGUAGE PREFERENCE OF RESPONDENTS (BY ETHNIC GROUPS)

ETHNIC LANGUAGE

Group	N	Can Speak Mother Tongue	Use Mother Tongue Often	Bilingual: Prefer MT in Home & Community	Bilingual: Prefer Eng. in Home & Community	Speak Only English
Hutterite	(6)	100.0%	100.0	100.0	—	—
French	(202)	99.0	78.2	48.0	20.8	1.0
Polish	(15)	100.0	86.7	33.3	13.3	—
Mennonite	(244)	97.2	68.9	52.5	28.3	2.9
Ukrainian Orthodox	(83)	100.0	62.6	33.7	37.3	—
Ukrainian Catholic	(154)	98.7	68.8	44.2	29.9	1.3
Doukhobor	(20)	95.0	70.0	25.0	25.0	5.0
Scandinavian	(86)	89.5	37.2	25.6	52.3	10.5
German Catholic	(190)	93.2	29.0	13.7	64.2	6.8
Total Sample	(1000)	96.6	60.4	38.5	36.2	3.4

Almost all of the respondents in the Anderson survey (1972, 1977a) could speak their ethnic mother tongue. While 97% of the Mennonites could use their mother tongue, nearly 70% actually used Low German often, hardly any (2.9%) could speak only English. Of those who were bilingual (German and English), over half (52.5%) preferred to speak their mother tongue in both the home and community. An additional 15% preferred to speak Low German at home and English in the community. About one-fourth (28.3%) preferred to speak English both at home and in the community. Thus, about two-thirds of the Mennonites preferred to speak Low German in the home, while most of the rest could do so if necessary.

Comparative research on linguistic trends in Saskatchewan (Anderson, 1976) has indicated that in their rural bloc settlements, a fairly high proportion of Mennonites, together with Hutterites, Poles and Ukrainians, Doukhobors, and French continue to use their traditional mother tongue often, unlike Scandinavians and German Catholics, who could speak their traditional languages but preferred English. Moreover, this research would seem to suggest that for Mennonites and most ethnic groups in this province, urbanization and generation differences are accounting for an inexorable (and in many cases rapid) loss of emphasis on the traditional languages.

Customs

As one anthropologist has commented, the sum total of the customs of similar individuals in a group or minority may be viewed as their culture or sub-culture. But to be more specific, we are equating customs with certain folkways contributing to the uniqueness of an ethnic group's identity. The sample respondents were asked specifically whether they cook or eat traditional food particular to their group, whether they produce any crafts (handicrafts, embroidery, etc.) typical of their group, and whether they have any special group taboos or norms (such as traditional prohibition of smoking or drinking). Among the Mennonites interviewed, about half (47.1%) reported that they prepared or ate traditional food, compared to only 21.7% who produced crafts, and 35.7% who observed customs of prudence, etc. Significant group differences are indicated in Table 4.

TABLE 4
SPECIFIED CUSTOMS OF MENNONITES COMPARED TO OTHER ETHNIC
GROUPS IN SAMPLE

Group	Foods	Crafts
Hutterite	100.0%	100.0%
Polish Catholic	100.0	100.0
Doukhobor	100.0	55.0
Ukrainian Catholic	92.2	92.2
Ukrainian Orthodox	86.5	86.7
Scandinavian	68.6	43.0
Mennonite	50.8	21.7
German Catholic	13.2	5.3
French	4.0	2.0
Total Sample	47.1	35.0

According to our sample (Anderson: 1972), all the Hutterites and Doukhobors, a high proportion of Slavs, most Scandinavians, half the Mennonites, and very few French and German Catholics regularly cook or eat the food unique to their group.

We have noted that all the Hutterites in our sample, a high proportion of the Ukrainian-Polish group, roughly half the Doukhobors and Scandinavians, less than a quarter of the Mennonites, and very few French and German Catholics produce traditional crafts. While Hutterites and some Doukhobors were still making much of their furniture and clothing in traditional style, few Mennonites continue to do so. Some Mennonite women still make quilts or do embroidery and needlework. Old Colony Mennonites are the only Mennonites in Saskatchewan who ever dress traditionally, but usually they do not (unlike Old Order Mennonites and Amish in Ontario). Some do on Sundays for church: the men often wear black shirts and dark outer clothing, but no ties, while the women wear long, floor-length, dark dresses, dark stockings and shoes, black bonnets or caps, and shawls (young girls may wear lighter, flowery dresses). Also related to crafts is interior home decor, as well as exterior home design. Traditional Old Colony Mennonite homes, and present-day Hutterite homes, were very simple: stark, clean and freshly painted, lacking adornments, with the absolute minimum of furniture. Old Colony Mennonites retained the Dutch custom of connecting homes with barns into one long building, and the Russian tradition of gabled roofs, but this is no longer the case.

Over a third of the Mennonites (mostly Old Colony) mentioned customs relating to taboos, particularly prudence, whereas none of the respondents in other groups mentioned any (except the Hutterites). Until roughly the 1930s, both Old Colony Mennonites and Hutterites were strictly opposed to riding in cars or tractors and using telephones. Punishment was shunning or ostracism in mild cases, excommunication from sect and kin in severe ones. Today, however, the emphasis is more on impassioned pleas by conservative elders and preachers to better one's life. Many of these taboos are changing, and the majority of Mennonites in the area (General Conference and Mennonite Brethren) always were more liberal.

Among other customs, the layout of some villages in the ethnic bloc settlements also constitutes a folkway. The collective or nucleated Doukhobor villages have long been eradicated, but present-day Old Colony Mennonite villages still exist. Traditional social gatherings are becoming infrequent among Mennonites. The Mennonites' hog-slaughters and building-bees are almost non-existent now. The agricultural fairs and auctions have become less leisure affairs and more business-like.

We conclude that a large number of Mennonites were generally concerned with preserving their identity. Most of them attended church regularly, most of them could speak their mother tongue, and a majority preferred to use it in the home and community, but their preparation of ethnic foods, creation of crafts, etc., were weakening. Compared to other ethno-religious groups, the Mennonite culture does not seem to be as strong as that of the Hutterites or some other ethnic groups in certain respects, yet it seems to be considerably stronger as a whole than that of most groups. In the next part we shall see whether this cultural "ground," as Lewin (1948) would put it, provides a support for a strong Mennonite family, or whether it is declining in importance. Given the considerable Mennonite cultural distinctiveness, we would expect, with Farber (1964), that elements of Mennonite norms, values, and socialization will be reflected in a distinctive family culture.

III. FAMILY AND KINSHIP

Normally, factors such as endogamy, intermarriage, and the family might be included in a discussion of cultural identity. However, as the focus of this book is on the family, we shall discuss several factors, such as attitudes to ethnic intermarriage, attitudes to religious intermarriage, and actual rates of intermarriage among Mennonites. We have attempted to show that ethnic group settlement in rural Saskatchewan, which remains demographically segregated, will permit maintenance of ethnic cultural enclaves as well. Let us now examine the extent of Mennonite family maintenance within this ethnic and religious milieu.

Mennonite Family Structure

In 1955 Driedger found that divorce in the Mennonite family was almost unheard of; by 1977 very few cases of divorce were found (Driedger: 1955, 1977). The Mennonite churches define divorce as sinful, and the community pressures for family solidarity are very strong. Since most of the dating and interaction takes place among Mennonites, uniformity of beliefs, traditions, customs, values, and norms seem to encourage family solidarity.

Family size has changed dramatically. When the Mennonites were farmers, children were an asset. Many families had ten children or more; a number had up to fifteen or more children (Driedger: 1955). Although the average family size in 1977 is still above the national average, many families now have between two and six children (Driedger: 1977). Since a small percentage of family heads are now in agriculture, children are less of an asset, and even farm families are much smaller. Extended kin networks may still be found among the Old Colony Mennonites, who seem particularly aware of such networks. Some Old Colony Mennonite respondents had more than a dozen near kin living in the immediate area. It is still not unusual for Old Colony Mennonite nuclear families to include a dozen or more, apart from the extended kin network. Both tradition and rural residence have contributed to large family size. Extended family gatherings, however, are still common; visiting with cousins, uncles, aunts, grandparents is popular. Most rural Mennonites keep track of their first and second cousins, and visit with them frequently as kin.

Sex roles are changing among the young. The Mennonite family was a typical patriarchal family, where the father was the head of the house and the mother and children took secondary roles. The children were to be seen but not heard. With the influences of the schools, children and youth are becoming increasingly more vocal, and sex roles are changing also. As more Mennonites work in the city, a number of women are working outside of the home. As the family size decreases, the woman spends less time raising children. Among the more liberal Mennonite young families, the equalitarian family is emerging, typical of the modern nuclear family.

There has been virtually no changing of surnames in the ethnic bloc settlements of north-central Saskatchewan. However, significant differences between ethnic groups exist with reference to changing given names (Anderson: 1976). For example, among the Mennonite farmers in the Rosthern settlement, German given names are still common; more than sixteen varieties may be found (e.g., Waldemar, Johannes, Karl, Helmuth, Konrad, Ludwig, etc.). Biblical names used in the German language are also common (e.g., Abram, Isaac, Jacob, etc.), and some English versions of Biblical names are quite common (e.g., Peter, John, etc.). But increasingly a variety of other names are becoming more prevalent than these traditional names (Driedger: 1977). As revealed in elementary school records and gravestones, the change from Biblical names to modern names began to occur after World War II among the more conservative Mennonites, so that by now the change to modern names among the third or fourth generation has been quite complete.

Finally, each group has unique socialization techniques. This is most apparent today in the case of the Hutterites, with their restricted opportunities for contact during adolescent dating, partially arranged marriages, incorporation of children into the functional specialization of labour as apprentices at an early age, separate children's dining room, etc. Whereas among conservative Old Colony Mennonites, with the movement away from collectivized village living several decades ago, such practices eventually disappeared, although restriction of contact with more liberal Mennonites (the majority of Mennonites) could be discussed until the past decade.

Attitudes Toward Ethnic Intermarriage

While most Canadian ethnic groups consider religion and language important factors in the development of ethnic group identity, endogamy is also considered to be of great importance. Endogamy will permit the parents to socialize their offspring into the ingroup culture and religion. Opposition to ethnic intermarriage has tended to vary considerably among ethnic groups in Saskatchewan (Table 5). While all of the Hutterites in the sample (Anderson: 1972) were opposed to marrying people of other (non-German) ethnic origins, only 10% of the German Catholics were. Over half (56.5%) of the Mennonites were opposed to ethnic intermarriage, but their opposition to ethnic intermarriage also declined with each generation. While three-quarters (76.2%) of the first generation opposed ethnic intermarriage, less than half (45.0%) of the third generation did so. While few of the other groups were more opposed to ethnic intermarriage, again the decline of opposition by generations is noteworthy.

It should be noted that the Mennonites have always been somewhat ambivalent about their ethnicity. The predecessors of Saskatchewan Mennonites were mostly of Dutch origin, moved later to Prussia (where they adopted the German language at the expense of their Dutch), then moved on to Russia (where they retained their German), and finally to Canada (where many Mennonites prefer to speak English more often than German). Thus, many Mennonites are often ambivalent about their national origin. Saskatchewan Mennonites are divided in claiming to be of Dutch or German origin. Perhaps the lack of opposition to ethnic intermarriage by the third generation is due to less stress on national ethnic origins. Would this hold true for religious intermarriage?

Attitudes Toward Religious Intermarriage

The Mennonites began as a religious sect, and have always stressed religion rather than ethnicity as the most important reason for their existence, even though we have noted that most of the Mennonites in the sample stress their ethnic identity. We would expect that their opposition to religious intermarriage would be greater than to ethnic intermarriage. Two-thirds (69.3% of the Mennonites in the sample opposed religious intermarriage; almost two-thirds (60.9%) of the third generation were still opposed to intermarriage (Table 6). Indeed, most of the groups compared with the Mennonites (except for the Doukhobors and Ukrainian Orthodox) are generally opposed to religious intermarriage.

TABLE 5
PROPORTION OF RESPONDENTS IN EACH GENERATION (BY ETHNIC GROUPS) OPPOSING ETHNIC INTERMARRIAGE

Group	Opposed to Ethnic Intermarriage %	N	By Generation First	Second	Third
Hutterite	100.0	(6)	—	100.0	100.0
Ukrainian Catholic	61.7	(95)	89.4	58.5	33.3
Mennonite	56.5	(138)	76.2	63.4	45.0
Scandinavian	52.3	(44)	95.0	90.2	61.5
French	45.6	(92)	70.0	48.9	27.2
Doukhobor	45.0	(9)	60.0	50.0	20.0
Ukrainian Orthodox	41.0	(34)	68.2	33.4	26.3
Polish	40.0	(6)	100.0	—	—
German Catholic	10.0	(19)	24.3	12.8	0.0
Total Sample	44.4	(443)			

TABLE 6
PROPORTION OF RESPONDENTS IN EACH GENERATION (BY ETHNIC GROUPS) OPPOSING RELIGIOUS INTERMARRIAGE

Group	Opposed to Religious Intermarriage %	N	By Generation First	Second	Third
Hutterite	100.0	(6)	—	100.0	100.0
French	81.2	(164)	95.0	90.2	61.5
Scandinavian	77.0	(66)	100.0	94.1	56.4
Polish	73.4	(11)	100.0	55.5	—
German Catholic	69.5	(132)	91.9	85.9	41.4
Mennonite	69.3	(169)	92.9	69.5	60.9
Ukrainian Catholic	68.8	(109)	89.4	66.3	48.1
Ukrainian Orthodox	43.4	(36)	68.2	33.4	36.8
Doukhobor	35.0	(7)	20.0	50.0	20.0
Total Sample	69.8	(698)			

Extent of Intermarriage

Intermarriage among ethnic groups in rural Saskatchewan is very low. The boundaries of the territorial communities, the cultural enclaves, and religious convictions seem to result in ethnic endogamy (Anderson: 1974; Driedger and Peters: 1973). Opposition to religious intermarriage seems to be declining, however, and opposition to ethnic intermarriage is declining even more. More than 90% (91.5) of the respondents in the total sample married within their own group; over two-thirds (69.8%) opposed religious intermarriage; and less than half (44.4%) opposed ethnic intermarriage.

With the consolidation of public schools, Mennonite children and youth are increasingly exposed to a greater variety of potential mates. However, since the elementary schools in Martensville, Warman, Osler, and Hague and the high schools in Warman and Hague are located in solid Mennonite territory, most of the students they come in contact with are Mennonite. However, more traditional Old Colony Mennonites go to school with more liberal General Conference Mennonites, which provides opportunities for some inter-Mennonite dating and intermarriage. A lot of dating takes place within the villages and hamlets and within the school context, which is largely Mennonite (Driedger: 1977). Inter-ethnic and inter-religious dating and marriage are likely to remain low for some time to come.

TABLE 7
SUMMARY OF THE EXTENT OF INTERMARRIAGE FOR MARRIED
RESPONDENTS, AND ATTITUDES TO RELIGIOUS AND ETHNIC
INTERMARRIAGE

Group	N	Extent of Actual Intermarriage	Opposed to Religious Intermarriage	Opposed to Ethnic Intermarriage
Hutterite	(6)	100.0%	100.0	100.0
Mennonite	(244)	97.6	69.3	56.5
Scandinavian	(86)	95.8	77.0	52.3
French	(15)	91.1	81.2	45.6
German Catholic	(190)	90.0	69.5	10.0
Ukrainian Orthodox	(83)	88.9	43.4	41.0
Ukrainian Catholic	(154)	87.5	68.8	61.7
Polish	(15)	69.2	73.4	40.0
Doukhobor	(20)	60.0	35.0	45.0
Total Sample	(1000)	91.5	69.8	44.4

Mobility in the Mennonite Family

In spite of a one-time avoidance of close social contact between Old Colony Mennonites and other Mennonites in the Rosthern settlement (mentioned above), recently there has been a significant increase in the mobility, affecting even conservative Mennonite families. Doubtless, this mobility (both physical and social) has been enhanced by such developments as the recent construction of a new link in the principal highway between the cities of Saskatoon and Prince Albert, for this new highway passes directly through the heart of the Old Colony (which was, until then, reached only by travelling miles over rough gravel and dirt roads). In fact, the sample data indicated that almost half (43.4%) of the Mennonite families interviewed mentioned recent "permanent" departure from the settlement of one or more members of each family. It is interesting to note that such a rate of physical mobility was appreciably higher than in the cross-ethnic sample as a whole (Anderson: 1972), possibly because of the location of the Rosthern settlement between, and in close proximity to, the second and third largest cities in the province. Moreover, 22.1% of the Mennonites interviewed were opposed to this trend of increasing physical mobility (particularly among Old Colony respondents), compared to 47.2% who were in favour (the remainder were indifferent). It was found that the more conservative Mennonites were more likely to oppose physical mobility than their liberal co-religionists; yet migration out of conservative families was just as high, if not higher, than out of more liberal ones.

To what extent do physical mobility and rural depopulation actually affect the preservation of ethnic identities and family solidarity? Many sociologists—including Shibutani and Kwan (1965), Schermerhorn (1970), and Greer (1964)—have stressed that improved transportation and increased physical mobility inevitably promote economic and social integration and urbanization, thereby having a profound effect on ethnic identity. Dawson and Younge described the Saskatchewan situation in similar terms as early as 1940. Greer (1964) has suggested that urbanization should refer not simply to a changing rural-urban proportion, but to what he calls the increasing scale of society. By this he means that changing technology is forcing formerly relatively isolated rural areas into a network of functional interdependence. A former emphasis on ethnic particularism comes to be replaced by a social structure emphasizing economic function and characterized by stratification, indifferent, if not antithetical, to considerations of ethnic origins (Driedger: 1968, 1972). Within a certain rural locality, therefore, individuals increasingly fail to regard local groups, such as their family, ethnic group or community, as primary reference groups.

The social changes and community reorganization resulting from population change may have a marked affect. It seems most apparent that a continuum of change parallels a continuum of conservative to liberal groupings. For example, among the Anabaptist groups, it has been suggested by some sociologists that even the Hutterites are adjusting to urbanization and mass culture influences; already they have adjusted technologically, unlike the Old Order Amish who are similar in other traditions. Many Old Colony Mennonites have abandoned their villages, sold their poor, small farms to larger-scale farmers of more liberal Mennonite groups, and ignored the traditional prohibition against living in town to move into Hague and Osler (Driedger: 1977). In turn, many of the more liberal Mennonite farmers are working part-time in Saskatoon; some have moved into Martensville, a solidly Mennonite town which grew very rapidly during the past decade and which is only 10 km out of the city, but still within the rural bloc settlement. By 1970, 64.6% of the more liberal General Conference Mennonites in Saskatchewan were classified as urban; 41.1% of them lived in Saskatoon; and only 32.3% of the gainfully employed ones were farmers (Anderson: 1972). Given this new mobility, the eventual merging of sectarian distinctions within the Mennonites is likely, as is the emergence of a new identity de-emphasizing the traditional family.

There has been frequent mention in the sociological literature on ethnic relations of social mobility raising the status of immigrants and their descendents, contributing to acculturation. However, in examining rural ethnic bloc settlements, we must be very careful not to misconstrue the relationship between physical mobility, social mobility, ethno-religious identity change, and changes in the family. It is possible to have physical mobility without social mobility or identity change; for example, there are unskilled labourers who commute to the city or farmers who live in the city but still carry on farming. It is possible to have identity change without physical or social mobility, or occupational integration without social integration, or economic integration at an early stage without affecting social segregation or cultural pluralism. We would suggest, though, that in most cases, physical mobility has been closely related to social mobility, identity change, and changes in the family structure, particularly for the younger generation. Many younger respondents asked why they should speak their mother-tongues and keep up their group's traditions when they didn't want to take over the family farm but get a "better job" in some city, where ethnic identity mattered little.

When asked whether their sons or daughters now had occupations requiring more education than the respondent had, 21.3% of the first and second generation Mennonites interviewed responded affirmatively (a higher proportion than the 15.9% in the total cross-ethnic sample). Half of the Mennonites interviewed were in favour of this social mobility, most of the remainder (42.6%) were indifferent, and only 5.3% (very conservative Mennonites) were opposed. Increased social mobility seems to contribute to changes in the Mennonite family structure and social interaction.

CONCLUSION

First, with reference to the demographic-ecological setting, we pointed out that most Mennonites in Saskatchewan remain quite highly segregated in rural bloc settlements. These Mennonite settlements are situated within a general context of a mosaic of similar bloc settlements established by other ethnic groups. The two Mennonite settlements studied represented almost half of the total Mennonite population in the province. Saskatchewan Mennonites are still predominantly rural, but urbanization of Mennonites is steadily increasing.

Second, with reference to Mennonite culture, we found that a high proportion of the Mennonites in the settlements studied revealed an interest in preserving, and considerable ability to maintain, their group identity as represented in religion, language, and customs. But at the same time we have argued that analysis of generation differences would seem to indicate clearly that this distinctive Mennonite identity is changing. Similarly, the identity of other ethnic groups is changing (with the possible exception of the Hutterites), although at a different rate and to a different extent, depending on the group.

Third, with reference to the Mennonite family, we have stressed that the Mennonite family is a *changing* social institution. This general conclusion has been illustrated in a variety of examples: family size has been changing, represented by a shift from large extended kin networks to small nuclear families; sex roles in the family are changing with the adoption of more liberal attitudes toward women; given names are becoming less traditional; attitudes toward ethnic and religious intermarriage have been changing with each new generation, although the actual extent of intermarriage has been limited.

Finally, it was pointed out that a new physical and social mobility could have a profound effect on Mennonite identity in general, and on the Mennonite family in particular. On the other hand, despite these changes, we have argued that Mennonites have revealed a continuing strong sense of family solidarity and a disinterest in divorce.

Perhaps the central theoretical problem posed by our study is at once deceptively simple yet actually quite complex; namely, to speculate whether the changing Mennonite culture and family represent social change in the general society, or the urbanization of rural prople, or the assimilation and acculturation of ethnic groups, or changes affecting Mennonites in particular. It must be our contention that the data which we have presented in this paper are indicative of social change at all of these levels.

In the past, Mennonites in rural Saskatchewan were successful in the orderly replacement of their traditional family. The conservative Old Colony Mennonites especially maintained traditional families and isolated villages. Changes toward the universal, permanent availability concept are setting in as Mennonites enter the urban industrial marketplace, but many are continuing orderly replacement of their families, albeit in a changed form. Farber's (1964) orderly replacement principle of the Mennonite family seems to continue, but more universal ability is making some inroads, especially as mobility increases.

The reason for some change in the Mennonite family seems to be closely linked with the changes taking place in the Mennonite rural community. Driedger (1977) has clearly shown that with the coming of the new highway, Saskatoon has increasingly come to the Mennonite community. A majority of Mennonites living in the villages no longer farm but work in the city, more and more Mennonites are moving to

Saskatoon, and urban goods and services have increasingly been adopted. These cultural changes seem to also effect family size and roles within the family, but there are still strong religious and ethnic boundaries which seem to encourage endogamy and retard extensive family separation and divorce. Urbanization and industrialization are changing the Mennonite family, but it would seem that the family will remain strongly Mennonite, albeit in a changed form.

NOTES

1. Two methods were used in collecting data for this study. One was a longitudinal community study made in 1955, with a follow-up in 1977 when the same community was revisited (Driedger: 1955 and 1977). The other was a sample study of the eighteen ethno-religious bloc settlements in north-central Saskatchewan, including two Mennonite settlements in 1969-72 (Anderson: 1972).

The Community Survey (Driedger: 1955 and 1977)
An in-depth community study of the Old Colony Mennonites in 1955 included intensive interviewing of original Mennonite settlers in Hague, Osler, and fifteen villages, to develop the social history of the area. The village organization, the social institutions (religious, educational, family, voluntary), and the ecological setting were studied in 1955, then restudied in 1977, to determine the social change which had taken place. Methodological details of the 1955 study (Driedger: 1955) and the 1977 study (Driedger: 1977) have been published for those who wish to examine the procedures in more depth.

The Sample Survey (Anderson: 1972)
The data were gathered during 1969-71 in eighteen ethno-religious bloc settlements (seven French Catholic, one German Catholic, two Mennonite, two Hutterite, three Ukrainian Orthodox, Ukrainian Catholic, and Polish Catholic, one Russian Doukhobor, and two Scandinavian Lutheran) located in the region between Saskatoon, North Battleford, and Prince Albert (Census Divisions Fifteen and Sixteen). A 2.00% controlled quota sample was stratified by age, generation, and sex, to represent as closely as possible the demographic structure of the total population of each settlement. In other words, one in every 50 persons of the relevant ethnic and religious category was interviewed in each settlement. Not more than one person was interviewed in a single nuclear family, and no respondent was less than 13 years of age. The extent of each settlement was statistically determined as the limit beyond which each relevant ethno-religious group comprised less than one-quarter of the total local population, although several of the communities sampled could be included in two overlapping bloc settlements. This sampling technique yielded a thousand cases. Respondents in 244 Mennonite families were interviewed, as well as in 202 French families, 6 Hutterite, 83 Ukrainian Orthodox, 154 Ukrainian Catholic, 15 Polish Catholic, 20 Russian Doukhobor, and 86 Scandinavian. The interviewing procedure employed in the study was focused interviewing; instead of designing a strictly structured questionnaire which would have yielded considerably less information, each respondent was personally interviewed in depth. Those who wish may write for a list containing the actual number of Mennonites interviewed in 23 towns and villages and the surrounding hinterland.

REFERENCES

Anderson, Alan B.
1972 "Assimilation in the Bloc Settlements of North-Central Sas-
      katchewan: A Comparative Study of Identity Change Among Seven
      Ethno-Religious Groups in a Canadian Prairie Region." Ph.D. thesis
      in sociology, University of Saskatchewan, Saskatoon.

1974 "Intermarriage in Ethnic Bloc Settlements in Saskatchewan: A Cross-
      Cultural Survey of Trends and Attitudes." Research paper presented
      at the annual meetings of the Western Association of Sociology and
      Anthropology, Banff.

1975 "Ethnic Groups: Implications of Criteria for the Examination of Sur-
      vival." A paradigm presented in the workshop on "Ethnicity and Eth-
      nic Groups in Canada," at the annual meetings of the Canadian Soci-
      ology and Anthropology Association, University of Alberta,
      Edmonton.

1976 "Linguistic Trends Among Saskatchewan Ethnic Groups." Research
      paper presented at the National Conference on Ethnic Studies and Re-
      search, University of Regina.

1977a "Ethnic identity in Saskatchewan Bloc Settlements: A Sociological
      Appraisal." In The Settlement of the West, edited by Howard Palmer.
      Calgary: Comprint Publishing, University of Calgary, pp. 187-225.

1977b "Emigration from German Settlements in Eastern Europe: A Study in
      Historical Demography." Proceedings of the First Banff Conference
      on Central and East European Studies, Edmonton: Central and East
      European Studies Society of Alberta, pp. 184-223.

Breton, Raymond
1964 "Institutional Completeness of Ethnic Communities and Personal Re-
      lations of Immigrants." American Journal of Sociology 70:193-205.

Dawson, C. A., and E. R. Younge
1940 Pioneering in the Prairie Provinces: The Social Side of the Settlement
      Process. Canadian Frontiers of Settlement Series, Vol. VIII. Toronto:
      Macmillan.

Driedger, Leo
1955 "A Sect in Modern Society: A Case Study of the Old Colony Mennon-
      ites of Saskatchewan." M.A. thesis in sociology, University of Chi-
      cago.

1968 "A Perspective on Canadian Mennonite Urbanization." In Mennon-
      ites in Urban Canada: Proceedings of the Conference on Urbanization
      of Mennonites in Canada, edited by Leo Driedger. University of Mani-
      toba, Winnipeg. Mennonite Life 23:147-159.

1972 "Urbanization of Mennonites in Canada." In Call to Faithfulness,
      edited by H. Poettcker and R. A. Regehr. Winnipeg: Canadian Men-
      nonite Bible College.

1973 "Impelled Group Migration: Minority Struggle to Maintain Institu-
      tional Completeness." International Migration Review 7:257-269.

1975   "In Search of Cultural Identity Factors: A Comparison of Ethnic Minorities in Manitoba." *Canadian Review of Sociology and Anthropology* 12:150-162.

1977   "Mennonite Change: The Old Colony Revisited, 1955-1977." *Mennonite Life* 32:4-12.

Driedger, Leo, and Jacob Peters
1973   "Ethnic Identity: A Comparison of Mennonite and Other German Students." *Mennonite Quarterly Review* 47:225-244.

Driedger, Leo, and Glenn Church
1974   "Residential Segregation and Institutional Completeness: A Comparison of Ethnic Minorities." *Canadian Review of Sociology and Anthropology* 11:30-52.

Epp, Frank H.
1962   *Mennonite Exodus*. Altona, Manitoba: D. W. Friesen and Sons Publishers.

1974   *Mennonites in Canada 1786-1920: The History of a Separate People*. Toronto: Macmillan.

Eshleman, J. Ross
1974   *The Family: An Introduction*. Boston: Allyn and Bacon.

Farber, Bernard
1964   *Family Organization and Interaction*. San Francisco: Chandler.

Francis, E. K.
1955   *In Search of Utopia*. Altona, Manitoba: D. W. Friesen and Sons Publishers.

Greer, Scott
1964   *The Emerging City*. Glencoe: Free Press.

Ramu, G. N.
1976   "The Family and Marriage in Canada." In *Introduction to Canadian Society*, edited by G. N. Ramu and Stuart D. Johnson. Toronto: Macmillan.

Schermerhorn, R. A.
1970   *Comparative Ethnic Relations: A Framework of Theory and Research*. New York: Random House.

Shibutani, Tamotsu, and Kian M. Kwan
1965   *Ethnic Stratification: A Comparative Approach*. New York: Macmillan.

10. The Doukhobors: Family and Rites of Passage

F. M. MEALING

I. INTRODUCTION

In 1899, some 7,427 immigrants passed quarantine at Halifax before ultimate arrival in north-central Saskatchewan; these were Doukhobors, the devout core of a sectarian group originated—and oppressed—in Russia since at least 1652. The religious revitalization of 1894 was marked by a major pacifist demonstration, "The Burning of Arms," which brought intense official punishment; international opinion and aid from Quaker groups expedited a Canadian refuge for the most committed.

Settlement in Canada was no more easy than adaptation to Canadian mores. The Doukhobors rejected the Oath of Allegiance, seeing it as a step towards military registration, and thus lost their homestead land by 1907; complex but apparently inequitable official dealings ensured the collapse of their communal enterprise, the Christian Community of Universal Brotherhood (CCUB), between 1929 and 1940. Doukhobors in British Columbia, whither the majority of the sect moved after 1907, did not for the most part own their own land again until the early 1960s. Along with economic stripping, they suffered social injuries, chiefly reflected by the collapse of industry and production, and the violent activity of some members of the *Svobodniki* (Sons of Freedom subsect).

Academic study of the Doukhobors—apart from rare Russian-language materials published by the sectarians themselves—began in Canada scarcely 20 years ago. Reliable sources to date are Hawthorne (1955), Tarasoff (1964 and 1969), Peacock (1966 and 1970), Woodcock and Avakumovic (1968), and myself (1972), dealing for the most part with history or traditional lore. There are thus minimal resources for the scholar; although journalistic production is copious, it better articulates Canadian prejudice than Doukhobor reality.

The focus of this discussion is the Doukhobors settled in the Boundary and Columbia districts of the West Kootenay region of British Columbia. The landscape is mountainous, inhabited on narrow valley bottoms and on river benches; the Boundary district, of which the town of Grand Forks is the centre, surrounds an ancient lake-bottom; the Columbia district, of which the town of Castlegar is the geographical centre only, is a complex of major and minor river gorges. During the period of communal living, Doukhobors developed village agriculture and forest industries. Since World War II, dominant forms of production in the area have been extractive, with forest and mining interests and the hydroelectric authority employing workers in an industrial context. Agriculture has become a symptom of a deliberately rural, alternative lifestyle, in the form of intensive gardening carried on by Doukhobors and aggressively "country" people. In the communal-life period, domicile for CCUB members consisted of unique village habitations; for those who withdrew from the organization, conventional houses served. In the late 1930s, *Svobodniki* withdrew to relatively isolated areas (Krestova, Gilpin) to dwell in small, impermanent (because inflammable) cabins, a style many have maintained to the present. With the collapse of the CCUB, some families lingered on in the village houses, many to be destroyed by arson; others squatted on their former land in small, self-constructed houses. With the return of land by resale in the early 1960s, most Doukhobors built houses which, to qualify for Central Mortgage and Housing Corporation support, followed Western Canadian conventions of plan, materials, and style. It may be held that such style was at least as desirable for its expression of achievement by Canadian standards, as for its mortgageability.

Demographic data on Doukhobors are not widely available. While the largest organization in the region, the Union of Spiritual Communities of Christ (USCC), lists children of over 1,000 families as school-attenders, this list does not cover children of Independent or *Svobodnik* families; and school boards do not maintain uniform ethnic statistics. Prejudice has discouraged most Doukhobors from identifying themselves more precisely than as Russian-Canadians. The religious identity suffices for religious contexts, and little is seen to be religious about industrial or bureacratic institutions now that the CCUB is gone. With commendable impartiality, just such identification has become obsolete among the institutions themselves. It is thus presently impossible to describe a normal or typical Doukhobor family with any degree of statistical accuracy, pending suitable large-scale research. Perhaps a useful picture can be given from subjective observation.

Settlement ranges through conventional town dwelling, rural settlements (form dictated by land resale conditions) of suburban style, with bungalows close-set on 1 to 4 acre lots; to contemporary or older-style houses on more-or-less isolated sites. Most men and a fair number of women work in local industry and trade; many women are energetic homemakers who maintain large (½ to one acre) gardens and put up many preserves. A significant number of older people did not adjust easily to the economic and ensuing social shutdown of c. 1938-1940. They live for the most part in small homes, garden, and carry out other work as opportunity is seen to arise, and depend for a portion of their subsistence upon government support. Families tend to be slightly larger than average, with two to three children common, and with both parents living at home. Slavic tradition endorses the maintenance of grandparents within or near the household. An informant comments that "It's a sin not to take care of the old folks"—a value not universally honoured, but producing a fair amount of guilt when defied.

The fundamental tenet of Doukhobor religion is the presence of God within every person, however cherished or repressed. Hence Doukhobor pacifism: taking life is not only an offense against the victim, but against the God whose presence is thus repudiated. Historically, Doukhobors have advanced their beliefs with strong reliance upon rationalistic argument, expressing them with great diversity. Thus, "identifiable" Doukhobors may include the literally and simply devout at one extreme, and the deliberately agnostic at the other.

This base implies a broad and egalitarian ideal, but it is blended with an administrative tradition of Russian origin, the Mir (village) reliance upon a council of Elders for normal conduct of everyday affairs, and with a belief that, as not all persons cherish their "divine spark" equally, so one must live in every age who best expresses the God within. Such a one, for many Doukhobors (though not all, including the sect of Independents), is their Spiritual Leader. There is no such leader at present for USCC people, although Honorary Chairman John Verigin has such a role expected of him by some older folk; a few among Svobodniki aspire to such a role, of whom Stefan Sorokin has most honour. This complex of beliefs and customs produced in the past a society accepting and supporting an efficient and usually benevolent authoritarianism of a theocratic style. Since the 1930s, most Doukhobors—drawing from the implications of their tradition at least as heavily as from the Protestant example of their Anglo-Canadian neighbours—have internalized much of that authority. It is important to see traditional Doukhobor authority as a counterfoil, conspicuous and exemplary, to the authority of the Czarist, Orthodox Russian state: God opposing Antichrist. By present custom, community affairs are carried on by assemblies of local representatives, advised by the Chairman (USCC), or by a Spiritual Leader (Svobodniki), or chaired informally (Independents).

The Svobodniki present too complex a case for full treatment here. They first appeared clearly as a functioning part of the British Columbian Doukhobor community in the late 1920s (Maloff MS, pp. 276-306). Pious and prophetically inclined individuals, viewing Community life as overly materialistic, withdrew to small homes on the edges of Community settlements, maintaining a very modest lifestyle and returning regularly to speak and preach on behalf of a spiritual outlook. Thus they came to occupy an alternate social slot for the CCUB. But as they found themselves increasingly at odds with both Community and outside world, and as the weight of external pressures (economic and social) grew more heavy upon all Doukhobors, the *Svobodniki* grew more rigid and narrow in their thought, more volatile and anti-social in their actions.

Between the 1930s and the mid-50s, political and religious acts expanded through nude demonstrations and destruction of one's own property (purgation of materialism) to arson and bombings. The press served only to nurse public prejudice; the provincial government overreacted massively on at least two occasions (Woodcock and Avakumovic: 1968, pp. 318-319, 340-343). In 1932 large numbers of *Svobodnik* adults were isolated in a prison camp (Piers Island), with no activities, work, retraining, or health care, their children distributed among orphanages and "industrial schools." In 1953, children were seized in violation of the prerogatives of the Children's Aid Society and were imprisoned in a guarded school (New Denver). Piers Island produced no amelioration of interaction; no consistent reporting appears on the New Denver experiment, which apparently produced some children who accepted academic education and many who became mistrustful, hostile, and seriously neurotic. Neither of these actions is the subject of any official or reliable external evaluation.

Following a trek to the Lower Mainland region in 1962, with experience of toleration and economic opportunity, *Svobodniki* appear to have broadened their techniques for evaluation of and dealing with external society; at any rate, the number and violence of actions has diminished since that time, indicating the possibility of amelioration. *Svobodniki* appear to me to have served as a functional complement to the Doukhobor majority, a role that will allow the dissident and deviant to maintain "Doukhobor" identity. Such was clearly the original function of the subsect; to it have been added presently the functions Western society chooses to impose upon the criminal and insane.

Large and durable historic forces have molded Doukhobor techniques and devices for the affirmation of unity. These are most apparent in various events in which community and family join, and which recur uniformly, allowing for minor local and subsectarian variation. Even the present distances between Doukhobors are less by far than those between the faithful and Czarist Orthodox Russian, against which early Doukhobors saw themselves silhouetted with hard-edged clarity.

The balance of this paper is based primarily upon folkloristic fieldwork carried out in the West Kootenay since 1970.

II. RELIGION IN LIFE

A. The Meeting

The Doukhobor family follows two times: human time, in the *rites de passage*, and chronological time, by which the community schedules regular and seasonal assemblies. The strongest marked passages are those of bethrothal and marriage, and death, burial, and commemoration, birth being dealt with only simply. Community assemblies consist of *molenye*, Sunday morning prayer, the primary worship service; great festivals focusing upon youth or upon Doukhobor history; Leaders' Commemorations; and quasi-secular entertainments.

When Doukhobors sing in assembly (*sobranie*, a generic term), they do so in a uniquely subtle musical tradition (Peacock: 1970, pp. 14-49; Mealing: 1972, pp. 28-36) that demands and elicits technical, conceptual, and emotional unity. Accompanying liturgics (Mealing: 1972, pp. 637-651) include mutual acknowledgement, assertion of unity with the dead (dead here, living with God), and committment to the absent.

Behaviour during community events takes two styles: many involve themselves intensely in the formal aspects of the assembly; many others, except at the more sacred moments, may spend a good part of their time talking with friends and kin, flirting modestly with other youth, playing with other children, or dozing securely. It is necessary to note that these others, too, participate fully in the underlying event of community assembly. Their unity is that of the broad group, not of the rite; but the rite is the bearing about which the more inchoate processes revolve.

Today mostly the elderly, and not very many of those, attend *molenye*, although in former times *molenye* was fully attended. The two causes for this change appear to be the pressure of the Anglo-Canadian example and prosperity, and the less pressing need for mechanisms opposed to violent persecution, in a context of weakened religious faith.

In these events, the family is varyingly visible. Men and women sit separately in *molenye* and sacred *sobrania*, though kin may cluster with sex groups. News at *sobrania* may include the travels of kin. Family groups are commonly involved in choral events at festivals. But it is during the low-intensity periods of assemblies that families become obvious: sitting together when audiences are not divided by sex; seated in groups at meals, for which kin assemble, often inviting guests to join them. When possible, the summertime festivals take place out-of-doors and meals are held picnic-style, families and guests sitting on the grass with their food, commonly arranged in long lines by settlement region. From outside, this placement by locale appears to limit family identification; but participants see it as rather affirming that there is a specific, permanent place for *their* family relative to all the rest.

B. Rites of Passage: Birth

At no recorded time have Doukhobors marked off birth by major observances, the only noted ceremony being an obligation, upon the first person to pick up the child after birth (or any subsequent person who raises it for the first time), to say "*Hospodi blagoslavi*," translated as Lord bless [us] (private communication). No ritual appears attached or reported to naming, which is sometimes told to be the responsibility of the grandparent of the same sex, who may give his own name; but naming is conducted simply, soon after parturition.

There are three independent, plausible reasons for such de-emphasis of birth. Firstly, most European radical sectarians attend more to a member's failure to conform (with subsequent shunning or expulsion) than to entry: birth is adequate entry. Secondly, Orthodox name-giving ceremonies were characteristically licentious. It would be natural for puritanical Doukhobors of the eighteenth century to reject the format of such recognition, as they limited license at marriages. Lastly, and of most import, Doukhobors traditionally were seen to postulate the entry of the individual into humanity as a slow, late process (Kravchinsky: 1888, p. 512):

> . . . The soul enters the child . . . from about the sixth to the fifteenth year of its life, the period during which the child is learning from the Book of Life. The newly born baby is only a piece of soul-less matter.

Compare this with a recent private communication:

> Used to be, a baby was born really handicapped, body or mind apparently. They wouldn't feed it for three days. If it died, it was meant to; but if it lived, they had to take real good care of it, because such was the will of God.

The place of the child within the community is defined in two psalms. Psalm 182 (Bonch-Bruevich numbering) identifies the virtue of the infant, going on to the devout child's behaviour and eventual adult witness for the faith:

> [The Lord] created the person, little fellow. The young lad grows up, he acts in God's will . . .

The late Psalm, *Basic Rules for Young Children* (Mealing: 1972, pp. 280-282), was composed (shortly before 1910?) by Peter Vasilievich Verigin, then Leader. It sets out a very wide range of simple regulations for children's life in the Community Villages of the period, leading to the assumption that the child is *already* a member of the community.

Children attained individual status as they learned, primarily through the father's teaching, a goodly bulk of the Living Book, the Doukhobor heritage of psalms, hymns, and other sacred oral texts. Today such material—along with the *molenye* liturgy—is also taught in Sunday Schools, which are scaled-down *molenye* managed by children under adult guidance. For Doukhobors, then, initiation into society depends upon the slow internalization of religious lore: who had the faith had real existence. It is important to note that, despite the apparently callous statement of social norms in tradition, actual treatment of infants, recognition of the prerogatives of children, and family emotions, are warm and strong, and apparently always have been. Early accounts and a recent study (Hawthorne: 1955, examples pp. 265-276 *passim*) show children to be objects of special concern. So the child's entry into society functions as a matter of accomplished fact, confirmed in the child's normal maturation and enculturation.

C. Rites of Passage: Marriage

Marriage, though religiously defined, departs furthest from *molenye* format. Mate selection has historically varied in form: while marriages were customarily arranged by parents in the nineteenth century, in both the eighteenth century and since settlement in Canada, the bride and groom have been responsible for their own choice (Chertkov: 1899, pp. 30-31, from material dated prior to 1804):

> Marriage . . . is accomplished merely by the mutual consent of the young couple. As, among the Spirit-Wrestlers, no preference is given to wealth or rank, the parents do not at all interfere in the marriage of their children.

With the security of isolated settlement in periods of the nineteenth century, parental preference apparently came to the fore. Mr. Harry Lebedeff of Thrums, British Columbia, reported from interviews with elders (1972, private communication):

> . . . Weddings performed in the native country were quite different in all respects to the concept of the word marriage . . . there was no real formality in the conduct of the marriages.
>
> Sometimes, but not always, the parents decided when to marry their children and to whom. The boy and girl had no say in the matter. Two families, who thought their son and daughter would make good marriage partners, would gather at the girl's parent's home and have a little party of their own. Close relatives were also present. The arrangement was very simple and consisted more or less of tea-drinking and a supper. It was typical to choose a girl who was older than the boy, because work was always a burden and an older person would have experience to cope with it.
>
> Next day, the parents would bring their son to the girl's house and would announce that they were married. The boy and girl would usually oppose the parents but would have no power to argue about their sudden union. The words of the parents were final . . . the girl would gather her belongings and go to the boy's home. . . . The couple had to live together, and most of the time the union worked out quite well.
>
> Weddings of this kind were common in Russia for a substantial time. Priests and churches were not recognized by the people, who therefore established their own customs . . .
>
> With the migration of the people to Canada, the customs changed. In the early 1900s, people were not married in that manner any more. The parents would gather at the girl's home, talk, recite or sing a hymn

[Psalm?], have a cup of tea, and then would pronounce the couple husband and wife, and wish them a happy life. The girl would then take her change-of-clothes and move in with her husband. The procedures of marriage were short and simple.

From this developed the style of the present. It is much more complicated than that given above, and seems much more appropriate. . . . It made marriage seem more real and have more definite meaning in the union of the couple.

Though all accounts of nineteenth century marriage stress parental dominance, such phrases as "sometimes but not always" suggest that compulsory marriage was exceptional enough to be most memorable. The concluding comments—as a summary of conscious present attitudes—gain weight through the voice of a member of the community. It seems that ceremony has evolved from a minimal form set in conscious opposition to the repudiated majority rites of the Orthodox Church, to recognition of a social urge (perhaps conditioned by Canadian example) for a rite revealing more dense social, symbolic, and material layers.

Contemporary marriage style has changed over the past few years, but exhibits consistent foundations. There are two clearly defined events, the latter further divided. Betrothal is recognized by a two-part rite. The couple, their parents, and close kin arrive at the girl's home, where the parents greet each other, using the Easter greeting and seeking guest status:

Slava Hospodi!	Glory to the Lord!
Slava blagodarim Boga za 'evo milost'	With glory we thank God for his favour!
Khristos voskris!	Christ is risen!
Vo istinnykh Khristos voskris!	In the righteous is Christ risen! [Bow]
Prinimayte nas zagostey	Accept us as guests
Milosty prosim	We ask your favour

A table near by bears the signs of Doukhobor worship: bread, salt, and water; the former, as loaf and shaker-full, were brought by the fiancé's parents. Those present form a circle with the fiancé's party on his left and the fiancée's party on her right; before the couple is a rug. *Be Devout* (Psalm 128) is commonly recited, a gnomic text traditional in this context, though other psalms are acceptable, then all bow. Next, any member recites the *Lord's Prayer* and all bow; then follows the psalm *Father of All*, with bows-to-the-ground being performed by family members. The fiancée's party approach the couple, who kneel on the carpet, bow-to-the-ground, rise, and kiss their parents or inlaws-to-be; in the same way, they repeat the ceremony with the fiancé's parents. A greeting, *Dobry chas* ("A good hour!" Good luck!), is offered. All present then take a meal, at which hymns and graces are used; the couple are again greeted with *Dobry chas*; and Borscht, *Pirohi* (Pirogis), and *Ploh* (rice pudding) are eaten, with other, non-obligatory foods. After a concluding grace, the evening becomes an ordinary social gathering, in which group singing commonly plays a large part. Lately, devout families have, on the earliest subsequent Sunday, repeated the initial greetings and announced the names of all concerned and the wedding date as a major feature of post-*molenye sobrania*.

The order for a wedding is essentially the same as that for a betrothal, with explicit elaborations. The ceremony is repeated twice, first at the bride's home and then at that of the groom. Both groups of parents carry bread and salt with them; at the groom's house the bride's loaf is sliced and placed on the table—perhaps symbolizing loss of virginity or the disruption of her family. A hymn is sung after the couple's bows and kisses, commonly *The Blessing of Trees in the Valley*, possibly *The Giving of Precious Moments by God* or *I Am Rich in the Land*. Lastly, the groom's parents kneel before the bride's and formally thank them for nurturing her and releasing her to their family; the parents then kiss each other.

The bride's parents may provide a dinner, after which wedding gifts are given. Till the present generation, this usually took place in the groom's home; now it often merges with the Supper, commonly given in the nearest Community Hall, to which gifts are brought. After the gift-giving or on the way to the groom's house, the bride customarily brings not only her gifts and personal belongings, but also linen and a quilt for a double bed. After the wedding supper, she must remove the linen carefully prepared by her mother-in-law, and will install her own in its place. This is said to symbolize her willingness to maintain the home she has joined and also "a happy married life," but seems to focus upon her sexual duties as a wife and her replacement of the mother as first woman in the groom's life.

Public recognition of the marriage now centres upon the local Community Hall, to which a large number (the greater, the more prestigious the event) of guests (500 would be "a nice total") is invited, perhaps to be fed in two sittings. These arrive early to greet the wedding party upon its arrival. The initial greeting is once more exchanged, but now the bride's parents ask to be guested, and are taken to speak for all guests present. More-acculturated families set up a receiving line just inside the hall, so that entering guests may greet the wedding party personally; this usage, acquired from Anglo-Canadians, seems to have peaked in the 1960s and to be moving into disuse. An invited choir performs intermittently during supper, which begins with the "Cooks' Greeting":

Slava Hospodi!	Glory to the Lord!
Slavim blagodarim Boga za evo milost'	We praise [and] thank God for his mercy
Zvol'te kushat'!	Come [and] eat!

Many of the commonplaces of Canadian weddings—toasts (usually non-alcoholic), real or preposterous, and bawdy congratulatory letters and telegrams, and applause or cup-tapping to make the couple kiss— are added to the Doukhobor core of grace, traditional food, choral song, and gift-giving. Gifts may be displayed unopened—they will be opened a day later, or during the honeymoon. An account (Hawthorne: 1955, p. 278) tells of a supper at which the guests gave small bills rapidly, the couple having to kiss as each bill fell. Supper and traditional observance end with grace.

An hour or so later, for many families, the evening will reopen with dancing. At this time, as in Russia before the revitalization, license extends to the use of alcohol. The break allows the devout and elderly (not always identical sets) time to depart without embarassment for the pious or licentious. As in most wedding traditions, mild bawdry is not unknown. The newlyweds will usually leave in the middle of the evening; while wedding trips are normal, simple home-going is still not unusual.

As in old Russia, a Doukhobor girl takes the patronymic. At marriage, she enters her husband's family. Marital residence is characteristically patrilocal. Until the present that meant precisely the groom's home; recently, while domicile is visibly neo-local, the home is typically donated or financed by the groom's father. The inlaw problems are thus not as impacting as in physical patrilocality, but unsuitable homes have been provided, tolerated as long as politeness demanded, then exchanged through the market for something better suited to the newlyweds' tastes.

Unsurprisingly, formal license—specifically reflected in acculturative elements and the toleration of otherwise reprehensible alcohol—is more observable in weddings than in any other recognizable event within the community. Chertkov's source (q.v. supra) comments: "Marriage among them is not regarded as a holy sacrament. . . ." Doukhobor marriage appears to have begun as a devout recognition of a secular fact; over two centuries the rite is evolving into a form affirming the place of religion in marriage and the right of the community to conspicuous witness and celebration. Note that despite the clearly analogous example of Quaker marriage, neither Doukhobor marriages nor offspring were legitimate in British Columbia until 1953, an example of gross governmental prejudice, but also an indication of the low visibility of the traditional ceremony.

Currently, the widest informal community approval is bestowed upon weddings in which North American extravagance is joined to maximum religious content. As the wedding is the most acculturated Doukhobor event, so is it also the vanguard of reaffirmation of identity, an identity keyed to a popular concept of "tradition," and hence creating a new tradition that will not resemble whatever really took place in, say, nineteenth century Russia, but is clearly distinct from, say, what takes place in English Canada.

Canadian folklore accords almost proverbial status to the phrase "Weddings aren't for the bride and groom, they're for the family." This is not an unsound insight: though the newlyweds are the focus and centre of the ceremony, they have, after all, already chosen each other; their attachments are settled. It is the families and close friends who have suddenly, with no real preparation, acquired bonds of new friendship and, variously compulsory, new kinship. All present must see and acknowledge the newlyweds (ostentatiously) and each other (surreptitiously), for whatever future reference may be desirable or unavoidable.

Doukhobor families live and lived in a close context. They shared an outcast faith that impelled them together; they shared their geographic community, and sometimes communal residence. The Russian tradition affirmed the relation of bride and groom, and the place of the parents in the life of each. In its present form, the Doukhobor wedding re-emphasizes bonding between the two families. Households are primary, even to the modified form of patrilocality, and so remain the site of the primary marriage rites. No priestly figure is present, since God— within the parents, as emphasized by the ritual bows— is present directly, precluding intercession. The family is not merely present at the wedding, it embodies the wedding.

Additional field material of high quality is found in Rhoads 1900 (pp. 26-29) and Hawthorne 1955 (pp. 277-279).

D. Rites of Passage: Death and Memory
Death presents an ultimate empirical challenge to all institutions: it removes their members from visible participation, unassailably changes the future. Beyond it nothing is materially documented; birth brings the known, but death the unknown. Institutions and members must thus find means to limit death. Doukhobors apply two techniques. Rationalism demands individual survival through corporate memory, that of the family and of the community; faith declares the entry of the dead believer into the Kingdom of God; Psalm texts tend to identify the goal of the living and the place of the righteous dead (Psalms 123, 130, 384).

Just as Doukhobor theology affirms human society to be in a state of constant progress—

5. The world is based upon going forward; all things strive for perfection, and through this process seek to rejoin their source. . . .
6. In all that is in our world, we see changing steps toward perfection. . . .

(Ps. 144)

—so the life of the believer is a journey, and death an overnight camp, a change of state but not of status for the soul.

All individuals, in or out of a bereaved family, are obliged to respond to the negation of death by an affirmation of integrity. Birth was primarily a family matter, from which the community traditionally held itself officially aloof. Marriage, involving more than one family, necessarily called for community recognition, but only that portion of the community known to both families was essential for witness. Death, however, is the business of the whole community; and while in practice the wedding and the funeral are open to the whole community and persons are invited to both, at the former, guests are expected; at the latter, everyone.

The only historic account of a funeral is necessarily sketchy (Fitzgibbon: 1899, pp. 59-61); the account given in Hawthorne (1955, p. 267) is incidental and impressionistic. The reluctance of Western scholars to examine Doukhobor funerals may be regretted. At present, local traditions vary, Grand Forks area style tending to limited services of about three to four hours; outside centres, twenty-seven-hour funerals remain common, in spite of gentle pressure from Anglo-Canadian undertakers.

The body of the dead is prepared as soon as possible, either by the undertaker or (not rarely) in the family home. In the past five years the use of homemade coffins, prepared quickly but carefully of plain materials by local joiners, has returned to some favour. The body is taken to the Community Hall on the second morning after death for a service beginning about noon; the coffin remains open conventionally, placed behind the usual head table. Often photographs of the dead made a few years earlier stand on the inside edge of the lid, "So people can see how they were when alive" (i.e., to remember the dead as living).

The service is the longest in duration of any conventional observance. As for weddings, a choir is specifically invited; but another honoured group is also present, the gravediggers. These are a half-dozen or more community men, rotating on a roster, but requested rather than expected to be present. They may include family members, and serve as exemplars of the community's duty to the dead.

The funeral is, like many services, supervised. Molenye is led by experienced elders, and festivals by appointed community members in committee; but the funeral's management is expressly the duty of the dead's family. At the service's opening and close, spoken psalms are recited by the family, and psalms are sung by all present. Many people will attend the first hour or so, and close friends will remain or return frequently. Attendance will flag in the afternoon, activities being limited to sporadic prayer and song, with long slack periods. During the night, family members and friends will stand vigil by the body; near its end, conversation will lighten, and jokes including bawdry may be used. As in most wake traditions, this serves not only to release emotional tension, but also to reaffirm the liveliness of the community in the face of apparent death. Through the following morning, community members return to stay at the hall, and intermittent song and prayer build up. About noon, there is more speaking and singing of psalms. The song and prayer are usually instigated by family members, who may also present opening lines, a duty in which even young children may share. At the service's end, the coffin is temporarily closed; if flowers have been used, it is often the youngsters who take these up, to line a walkingspace for the coffin and its bearers.

The funeral party proceeds out-of-doors. In earlier times, the coffin was carried, usually some distance, to the cemetary; today it is commonly taken in a hearse, and the assembly either drive or process behind the hearse to the cemetary, depending upon weather, road, and distance. When it arrives, the undertaker, if present, ends his duties. The family gathers on the south or east of the grave, beside the re-opened coffin. The choir sing a psalm and the *Lord's Prayer* and *Father of All* are recited. The gravediggers close the coffin, after a prayer of their own, and lower it into the grave. This is usually the moment of greatest tension: the family has formally dismissed the dead, the community does so through the gravediggers, who take over care of the body. Family members, including children and friends, will cast a number of clods of earth into the grave, and friends commonly join the diggers in completing backfill and topping-off. With this finality, pressure eases, conversation begins, and the assembly returns to the hall. Throughout, a special greeting, *Tsarstviye Nebesnoye Pokoinom!* (The Kingdom of Heaven for the Dead!), is used formally and informally. All now join in a funeral meal. Food is essentially the same as that for a wedding, with a remarkable exception: *Pirohi* is obligatorily replaced by *Lapshi*, noodles. Young women of the community serve food, and the family, gravediggers, choir, undertaker, and specially invited friends have the right to eat at the first sitting. A psalm and funeral hymns will be sung. With this meal, which usually ends around four or five in the evening, the funeral ends.

Observance, though, does not end; a special process affirms essential immortality indefinitely. About six weeks after death, the same day-of-the-week as that of burial, the family returns to the graveside for *Paminki*, Commemoration, a short rite of family prayers and perhaps the singing of psalms, followed by another formal meal. The time period, about 40 days, recalls not only ancient beliefs known throughout Europe (at least), regarding the slow departure of the soul from the body's vicinity, but also, by analogy, the ascension of Christ. The believer would not be expected to arrive in Heaven earlier than did his Lord. Seen rationalistically, this period also allows the living to become accustomed to the absence of the dead. The service may be repeated a year later and subsequently on the anniversary, as in the ancient European custom of Yearmind, or it may be rescheduled to a brief observance at Easter next. In the latter case, it obviously moves to association with Christ's resurrection, and affirms the functional identity of both passages, that of Christ and of the commemorated dead, into a transcendental life. With such an identity, commemoration of the individual becomes indeed as perpetual as the church's commemoration of Christ, and immortality becomes absolute as any other tenet of faith.

Graves are customarily marked, with noteworthy variety in style, depending largely upon family taste. Markers usually record the name and kinship role of the dead, and often include the phrase *Vechnaya Pamyat*, Eternal Memory.

While deaths of the very young and of the aged are generally regretted but felt to fall within the scheme of things, untimely death at any point between the age of six to seven years and around 70 years is viewed as abnormal and deeply regrettable. Especially mourned are the deaths of adolescents and persons in their twenties; grief will be unrestrained, and the grave correspondingly ornate.

The only ghost legend collected thus far deals expressly with personal conflicts arising from a death, and their transcendental resolution (Mealing: 1972, p. 585):

> N- and his wife, both in their early twenties, were coming home . . . after a meeting one night, and their car went off the road, they were both killed. Well, old Mr. N-, the father, was really upset even after the funeral and all. He couldn't sleep nights, and finally he went out to the barn very early one morning, not on schedule, you know, and started to milk the cow. Then he heard very quiet steps behind him and someone said, "Dad, Dad." But he didn't turn around, he was shocked, you know, it was N-'s voice. Then he said "Dad" again, and Mr. N- turned around, it was his son standing there. And he said to him, "Don't worry about us, Dad, we're all right. Don't worry anymore." and Mr. N- didn't feel shocked or upset anymore, you know, he just got up and started to go indoors. Then he looked around for a minute, there wasn't anyone there anymore. And he went inside and went right to sleep without thinking about it at all. But when he woke up in the morning, he was a little upset about it, because he realized what had happened, and things like that don't happen very often, it never happened to him or anyone in his family before, he's not that kind of person. And he got in touch or told all the members of the family that N- had come to see him and that they were all right. So nobody was upset anymore.

In this story, belonging to an ancient tradition (cf. Child 76, *Unquiet Grave*, in which the dead bids mourning cease, to give him peace), but perhaps anecdotal for all that, the father—the central figure—has an experience which resolves his grief. Transcendental or hallucinatory, the experience serves personal adjustment and confirms underlying integrity (". . . We're all right.") in a universe that had displayed confusing, improper events (in their early twenties . . . were both killed). Again the experience is not merely hoarded: the entire family is addressed and the happy affirmation confirmed.

In this observance of death, the last and, by the evidence, the greatest any Doukhobor can make, two foci appear. For the family, death observance itself begins with the last care of the body, laying-out, and continues over three days. The sorrow that in some other observances is made or allowed to become deeply obsessive is here inhibited both by formalization and by practical involvement of the family with other duties. In the very act of successfully playing the role prescribed for mourners, the family is compelled to commit its attention not to the dead, but to the living. In turn, the community at large shares in this communication, and affirms to the family its own life, with the compassionate concern, cheerful conversation, youthful flirting, dozing, inattention, and devout worship that are all parts of its presence. The bereaved family will, no doubt, be exhausted at the funeral's end; they will also be purged of much of the injury done them by this death. Their personal experience is blended precisely into a familiar, formal ritual; the necessary memory of the dead has already begun to prevail, because the dead has become, with his or her family, a part of that aspect of community ritual life that is directed toward memory. All the subsequent observances—casting earth on the coffin, sharing in the burial, *Paminki*, and the erection of a gravemarker—affirm the fundamental tenet: the dead is not *here* and therefore has become immortal.

Discrepant and light incidents at a funeral are matter for critical community comment, and the duties of the family are held to be onerous. The community need not be conscious of all the implications of its actions, merely to carry them out, and what it essentially carries out is the affirmation of its own life. Its integrity is challenged but undiminished by the loss of a member, who indeed is held not to have been lost, but simply to have carried community representation into another mode of existence. So the community for the most part enjoys the funeral, in several senses, and through identification with choir and gravediggers, extends special services, affirming its stake in the passage to immortal memory.

This passage more than any other affirms integrity of family and community. Each is indispensible to the other, each fundamentally involved in the state beyond-the-grave. The family has a representative there, the community is moving in time to a period when there will be no distinction either side of death, but all will be perfect. Life with God and his angels, in company with all the faithful departed, is affirmed; ordinary life, with its flowers and bruises, goes on in fact, and no mere death is allowed to interrupt that. As the family is that part of the community most threatened and injured by death, so the community affirms the strength and vigour of the family and honours it as its own agent in the conduct of ritual, the people most qualified to lead the rest. The apprehended effect of death is division: the rite of passage retaliates with union and proposes eternal union. Under historic pressure, most Doukhobor customs stress processes of unification; death, the extreme pressure, calls up the strongest rebuttal.

III. CONCLUSION

Before summing up, a caution is in order. This discussion is based directly upon field observation—unrepeatable contexts—and from review of traditional texts. Outside the culture or within it, evidence is only open to interpretation, rarely to proof beyond accuracy of reporting. Folkloric analysis, given the kinds of evidence available, rests much upon the fieldworker's ability to enter the mores and philosophy of a society as well as its more overt behaviours and communication. What is presented here is not the Law of the Medes and Persians Which Changeth Not, but the analysis fieldwork trains me to make of the raw materials Doukhobors offer through their tradition. The reviewer must not expect to go to any isolated Doukhobor and ask, "Do you believe this? Is this a fact?" He or she might, however, profitably ask, "Does this make sense to Doukhobors?"

Doukhobor *rites de passage* concern themselves with changes in human status, as do any rites of passage. They do so in the context of a society that has been educated by history to see itself as threatened, righteous, exemplary, and ultimately vindicated (Ps. 150). This society not only sees itself in a presently imperfect circumstance, but it sees its circumstances as continually progressing to perfection. The pessimistic implication of history is opposed by an optimistic social ideological goal.

For the Doukhobor family, integrity must involve Doukhobor identity. Birth assumes this identity to be a fact needing no special confirmation: such will come developmentally. Marriage includes the psalm *Be Devout*, in which the newlywed hearers are enjoined to Doukhobor behaviour; the rite has moved from integrity by opposition to an established form, to identity by distinction from local, surrounding forms. Death causes the strongest possible affirmation of family and community integrity.

But Doukhobor identity is not simply a matter of formal behaviour. Indeed, it is a credal matter that ". . . we see changing steps toward perfection . . ." (Ps. 144/6). In spite of their natural inertia, customs will be adapted, observances will alter. This process need not be destructive: it may, as the psalms suggest, imply the correct progress of Doukhobor society. Hasty change is not commended, of course:

> [Doukhobor children . . . ought] to restrain themselves sensibly in adaptation to the times. . . .
> (*Basic Rules for Young Children*, Sixthly; Mealing: 1972, pp. 280-282)

Thus their faith calls Doukhobors to tread a narrow path: to affirm an identity, but to accept changes in the accidental phenomena of that identity. Armed with the historically conditioned emphases of community assemblies and defended by the expectation of ameliorative change, the traditional Doukhobor family stands not only in benefit of, but an agent of, unity.

REFERENCES

Bonch-Bruevich, Vladimir
1954   Zhivotnaia Kniga Dukhobortsev (From the Book of Life of the Douk-
        hobors). Reprint of 1910 ed. Winnipeg: Regehr's Printing.

Chertkov, Vladimir
1899   Christian Martyrdom in Russia. Toronto: Morang.

Fitzgibbon, May
1899   The Canadian Doukhobor Settlements. Pamphlet by Lally Bernard
        (pseud.). Toronto: William Briggs.

Hawthorne, Harry, ed.
1955   The Doukhobors of British Columbia. Vancouver: Dent & U.B.C.

Kravchinsky, Sergei M.
1882   Russian Peasantry, Their Agrarian Condition, Social Life, and Reli-
        gion. By Stepniak (pseud.). London: Sonnenschein, Vol. II, pp. 505-
        549.

Mealing, F. Mark
1972   Our People's Way: A Survey in Doukhobor Hymnody and Folklife.
        Ph.D. (Folklore and Folklife) dissertation, University of Pennsylvania,
        Philadelphia.

Maloff, Peter
1948   The Doukhobors, Their History, Life, and Struggle. Unpublished type-
        script, partial translation of Dukhobortsi: ikh Instori'ia, Zhizn', i
        Bor'ba. Thrums, British Columbia.

Peacock, Kenneth
1966   Twenty Ethnic Songs from Western Canada. Ottawa: National Mu-
        seum.

1970   The Songs of the Doukhobors. Ottawa: National Museum of Man.

Rhoades, Jonathan
1900   A Day with the Doukhobors. Philadelphia [?], pamphlet.

Tarasoff, Koozma
1964   In Search of Brotherhood: A History of the Doukhobors. Vancouver,
        p.p., Vol. III. Mimeograph edition of 10.

1969   Pictorial History of the Doukhobors. Saskatoon: Prairie Books/West-
        ern Producer.

Woodcock, George, and Ivan Avakumovic
1968   The Doukhobors. Toronto: Oxford University Press.

11. Time, Space, and Family Relationships in a Rural Dutch Community

K. ISHWARAN AND KWOK B. CHAN

THE PROBLEM AND THE METHOD

Against the background of a community development process within a developmental framework,[1] this paper attempts to examine the changing patterns of relationship between time, space, and intra- and interfamily relationships in the Dutch Canadian community of Holland Marsh in the province of Ontario. The data to be reported in this paper came from a larger pool of information we gathered between October 1977 and March 1978, on the family life of the rural Dutch in the Holland Marsh. Since one of us had done some intensive field work in the community between 1965 and 1971, with the gathered data resulting in a community study monograph (Ishwaran: 1977), prior working relationships with key informants of the community and heads of households, which were essentially pleasant and satisfactory, greatly facilitated attempts in soliciting agreement of the respondents to participate in this study and in making arrangements for conducting interviews.

We conducted all interviews with the parents (from a total of twenty-five households) in the evening in their homes for between two and three hours. While these interviews were intended to be intensive, in-depth, and semi-structured, the two-man research team enabled one of us to concentrate on making detailed and comprehensive notes of the dialogues, and the other to pose questions to the respondents, to establish rapport, to maintain the continuity of the interview, and to effect the eventual completion of the interview process. Since we did not adhere visibly to a set of preconceived questions, the resultant flexibility and ease of the interview situations were conducive to pursuing issues and concerns which were deemed interesting or important on particular occasions. In general, we usually started an interview with basic questions eliciting demographic and socio-economic data; then with questions on marital stability and commitment; and on attitudes, values, and patterns of behaviour of the adolescents in the community; and ended with a discussion of the conceptions of time and space of rural Dutch Canadians. Data on the socialization of rural adolescents and marital stability and commitment are reported in two separate papers by us (Ishwaran and Chan: 1979a; Ishwaran and Chan: 1979b).

The Dutch Canadians of Holland Marsh have settled in two territorial centres. The older one, Ansnorveldt, was established in 1934, and Springdale, an offshoot of the older unit, was established some four years later in 1938. The two settlements are located on both sides of Highway 400, some forty miles north of Toronto. The general area in which they are located is called Holland Marsh, so named to commemorate Major Holland, who landed at the East Branch of Schomeberg river. Ansnorveldt was pioneered by 11 Dutch immigrant families, while Springdale was established by 4 families.

The Springdale village, an outgrowth of Ansnorveldt and a product of its efforts and resources, both material and spiritual, is a virtual replica of the parent community. It shares a common ethnicity, religion, and socio-cultural values. Ansnorveldt had 118 families and Springdale 80 families at the time of our second survey (from the winter of 1977 to the early part of 1978). The Dutch communities of the Marsh can be characterized as near-total communities, each provided with its own Church, school, and even recreational institution linked to the Church, its own ethnic media connected to agencies in Toronto and Grand Rapids (Michigan), its own co-operative society, horticultural system, and its own storage facilities. Economically they are part of the wider, surrounding society. They live in an environment that is predominantly Protestant but co-exist with Catholic minority groups from Poland, Hungary, and Austria. The latter merely share a common physical space and exist in complete cultural and social isolation from the former. Though they may be internally differentiated, the Dutch regard themselves as a people distinct from the non-Dutch groups in terms of lifestyle, values, and ideology.

Within the Dutch community, the dominant group is the one whose original home was Groningen in northern Holland. It considers itself superior to the other groups hailing from other parts of Holland, such as the Frisians and Zeelanders. But cutting across such internal differences, the Dutch as a whole display a distinctive group identity characterized by familistic, religious, and occupational values. They are also predominantly authoritarian, ascetic, frugal, and work-oriented. They share not only a common physical space, but also a common and distinctive socio-cultural space. They are not significantly politicized, show little inclination for political involvement, and take very little interest in national and international matters. They display a notable lack of interest in what goes on in the outside world, as the main focus of their interest remains centred upon themselves.

Ever since their birth in 1934 and 1938, the two Dutch communities of the Marsh have been undergoing a process of change from systematic localism to centralization, resulting in a structural and substantive transformation in their socio-cultural system. This development can be traced through three distinctive but interconnected and successive historical stages—the exploratory, the consolidatory, and the ramificatory.

Exploratory Stage The exploratory stage is characterized by localism, during which social and cultural institutions of the community are structurally and functionally decentralized. The absence of functional differentiation made institutional organization unnecessary. Without a centralized Church, religious activities were informally organized in different homes by turn. Here they prayed together. There was no pastor to conduct formal services, and the members of the congregation officiated as ministers to conduct the worship of the Lord. As they had no schools of their own, they had to send their children to a public school in the neighbourhood. The children, therefore, had to mix with other ethnic groups. The economic resources of the community were not adequate to enable the extension of their agricultural production. Each family owned a five-acre piece of land, and this was made possible by the financial assistance of the Netherlands Government and the concerned provincial governments in Canada. The agricultural system was not mechanized, and the members of the community had to work with their own hands and on their knees, as one respondent put it vividly. The normal labour support came mainly from the members of one's family and kinsmen, though, during times of crisis, neighbours came to be enlisted. There was virtually no status difference among the members of the community.

Consolidatory Stage In this stage, specialized institutions emerge. The communities had become economically more productive, and were able to build two parochial schools of their own, the Ansnorveldt school in 1942 and the Springdale school in 1959. Aided entirely by community resources, the two schools were maintained and run as separate institutions. Two separate Churches then emerged to serve the two communities; the Church in Ansnorveldt was established in 1938, while the one in Springdale was set up in 1959. The onset of agricultural mechanization contributed to the slow weakening of the earlier pattern of community cohesiveness. The two communities became highly differentiated from each other, each becoming virtually an independent functioning unit. Though neighbourliness did not disappear totally, it was significantly reduced. Apparently perceptible in the lives of individuals was the increasingly significant role played by the community and its specialized agencies, the Church and the school. However, there was still the continuation of the role of the family in exerting influence on the individual's growth of identity, and on the development of his or her attitudes towards the Church and the community.

Ramificatory Stage   The life of the community, and its socio-cultural and economic institutions, had become significantly differentiated by the time the community reached this stage. This involved a significant level of centralization of the Church, the school, and the economy, resulting in their dominance in community life. The more primordial structures, such as the family and the kin group, became weakened, leading to a substantial degree of atomization of the individual. Released from the immediate constraints of these structures, the individual found himself increasingly subordinated to the remote and impersonal constraints of the bureaucratized institutions of the community.

The total impact of the differentiation and "modernization" of the community can be understood in terms of a historical shift from a solidary, *gemeinschaft* structure to a mechanical, *gesellschaft* structure. A gradual movement away from organized religious life could be noticed among a minority segment of the population, though the majority continued their allegiance to the Church. One also witnesses the emergence of disinterestedness of some teenagers in the Church, the gradual disruption of the traditional sense of neighbourliness, the increasing presence of individualism, and the undermining of marital relations.

THE CHANGING FAMILY CONCEPT

The concept of the family, both as a subjectively perceived experience by the members of the community and as an objective physical entity in correspondence with the subjective, underwent change with the changing developmental stages in the life-history of the community. In the exploratory stage, the family came to be conceptualized as the most important institution, performing a variety of essential functions necessary for social survival and progress. As a result, the community was predominantly familistic in its orientation. The pioneers who established the community had yet to develop a full-fledged community, and therefore, the family became in this context the most viable and dependable institution to which the individuals could look for psychological, socio-cultural, and economic security. In this stage, the family provided religious service, since the organized church had not yet emerged. Like religious life, educational activities also were carried on within a family framework. The main source of manpower for the rudimentary agricultural operations was the family. What little recreational activities that took place were also centred around the family. The fact that the immigrants brought with them the original familistic culture, value system, and ideology, contributed significantly to the development of a familistic orientation. This development hinged on the concept of the family as a multipurpose, multifunctional institution, catering to a wide range of individual needs and demands.

In the consolidatory stage, the occurrence of the most important structural changes in conceiving the family may be conceptualized as a process of differentiation during which basic functions in the community became clearly differentiated through the development of specialized institutions capable of handling specific functions. In the context of this process, the family was seen as shifting both conceptually and empirically from a multi-functional structure to a more specialized, functionally specific structure. The emergence and consolidation of the school system, the church, and the class system involved a considerable reduction in the functions of the family. However, this did not mean that the family became less important in the life of the community. As a matter of fact, the family continued to be the dominant institution it was in the traditional Dutch society by performing the crucial function of reinforcing the community's commitment to the other specialized institutional structures. There was thus a structural and functional mutuality and interdependence between the differentiated institutional structures. Contrary to the conventional modernization paradigm in which the family is seen as suffering from a decline in the face of increasing structural differentiation, we find that the family in the Marsh, instead of declining, becomes a structure essential to the initiation and continuation of the modernization process itself. No doubt, this is not the same family that once dominated the less-developed community system in earlier times.

In the ramificatory stage, there is evidence that the earlier conception of the family finds itself significantly threatened by forces released by an increasing exposure to, as well as integration into, the wider Canadian society. The mechanization in the farming and horticultural system, the commercialization of the economy, the increasing involvement of the local economy in the wider market system, the infiltration of the mass media influence, and the availability of unprecedented opportunities for holiday travelling provided by the rising prosperity of the farmers have all combined to undermine the traditional familistic culture and ideology of the Dutch community in the Marsh. One respondent was referring to the changes in ideology and behaviour brought about by the introduction of the new mechanized agricultural technology in the Marsh in the late fifties, when he declared:

> Our family life is now adapted to the machinery. Earlier, children had always chores in the family and on the farm. Now we do not need them in the family because of gadgets and one man can take care of 25 acres, though we take help of children during harvest time.

The earlier, traditional concept of the family as a tightly organized and essentially self-sufficient institution anchored firmly in the traditional Dutch religious culture becomes blurred and weakened in the ramificatory stage. While there is evidence that the Dutch family system has been pushed closer ideologically and structurally to the North American family norm, it is equally important to note that this is a very complex process punctuated by counteracting forces of traditionality. The emerging concept of the family, therefore, is clearing towards a compromise model in which the traditional and the modernizing forces are structurally contained. The problem of conceptual clarification would then be one of identifying the historically changing patterns of interrelationship and interaction between the traditional Dutch system, and the external, modernizing pressure radiating from the external sociocultural environment.

Husband-Wife relationships   In the exploratory stage of the evolution of the community, the family performed its multifarious tasks within a framework of considerable internal stability and cohesiveness. The source of such solidarity and stability must be traced to the nature of the internal role relationships in the family. In this context, the relationship between the roles of husband and wife acquires special significance. The traditional Dutch family, carried over by the immigrants into their new environment, proved to be a basic socio-cultural resource in the struggle of the community to establish itself in an alien, even hostile, ecological environment. In essence, the immigrants found it imperative and necessary to continue the patterns of role relationship inherited from the original model of the Dutch family. The traditional Dutch family was broadly patriarchal, in which the male head of the family occupied a central position in the authority structure. He took the initiative and invariably played a definitive role in familial decision-making. While the wife was associated with the decision-making process functionally, in the sense that her specialized role was sometimes accommodated, the final decision remained with the husband. Such a system of centralized decision-making within the family contributed to the stability and cohesiveness of the structure of the traditional Dutch family.[2] The fact that the pioneers (in the exploratory stage) had little time or opportunity to function in a social space wider than the family also contributed to the maintenance of an authoritarian relationship between the husband and the wife. However, it needs to be emphasized that this authoritarian relationship was a functional one, insofar as it was necessary for the realization of the individual and community goals in the given historical-developmental context. Functional authoritarian relationship between the husband and the wife, role differentiation between the husband as bread-winner and the wife as the manager of the internal affairs of the household, together with ecological pressures, contributed to the preservation and strengthening of the traditional husband-wife relationship within the Dutch family.

The consolidatory stage demonstrates a situation that can be best characterized as transitional. The patterns of internal family role relationships predominant in the first stage continued but weakened to some extent. These changes took on additional significance in the ramificatory stage. The increasing structural differentiation in the community's institutional system as a response to the environmental challenges from the outside, the internal technological changes such as the use of mechanized farming, the widening of the social space, the increasing availability of opportunities for activities outside the family and outside the community, and, finally, the expanding opportunities for the individuals both within and beyond the community have tended to weaken but not destroy the traditional husband-wife relationships. The increasing role specialization of the wife within the household has meant a weakening of the dominance of the husband. With regard to such decision-making situations as the purchase of household equipment, the choice of career for children, and the organization of holiday activities, the wife has come to share more power with the husband. This does not, however, mean that the husband has ceased to play a decisive role in these matters. The sheer fact that the woman is necessarily more involved in the immediate household activities has enabled her to strengthen and consolidate her role in these activities in relation to the husband.

Parent-Children Relationships   In the exploratory stage, the children were fully integrated into the family authoritarian structure. The nature of the farming work in this stage necessitated total participation of the children in the work process (Ishwaran and Chan: 1979). One pioneer respondent recalled:

> "Before machinery, parents collected their children and worked together with their hands. Their team work together in the field was also reflected in the togetherness of the family."

In such a collectivistic and cohesive family atmosphere, the relationship between the parents and the children became functionally interlinked. Parent-child relationships were further strengthened by the traditional Dutch ideology of parent dominance and filial obedience, the religious ideology embodied in the teachings of the Church, and the severe constrictions on the social space in the Marsh.

The lack of structural differentiation and functional specialization meant that the child's world was only as large as his or her family. In such a situation, the traditional authoritarian pattern of relationship between the generations was easy to maintain. The children had little freedom, as they were subjected to a very rigid family discipline, essentially symbolized and manifested in the authority of the father. Two respondents recollected the situation as it existed in the exploratory and pioneering days as follows:

"As teenagers we were brought up in a strict environment. . ."

"In those days, boys and girls did not talk to each other and mix freely. . ."

"It was a tough time during the war, and there was nothing. I was never allowed to go to a party to drink or to go to a show when I was a teenager. These days the teenagers have more money, drink a little more—more dancing in parties and more smoking. They go out of the Marsh on Saturday nights to have parties and drink."

"In the old days, we had little contact with the outside world. There was little chance to have social contact with people other than our own."

The most visible manifestation of the changes in the intergenerational relations that have been taking place in the ramificatory stage is the sharp changes in the lifestyle of the adolescents in the Marsh. One notices that the overall attitude of the young to things in general is more easy-going. This is seen, for instance, in their attitude to work at school. One respondent explained the situation in this way:

"When I was a teenager I never went out in the evenings. We worked in the field in the summer, in winter we did housework. These days teenagers are not interested in school work. They are interested in drinking and dancing."

There have also been changes in the relations between sexes. While in earlier times, boys and girls followed the original Dutch pattern of in-group dating, now they are seen to follow the dominant Canadian pattern. They go out as couples, and dating has become a normal part of adolescent behaviour since the early 1960s. Nevertheless, there is also a tendency towards inconstancy in the dating partners. One parent put it thus:

"Youngsters in the Marsh are not interested in steady dating. Most go out with one partner for a year or so and then break off. Early marriages are common and they get married at the ages of 17 or 18."

Early marriages leading to marital instability among the adolescents weakens the earlier structure of authoritarian relationships between parents and children. While those adolescents who get married very early tend to be disinclined to accept an authoritarian parent model, they continue to reject this model when they have become parents themselves. The older generation view the situation as one of "limitless freedom," capable of undermining the stability of the family system. Finally, the independence of the young has increased, as a result of the opportunities they get to earn on their own. One parent drew attention to this development when he stated:

"Somehow they manage to find something to occupy themselves; they keep the money they earn and spend it on their clothing and education. . ."

"In some immigrant families, the parents are losing control over their children. Children used to work and put all the money they earned on the table. Now, I don't think the children are still doing it any more.

For other families, parental authority is losing ground. Children are walking around with long hair on, and parents can't do anything about it. However, I don't consider these things as problems, but as a change in lifestyle."

"Children nowadays wouldn't amuse themselves within the home any more. There is a lot more freedom. With better access to means of transportation, they now go out a lot more often. Nowadays, boys and girls talk more freely among each other, including sex. For the teenagers, going outside the Marsh could be a good thing, a blessing. Young people now are a lot more progressive."

"Children grow more freely now. Maybe they've too much freedom. Now, parents do not punish children as hard as before, and, instead, will occupy them with something else. Children don't like to work in the field anyway."

"Recently, there have been conflicts between parents and children stemming from young people questioning old values of their folks. For some young people, growing up is tough enough. There seem to be more adolescent problems in Ansnorveldt than in Springdale. Children in Ansnorveldt are less respectful. There is a gradual breakdown of the traditional system of the Dutch community as a result of more exposure to the outside world. More and more teenagers are reaching out to the outside world."

"In some cases in the Marsh, the family is gradually losing ground. The parents preach some important values (e.g. Love Thy Neighbour As Thyself), but children will tend to see some phoniness in them. Even some parents drink frequently. There is a greater acceptance of addiction in the community."

Together with the increased sense of independence of the young is the simultaneous assumption of more responsibility. The parents feel happy about this and attribute it to the fact they had brought up their children in the fear of God. The changes noted in the adolescents seem to be matched by certain counter-developments which point to a pattern of persisting behaviour. Some parents maintained that, despite changes, the situation was not beyond control. They felt that there was a basic continuity with the past. Two of our respondents stated:

"Family, church, and school form a triangle. It is difficult for a teenager to step beyond it."

"Generation-gap does not exist here. It is invented by the outside world. We have more community problems because of our conservative nature. However, parents and children get on very well."

Another factor that has weakened the authoritarian parental control pattern is the increasing knowledgeability and technical ability of the younger generation. The young are born into a highly technological culture. In the words of a senior resident:

"Teenagers have a lot of know-how of agriculture . . . Learning to handle machinery has become part of the farm culture in the Marsh."

When one examines the aspirations of the young people today, one finds evidence for contradictory tendencies—the desire to go beyond the Marsh and the desire to stay home. No doubt, their aspirations are less locally oriented than those of comparable age-groups during the pioneering stage of the Marsh community history, but nonetheless, they do not amount to a sharp break with the traditional behavioural and normative patterns.

Family-Community Relationships When the pioneers started to sweat and toil to create a habitable world for themselves, they found that the major, or perhaps the only, source of manpower in these efforts was the immediate family. In the earliest pioneering days, the sense of family identity and solidarity came to be intensified as families operated on the principle of "each family for itself" (Ishwaran: 1977). This, however, did not mean that there was no sense of community. The pioneers had brought with them into the New World their original socio-cultural community identity, based on the Dutch traditional familistic and religious ideology. In the absence of appropriate environmental conditions and challenges in the beginning, this community sense remained submerged as a potentiality.

As soon as the families discovered that the hostile and intractable Marsh ecology could not be tackled on the basis of isolated family effort, the pioneers had to develop a working strategy of inter-family co-operation and collaboration during the exploratory stage. This development took place as a response to two types of needs. On the one hand, each family required physical support of other families in the form of manpower in the process of production. On the other hand, each family had to develop a socio-cultural institutional community system (in order to survive). While the former type of need led indirectly to the growth of a community system, the latter type of need, involving the notion of common tasks and common challenges to be tackled on a co-operative basis, led directly to the growth of a strong community sense with organizational consequences. This process of community development on the basis of a reduced family separatism dominated both the exploratory and consolidatory stages. One of our respondents narrated how the original fifteen pioneer families prepared roads, built houses, drained the land for cultivation, and helped each other for harvesting. The sense of neighbourhood, as distinct from kin solidarity, was strong, and it contributed to the growth of community sense. The situation as it then existed was summed up by our respondents as follows:

"... Those were the days of cooperation and sharing. Those who had transport gave us lifts to the farm, though we often walked to buy things for the week. In the first summer Mom worked on the farm picking up onions, we earned hundred dollars for the whole summer. Without family unity and solidarity and community help, we would not have made it in the Marsh."

"In the old days, everybody was poor. They were all in the same situation, worked with each other, and all shared the same property. They ate common meals; there was so much fun in those days, sharing among themselves the cooking. Eating place, and worship place were all in the same place—again, sharing was both necessary and compulsory. They helped each other in the fall with the crops. Every Sunday night, they used to gather among themselves singing songs.

"Though the neighbours still help each other out now (e.g. lending out equipment), they were a lot closer in the past."

"Pioneer houses were closer with each other. But now, houses are built to spread out over a larger space. Homes are bigger now. Expansion of house means changes in family relationships."

"There was this isolated living: roads were bad and transportation was limited. We lived quite close to each other. There were no shows, no theatres, but we had good time together. We did a lot of drop-in visits to families during long winter months and played a lot of chess and various other games. Picnics were for the summer time. We always had Thanksgiving dinner together. Friends and relatives gathered around on festive and wedding occasions. It was a very simple social life, especially during winter. In those days, work was hard and physical, and there was very little else one can do."

In short, both the sense of family identity and community identity co-existed. They were not in conflict in the first two stages in the process of community evolution. The dependence of the family on the community, however, did tend to reduce, but not significantly weaken, the family identity. The relationship between the individual families and the community were most cordial and mutually supportive. A high level of structural interdependence characterized this relationship.

As indicated by our respondent in their above-noted remarks, the family-community relationship underwent a clear change in the ramificatory stage. With the economic development of the community as a result of cumulative efforts and increasing use of better technology, economic inequalities between families became sharpened as more successful families came to look down upon the less successful ones. The emerging class system tended to weaken interfamily co-operation by generating a process of family individualization. This process was further strengthened by the external ecological pressures working in favour of the more individualistic, secular, and permissive Canadian ethos. These socio-structural and personal changes were vividly identified in the following remarks by our respondents:

"Individual families still have informal visits with friends and relatives. There is still social activity, but social circles are contracting and getting smaller and smaller. They have begun to associate only with "close people," with own friends and own neighbours, and never with people from other nationalities."

"People were a lot more like one, a lot closer to one another."

"People used to visit others very often. Very seldom do they get visited now—perhaps once per year."

"I see a tendency toward wider spacing of houses. It is not surprising to see new houses getting bigger and bigger."

"Nowadays, farmers here are trying to out-do each other, and are more competitive. The friendly atmosphere in the old days in the farm is no longer there any more. People are more inclined isolating themselves into circles or their own families. In general, people are a lot more selfish. Big shots want to be bigger (people can make a good living with 15 acres) and bigger. The farms have become so big, with the help of machinery, that you cannot find too many small farmers any more. Big farmers started buying the small farmers out. You have this constant craving for expansion among some big farmers. There are at least a dozen of well-to-do farmers in both villages.

"With easy access to means of transportation and contact with the outside world, there is a tendency for young people to get out.

"Family ties are a lot looser now. Gardening was more like a family living. Without machinery the whole family had to work together to make a living. I help you and you help me.

"Luxury is almost a necessity, something taken for granted.There is not much difference between big farmers and big business men—they dine in CN Tower, accumulate wealth, and live luxuriously and competitively."

"With children growing up, our lifestyle changed, and we travelled a lot more often. Travelling has become part of our lives now. I don't think you can find a Dutch farmer who doesn't go back to Holland. Some don't tend to visit the home country as a vacation, but as a family gathering and re-union.

"We go out of the Marsh to do shopping and have supper there—at least once per week now.

"Now families are more independent, and lead a more independent style of life. In old days, we worked hard and did try to cooperate with each other. But independence does not necessarily generate selfishness."

As a consequence, the family identity has now become stronger, though, paradoxically, the internal family structure itself has become weaker in response to a similar challenge. The increasing bureaucratization of the central institutions of the community—the Church and the school—coupled with the emerging sense of alienation of the individual from the community, have contributed to an increasing sense of loss of community, especially among the younger generations. The differentiated community system can no longer perform the social function of providing a strong primordial community identity and solidarity. The families now relate not to an undifferentiated close-knit community per se, but to the separable and differentiated bureaucratic structures through a complex system of multiple linkages.

TIME

Two considerations are integral to our exploration into and analysis of the meaning of time as both an entity of phenomenon and as a concept:

time is sociologically transformed and culture-specific. Different socio-cultural systems may express the time sense in different ways, ways which are deeply rooted in the history, tradition, and experience of their people. Our earlier analysis and interpretation of the changing patterns of family relationships have employed the "dynamic" and "historical" aspects of the time concept in constructing and delineating the three evolutionary stages of the development of the two Marsh communities. However, a more meaningful understanding of a community and its social organization cannot arise without a clear understanding of the culturally conditioned and specific ways in which time is experienced by the community itself. The tribal society, the agricultural society, and the modern industrial society may express their time sense in culturally different ways. The identification and explication of the entity and concept of time intrinsic to a specific cultural system would involve a systematic examination of the socio-cultural contexts in which time concept is relevant. But since the community is involved in a dynamic and evolutionary process, its time sense becomes necessarily enmeshed with its changing contexts. In fact, this fact is itself a clear demonstration of the culture-specificity of intrinsic time. In the case of the two Marsh communities, two different conceptions of time are observable. The earlier conception was intrinsic to the first stage as well as to a considerable part of the second stage. The second conception relates to the last part of the consolidatory stage and the later ramificatory stage. We shall designate them as Time Then and Time Now.

Time Then Time Then was not reckoned in terms of specific units, because it was not conceived of in terms of divisibility and measurement. This sense of time was bound up with the notion of work as a continuous, self-generating, and endless process. There was no clear-cut idea of leisure as an activity separate from work. In fact, work on the Marsh was then a continuous exercise of human labour necessitated by the pressures of a very harsh and arduous physical environment. Work was totally manual up until 1958, when mechanization was introduced for the first time to the Marsh farms. Recalling the pre-mechanization days, one respondent stated:

> "We never took holidays in summer. We were lucky if we had a long weekend."

> "The amount of work time and the amount of work to be done was determined by weather conditions. There was much less sharp division between work time and play time. Only nature was taken into consideration, which explains why we sometimes had to work into midnight. Lots of discretion was exercised regarding work assignment, mostly in accordance with the weather."

Prior to the introduction of scientific agriculture, people forecast weather by simply sky-gazing. The sight of a full moon meant frost, early spring, and early fall. A red sky was indicative of a clear, cloudless day, but a red sky in summer meant day-long rains. A grey sky or the east wind also signified a rainy day. Dew in the morning pointed to a clear day. A respondent contrasted time then with time now as follows:

> "Today we believe in listening to the radio reports for weather forecast, or we telephone the agricultural station for information and listen to the taped version of a scientific weather report."

In the earlier days, a summer day meant hard toiling in the fields from seven in the morning to dusk. The time concept then was more directly and immediately bound up with the processes and phenomena of nature. "In early days, we worked by day light. The sky was our dial and we stopped when it began to grow dark," one respondent said poetically.

The relentless and tight work schedule left them no time for Church activities, though they invariably attended the Sunday service. Their weekends were wholly devoid of any entertainment. Winter was less rigorous and taxing. It was the season for intensive social activity, when the families got together and played a great deal of chess.

Time Then was also conceptualized in terms of the sacred. It is to this sacred time that a respondent was referring, when he declared, "Sunday is a holiday for us. We do not work on that day. All of Sunday is a religious day for us. It is our response to Lord's love." Even the time spent in working and earning one's living was conceived of in sacred terms. In fact, in a sense, all time was regarded as sacred, as a gift of the Lord. According to a respondent, "A Christian has an obligation to his religion. He must practise its precepts. . . . The big farmer who has succeeded here in the Marsh makes it through the Grace of God." A rich farmer related an incident that happened some twenty-five years ago, illustrative of the dominance of sacred time. On a certain Sunday, he felt obliged to work in the fields because a threat of frost had been anticipated. Some of the Church elders disapproved of this and were very angry with him. Since then he had never committed the sin of working on a Sunday.

Time Now   Within the context of Time Now, the year is functionally divided into three socio-culturally meaningful seasons: summer, fall, and winter. A more detailed work-time schedule of the communities today would run as follows:

Summer
April-May
> This is the time for preparing the land for agricultural operations. Then follow the operations of ploughing and seeding. This is a period of hard labour, involving a strenuous working day stretching from 7 a.m. to around dusk (8 p.m.).

May-June
> This time is occupied with spraying and weeding. Then follow the harvesting of the first crop of celery, carrots, etc.

June-July-August
> The community finds itself involved in full-time work. This is without question the busiest part of the year. Spraying takes place in the night when there is wind blowing; otherwise the farmer fears that he may spray his neighbour's field! This is the period when lettuce, cabbage, etc., are harvested.

Fall
September-October
> This is the time for the big harvest. The produce harvested includes onions, carrots, potatoes. The produce are systematically stored in cold storage facilities, to be preserved for future selling during the winter.

November
> This time is spent in clearing the land, levelling it, and getting it ready for winter.

Winter
January-February
> This period is devoted to the marketing of onions, carrots, etc., and to the job of repairing the machinery.

March
> Lord willing, the farmer may visit Florida and Holland.

Time Now is reckoned in terms of specific units, and there is a clear distinction made between the time meant for work and the time meant for leisure. Now the farmers are able to take off for holidays, and the more successful ones are able to make a trip to Florida or Holland in summer. Today the farmers depend for weather forecast on scientific reports, disseminated through the specialized services of the local agricultural station. Just as increasing mechanization has altered the nature of the weather forecasting system, it has also altered the nature of work, especially releasing more time for leisure and recreational activities. But mechanization has also increased to some extent the work involvement of the farmers. As one of them put it, "We work longer in order to keep our machinery busy. We do more spraying, build more boxes." In winter, nowadays, the more fortunate farmers head for warmer climates of Florida, the Caribbean Islands, or California. The new situation has not been altogether welcomed by some. One respondent stated:

> "Now we have more labour-saving devices, both in the house and on the farm. So we have more leisure time compared with the pioneering days of

1934-1944. I must confess that we don't get together as families, though we have time for ourselves. Often times I wonder if we are happy here."

Social time is still mostly Church-centred and Church-sponsored, as in the earlier times. Age-graded clubs are organized around the Church to cater to the social and recreational needs of both the young and the old. A citizens' club was built in September 1977. There is now a clear conception of payment for work by measuring the work-time. In the words of a respondent, "When we work we do not look at time, but we pay the workers on hourly basis." However, despite the changes, the people still tend to cling to the past. They express this in terms of an attachment to the old, taking pride in the slow pace of change and tending to value highly the continuity with the past: "We have changed with time but gradually and slowly, unlike the outside world."

Though there is some decline in religious commitment today, the notion of sacred time continues to govern community life. This is most clearly manifested in the practice of setting apart Sundays for religious activities. This has become an essential part of the ideal Christian life. However, there is also a tendency to mingle Church activities with recreational activities under the auspices of the Church. A brief account of the weekly time of an average member of the community is indicative of the dominance of religion in the life of Marsh people. The Weekly Schedule runs as follows:

Monday: Ladies' Aid Societies
Tuesday: *Harken* night
Wednesday: Catechism classes
Thursday: Cadet Corps Day
Friday: Kept open
Saturday: Shopping, etc.
Sunday: Relaxation

The weekly schedule represents more specifically the family context. Through this weekly calendar, we can see family activities based on a high degree of functional differentiation within the family structure. In particular, we can note the distinction between the sacred and secular time.

SPACE

The most important and immediately recognizable dimension of space as a conceptualized historic ally in the Marsh community is one of closed communities. The outside world becomes space that is not structurally and functionally linked to the social space of the community. That the community itself perceives social space in this way is clear from the following statement made by one of the respondents:

"We have a tendency to stick with our own kind and we do not move beyond this world of ours bound by social barriers."

But this sense of a socially bounded space is closely connected with the dominance of a community central institutional structure which demarcates the community from the surrounding socio-physical space. In the generation and maintenance of this community identity, the Church, the school, and the family combine in their influence to reinforce this perception and conception of a socially bounded space which becomes the spatial context for the manifestation of a strong community identity.

In conjunction with the opening up of the community system as a consequence of cultural and economic exchange with the external environment, the community social space has been expanding empirically. The following responses underscore the emergence of processes that threaten the boundaries of the community social space, and point to the gradual undermining of the predominantly religious and traditional basis of the community spatial perceptions:

> "I have lived 35 years in the Marsh. When I was a teenager (17), I visited Toronto once a year. Now we are frequently visiting the city."

> "Some parents are neglecting our Church and school and this has widened our contact with the outside world. We have brought into our Church and school the Dutch families living around Bradford and Newmarket. Secularism is creeping into the Marsh."

> "Children don't stay in the community as often as we used to. They go out to Bradford, Newmarket, and many other outside places."

> "As teenagers, we never went out of our own town. The outside didn't have much influence on me, and I had my own mind made up. Grandfather is personally very much against 'shows,' though now he has no control over his grandchildren. Then my 17-year-old daughter has a licence and grabs the car to go around."

> "Space was limited in earlier days. We moved then within the limited world of the Marsh. Because of widening of our social space and life, our life is degenerating."

Sacred Space   The local community perception assigns to all sociocultural institutions a clearly religious framework. As a consequence, all social space tends to become sacred space. The notion of sacred space involves the idea that certain places are demarcated for sacred functions and activities. The community sees its socio-cultural foundations as basically religious. One of our respondents gave expression to such an understanding of his community:

> "The family and the Church are our sacred institutions. The house and Church buildings themselves may not be sacred, but what goes on inside is sacred. Their environment must be protected. The sanctity of familial and marital institutions and of the Church are very meaningful in our lives. We frown on drinks in our homes, and forbid smoking in the Church. We also forbid commercial sales within the precincts of the Church, though, of course, we organize Church bazaars."

It is worth noting that the respondent makes a distinction between the physical structure of the building and its functionality, the implication of which is that physical space has to be transformed functionally before it can claim the status of sacred space, and equally importantly, that the community institutions strive to exercise regulatory pressure to preserve the sanctity of physical space that has earned the status of being sacred.

The Dutch Home   The Dutch homes in Holland Marsh are located in a distinctive area, constituting a distinctive spatio-ethnic neighbourhood in which the Dutch live in very close physical proximity to each other. On rare occasions of social interaction with the non-Dutch, active attempts are made by the Dutch to maintain social and cultural aloofness for reinforcement of community identity and Dutchness. Intricate and subtle patterns of explicit avoidance of inter-ethnic interactions by the Dutch and the non-Dutch are real and have made considerable impression upon the few non-Dutch residents who are peripheral to the Marsh community:

> "I have been living in Ansnorveldt for 45 years, but have never gone inside a Dutch home. Of course, we carry on conversation when we meet in the streets. We are chums only with other non-Dutch—the Germans and other ethnics, with whom we even have considerable intermarriage."

> "We don't mix with the Dutch too much. Now they are moving into my neighbourhood. I have begun to hear a little more about them a little more often, e.g. about their Church divisions. There are imaginary boundaries between them and us. We go to our own Church, where we centre our lives. In a social way, sometimes these boundaries are real. But there are boundaries almost everywhere."

> "The ethnic people socialize among themselves—the Germans, the Italians, and the Dutch. It's not exactly a matter of language."

> "In the past 39 years, I have not really been in any Dutch home. I guess I can be off hand. I know a lot of Dutch people, but not really associate with them very much. A few Dutch people come into my home for business and have a few drinks. They are usually young people."

> "Our family does not have close Dutch friends. Even my children do not hang closely with the Dutch children."

> "I cannot remember having received invitations into the Dutch homes. They have their friends, we have ours. Dutch and non-Dutch people do not mix with each other. Inter-ethnic segregation is exclusive and mutual. I can't remember I have ever sent out invitations to the Dutch people either. Dutch and non-Dutch children do not intermingle with each other. Hungarians get along well with the Germans. Intermarriage between the two nationalities has been frequent enough. I sometimes think that the Dutch shouldn't be throwing stones at the non-Dutch people. Don't ever think that you have only Dutch in this world."

> "I have never gone to Dutch homes. They have never been in here either. We have some relationships with the non-Dutch (e.g., Hungarians). I don't know those Dutch people in the Marsh. If you don't communicate, you don't know much about them."

"I can't tell you the names of non-Dutch people. I don't know them and I don't want to impose."

"The Dutch people hang together well, trying to keep themselves from pollution of secular lives."

"It was 10 to 15 years ago when we had Dutch people in our home for supper. We don't know the other side of the story. We don't associate with them. Not only that, we have a tendency to hold back."

The physical morphology—the external architecture and the interior spatial arrangements—of the present Dutch homes remains traditionally Dutch, replicating the original style in Holland. This was true of the pioneering period, and is true today, though there are changes in detail. A Dutch house stands out as a distinctive entity, strikingly distinguishable from the non-Dutch houses. A Dutch house has its own characteristic features, such as lace-curtained windows, reproductions of Dutch paintings, and the invariable cuckoo clock, and reminds one very strongly of the original Dutch homes back in Holland.

The Marsh Dutch homes preserve the traditional Dutch concern for cleanliness and tidiness. The entrance to the house is always through a garage door. One is expected to take off one's shoes, though it is customary for the host to say politely, "Please do not bother to remove your shoes." One informant mentioned that his next door neighour built a new house with an entrance through the back-door simply to maintain his ideal of cleanliness.

The morphological and spatial repetitions of the forms and styles of the traditional Dutch homes tend to strengthen the bond with Holland. Holland, though physically absent, is very strongly present socio-culturally. This sense of socio-cultural continuity and identity with the old country is constantly reinforced by visits to Holland and reciprocal visits to the Marsh. The interchange between the two social systems is best described in the words of a respondent:

"There has been not much change in the visits to the old country. A lot of people in the Marsh go to Holland every year, and relatives, in turn, visit the Marsh. The two bonds between these two worlds is a continuing one, though we have yet to see if this visiting relationship is going to be affected, with the coming age of the first generation of children born in the Marsh."

The socio-cultural space which the Marsh Dutch share with the old country becomes temporarily converted into a physical-spatial continuum between Marsh and Holland through this system of visiting relationships.

What, then, is the function of the social space? It can be seen as a potent ecological force strengthening community ethnic identity and cohesion. Self-enclosure as a result of closing the system implies close bonds amongst members of the community and separateness from the non-Dutch by widening the social distance between the two qualitatively different social spaces—the Dutch and the non-Dutch. However, simultaneously, the same system also tends to emphasize the mutuality relationship between the immigrants and their old country by strengthening the identity and continuity of social space between the two. The Dutch in the Marsh are very much aware of the dynamics and processes of the situation.

Within a developmental framework, the identity-reinforcing functions of the Dutch social space in Holland Marsh need to be viewed in the context of the changes that are taking place, however gradually, in the area. Such changes include the appearance of ranch-style houses built by big farmers in their efforts to keep up with non-Dutch outside; the organization of hockey teams by the young people since 1971 to play matches in places outside the Marsh; the increasing tendency to spend weekends and leisure time outside homes and the community, a development facilitated by the automobile; the increasing comforts and facilities in the Dutch household; and the tremendous growth in communication and means of transportation. In the face of such changes, the community has developed the notion of closed social space, emphasizing separations and differences from whatever is non-Dutch as a strategy of defence. Understandably, the older people are more inclined to express regrets at the changes and consider them in largely negative terms. A great deal of lament has been expressed for the loss of the co-operative community life, which is poetically romanticized to have existed in the good, old pioneering days.

INTERPRETATION AND DISCUSSION

The evolution of the Dutch community in Holland Marsh can be best conceptualized and understood in terms of an historical process of ecological adaptation which takes place in space and through time. The developmental framework adopted in this study and delineated in our writings elsewhere (Ishwaran: 1977) attempts to view the concept of time as a starting point for theoretical analysis, and as a device in conceptualization and construction of typologies and phases of development. The developmental approach looks upon changes as the primary units of analysis, and characterizes them as essentially directional, purposive, and goal-oriented. The construction of stages or phases within the broader framework alerts the researcher's attention to the identification of the differentials in changes attendant to each phase, and perhaps more importantly, the historical conditions under which these changes are activated and rendered possible to exercise their impact on the evolving community.

While a substantial amount of our research efforts have been expanded on the "time" dimensions of the ecological adaptation process, it is equally important to emphasize that adaptation is essentially ecological in the sense that it takes place "in space" within a specific ecological environment. Our primary empirical concern is then with the historical dynamics underlying the differences in definition and maintenance of boundary in different stages of community development. The important research question is two-fold: First, how is space as both a physical and social entity conceived, constricted, and expanded within the community historically; and second, how do changes in conception of space affect relationships between individuals, family, and community?

We have traced the entire development of the community's definitions of physical and social space and their maintenance. Perhaps it is of some theoretical utility to conceptualize and recapitulate changes in terms of the historical shifts between "closing the system" and "opening the system" in different stages of community evolution. During the early, pioneering days of ecological adaptation, one witnesses the functional necessity of a self-imposed, self-defined, and self-constructed model of a community based on isolation and separation from the broader, environmental context. The system is closed, and its boundary very rigidly defined, with physical survival as the only common goal within an unknown, primitive, and hostile physical environment. The occupation of agriculture highlights the extreme vulnerability of human activities to the forces of nature in the absence of technological innovations and mechanization. The core of the physical universe is not the individual, nor the few individuals who comprise the family units, but the collectivity, which is made up by every individual who happens to be there, and therefore, is larger and more important than the individual. Collectivism, necessitated by survival and consolidated by a unifying religious and cultural bondage, becomes a dominant operating spirit, giving birth to inter-individual solidarity, cohesiveness, and co-operation. Physicial survival within an ecological context makes human solidarity a fundamental pre-requisite. Within a physically and structurally closed system, the meaning of individual existence is understood in terms of the existence of the collective unit.

The advent of technological innovation and mechanization has converted mutual interdependence among individuals on the one hand and families on the other, from a condition of absolute necessity to one of optional choice. Technology takes the place of hard human toil as collectivity, and consequently removes the bondage between individuals. More importantly, toward the end of the consolidatory stage and the beginning of the ramifactory stage, one witnesses the gradual opening up of the hitherto closed system, a phenomenon punctuated by increasing modernization and mechanization, and by the continuation of productive prosperity of the agricultural economy through relations of exchange with the outside economy.

Concomitant with the processes of modernization are parallel forces pressing toward institutional specialization and differentiation. The community which was once a total, all-inclusive unit of solidarity and cohesiveness is heading toward functional independence in the sense that such human-created institutions as church, school, economy, and family mediate and intervene between individuals and the community.

Precisely, what has happened to the individual and the family? We have noted earlier the functional eminence of the family as a multi-faceted, multi-functional, and all-encompassing unit during the exploration stage of development of the Marsh community. Social differentiation of the community in terms of functional specialization by evolving institutions leads to the gradual loss of some family functions, and the decline of the prominence of the family. There is then the nuclearization of individual families, and then gradual functional and emotional detachment from the community and the kinship networks, which are considerably enhanced and perpetuated by differentials in economic success and prosperity among individual families. The slow ascendency of social stratification within the community, which differentiates the successful families from the less successful ones, has contributed much to the undermining of community solidarity and cohesiveness. The model of the community is eventually transformed from one of structural interdependence to functional interdependence.

Economic prosperity and technology have transformed families into self-sufficient operating units. In the ramificatory stage, space is defined as family space (my family versus your family and other families) and individuals are thrown into the household unit within the boundary of which individual family members strive to satisfy each other's emotional and psychological needs.

In conjunction with the overall trend of the community over time to initiate and cultivate functional exchange with the external environment, such that internal community space is expanded and old boundary is re-defined, distance between individuals is rigidly defined and consequently increased. Within this perspective, one seems to be talking about the gradual atomization and individuation of the individual. The functionality and desirability of the community as a collective unit is then assessed in terms of its extent of conducivenss to individual well-being. Hall (1959: 146), the pioneering researcher on the socio-cultural meanings of time and space, once stated:

> "Every living thing has a physical boundary that separates it from its external environment. . . . We call this the 'organism's territory.' The art of taking claim to and defending a territory is termed territoriality."

Anthropologists have long emphasized the salience of such human activities as defending territoriality and marking fine graduations of time and space within the value framework man brings into the situation. Our study of the development of the Marsh community and the historical changes in patterning, forming, and structuring space within a time framework epitomizes the articulation of space as a focal human concern in a developing community. Old conception of space in terms of within and without the system are gradually replaced by institutional space, family space, and finally, personal space.

NOTES

1. A detailed account of the Holland Marsh community in a developmental perspective has been reported elsewhere (Ishwaran: 1977).
2. For further analysis and interpretation of data on marital stability and commitment in the Canadian-Dutch family, read another paper of ours (Ishwaran and Chan: 1979b).

REFERENCES

Hall, Edward T.
   1959   *The Silent Language.* New York: Premier Book, Fawcett World Library.

Ishwaran, K.
   1977   *Family, Kinship, and Community: A Study of Dutch Canadians, A Developmental Approach.* Toronto: McGraw-Hill Ryerson.

Ishwaran, K., and Kwok B. Chan
   1979a   "The Socialization of Rural Adolescents." In *Childhood and Adolescence in Canada,* edited by K. Ishwaran. Toronto: McGraw-Hill Ryerson.

   1979b   "Marital Stability and Marital Commitment in a Rural Dutch Community." In *Marriage and Divorce in Canada,* edited by K. Ishwaran. Toronto: McGraw-Hill Ryerson.

12. Problems in the Family, Community, and Culture of Hutterites

KARL A. PETER

INTRODUCTION

Hutterite institutions and patterns of behaviour have become the focus of considerable sociological attention in recent years. The question, how an institutionally complete *Gemeinschaft*-culture can be maintained and kept distinct in the middle of an industrialized, fast-changing society generated some interest among sociologists and anthropologists alike. But very little attention so far has been paid to Hutterite individuals filling these institutions and roles on a day to day behavioural basis. Could it be true that Hutterites in fact form a "community of Saints," as they like to call themselves, living a serene, carefree, and conflict-free life as suggested by the ideal patterns of the culture? The absence of data on crime and social problems among Hutterites seems to suggest an idyllic, if not perfect, society. Yet there is some evidence that conflict and competition, strains and stresses, are neither absent nor particularly rare among Hutterites; they seem to be exceptionally well managed and kept out of view of outsiders.

THE PROBLEMS OF CULTURAL SELF-DETERMINATION

A cultural group like the Hutterites, which over the centuries maintained a process of dissimilarity from its ethnic base as well as from its host society, is compelled to achieve this goal through degrees of cultural self-determination and social independence. The latter are by no means total because Hutterites require a host society as a basis for their own existence, and the adaptive responses to the social and cultural environment of the host, determine, to a large extent, the degrees of cultural self-determination and social independence, possible under any specific conditions.

Cultural self-determination and social independence above all require economic strength and the ability to solve one's own internal problems, whether they be economic, religious, or social. To the extent that the group must resort to outside assistance to solve its own inherent strains and stresses, such assistance endangers the legitimacy of its own institutions and consequently endangers its existence as a distinct ethnic group.

Hutterites have institutionalized their determination to solve their own internal problems. This went so far as to enter into contractual relations with their respective feudal hosts during the sixteenth and seventeenth centuries, stipulating clearly the boundaries beyond which Hutterites would not tolerate any interference into their internal affairs. In today's society, laws, social services, and welfare measures are carefully scrutinized as to their actual and potential consequences in impeding the socio-cultural independence of the group. Hutterites have found, for example, that universal hospital coverage is no threat to their cultural fabric, but old age pensions and children's allowances are. The latter are social services bypassing the Hutterite community and providing economic assistance to selected group members. Not only are these members partially freed from their total dependency on the resources of the group, but the institutionalized access to the resources of the group is being disturbed, leading to disunity and discontent of disadvantaged members.

SOCIAL PROBLEMS AND RESTRICTION OF INFORMATION

The Hutterites resistance to outside interference above all compelled them to build a wall of secrecy around their internal affairs. There is not anything intentionally sinister or deceptive about such secrecy, although throughout the centuries it has often been interpreted in a conspiratorial fashion and has given rise to a great many prejudices against them. Secrecy about one's internal affairs is an attempt to limit the flow of information to the outsider and thereby limit his means of interference. It is a simple but essential mechanism of group survival, particularly if the outside world is either very hostile or uncomfortably paternalistic.

It is from this point of view that certain data on social problems among Hutterites cannot be taken at face value but must be very carefully investigated as to their actual significance. The virtual absence of divorce among Hutterites might not readily be interpreted that the Hutterite family is unusually stable and free from difficulties. It might mean that the group chooses not to have marriage counselors and courts interfere in its own social problems. Hutterite preachers have the legal power to marry their people, but they cannot divorce them. It is, therefore, perceivable that the stability of the Hutterite family is at least in part due to the refusal of the group to have its internal social problems referred to outsiders for solutions.

Statistical data, therefore, are not reliable indicators regarding the nature of the frequency of social problems among Hutterites, nor are they a reflection of the true nature of interaction among the members of the group. Survey research in most cases does not penetrate the wall of secrecy, and if it does, is extremely difficult to interpret. Participant observation, case studies, and individual biographies are only of value if they are obtained from inside the wall of secrecy, that is to say, under conditions of trust. This condition puts the observer under the moral constraint not to abuse his information.

The following inquiry is an attempt to look behind the wall of secrecy and to map out some problems which Hutterites encounter in their families and communities. It is based on a combination of participant observation and individual biography. The inquiry opens with an autobiographical sketch written by a Hutterite woman at the age of 22, describing her childhood relations, adolescent relations, the school, community work patterns, social control, and family relations.[1] To complement these descriptions, the author will bring to bear additional data obtained as a participant observer in the family and community under discussion. Finally, an in-depth analysis of certain selected aspects of Hutterite life and culture will be made.

THE SOCIO-PSYCHOLOGICAL BACKGROUND OF THE AUTOBIOGRAPHER

To better comprehend the background of this inquiry, it must be noted that the Hutterite woman who wrote this autobiography went through a profound personal crisis at the time of writing. There were three interrelated processes which preoccupied her state of mind. For at least three years she had refused to receive baptism and thereby postponed her marriage, since marriage customarily is expected soon after baptism. Secondly, she was romantically linked to a young ex-Hutterite to whom she could not get married unless he rejoined his community and became properly baptized. Moreover, the exchange of letters and the occasional meetings which she had with this young man had to be kept secret from the rest of the community and her family, placing her under considerable mental strain. Thirdly, she became involved in the fundamentalist religious orientation which this ex-Hutterite had acquired, going so far as to enroll in a correspondence Bible course. This fundamentalist orientation served her as the major vehicle of criticism toward Hutterite life and religion.

The combined result of these processes were that the woman on occasions fantasized leaving the community, despite the fact that her father happened to be the first preacher. However, she could not bring herself to take the initiative, but began to focus on outsiders, whom she hoped could provide her with a solution. One of her uncles, who had defected from a Hutterite community 25 years earlier and now lived in California, became the focus of her desire "to be taken away." Of course the uncle never took this initiative.

It is this experience of confusion and dissatisfaction which made her see things and say things which otherwise might never have occurred to her. What to the reader might appear as rather mild statements of criticism here and there are rather remarkable statements of a vigorous young mind, bewildered by the disagreeable choices that were lying ahead of her.

As it happened, the woman eventually left her family and community in the middle of the night and joined a group of ex-Hutterites near by, who maintained a quasi-Hutterite group life. She could not endure to face her parents and her community with her decision beforehand, knowing very well that if she tried, she would not be able to go through with it—not because of any coercion, but because of the moral strains and pains which such a decision would impose on everyone.

A few months later she and her boyfriend got married, and for the next few years they participated in the life patterns of the group mentioned. The unrelenting pains of having separated herself from her family and community nevertheless caught up with her. Her husband found himself in a similar position. Eventually both rejoined the Hutterite community of the husband in a reconciliation ceremony, followed by baptism and marriage according to the Hutterite ritual. They have been seemingly solid and satisfied members of this community ever since.

THE AUTOBIOGRAPHY

I can remember the time when I was going to kindergarten. This was from three to six years of age. I guess my mother and dad took good care of me the first two years.

Each year, winter or summer, we had to get up and get dressed. By 8 o'clock we were on our way to kindergarten school. There we had our breakfast, but first of all we thanked the Lord for our food. After breakfast, the mother who was looking after us for the day recited a number of songs and prayers, while we repeated them with her. When we were through with this 10 or 15 minute recital, we could go out and play together until 10 o'clock, at which time our dinner was brought over from the kitchen. These were only simple meals, milk with potatoes or soup. On Sunday it was special, soup with duck and fruit. When the bell rang at 11:30 a.m., all the children had to take a nap, no questions asked. Most of the time we slept because the mother was watching over us. When we got up after an hour or so, we could play until lunch time, after this we had to recite a couple of songs, say our prayers, and then we could go home by 3 or 3:30 p.m.

So the days dragged by, every day the same. All the enjoyment we had was when we kids played together—whatever came to our mind, hide-and-seek, tag. We could go on the swing or see-saw when there was one. We climbed fences and often tore our skirts. Oh, many things happened. One time I remember two boys, another girl, and I planned on running away from school. Sure enough, when we were alone in the afternoon when the other kids were taking a nap, we sneaked through the fence and walked away. It did not take long and an older girl followed us to take us back, and then we got such a spanking, I don't think we ever dared to run away again.

From six to seven was a wasted year as far as I am concerned. We joined the children from seven to 15 years old and had to help with the dishes and sweep the dining room after each meal, but I did associate only with children my own age. Rules and regulations began and were expected to be followed. When 15 years old, we had to join the women in all the work there was to do; whenever the bell rang we had to go.

Spring is the beginning of a busy time in the colony, although daily work is carried out through the winter months. Spring brings its extra work, with house cleaning, and many are quite anxious to spring clean all the community buildings, such as the kitchen, cooler, milking parlor, school house, and church house. When all the women and girls help, it takes only two to three hours and all is clean. The girls have to do the finishing touches, like cleaning windows, or if there is something to paint or varnish.

When the garden is ready and prepared for seeding, all the women and girls age 15 to 45 help in cutting potatoes. It takes about two days to cut enough potatoes, that is five tons. We help plant the onions and garlic, the rest of the vegetables are seeded by the gardener. Then hoeing begins, twice a week early in June until July, at which time some of the vegetables are picked for canning. As soon as the pears are ready, they are picked and put into jars, we can about 50 to 60 jars, depending on the harvest. The same with beets and cucumbers, but cucumbers are canned in three different ways. This is the time when the girls are together most of the time during the day. In the month of July we go swimming to cool off in the river from the hot kitchen, as the girls take turns in cooking the vegetables and put them in order on shelves in the cellar. During July and August we get into the fruit. Cherries and strawberries are picked in British Columbia; in the fall, apples and plums and pears are also picked there. The rest of the fruit, like apricots and peaches, is bought. Ever so often we girls enjoyed ourselves, we sang songs together a lot, and if we didn't, our women asked us to, I guess the work goes faster. Ducks and geese are butchered in the fall, but here the men folk helped, because it took all day to clean 300 or so.

The girl who was cooking did not help with this work because she was preparing the meals, as the head cook told her. The relatives helped to clean the kitchen after each meal. Since we were divided into three groups, the women took turns in washing dishes and tables, as we had so many.

Girls have to begin to cook and bake when they are 17 years of age, but with 15 we start milking. This is a hard job and I wish the men would milk, but it seems our men will not do this.

So this all takes care of the rules we are to follow. If we don't, we are talked to and asked why, or where we have been. Unless we are sick, we have to attend to the work. The person is excused of the work in times of emergency.

This way food and clothing is provided for all who work for the colony. Even furniture is given. At the age of 15 we get a chest to store our clothes or whatever we please.

As for the women, they do not have much to say outside their business; they have to learn to be quiet.

In the colony much talk is going on, you can be talked of in one of the two ways. In a thoughtful way and a thoughtless way, and the girl gets to hear either one. If a girl does only things which please her, she is not favored or liked by others. She becomes a hindrance instead of a help to other girls. This covers a great area, but I will not go into details. Unless the girl becomes mindful of others, nothing will change her and she is subject to be talked of because of carelessness, and the personality shows the character she has.

I think the elder women think much of how they have lived in the colony and want to set an example to the younger ones, but most of all, they are concerned with the welfare of their own children. They are happy to see their children be subject to the colony rules and regulations without complaining, and they want them to remain in the colony because security is provided for them.

Some parents really see to it that their children receive proper training, and help them under discipline, while there are those who neglect the responsibility to instruct their children.

Since I was the only girl in our family with half a dozen boys, there was always a lot of work in our home. Responsibilities were put on me very early in life. I had to wash and polish floors in a number of rooms. At the age of ten I had my own room, and I arranged it the way I wanted to. I remember when I cleaned up and did not do it nicely, mother made me go back and do it all over again. I didn't like it at that time, but this is how I have been taught and now it cannot be otherwise. I want everything nice and in order. Now I have the nicest rooms of all the girls in the colony; this is what I have heard others say too.

I needed a girl's companionship. When I was eleven years old I became close friends with Sarah. She always was so nice to me and helped wherever she could. She was only ten months older than I and had seven sisters. She knew more about the facts of life and she passed it on to me. Some of the things frightened me at first, because I did not know about them. Our parents, who should tell us about this, did not tell us children. The change from girlhood to womanhood is unknown to us.

So Sarah helped me to be better prepared to meet these changes and I was glad I was not the only one who had to face this. We got to know each other quite well, for we were cleaning chicken eggs every evening for some years. Sarah is married now, nevertheless we are very happy to see each other; and if we have time, we enjoy to recall the past and talk about bygone days which were wonderful. We shared our joys and disappointments, which made double the joy and half the sorrow. We also had a lot of fun in cleaning three to six pails of eggs daily. On our birthdays we gave each other gifts, not much, but one time Sarah cross-stitched me a pair of pillowcases with my initials on. I still have them and I still have the presents Dad gave me and Sarah at Christmas time, for cleaning eggs. Often we had ice cream or a chocolate bar. In the summer evenings we would go for a walk. Sometimes boys followed us and we all walked home together.

I guess I was 13 years old when I had my first date. And this same boy, who is here on the colony, is still after me; he wants me to be his wife. There is nothing more his mother and all the family would like better than this to happen, but . . .

I remember I was still very young when my mother and dad had an argument. I didn't want to hear what they said; I thought to myself, "I am going to think twice before I will marry."

I cannot stand it when people argue and get angry, sometimes over nothing. I know it is in our nature, but we must learn to control our emotions. Our parents could teach us children by telling us we may quarrel as much as we like, if we hear mother and dad quarrel, but if mother and dad don't, then we children are not supposed to quarrel with each other.

Now I would not know how much love is received by either husband or wife. I think it is taken for granted, while others are quite happy when a woman gives birth to a child. As soon as the woman knows she is expecting a child, preparations are made for the little one with the help of the husband. Everyone thinks it is quite natural, I guess. Young parents receive gifts, help, and advice, and anyone may feel free to give it. Clothes and bedding is provided for the child and given by the boss in the colony. One woman is elected to cook extra and special meals for the mother for four weeks. Her work in the colony is carried out by others for the next 13 weeks. After that she slowly begins to join in the work with the rest.

Husband and wife support each other in the colony. It all depends on the person, and at times the man does not receive the stand he could have, on account of his wife. Then again, in some cases it is quite the opposite, on account of his wife the man might get a job because of the help and influence given by his wife.

Sometimes the man will refuse the position or job he is appointed to, because he didn't like it or would not go for this particular job. I guess this causes disagreement between husband and wife, especially if he is careless and tries to get by without a job, and someone else is elected. Then I guess husband and wife are faced daily with decisions, and if there is no consideration or understanding, this can cause a quarrel between the two. But not all people have the same personalities; much depends on how you are taught.

As the parents are, this is how the children will be. They lose all respect even when the parents are around.

I could tell of incidents with my brothers and me. Once my brother and I had a long discussion, he can be understandng if he wants to, but he tried not to. I came to the point of speaking harshly to him and it ended in an argument, but at night before going to bed, I just waited for my brother to get home. It was not easy to apologize, but after this I was so happy, I had peace in my heart. Doing this helps me to be conscious of the fact that I must be careful, because there are so many who watch me.

I am sure if all of us in our family would obey this rule, we would have a happier home, but how do they burden and discourage dad by doing things he does not approve of. I am reminded of the verse: "Train a child in the way he should go, and when he is old, he will not depart from it." Proverbs 22:6.

If only dad would sit down and take the time and speak in love and explain the wasted time and money spent on liquor, smoking, going to shows, and the many other evil influences that have the tendency to lead wayward. I am so glad the colony objects to this; that is how I have been kept from youth until I was old enough to choose. More could be said about this, but this is sufficient for now. Anyway, I still have to see my first show. 1 Cor. 6: 19-20.

I like to recall my school days, taught by our good teacher who was teaching at our colony for a long time. Much respect, praise, and honor was given to him. Not only by the many school children who were going through grades 1 to 8, but also by the inspector, for the best teaching in colonies and regular attendance by the children. Our daily record proved to be so.

These were 8 wonderful years of much study and strict discipline, and all that goes with it. I am thankful for all this now and the way I was taught in school. I have learned many valuable lessons, because our teacher talked to us about the Bible story, which he read to us every morning. It was then that we began to read the Bible each day, and I still do so, not only out of habit, but to satisfy my longing and searching heart. What a help this has been and so many questions have been answered.

Our teacher strongly emphasized the wrong and right. He was very much against taking what is not ours—he called it stealing—or speaking untruths (lying), dishonesty, cheating, using bad language (swearing), bad habits, such as drinking, smoking, etc. If we were found out doing any of these while still going to school, we did not get by, we had to face the consequences. Our teacher not only taught the subjects in school, but also how to build an honest and upright character. How glad and thankful I am for having had a teacher like him who was strict and demanded obedience upon his word. In English periods we were not supposed to speak German, and in German school not to speak English. We had enjoyable times as well. We had parties on special occasions—like on Valentine's Day, we kids sent each other cards. On the teacher's birthday we played a number of games, and each child gave him a present. Then we had lunch.

As soon as spring weather was here we played baseball, and most of the year round. We did have some excellent ball players, girls as well as boys. Picnic on June the last was always an exciting time for all, even for those older boys and girls who were already out of school. They came to join the ball games. We picked two teams and the one who had the most innings was the winner. We also had different games, like racing, jumping in a sack, threading needles while walking, walking with a potato on head. Everyone tried to be a winner in order to win a prize.

At Christmas time we had programs, and every child had to know their pieces well. We had to act when on stage, and not just stand. Some of the plays were a great success. Once we had to charge 50 cents a seat from the visitors who came from far and near. Still this did not stop them from coming, the school house was just packed, the children had to stand.

The teacher who came after our longtime teacher left and moved away also had a program he asked us to join, even those who were out of school. So there were six girls and four boys who took part in singing the

Christmas carols. We could hardly believe our young people could per-form such good singing.

In the winter time we were sleigh riding on the hill. Most every child had something to go down on, even if it was only a piece of tin. I had many rides with boys. In the evening when we were too loud with shouting, the German schoolteacher came and send us home and we all had to go. When the ice was thick on the duckpond, the kids were on, the boys who had skates were skating.

In the summer time we went swimming in the river—we were more in the water than out on some days. As we grew older, we girls did not like to swim with the boys, as they were too rough. The teacher told the boys to leave when the girls came for a swim, or else look for another place. Sure enough, the boys found another place, a good place, where they could dive, and so we were left alone. Our teacher was careful, he did not want anything to happen which he did not approve of. He was responsible for us kids and rightly so. He felt it was his duty.

My dad was German schoolteacher at my time and he taught us in this same way. I guess he resembled his father very much. I do respect him for his rightness and honesty, which he leaves as an example for his children to follow.

THE ANALYSIS

Running Away from What?

The first part of the woman's autobiography is concerned with her childhood experiences in the kindergarten or "little school." This school for the three to six year old children usually is situated at the periphery of the Hutterite community and contains two rooms, one for sleeping purposes, the other being a dining and playing facility. All children sit at the dining table separated by sex and in the order of their age.

There is an air of monotony in the narrative of the woman which is rather remarkable, in that a 22 year old is able to remember it with the intensity that flows from her account. It seems to reflect a lack of outside stimulation during this period of her childhood. Hutterites seldom allow individually owned toys, although a few collectively used ones are provided. The "mothers" who look after the children change frequently and do not initiate any games or plays, nor do they participate in any. Their duties are largely custodial, with the exception of teaching songs, prayers, and watching over the moral conduct of the children.

It is rather interesting to inquire why a couple of youngsters at such an early age might be motivated to run away from the community, which after all constitutes the totality of the world known to them. While there might be any number of situational factors which might have triggered such behaviour in this particular case, some important contributary social conditions nevertheless seem worthwhile to be investigated.

When children run away from their family it is usually either the attraction of some idealized world beyond the boundaries of the family and community, or the repulsion of some experiences or relations within the family, or both. These young Hutterites had no conception of the world beyond the boundaries of their community, therefore no focus of attraction could be formed. If one assumes that they were repulsed by relations in their school, family, or community, one would have to find conditions leading to such feelings of repulsion in some patterns of these institutions.

For the young Hutterite, entering the little school coincides with the partial withdrawal of parental affection and the affection of relatives. During the first two years the Hutterite child is lavishly subjected to signs of affection from all family members and relatives. This does not cease entirely, but changes greatly in nature and frequency with the coming of its third birthday, when it enters the little school. Usually a younger child has already taken its place in the family as a focus of affection, and the imposition of a non-affectionate supervisory relationship in the little school, combined with the expected adherence to unfamiliar norms of older peers, can produce a traumatic experience of estrangement in the child. It is bound to lose at least part of a sense of security provided formerly by the affection of relatives. The adjustment to a set of impersonal rules, to changing, non-affectionate supervisors, combined with a lack of outside stimulation, might very well not only produce a feeling of monotony, but one of temporary rejection and dissatisfaction as well. In its third year of life, a Hutterite child becomes socialized into the structured rules, regulations, and norms of the community with an intensity which stands in contrast to its former permissive treatment in the family. It becomes obvious that the child is forced to make a major adjustment, not only in its conduct, but in its attitudes and expectations as well.

Human Nature and the Functions of Love and Lash

According to the testimony of the woman, corporal punishment seems to be an effective treatment to the kind of problem they encountered. Physical punishment at this age can only be responded to by total submission of the child. To the extent that this submission is achieved, it can possibly substitute for the missing emotional states previously induced by affection. Submission, it should be remembered, is a rather comfortable, if passive, emotional state, particularly if it is directed toward a powerful and admired figure, as fathers at this stage usually are.

Hutterites are consciously aware of the fact that love alone is insufficient as a mode of socialization for the type of personality which they envision. Physical punishment of children is seen as a means to suppress man's carnal nature, its animal desires and wants, until the time arrives when knowledge and reason can take over these functions.

Underlying these convictions are certain assumptions regarding the nature of human nature. Hutterites see man's nature as a duality.[2] There is the carnal part of drives and desires which Hutterites assume to be put there by God as the result of man's fall from grace. This powerful entity is the first to assert itself in selfish and asocial behaviour. In this sense it is not very different from Freud's concept of the "Id," and Georg Herbert Mead's concept of the "I".[3] The second part consists of knowledge, reason, and faith, all of which are acquired in the social context, through socialization and education. Again, the similarity to Freud and Mead is striking. The necessity of physical punishment is due to the fact that the carnal part of men's nature develops very quickly after birth, while the acquisition of reason, knowledge, and morality takes a very long time. Corporal punishment, therefore, is a temporary tool to suppress asocial behaviour until reason and morality are developed and act as a guide to conduct. While it is assumed that a child of 15 has fully developed these means of self-control, and therefore corporal punishment ceases at this age, the changeover from the control of behaviour through corporal punishment to individual self-control is seen as proceeding throughout childhood, but at different speeds. Most important, Hutterites have clearly staked out the limitations of corporal punishment by not making any assumption that corporal punishment could teach anything. While it is effective in temporarily preventing unacceptable behaviour, a change in behaviour toward more acceptable forms can only be achieved through an increase in self-control, for which the appropriate means are education and socialization.

Education, aiming at the acquisition of knowledge and reason, is a very modern concept and has become widespread in Western societies only after the Enlightenment. The rationality of the Enlightenment rejected religious and traditional legitimacies as the sole criteria of the validity of social phenomena (and physical as well), and substituted a new concept, that of human credibility. What is credible to the human mind on the basis of existential experiences became the main criteria in the construction of social institutions and human relations.

Hutterites were never touched by the spirit of the Enlightenment due to their geographic and social isolation at the time. Their understanding of what constitutes knowledge and reason is very different from those concepts generated by the Enlightenment. It is based on conceptions essentially going back to the Protestant Reformation two centuries before the Enlightenment. The religious tenets of Anabaptism adapted to and sanctified in the traditionally oriented communal lifestyle of the group provides the raw material of what constitutes knowledge and reason among Hutterites.

Verbal Morality Versus Moral Action
The woman's account of her experiences in school sheds some light on some of these fundamental differences and problems. The Hutterite school is a form of Public School, in the sense that the teacher is ap-

pointed by the local School Board and teaches the provincial curriculum. The school is, however, located on community property, maintained by the community, and forms part of the communal set of interaction. The German school solely conducted by Hutterites themselves for about one hour every day is mainly concerned with the reading and writing of German, the memorization of Bible quotations, and singing. Its teaching methods and curriculum are highly ritualized, and the woman mentions this school only in passing, when at one time she refers to her father as being the school teacher at the time.

The public school teacher referred to in her autobiography was a much respected Mennonite, who perfectly spoke and understood the Hutterite German dialect. What is so remarkable in her description of him is her emphasis on moral definitions like lying, stealing, etc. She describes these definitions as if they were enormous moral discoveries never before heard of in Hutterite communities. While Hutterites would strenuously argue that lying and stealing, etc., are strictly disapproved of and severely punished if engaged in, the conceptual context in which this Mennonite teacher approached such definitions seems to have surprised the woman very much.

Indeed, Hutterite socialization is geared not so much to the teaching of general moral principles from which conscious moral decisions can be deduced, but to teach situationally appropriate norms containing specific aspects of behaviour and morality. This distinction is best emphasized by the contrast between *Gemeinschaft* and *Gesellschaft* types of socialization, a major sociological concern since Toennies and Weber.

The limited range of social interaction in the Hutterite *Gemeinschaft* is fully regulated by behavioural norms appropriate for any specific situation. To know the norm also means to know the morality that goes with it. *Gesellschaft* types of interaction, in contrast, are only partially covered by situational norms. Much behaviour must be deduced from general values or principles of behaviour in order to attain a degree of predictability and stability of interaction. The latter, in turn, demand that such deductions must be logically derived and must consistently be applied to diverse situations.

HISTORY, TRADITION, AND THE LOGIC OF NORMS

The Hutterite situational normative approach toward behaviour to a large extent lacks this internal logic and consistency. Norms have developed historically, and while their development certainly was guided by values, historical accidents, and precedents, injected inconsistencies and illogicalities which accumulatively defined normative behaviour and morality in non-logical situational specifics. The intense and life-long primary interaction in Hutterite communities of course is the major vehicle by which this process takes place.

What Hutterites call knowledge and reason therefore is, in fact, codified in situational norms, and it is these situational norms which not only apply to all behavioural situations in their communities, but they also form the content of much of their education and all of their socialization. These norms need not be logically consistent, in the sense in which conduct deduced from generalized principle is understood to be consistent, but yield to some social, religious, or traditional consistency which might appear arbitrary if not properly understood by the observer. An example might shed some light on this problem. All Hutterites are required to attend their common dining hall for their daily meals unless someone is temporarily excused because of illness or other legitimate reasons. The two preachers of each community, however, are exempted from this common norm on the basis of an historical precedent going back to the year 1537, when a disagreement over the eating facilities of preachers was solved by allowing preachers to take their meals in their own homes. While the logic of communal meals is powerfully supported by religious principles (the Lord's supper, etc.) and by the whole communal orientation of the group, this logic as a general principle of conduct nevertheless is being rendered useless by a historical precedent which justified a deviation from the norm for specific persons. Given the communal emphasis of Hutterites regarding the sharing of spiritual things and material goods between man and man, nothing can be more contradictory than excepting "the servants of the word" (the preachers) from participating in the communal meals of their flock. Yet this behaviour is strictly observed in all communities.

Jewish Law, in comparison, which originated to a large extent as situational norms (The Commandments, etc.) similar to those of Hutterites, was subsequently subjected to profound philosophical analyses to illicit its basic principles by generation after generation of scholars. The principles such abstracted not only established the universal character of Jewish Law, but also gave Jews of all ages the means of modifying their behaviour according to new situations yet remain within the principles of the Law.

THE COLLAPSE OF RELIGIOUS SCHOLARSHIP

In contrast, scholarship among Hutterites, which was profound during the sixteenth century, died out in the seventeenth century and has never been revived. All church sermons used in Hutterite services today were written before 1665. No Hutterite feels able to produce new interpretations of religious principles.

With religious scholarship at a standstill for more than 300 years, social adaptation with the help of continuous religious reinterpretations is impossible. The absence of any creative religious activity facilitated the emergence of traditionalism among Hutterites, which was already well underway at the end of the sixteenth century. The issuing of community ordinances during the latter half of the sixteenth century, and the periodic renewal of these same ordinances time after time, testifies to a process of progressive traditionalization of the group.

But traditionalism is non-adaptive in a fast changing environment which demands flexible responses to changing conditions. Successive migrations and the industrial revolution rendered traditional Hutterite economic designs obsolete. It was at this point that Hutterites decided on a two-prong development of their culture. This strategy tried to maintain a traditional configuration wherever this was possible, and to modernize wherever such modernization contributed to the survival of the group as a whole. Modernization of course affected mostly the economic institution, and traditionalism was maintained predominantly in social relations and religious observances. The educational institution was caught somewhat in the middle, insofar as it became necessary to educate Hutterites for adequate roles in their traditional as well as in their modernized institutions.

THE MARGINALITY OF TRADITION AND MODERNIZATION

There is, however, a basic incompatibility between traditionalism and modernization which poses a dire threat to the group. The manager of a Hutterite community, for example, handles a cash flow of close to a million dollars a year, which, if done adequately, as is most often the case, requires countless well-informed, hard-nosed decisions. To the extent that he is capable of doing so, he is also required to accept such traditional rules which forbid him to possess a radio or TV and even forbid him to hang a picture on the wall of his bedroom. How is the credibility of these traditional rules maintained?

The woman's description of her family relations throws some light on this question. She feels that they could have a happier home if only the sons would not discourage and burden their father with "wasted time and money spent on liquor, smoking, going to shows." Then she laments the fact that the family cannot sit down together "to speak in love" and discuss these matters. Hutterites are unable to justify their norms in other than religious and traditional terms. But these terms have lost much of their credibility because religious scholarship has failed to update them, and the modernizing influences which have found entry into the communities have rendered many of them obsolete.

COMPARTMENTALIZATION AND INTELLECTUAL SELF-LIMITATION

Faced with the dilemma of not being able to justify their norms in modern, more credible terms, Hutterites have only one choice if they want to maintain their group life: to compartmentalize the contradictions and leave them unexamined. Much of the socialization process, therefore, is geared toward such compartmentalization of contradictory elements. The emphasis on behavioural norms and the de-emphasis on abstract principles and values produces a personality structure which is well equipped to endure such compartmentalization without suffering too many anxieties.

As a result, the Hutterite personality structure differs markedly from those encountered in most parts of North American society. Hutterites emphasize appropriate behaviour not as much as appropriate motives, attitudes, intentions, or generalized values. They look for and judge a person by his or her behaviour, not so much by his or her attitudes. A silent prayer is no prayer at all; one must be able to hear the spoken word.

With only a slight exaggeration, one can say that a Hutterite is free to think what he pleases; as long as he behaves according to prescribed and appropriate norms, he is fully acceptable to his fellow men. Norms, as the embodiment of religious and traditional legitimacies, do not require as much the mental consensus of Hutterites as they require behavioural adherence.

George Herbert Mead's notion of the "generalized other" as a level of orientation from which to judge oneself and others seems relatively localized among Hutterites. The reference group is the community, and there is little beyond the group which a Hutterite can systematically build into his personality.

The scarcity of role models and role varieties not only perpetuates a relatively homogeneous personality structure within the communities, but of course limits the development of individual capacities and talents to the predominant model. In this sense Hutterites put intellectual restrictions onto themselves and their offsprings. They recognize very clearly that intellectual variety among their members creates problems in communal decision-making and conduct detrimental to the co-operative functioning of the communities. "Being of one mind," the desired goal of the religious and economic community, is paid for by intellectual and educational limitations imposed on the Hutterite individual. Whether he suffers from such limitations or whether he enjoys them is dependent on the degree of objectivity, or lack of it, with which the individual can see himself as being distinct from the group.

THE FORCE OF SOCIAL CONTROLS

The group's preoccupation with behavioural specifics of course enhances the forces of social control enormously. The detailed knowledge of each other's behavioural obligations injects an intensity into the process of social control which forced the woman to say after she apologized to her brother: "Doing this helps me to be conscious of the fact that I must be careful, because there are so many who watch me."

The forces of social control among Hutterites do not allow for any withdrawal or escape, save that of leaving the community. The individual has no other choice but to live with it, and to swim against the stream might be possible only for a limited period of time. While many

Hutterites try it, it usually exceeds the powers of any individual if it is attempted for life. The social cohesion of the group rests on the simple fact that the group at all times is stronger than any individual. Once the individual has been socialized, it has the power to bend him to meet its own terms or to force him out. The latter decision is exremely painful and, as shown in this inquiry, hardly a solution for life.

NOTES

1. The study of life histories and biographies is not a major methodological device among contemporary sociologists, but earlier sociologists found such material extremely useful in the study of social conduct. Studies such as Thomas and Znanieki's "The Polish Peasant in Europe and America" and Shaw's "The Jackroller" made significant contributions to the understanding of human action. As pointed out by Howard Becker in the 1966 edition of Shaw's book, life histories reveal useful information in at least three important areas of human conduct: (1) They reveal the point of view of the actor; (2) They elaborate on the socio-cultural context to which the actor is responsive; (3) They reveal the sequences and the interconnectedness of past experiences and situations in the life of the actor.

The methodological problems associated with the study of life histories are authenticity, accuracy, and representativeness. In the present study, the first two problems were overcome through the author having the opportunity to check his data against those collected through participant observation. From the literature it is further evident that the woman's description of life and routine activities is highly representative of conduct in Hutterite communities. But this is of minor interest to the author. The real task is to select from this autobiography those crucial descriptions which provide insights into problematic areas of the socio-cultural life of Hutterites, and to present them in their logical, religious, and socio-cultural connectedness. To do so required drawing on additional information not contained in the woman's autobiography. Nor is this analysis meant to present a definitive statement of socio-cultural problems among Hutterites, but it is being put forward as hypothetical, awaiting further confirmation or refutation.

2. Peter Rideman, "Rechenschaft unserer Religion, Lehre, und Glaubens. Von den Bruedern, die man die Huterischen nennt." (Cayley, Alberta, Canada, 1962), pp. 48-52.

3. George H. Mead, "Mind, Self and Society," (Chicago: The University of Chicago Press, 1963).

IV
ETHNIC FAMILIES AND CANADIAN INDIGENOUS SYSTEMS

INTRODUCTION

In this section, the studies are concerned with the problems of change and adaptation among ethnics indigenous to the Canadian physical environment. However, they share with the immigrants the problems of cultural adaptation. Though they are not strictly immigrant groups, they are cultural aliens like the immigrants. They represent what may be described as a case of indigenous modernization. The groups examined—the Kutchin, the Inuit, and the Hare Indians—represent the original North American groups, which may be regarded as "primitive" from certain theoretical perspectives, such as modernization and industrialization. Their case, therefore, is not identical with that of the other ethnic communities so far examined. Basically the other groups constitute part of historical processes associated with industrialization either through internal dynamics or through external stimulation. But the three groups discussed here have been less structurally involved in such processes. In a sense, they have been outside the main global historical developments, and forced into such processes abruptly and involuntarily. They have found themselves historically in a situation overwhelmingly and comprehensively dominated by social and cultural systems produced by historical processes in whose making they had less role to play. Their problems of adaptation, acculturation, and survival are bound to be qualitatively distinctive. No doubt they have had to adapt themselves to more powerful and alien systems in order to maintain a minimal physical survival in the outpost region of the country. A study of their problems reveals yet another dimension of the complex multi-ethnic family sociology in Canada.

Ann W. Acheson's paper examines the transformations that have taken place in the family system of the Kutchin, a Northern nomadic hunter community. The time-frame of this analysis is the preceding century, and a period long enough to provide an empirical basis for generalisations. The first shift in their traditional way of life occurred when they turned commercial trappers. In a more recent shift, they have become transformed into sedentary inhabitants of settled townships. These overall societal shifts have exerted fundamental influence on their family system. In particular, the impact of Christianity and the new economic structures have produced noticeable changes in the marriage pattern and the family system at the level of formal structure. This visible surface shift has not made any basic alteration in some of the principles involving the marriage pattern and the family organization. It is this fact that has determined the historical continuity of the Kutchin community. The core of the traditional family was at least one adult hunter, sometimes teamed up with another associate. The practice of polygamy prevailed, and it was accompanied by a system of matrilocal residence and free adoption of children. This meant that a winter camp could comprise one or more men, their wives, natural and adopted children, and possibly some dependents, such as orphans or elderly persons. The resulting pattern of family structure was complicated by its location within a wider structure of three exogamous, matrilineal clans. The families were also grouped into flexible units with members drawn from regional and local bands. But during the historical phase when the Kutchin became fur-traders, polygamy was abolished, the clan exogamy disintegrated, matrilocal residence significantly weakened, and Christian marriage rites came to be adopted.

In its examination of the more recent changes, the paper limits its focus to a single territorial settlement, the Old Crow, in the northern Yukon Territory. Some two hundred Kutchin families have become permanently settled for the last decade. An exploration of the situation in this phase of change might give a superficial impression of a family system radically ruptured or transformed, as indicated by such observed facts as the low rate of marriage, a perceptible rise in illegitimacy, a pronounced growth in households headed by women, and the sheer size of the household. However, the earlier practice of adoption continues.

The author argues that the changes mentioned above should be most meaningfully interpreted as adaptive responses to the shift of sedentariness, the emergence of the system of government benefits, and the system of wages. At the same time, she emphasizes that these changes have not affected the continuing Kutchin evaluation of marriage as the normal state for adults, and the acceptance of a household ideal in which a single provider heads the household. The new forms of income-earning through wages and government benefits have involved a variety of income-earners, such as widows, unmarried women with children, the disabled, and the old. Such persons with regular income have turned household heads. While the practice of a male heading the household has changed, the principle that a single person should be the head continues. In the concluding section, Acheson discussed the controversial issue of the matrifocal family. Focussing on the relationship between Kutchin norms and behaviour, she formulates it as a case of adaptive transformation.

In his analysis of the changing structure of the Inuit family, Matthiasson concentrates on the process of centralization in the development of the traditional family. He draws attention to the changes in such aspects as the socialization practice, and the systems of alliances and partnerships evolved as part of a strategy to deal with a hardy and hostile environment. Further, the author relates the problem of adaptive change to two ecological dimensions—subsistence and settlement patterns. In the Inuit family, connections on both the mother's and father's side are equally significant, since descent and inheritance take place through both channels. As a result, the individual unmarried male or females constitute the core of the kinship group or family. Family itself is a mere social group which brings together the individual, his or her siblings and parents, or, in the case of the married, the spouse and the unmarried children. The nuclear family becomes the basic family unit.

Matthiasson confines his attention to the Inuit of Arctic Canada. The division of labour in the nuclear family is based on sex division—men as hunters and women as domestic managers. But as a matter of fact, women also take part in the economic process in being engaged in fishing, a major source of food. Socialization of the young is a joint affair of both the parents, though it is probable that women have a greater role in the transmission of cultural values. In this process, one child, usually a male, is marked out for favoured attention. In addition to the basic nuclear family, there is a secondary and supportive system of extended family. The kinship system is characterized by the special tie between brothers-in-law and *angayungog-nukangor*, and the partnership based on wife-exchange. Most recently, the Inuit have taken to settlements and thus have come to be involved in extensive contacts with the federal government. This phase is what the author calls the centralization phase. The changes brought about in this phase, however, have yet to be studied in depth and detail. The author speculates that the Inuit people, one of the world's most hardy and adaptive, are likely to restructure their family system to accommodate the more fundamental environmental changes that have been taking place.

Joel Savishinsky and Susan Frimmer Savishinsky examine the case of the Hare Indian community in terms of the impact made on them by a specific Euro-Canadian trait—alcohol consumption. Through this framework, they attempt to examine the adaptive pattern of family structure of the community in response to the Euro-Canadian cultural environment. Their central focus, therefore, is drinking behaviour. Recording the fact that drinking behaviour is sometimes characterized by aggressive and demonstrative action, which contravene the drinking norms of the community, they attempt to explain the surface contradictions in behaviour in terms of the overall normative and behavioural system of the community. They also observe that drinking situations are considerably circumscribed by the economic processes of hunting, fishing, and trapping, and the associated ecological variables. They find that drinking pattern correlates with specific types of life situations.

In a complex analysis, the authors establish the interconnection between this pattern and psychological-normative notions like interdependence, generosity, responsibility, autonomy, emotional restraint, and inter-ethnic relations. Both motives for drinking and the kinds of satisfaction derived present a considerable variety and range. Some of these include generosity, sociability, euphoria and sense of liberation, the need for emotional security arising from drinking in company, affirmation of group solidarity, relief from anxiety, response to certain socially discredited behaviour, status-seeking, and identity-search. In the context of family life, the individual imbibes by the time of adolescence drinking behaviour and a specific cultural definition of drinking. Age and sex are taken into account in drinking behaviour by the authors in their interpretation, but they also note and analyze interfamily differences in such behaviour. They find that there is a general ambiguity in the attitude towards the habit, and attribute this to the opposed effects of the behaviour. In particular, they draw attention to the cultural fact that the indigenous socio-cultural system lacks any structured mechanisms for retraining excesses. There is reliance on the white neighbours restraining mediation. The community's special sensitivity to the white man's critical comments on the behaviour of the Indian, together with the reliance on the former's intervention, contribute to the emergence of an ambivalent orientation towards drinking in the community. At the same time, the socio-cultural functionality of drinking is substantial, and the positive satisfaction derived from it is clearly acknowledged. The main thrust of the paper is to demonstrate the need for analyzing the drinking problem among the Hare Indians in relation to the highly complex cultural ramifications of the drinking pattern, potentially availabe to the members of the community. Further, they also show that the drinking act, within the context of the family, cannot be understood without some understanding of these cultural ramifications.

13. The Kutchin Family: Past and Present

ANN W. ACHESON

INTRODUCTION

The Athapaskan-speaking Kutchin Indians, dwelling in the northwest corner of Canada and adjacent portions of Alaska, have undergone very rapid cultural change since their first contact with the "Whiteman" in the mid-1800s. Family structure, in particular, seems to have undergone a great transformation, as this group of formerly nomadic hunter-gatherers shifted to a way of life first as commercial trappers and, more recently, as sedentary town-dwellers. In this presentation, it will be pointed out that even though the *form* of the marriage and family system has indeed changed under the impact of such things as Christianity and a new economic system, some key *principles* are still important, and provide the Kutchin with an important link with their past. Changes of particular significance include the introduction of wages and government benefits, a declining rate of marriage, and an increase in the number of households headed by women. In discussing the modern period, an attempt will be made to present Kutchin ideals concerning marriage and family, as well as a structural description of various aspects of family life at Old Crow, a Kutchin village of about two hundred inhabitants in the northern Yukon Territory. Some attention will be paid in the concluding section to the much-debated issue of the "matrifocal family," and the degree to which conditions at Old Crow may or may not be promoting this kind of pattern.

The picture given here is drawn from information gathered during nine months of fieldwork in Old Crow in 1968-1969, and from ethnographic and historical sources (Acheson: 1977; Balikci: 1963; Hardisty: 1866; Jones: 1866; Morlan: 1973; Murray: 1910; Nelson: 1973; Osgood: 1936; Slobodin: 1962; Welsh: 1970).[1]

TRADITIONAL KUTCHIN CULTURE

When the Kutchin were first contacted by Whites in the 1840s, they numbered about 1,200 and occupied a total area of about 37,500 km² (Osgood: 1936, p. 15).² Like most other hunting peoples, they lacked any overall sense of "tribal" identity, had no centralized political authority, and never came together as a group. Indeed, the term "Kutchin" is meaningless in the Indians' own language without an attached place designation, such as "Vuntakutchin"—"dwellers among (or at) the lakes."

The largest unit formally recognized by the people themselves were a series of nine "regional bands." Each of these groups was named after the area it habitually used, such as the Peel River, Arctic Red River, Crow Flats region, and so on (Osgood: 1936, pp. 13-15). The population of such a band in traditional times is difficult to estimate, but a range of 150 to 200 seems reasonable (McKennan: 1965, pp. 20-21; Osgood: 1936, p. 15). This kind of organization is quite typical of Northern hunting Indians, as suggested by June Helm (1965: p. 376). She defines a regional band as a group of people (usually named) who share an orientation to an extensive exploitive zone or territory, and who are linked more closely by marriage and kinship to one another than they are to people in other areas. Individuals usually lived their whole lives in the region in which they were born, and ordinarily they married in that area as well. However, membership in a regional band was not fixed or rigid, and individuals or whole families would sometimes move to another region where they had relatives. (In anthropological terms, we would say that regional bands were not corporate groups.) Given the nature of Kutchin subsistence patterns and social structure, members of a regional band did not come together regularly, though at least one band did have a tradition of periodic assembly for trade and large-scale ceremonial (Slobodin: 1962. p. 69).

Over the course of the yearly cycle, the most important unit of economic co-operation was a smaller group, a "local band." Ordinarily, this was made up of closely related families who associated themselves with a successful and respected hunter, considered the group's informal leader. The number of local bands within a given region varied a good deal over the years, and membership in this kind of group was even more fluid than the membership of a regional band. Usually, there were at least two or three local bands in a region, whose members tended to congregate seasonally at certain traditional fishing and caribou hunting sites (McKennan: 1969, p. 104).

The Kutchin's seasonal cycle was like that of most hunting-gathering peoples, with alternating periods of population gathering and dispersal. Their major sources of food were caribou, moose, and fish, with important supplements provided by small game and birds. Exact species used, as well as the seasonal cycle, varied from one regional band to another because of local environmental differences. For the Vunta Kutchin band (in whose area the modern village of Old Crow is located), summer and fall were the best seasons for caribou hunting and fishing. During these times, fairly large groups came together at traditional sites, where communally operated caribou surrounds and fish traps were located. People looked forward to such periods of population concentration, when social ties could be renewed and established through activities such as feasting, trade, courtship, and ceremonies. During much of the year, especially during the long months of winter, people were dispersed in small and isolated groups in search of scarce and scattered game. A single nuclear family could operate on its own, but winter groups of at least two or three families from the same local band were more common.

Cross-cutting the regional bands were three non-localized, exogamous matrilineal clans. That is, individuals inherited permanent clan membership from their mothers, and were supposed to select a spouse from outside their own clan. Besides regulating marriage, clans had specialized duties to perform at certain ceremonies, such as the "death memorial feast." Clans owned no property or territory, and were not particularly important in day-to-day activities, however (Osgood: 1936, pp. 107, 122-123, 128-129).

Girls married shortly after their first menstrual period, while young men usually married later—in their late teens or early twenties—because they had to prove themselves as hunters before they could attract a spouse. Parents or other relatives usually played a large role in arranging marriages, though mutual desire on the part of the young couple was definitely considered (Osgood: 1936, pp. 141-143, 148, 151). Pre-marital sexual relations were not frowned upon, and pregnant brides were apparently not unknown. Since a husband and wife formed an important economic unit, there was a good deal of pressure on young people to get married, and on married people to stay together. In spite of this, there seems to have been a fair degree of marital instability and conflict in traditional times. Early writers on the Kutchin make mention of jealousies, wife stealing, adultery, and wife beating, and a large proportion of inter-group feuds and conflict stemmed initially from controversies regarding marriage or sexual relations (e.g., Hardisty: 1866; Jones: 1866; Murray: 1910). Nonetheless, actual divorce was probably not common, and relatives usually pressured spouses to remain together (Osgood: 1936, p. 144).

Men were allowed to have more than one wife, but this practice of polygymy was not common, because a man had to be an unusually successful hunter and fisherman to be able to support more than one woman and one set of children. Band leaders and those with extraordinary spiritual powers (the shamans) were more apt to be able to support more than one wife (Osgood: 1936, p. 143).

Immediately following marriage, the young couple usually lived with the bride's parents. This period of matrilocal residence would continue at least until the birth of the first child (McKennan: 1965, p. 56). During this time, the young man was expected to "work for" his inlaws, a type of "bride service." Later, the couple could live where they wished, though they almost always chose to camp with close relatives, such as the parents or siblings of either spouse.

At any given time, nuclear families of father, mother, and children predominated, although extended family households of various kinds were not uncommon. It was not that the Kutchin had several different types of families, but rather that the constellation of people belonging to a family unit changed as children grew up, sons-in-law came to do bride service, and relatives attached themselves for varying lengths of time. Regardless of the exact residential arrangement, almost every household (with very few exceptions) had at its core at least one mature male hunter. Although women, children, and elderly people could acquire some food through snaring small game and fishing, it was the male hunter who provided the bulk of the sustenance, and it was his role that was essential for the Kutchin's survival from one season to the next. Elderly people who could no longer provide fully for themselves would be attached to the household of a good hunter, preferably a son or other close relative. Grandparents would sometimes adopt a grandson, who was expected to hunt for his adoptive "parents" when he was able to do so. Widows usually remarried as soon as possible, unless they had adult sons living with them, so that they would not have to be dependent on the generosity of more distant kinsmen, who might themselves have too many mouths to feed.

Sometimes two families would remain together throughout the year in a "paired family" household for purposes of companionship and mutual assistance. The heads of the two families were usually about the same age, and were not necessarily closely related to one another. Such a unit normally occupied a single large skin house, and the members co-operated with one another in economic activities and shared the proceeds of hunting and fishing (Slobodin: 1962, p. 43).

CONTACT WITH THE WHITE WORLD

White explorers and traders began to enter the Kutchin area in the 1800s, followed shortly by missionaries. Major trading posts were established by the Hudson's Bay Company at Fort McPherson, N.W.T., and at Fort Yukon, at the confluence of the Porcupine and Yukon Rivers in what was then Russian Alaska (Osgood: 1936, pp. 17-18; Slobodin: 1962, pp. 22-23). Later, independent traders opened stores in places such as Old Crow. The Royal Canadian Mounted Police also extended their jurisdiction over the area. During this early contact period, which lasted until the latter part of the 1800s, the Indians had only sporadic contact with Whites. Most of the Kutchin were converted to Christianity (some becoming Catholic, others Anglican).

More significant, many Western goods were introduced; most important of these were metal tools, such as knives and axes, along with guns, twine fish nets, and traps. These items made it much easier to cut wood and to acquire food (Balikci: 1963, pp. 36-48 has a detailed description of such changes).

As their desire for trade goods increased, the Kutchin became more and more drawn into commercial trapping. From the late 1800s to the 1940s, fur-trapping was the most important economic activity (Balikci: 1963, chap. 4; Slobodin: 1962, chaps. 5-7).

The fur-trade period saw a large number of changes in Kutchin culture. Besides a shift to more individualistic subsistence techniques, there was a major change in the seasonal round and in the kind of common social groupings. In order to trap, the population had to disperse in small groups of about one to four families, which settled at trapping or fishing camps throughout much of each year. Gatherings now took place at trading post settlements, at times of year determined by the trapping seasons and by Christian holidays. Regional band identification began to break down, to be replaced by a unit based on trading post attendance or residence (Acheson: 1977, pp. 93-95; Slobodin: 1962, chap. 12).

The male hunter-trapper was still the focal point of family structure during the fur-trade period. However, conversion to Christianity and certain economic changes affected the nature of household composition, marriage, and residence arrangements. Polygamy was strongly opposed by the missionaries, and ceased to be practised by the late 1800s (Balikci: 1963, p. 53). Clan organization began to break down, and clan exogamous marriages became less frequent (Acheson: 1977, pp. 119-121). Couples were encouraged to marry within the Church, and divorce was opposed by both Anglican and Catholic missionaries. According to modern informants, pre- and extra-marital sexual activities do not appear to have diminished as a result of the missionaries' teachings. Family histories collected at Old Crow indicate that pregnancy was still a common reason for marriage as recently as the 1950s. Medical care and other services given by the missionaries made life a little easier for the elderly and the needy, thereby reducing somewhat the economic need for certain kinds of extended family households. Individuals who formerly had to accept dependent status in someone else's household began to spend longer times dwelling in relative security at the trading post.

Throughout the fur-trade period, there was a gradual tendency for people to become more and more sedentary. Most of the year was spent either at camps in the bush or at the trading posts. As the fur-trade period drew to a close, families spent longer and longer periods of time at the trading post, and less on the trap lines. Sometimes, women and children would stay at the post, while men went out alone or with partners to trap far from town. During the late 1940s and early 1950s, fur prices began to drop. At the same time, the Canadian Government instituted an accelerated program of assistance for native peoples of the north. Schools, hospitals, communication services, housing, and direct financial benefits, such as family allowances, old age pensions, and welfare assistance, were introduced. More full- and part-time jobs became available at mines, government installations, and in the expanding settlements and towns. By the 1960s and 1970s, almost all of the Canadian Kutchin had shifted to dwelling for most of each year in permanent towns; most are to be found at Old Crow, Y.T., and at Fort McPherson, Aklavik, Inuvik, and Arctic Red River, in the Northwest Territories. A comparable process of sedentarization has taken place in Alaska, though trapping seems to have continued to a greater extent there, and some of the Kutchin settlements are smaller than those in Canada (Nelson: 1973).

THE FAMILY IN OLD CROW VILLAGE: 1968-1969

The village of Old Crow began its existence as a trading post in the first decades of the twentieth century. Located at the junction of the Porcupine and Crow Rivers, it soon attracted members of the Vunta (Crow Flats) and Tukkuth (Upper Porcupine River) bands, who began to trade there in increasing numbers. The establishment of a Royal Canadian Police post and an Anglican mission further enhanced the attraction of the embryo settlement during the 1920s and thereafter. However, even through the 1950s most of the Kutchin in the area around Old Crow still spent most of the year in trapping or fishing camps. In the early 1960s, a combination of factors caused them to all but abandon serious winter trapping and to move to Old Crow. First, low fur prices decreased the attractiveness of trapping. Second, a school and nursing station were built at Old Crow, providing educational and medical services greatly valued by the Kutchin, as well as several additional full- and part-time permanent jobs.

In 1968-1969, when I carried out field research at Old Crow, the "native" population consisted of 186 Indians and Metis, dwelling in 35 long-cabin households.[3] There were also several Canadian Government and private institutions staffed by a rotating group of officials. (In all, there were ten white adults and three children in 1968-1969.) These included a private trading post run by a local Indian man, Anglican and Roman Catholic Missions, and a nursing station, post office, Royal Canadian Mounted Police unit, and a three-room school run by the government. These institutions provided eight full-time, year-round jobs, as well as several permanent part-time ones, for the native residents of the town. Summer employment in construction guiding, scientific research, unloading freight, and other activities provided temporary wages for another significant section of the local male population. About half the families in town in 1968 earned some income from muskratting, and three men trapped for fine furs on a fairly regular basis. Cutting wood for sale, for construction, and firewood, provided an important income supplement in several households. Besides cash income, the people of Old Crow in 1968-1969 still gained a fair portion of their livelihood directly from "the bush." I estimated that close to 50% of the food consumed by people and dogs was acquired through hunting and fishing. Finally, almost every household except young adults with no children received some form of direct or indirect government aid: old age pensions, family allowances, welfare, or housing subsidies.

Old Crow itself has no formal political structure. The Indian-status natives, but not the Metis, are "enrolled" in the "Old Crow Band," which elects a chief and three or four council persons. In 1968-1969, this organization had little real power, however. The Kutchin had never had any kind of formal leadership roles, and are not accustomed to the kinds of structures and procedures introduced by the government. More important, all significant decisions were being made by agencies outside the community, and the local people played only an advisory or consultative role, if that. In the 1970s, there has been some move toward greater political activity, spearheaded by some of the younger, more educated, more widely travelled people whose political activism has been triggered in large part by concern over oil and gas exploration and pipeline survey.[4]

Old Crow is a close-knit settlement. In 1968-1969, there were only four households out of 35 which did not have close, primary links (parent-child or sibling-sibling) with other households. Even people in these four did have distant kinsmen in the village.

The networks of close kin ties are reflected in settlement patterns. Twenty-three of the 35 households in 1968-1969 had dwellings placed close to those of one or more sets of close kinsmen. There were seven such "kin clusters," ranging in size from two to five households, with each household occupying its own cabin (Acheson: 1977, pp. 205-211).

Even though kinship continues to be an important organizing principle at Old Crow, the formal clan organization has all but vanished. Clan exogamy rules are no longer observed, and many younger people do not know their own or their parents' clan membership.

Marriage, family relations, and household composition have changed a good deal in recent years, both according to people alive today and to available written records. Many of these changes are interrelated, but for purposes of clarity I shall first describe them separately, and then point out some of the linkages between them in a general discussion section.

Marriage

There is currently a very low rate of both first marriages and remarriages at Old Crow. Only three marriages took place between 1964 and

1971, and two of these were marriages of White men and Indian women. There is a large proportion of men in Old Crow who have never married, and a growing number of single women. There are also more widows and widowers than there were formerly, according to informants. All told, close to half the adults in 1968 were "unattached" (Acheson: 1977, pp. 211-212).

TABLE 1
MARITAL STATUS, ADULTS AGED 20 AND OVER
DECEMBER 1968

	Men		Women	
Married	20 (50%		20 (54.1%	
Never Married	16 (40%		4 (10.8%	
Separated	2 (5%	50%	3 (8.1%	45.9%
Widowed	2 (5%		10 (27%	
Totals	40 (100%)		37 (100%)	

Marriages are no longer arranged by parents or kinsmen, though in cases of pre-marital pregnancy there is still some pressure applied on the young couple. For example, in 1968 a girl in her late teens became pregnant. She was known to have been going with a young man on a fairly regular basis for some months, and older persons in town assumed that the girl's pregnancy would surely lead to marriage taking place. The young man, however, was apparently reluctant. His uncle told me that he had been asked to speak to young Ben, to try to persuade him to marry Ellen, "because I'm his uncle" (his mother's brother, traditionally an important relationship when the matrilineal clan system was in operation). The marriage did not take place, and the child was born out of wedlock several months later.

Following marriage today, the young couple always sets up its own household, and there is no longer any matrilocal residence. Parents or other close relatives of the bride or groom do often give a house if they are in a position to do so. There was only one instance of a young couple in 1968 living with parents, and this was only for a few months. The son and daughter-in-law in this case usually bought and fixed their own food, and did not appear to contribute anything else to the maintenance of the household.

There is some degree of marital instability at Old Crow (Balikci: 1963, pp. 125-133), though no formal divorces have taken place. In 1968-1969, there were 22 married couples living in the village. Three of these marriages had broken up some years before, and the couples remained permanently separated. Of the remaining couples, at least six of the marriages were, by local standards, "in bad shape," meaning that the spouses live in the same house, but are having serious difficulties. Some forms of intramarital friction are fairly common, and are not con-

sidered by the local people to be "abnormal." This would include behaviour such as loud arguments when the spouses have been drinking,
the "silent treatment" (when one spouse refuses to talk to the other for
a period of days or even longer), or going away on long trips without
the spouse (usually a male ploy). A marriage is considered by the local
people to be in more serious difficulty if there is repeated physical
abuse, or if there are flagrant extramarital relations, especially if the
husband or wife has a steady lover. More subtle signs of marital problems, according to the villagers, are such things as a woman keeping a
very poor house, refusing to cook, sending her children to school in
torn or dirty clothes, or spending a lot of time visiting around town or
attending brew parties. The failure of a man to provide adequate food,
fuel, or other goods for his family is considered a similar sign.

Marital problems are not a new phenomenon to the Kutchin. In particular, recent changes have only exacerbated what continues to be the
most serious cause of marital friction—infidelity. Standards of morality
have probably not changed greatly. Rather, as Balikci points out (1963,
p. 112), "The concentration of all the people . . . in a single locality, Old
Crow, has greatly increased the opportunity for pre- and post-marital
promiscuity." The large proportion of unattached adults, particularly
of unmarried younger men, is also an important factor. One elderly
man at Old Crow phrased it in this way:

> Those young boys and girls, all they do is "walk around" all night.
> There's "fooling around" [the local term for sexual activity of any kind]
> all the time. Older ones too—like that Charlie, all the time after young
> girls, gets them drunk and takes what he wants. My day, everyone
> worked hard, out trapping, snaring rabbits, getting wood—none of this
> living in town business.

This man's wife remarked with a chuckle that before they married,
"Old man, he come back from school, hang around my tent all the time,
try to 'fool around.' Then our parents say we better get married." In
their eyes, pre- and extra-marital sexual behaviour had not changed a
great deal, but the external circumstances surrounding it have, as has
the willingness of individuals to marry.

The influence of kinsmen or respected elders in family relationships
is much less today than it was formerly. Now, neutral parties rarely try
to mediate between husbands and wives, as they did as recently as the
1950s (Acheson: 1977, p. 216). Some White officials and missionaries
at times deplore the "loose morals" of the Indians, but White institutions have not operated in ways to deal effectively with marital problems. For example, the Anglican church (to which all the natives at Old
Crow belong) discourages divorce. The Indians do not now feel that
they can end a bad marriage and begin again with another spouse. Several women who have been separated from their husbands for years
have had a succession of children by different men. These women re-

ported that they have not sought divorce because they believe it is both "immoral" and expensive. Their behaviour would be viewed as scandalous in many White, middle-class circles, yet adultery of this type appears to be considered preferable to divorce.

Illegitimacy
Prior to the introduction of the Christian marriage form, there was no "illegitimacy" in the legal sense among the Kutchin. Women did get pregnant before marriage, but by the time the child was born, a marriage had been arranged. Modern villagers and church and band records suggest that illegitimacy is increasing at Old Crow. If we define an "illegitimate child" as one born to an unwed mother (including widows), thirteen of the 80 children aged 14 and under (or 16.3%) in 1968 were illegitimate. Seven of these were born to young women who had moved away and who brought or sent the children back to be adopted or raised by kinsmen. The other six were born in Old Crow and live with their mothers. One of these is the child of a teenage girl who lives at home with her parents, while the remainder belong to three older women—two widows, and one who has never been married—who each maintain a separate household. Shortly after my departure, three unmarried teenage girls had babies, and there have been more since. There are ten additional children born to women who have long been separated from their husbands. Though not technically "illegitimate," it is common knowledge that these children were not fathered by their mother's legal husband. Adding these with the thirteen discussed above, the illegitimacy rate rises to 28.7%. Finally, it was rumoured that several children in the village were not sired by their legal fathers, even though the husband and wife continued to live together. In a number of these cases, the child was said to bear a strong resemblance to the purported father.[5]

No very great stigma seems to attach to illegitimacy, though being an unwed mother is not considered a desirable state of affairs for a number of reasons. People feel sorry for a woman with no husband, whose children are deprived not only of a father, but of desired products such as meat and fish. There is also some suspicion and a degree of hostility felt by some married women toward those unmarried women who are believed to flaunt their sexuality. One middle-aged woman remarked:

> That Maggie, she and her husband didn't stay together for years. But she's got four kids anyway, and I don't think she knows who's their fathers. Poor kids, their clothes're torn and dirty; sometimes they're so hungry I feel bad and feed them. No daddy, that's not good way.

Whatever degree of disapproval may attach to the mother, the children are spared. No one in town would ever throw up the issue of a child's legitimacy to the child, and there is no arena of native activity where legitimate and illegitimate children are treated any differently.

The one exception to this is the incidence of adoption, to be discussed shortly. Even in several instances where a married woman has borne children by another man, the husband does not overtly seem to mind, and the children are apparently treated no differently from his own.

Adoption
The rate of adoption and the kinds of kin ties between the child and the adoptive parents are much the same as in the past, at least so far as can be reconstructed. There has, however, been a change in the situations under which adoptions take place, and in the legal circumstances. Several case examples will provide a useful background for examining adoption.

Case 1 Charlie and Maggie Robert
According to rumour, Charlie Robert "can't make no kids," though he and his wife do have a natural daughter and son (the latter is rumoured to have been sired by another man, however). Maggie's widowed sister "gave" her son Isaac to be raised by Charlie and Maggie when he was seven or eight, at a time when she was in great economic difficulty. Legally, he is called "Isaac Paul" (his original name), but many in town refer to him as "Isaac Robert," because he has lived in the Robert household so long. Now in his thirties, unmarried and living at home, he calls Maggie and Charlie "Auntie" and "Uncle," though he does not have much to do with his biological mother. He does, however, frequently hunt and undertake other activities with several of his full brothers, who were themselves "adopted" into other households. Next, Maggie's sister-in-law (her brother's wife) gave an infant son, Charlie, to the Robert family. He is always referred to as "Charlie Robert, Jr.," and he calls Charlie and Maggie "Mother" and "Dad." However, like the adoption of Isaac, this was not a formal one, and both young men are listed on the band list by their original names. More recently, Charlie and Maggie acquired a little girl, born out of wedlock at Fort Yukon (Alaska) to a former Old Crow resident. According to one informant, "She was born, and Maggie happened to be over there and she took her." This is also not a legal adoption. Finally, Charlie and Maggie, who were then in their 50s, in 1968 were in the process of legally adopting an infant boy, the illegitimate son of a girl referred to as Maggie's "niece," who is actually Maggie's step-mother's grandaughter, descended from a previous marriage, and not a true biological "niece."

Case 2 A Childless Woman
Rosalie had been married for many years, without bearing any children, when her husband left her. Her sister had many chil-

dren, and gave her one of the older girls a few years ago "because Rosalie was lonely." The girl was in her early teens in 1968, and lived with her adoptive mother, grandfather, and unmarried uncle. One man noted that the adoptive mother was somewhat unstable mentally, and that the girl's parents "could take her back any time because they don't have no papers for it."

Case 3 Illegitimacy

Elizabeth Joe, a young woman who now lives in a large town in the Mackenzie River area, has had three illegitimate sons. She "gave away" all three at Old Crow: two to her parents, and a third to her terminological "aunt" (genealogically, the "aunt" is her grandmother's brother's daughter, in English terminology, her mother's "first cousin"). The boys' grandparents still have many younger children living at home, but they willingly took in the additional youngsters. The "aunt" and her husband had three older (11 to 15 years old) children, but wished to have some more. None of these are legal adoptions.

In the past, "adoption" was considered to have taken place when the parents (or parent, in the case of separation or death of the spouse) gave a child to someone else to raise—usually a close relative. No legal agreement or compensation were involved. A majority of the adoptions in Old Crow still take place in this way, as the above examples illustrate. The nurse, Indian agent, and R.C.M.P., in 1968 were urging people to follow the formal procedures to avoid possible future controversies, misunderstanding, or confusion. Although there are several cases where legal procedures have been followed, there is no great behavioural or conceptual distinction between legal and traditional adoption. All instances where a child is given permanently by its mother to another family are referred to as "adoption" by those who are fluent in English; in all cases the woman is said to have "given away" her child. The more sophisticated people do recognize that the biological parents can reassert their legal claim, if the proper "papers" have not been filed. Indeed, there were at least two cases in the 1960s when this had happened. In one, a woman gave her sister a baby girl, but she did not feel the infant was being properly cared for so she took her back shortly and gave her away to someone in Inuvik. In another instance, Miss Edith Josie describes how she gave away her newborn son:[6] "At 8:30 p.m. I had baby boy and he's 6 lb. Miss Edith Josie had baby boy and I gave it to Mrs. Ellen Abel to have him for her little boy. She was very glad to have him cause he's boy." (Josie: 1966, p. 23) (Mrs. Abel had two older girls at the time.) For reasons unknown to me, Miss Josie took back her son, and was raising him with her other two children.

There were 108 children and young people under age 19 in 1968, of whom 12 (or 11%) were adopted. As in the past, almost all were adopted by close relatives, the grandparents being the most common (three cases), followed by aunts (mother's sister and father's sister), two cases.

As in the past, children are highly desired, and couples who remain childless usually make an effort to adopt. They almost always find someone who is willing to "give away" a child, preferably a newborn or an infant. Elderly couples or individuals still sometimes adopt a school-age grandson or other kinsman, with the expectation that he will hunt for them when he becomes a young man.

Formerly, poverty was an important factor forcing people to give up their children. Widows who did not remarry right away were in especially bad circumstances, and often had to "give away" one or more children (as in the case of Isaac Paul, example 1). Eleven persons living at Old Crow in 1968 had been adopted during the period from the 1880s through the 1950s. Almost all had been orphans, or had one parent deceased, or came from very poor families. All were legitimate. At present, an increasing proportion of children offered for adoption are illegitimate—seven out of twelve in 1968-1969. To some extent, Old Crow is becoming a haven for illegitimate children born to women who have moved away from town (see Cases 1 and 3, for example). Such women still have strong ties to the village, and see it as a desirable place to have their children raised. Poverty is rarely cited today as a reason for giving up children, now that people are living in town and government financial aid is available for dependent children.

Adopted children are reportedly treated in the family exactly as non-adopted ones, unless they are adopted when they are over five or six years of age. No instances were observed where adopted children received overtly differential treatment in the household. No attempt is made to conceal the fact that a person was adopted or raised by someone else. Both the child and the rest of the villagers usually know who the biological parents are.[7] Adoptive parents are addressed as parents if the child is adopted as an infant or toddler. If the child comes to the family at an older age, kin terms designating the original relationship are usually used, for example "grandfather," "aunt," and so on (see Case 1).

Household composition
In the past, as we have seen, households were almost always headed by men. Nuclear families were the ideal, but there was probably a substantial minority of paired family households at any given time. There were also variations from the "ideal," due to the normal developmental cycle of the family. For example, at some point there might be a married daughter and son-in-law living matrilocally, or there might be a dependent elderly or orphaned relative attached for a short time.

Today, paired family households no longer exist. Furthermore, there is no longer any matrilocal residence. The number of simple nuclear families has gone down, however, informants believe. While it is impossible to verify their impressions with hard data from the past, in 1968 only slightly over half (57%) of the households in Old Crow were of the nuclear family type (mother, father, and children); and two of these might technically be considered extended families, since they also included grandchildren.[8] One especially significant change is the relatively large proportion of households headed by women (37%), a situation almost unknown in traditional times (See Table 2).

TABLE 2
HOUSEHOLD COMPOSITION, 1968

Nuclear Family Households	Number
(a) With young children only	11
(b) Including adult children*	6
(c) Three generational, including grandchildren**	2
(d) No children	1
	20 (57%)

Female-Headed Households	
(a) Widows alone	3
(b) Widows with adult, unmarried children	5
(c) Widows and young children	1
(d) Separated from husband or never married***	4
	13 (37%)

Widowers	
(a) Man plus grandchildren	1
(b) Man, adult children, adopted grandchild	1
	2 (6%)

   * Includes elderly couple with adult adopted grandson.
  ** One case involves children of a daughter living outside Old Crow; the other involves teenage daughter with her illegitimate infant.
*** One contains a woman, her children, and her brother (separated from wife).

Household size also seems to have changed, though this is even more difficult to substantiate, since accurate figures for the traditional period are lacking. However, according to elderly individuals now living at Old Crow, there are today more very small (one or two person) and very large households than there were in the past (Table 3).

TABLE 3
HOUSEHOLD SIZE, 1968

No. of People	1	2	3	4	5	6	7	8	9	12	16	186
No. of Households	3	5	6	2	4	2	3	6	2	1	1	35

Average Per Household = 5.31   Totals

One important fact which is not evident from the above tables is the increase in the proportion of households containing attached, single, able-bodied adults (almost entirely men). It is not at all uncommon to have a household headed by an aged man or woman, with an unmarried son or sons living at home. In fact, in 1968 there were no unmarried individuals living alone or maintaining a permanent separate household.[9] (Some unmarried men did live alone when they were in the bush, however.) (Acheson: 1977, p. 225.) Unmarried individuals in the past did not usually maintain separate households either. However, marriage took place at an early age, so there were formerly few unmarried young adults, and the kind of situation common at Old Crow today did not exist.

The recent pattern may be partly due to shortage of housing, since Balikci found single men living alone to a greater degree in 1961—six out of the forty houses or tents being occupied by single men (Balikci: 1963, p. 130). However, the fact that single men in 1968—even those in their forties—were seemingly content to live with their parents is still significant. These men could have built houses or set up tents for themselves, but were not doing so.[10]

Such single men are attached to their parents' households not only by virtue of co-residence. Many are also dependent on their parents for support to at least some degree. The majority of these unmarried men do not have regular local jobs, since preference in such positions is given to men with families to support. They do provide labour, wood, meat, and fish to the household in many cases. However, it is the elderly parents, with their monthly old-age pension (and sometimes a government-built house) who have the regular income and who are considered to head the household. Interestingly, there are two men permanently separated from their spouses who are both also living as attached household members with kinsmen who are considered to head the household. (One lives with his elderly mother, the other with an unmarried sister who is receiving family allowance and welfare aid for her illegitimate minor children; the women in both instances are considered by the native community members to be the owners of the house.) In contrast, the three separated women do receive regular monthly government aid, and each owns a house and heads her own household.

Discussion
The major structural changes in Kutchin family and marriage pratices may be briefly summarized: the abolition of polygymy, disappearance of the paired family household, breakdown of clan exogamy, decline in the importance of matrilocal residence, and the introduction of formal Christian marriage practices. Several statistical tendencies evident at Old Crow are also highly significant: the low rate of new marriages and remarriages; the increase in illegitimacy; the high incidence of female-headed households; and the apparent change in household size.

The factors behind these statistical tendencies are interrelated, and deserve further examination. To a great extent, these tendencies may be seen as responses by the Kutchin to the changed economic and social circumstances brought about by sedentary village dwelling and by government benefits and wages. The story is certainly not a unique one, and similar processes are at work throughout the Canadian North, and in many other parts of the world.

Simply put, the introduction of wages and of government aid and other benefits has greatly reduced people's reliance on making a living off the land. This has combined with changes introduced by other sources, for example, education and conversion to Christianity, to lead to a breakdown of the older social and family structure which had been based on the necessity for economic co-operation and for social flexibility in the face of harsh environmental circumstances.

The impact of wages, government benefits, and a sedentary existence on household size is relatively easy to understand. With regular medical attention and the more secure circumstances of town living, infant mortality has been greatly decreased (Acheson: 1977, pp. 267-268), and many more people survive into old age. With more surviving children (and the continuation of older adoption practices), household size at the upper end of the range has increased a good deal. The larger number of old people now also have regular pensions and usually free housing as well. This enables them to maintain themselves separate from kinsmen, and helps account for the increase in numbers of very small households, most of which are composed of elderly persons. Thus, government benefits and medical care have increased the proportion of both very large and very small households.

The presence of government benefits is also a significant factor in explaining the low rate of marriage, the increase in female-headed households, and the increase in illegitimacy. However, these are interconnected phenomena, and cannot be understood solely with reference to the availability of these benefits.

It is easy to understand how a low rate of marriage, combined with the Kutchin's traditional sexual morality, leads to an increase in illegitimacy. There is probably a relationship between the low rate of marriage and the high incidence of female-headed households, but this is a much less obvious relationship. What is clear is that elderly widows or women with children but no husbands always form independent households. In 1968-69, there was only one instance of such a woman (actually a teenage girl) living as a dependent in someone else's household, in contrast to the situation among unmarried men. These women are economically able to maintain separate households, and at least some of them prefer this kind of living arrangement. Widows or women with children are assured of a cash income and other benefits. All of the younger widows and a majority of the older ones reported that they prefer their independent state, and had turned down offers of marriage.

If the low rate of marriage is connected with a rise in the rate of illegitimacy and of female-headed households, a critical question then becomes: What causes the low rate of marriage in the first place? First, the ready availability of sexual partners in the permanent town setting removes one of the former incentives for marriage. More important, the economic circumstances are very different today. Having a spouse is no longer necessary for survival as it once was when the Kutchin lived in the bush. However, marriage still brings certain economic responsibilities, especially after children are born. One of the problems is that the economic situation of the young men is generally so uncertain that many appear to be reluctant to marry. Younger men, who have spent most of their growing-up years either in town or away at school, lack many of the bush skills which would enable them to trap, even if fur prices should continue to rise as they began to in the early 1970s; many of these young men are not even especially productive at hunting and fishing. The number of regular jobs available in town is small, and these are already held by the older married men.[11] One might ask if the young men would marry if their economic circumstances were to improve. While this cannot be predicted exactly, I have a distinct impression that some men, at least, are not all that unhappy in their present, relatively carefree, unmarried state.

Even in cases where a man gets a woman pregnant, marriage is not taking place as it used to. (See example of Ben and Ellen, page 248.) The men involved offered two kinds of reasons. First, in a few instances the man argued that he could not be sure he was the father, since the woman had ostensibly had sexual relations with several men. Since this kind of sexual activity probably took place in the past also, this excuse may reflect the adoption of at least certain aspects of Christian morality and the Western double standard. More significant, the men involved, and other villagers as well, pointed out that "the Indian agent" (i.e., the government) would "take care of" children with no father in the household. Being an unwed mother at Old Crow is far from an ideal condition, but women and children with no male provider can today at least survive in relative comfort.

Finally, the experiences of young men and women outside Old Crow are affecting their decisions about marriage. Both boys and girls now go away to high school in Whitehorse, and many of them have work experiences there and in other towns. Women, interestingly, seem to make a better adjustment to living away from Old Crow, and are less apt to return than men are. For one thing, there is a shortage of women in most larger northern towns and cities, so women from Old Crow have a better chance of finding regular employment than do the men. They also have an easier time than men in finding spouses or, more frequently, partners with whom to set up a temporary living arrangement (see Cruikshank: 1976, for a discussion of Indian women living in Whitehorse, Y.T.). Even when young men do find employment, many of them do not like life "on the outside." Drinking is a major problem, as is the prejudice which they face in larger, White-dominated towns. Younger women have acquired certain economic and romantic aspirations which local boys and men find difficult to satisfy. In spite of some of their aspirations, however, most girls in their late teens and early twenties at Old Crow reported that they would prefer to marry locally and remain in town.[12] If a young woman does not marry, she may leave the village when she is in her mid-twenties to seek employment or romantic opportunities elsewhere. It is noteworthy that only one of the four never-married women in town was past her early twenties in 1968, while half (eight) of the men were in this age category.

In short, an unmarried man who leaves Old Crow is apt to return unmarried and stay that way. If a woman leaves Old Crow, she is more apt to remain "outside." If she returns unmarried, she does not usually find anyone satisfactory in Old Crow who is willing to marry her. The result is a high rate of unmarried people in the village.

Even though marriage is not as much of an economic necessity as it once was, and even though there is now a high rate of unmarried people, most Kutchin still believe marriage to be the normal state of affairs for an adult. Marriage is still considered to be a serious undertaking, requiring responsibility and maturity. Children are especially valued, as we have seen, and adults who neglect their responsibilities to their youngsters are condemned by young and old alike. Because of this continuation of the traditional Kutchin ideology concerning marriage, those who have never married occupy a rather anomalous position. For example, in 1968-1969, unmarried men, even those in their thirties and forties, rarely spoke at band meetings, and only one had been elected to band office. Furthermore, unmarried men are much less apt to hold regular jobs or to engage in serious trapping (Acheson: 1977, pp. 178-182). Unmarried women are never fully accepted as full members of women's groups or gatherings. Following the older Kutchin principle, marriage, especially when followed by children, still confers full adult status.[13] Once a person has married, this status is never taken away, even in cases of separation or the death of the spouse. Hence, widowed or separated women, who are now economically in a much better position than they were formerly, do not have a great incentive to remarry. Almost all the female-headed households are headed by women in this category, with only the one headed by a woman who has never married.

CONCLUSIONS

One of the key principles underlying past and present Kutchin family structure and behaviour is that of flexibility. Recent anthropological studies on family and social structure among hunting-gathering groups living under severe environmental circumstances have stressed the long-term adaptive advantages of such structural and behavioural flexibility (see, for example, Damas: 1969; Helm: 1965; articles in Lee and

DeVore: 1968; McElroy: 1975; Savishinsky: 1970, 1974). The variability of family types in the past, the lack of rigid social structural principles, and the responsiveness of the family to introduced changes in the present give evidence for this kind of flexibility among the Kutchin.

In the past, the adult male hunter provided the bulk of the Kutchin's subsistence. He was the focal point around whom the family—in all its various types—was organized. With the decline in importance of wages and government benefits, the male hunter-trapper is no longer this kind of "focal point." On an ideological level, however, the family is still seen as a unit in which an adult man is the "rustler," the provider. Today, he must "rustle" not only meat, fish, and wood, but cash as well. In several Old Crow families, the male household head did not have a regular job in 1968-1969, though he worked hard at hunting, fishing, woodcutting, and trapping; these families were said to be "very poor." In other words, the Kutchin have become involved in the White man's economy and have acquired certain material aspirations which cannot be satisfied by bush activities alone. Indeed, it would almost seem that they have come to value regular cash income more highly than the products they derive from the bush. Money is in many ways easier (or less risky) to obtain than game, fish, and furs; certainly the returns from wage employment or government benefits are more predictable than those from hunting, fishing, or trapping. It was noted earlier that unemployed, unmarried men who live with their elderly parents are not considered household heads, even if they provide most of the meat, fish, wood, and labour, since it is the parents who have the regular cash income and who own the house.

On the surface, it would appear that these are massive—if not potentially disruptive—changes. However, several important organizing principles of the Kutchin family remain remarkably the same. Formation and continuity of a family are still based on a concept of regular income. Today, with wages and government benefits, money is a much surer source of family security than the "income" of animals, fish, and furs. Because of the addition of this new kind of income, the role of provider is no longer as focused on mature men. The channelling of regular income in the household unit can take place through categories of persons who had never before been able to perform this function: unmarried women or widows with children, the disabled, and the elderly of both sexes.

Ideologically, highest prestige still attaches to the male-hunter role, yet pragmatically the Kutchin also recognize that money is a necessity if they are to obtain the goods and supplementary foods they desire. Thus, the ideal household is one in which there is an adequate balance between cash income and desired bush products. Female-headed households or those of elderly persons with no younger male hunter are far from the ideal in this regard. No matter how much cash is coming in, most women and older people do not do enough hunting or fishing to satisfy their family's desires. As in the past, such women or older people are dependent at least to some degree on the generosity of kinsmen (or lovers), though they would not starve without it.

There has been some suggestion that rapid acculturation and government policies may be producing an increase in the true "matrifocal family" type among Northern natives (e.g., Balikci: 1963, pp. 130-133; Cruikshank: 1976). The household picture at Old Crow in some ways seems to support this. However, there are several factors which complicate this generalization. First, there is a definitional and structural issue. Are all kinds of households headed by females truly "matrifocal"? There is no doubt that there are more female-headed households than there were formerly among the Kutchin. However, unlike the situation among certain groups of New World Blacks, there are no three generation matrifocal households (grandmother, mother, children, with no permanent male members) (Henriques: 1953; Queen and Habenstein: 1967, p. 329). Furthermore, in most families classified elsewhere as matrifocal, there are usually males, more likely a succession of males who live or visit in the household, whether as legal husbands or as lovers (Ashcraft: 1968; Cruikshank: 1976; Gonzales: 1970). In Old Crow this is not the case. There are currently no unmarried, widowed, or separated women with unrelated men living in the household. (Though there was at least one instance of such an arrangement in the recent past, the woman in question had returned to her legal husband by 1968-1969). Nancy Gonzales offers a more functional characterization of matrifocality, relating the concept to "female stability, role dominance, and authority patterns" (1970, p. 238). The female-headed households at Old Crow do not currently fit this characterization either, though it is possible that they could evolve in that direction over a period of time. Although the "matrifocal" households among Indians in Whitehorse reported by Cruikshank come somewhat closer to Gonzales's model, the pattern may only be a temporary one, an "adaptive response to a changing and often stressful situation" (Cruikshank: 1976, p. 119).

Second, there is the question of Kutchin norms. In spite of the fact that an increasing number of people are remaining unmarried or are choosing not to remarry, marriage is still deemed to be an important institution. The Kutchin at Old Crow still maintain that it is improper for a man and woman to live together without benefit of marriage, and they speak disparagingly of Indians in larger towns who do this. Pre- and extra-marital sexual activities are still carried out with a marked degree of secretiveness, even when a man and woman have a long-standing relationship. The nuclear family type of household is still considered the ideal type, though another acceptable alternative is one where there is an adult male hunter (for example, an elderly widow with her unmarried son).

At the same time, some individuals are indeed beginning to worry about what the future will bring, given current marital patterns and family structure. The pace of change and pressures from the "outside" have increased greatly in recent years. Many Old Crow residents, for example, are fearful that oil and gas exploration, the building of a pipeline, or other "industrial" developments might spell the end of their society as they know it today. Stager (1974, pp. 197-200) reports that their concerns focus around increased drinking, the possible presence of large numbers of single male workers from "outside," and the effects of both of these on family life.

Clearly, the family as it exists today among the Old Crow Kutchin is in a precarious balance. There is an increasing gap between an older ideology and a newer form of family structure where there is no longer as clear-cut a focus around the male-provider status. In other areas, loss or drastic change in the male-provider role has often been said to lead to rapid disintegration of family functioning, as well as to other major social and psychological problems, such as violence, alcoholism, mental illness, child abuse and neglect, and so on (see, for example, Mac-Gregor: 1946; Moynihan: 1965; L. Spindler: 1962; TenHouten: 1970). So far, however, the Old Crow Kutchin seem to have escaped many of these negative features associated with rapid change in family structure. Overall, they seem to be making a fairly successful adaptation to the new circumstances of their society and economy. "Success" here is used in a relative sense, and may be measured in at least two ways: first, with regard to the Kutchin's own perception of their current situation, and second, with reference to conditions among other comparable groups.

Without exception, all persons interviewed expressed their general satisfaction with life in Old Crow, though there were of course various minor specific complaints. Material well-being and security were the main positive factors stressed. When one remembers that starvation haunted the Kutchin until as recently as the 1930s, one can perhaps understand why they place such emphasis on the security offered by their current way of life. A middle-aged man, after describing how he and his family nearly starved in the 1930s when they were out trapping, concluded:

> I like the way it is now. No one's ever hungry, got plenty of grub. Our kids aren't going to be like us—they'll get education, get good jobs. Used to be a lot of kids died. Sometimes a family might have ten kids, and pretty soon there'd only be two left. Now, there's nurse and hospital. We got lights, airplane, everything.

Traditional social science measures of "social breakdown" (for example, incidence of alcoholism and mental illness, divorce rates, crime, and so on) confirm the judgment of the Old Crow Kutchin. When compared with native people in many other northern communities, those in Old Crow are clearly making a more successful adaptation to the rapid changes in the context and fabric of their society (see, for example, Clairmont: 1962, 1963; Honigmann: 1965; Wintrob: 1968). The Kutchin's isolation has probably been a significant factor affecting the nature of change in the family, as has their continued residence in their traditional homeland. Changes in the family and in other aspects of Kutchin culture have not come about through the massive influx of members of a dominant culture, as happened in so many native North American groups further south. Rather, the family has so far been able to adapt to changing social and economic conditions through a process which has been called acculturation "at a distance" (Dunning: 1959, p. 208). External conditions and family forms are continuing to change, but certain important core values concerning children, the importance of economic security, and the preservation of the village continue to be important factors influencing the future direction of change among the Old Crow Kutchin.

NOTES

1. Fieldwork on which this article is based was carried out under a predoctoral grant from the United States National Institute of Health. James M. Acheson and Toby Lazarowitz provided helpful commentary on preliminary drafts; deficiencies in this version are, of course, solely my responsibility. To protect confidentiality, names of Old Crow villagers mentioned have been changed, unless otherwise noted. The present tense used here refers generally to the 1968-1969 period.

2. The easternmost bands, near the Mackenzie River, were the first to be contacted, and were referred to by early visitors as "Loucheux." This appellation is still used in that area to some extent.

3. In the Mackenzie River area, "half-breeds" are usually referred to as "Metis." Although the term Metis is not in general use at Old Crow, it will be used henceforth here, as it is a more respectable alternative than "half-breed." Thirty-eight of the 186 natives had White ancestry on the paternal side, and were legally classified as "White"; this is the group that will be here referred to as Metis. Socially and culturally, the Metis are to some degree "middlemen" between the White and Indian worlds. Most of the general information contained here, however, applies to the Metis at Old Crow, as well as to those who are legally "Indian." For further discussion on the Old Crow situation see Acheson: 1977, pp. 190-193; and on those of the nearby Mackenzie River area, Slobodin: 1966.

4. Although the Kutchin never signed a treaty ceding over their lands, the area is nonetheless considered by the Canadian government to be its property. Oil leases, etc., are signed by the government, not by the Kutchin. The legal status of Kutchin lands remains an open issue at the time of this writing. See Stager: 1974 for a recent study of issues related to Old Crow and the northern gas pipeline.

5. Balikci, who worked at Old Crow in the summer of 1961, groups all these categories together as "illegitimate." Following that procedure, in 1961 he found that 39 out of 94 children and young people (or 41%) were illegitimate (Balikci: 1963, 128).

6. Edith Josie has been writing an Old Crow news column for the *Whitehorse* (Y.T.) *Star* since 1962. A collection of her articles was published in book form.

7. In a very few of the recent cases, the biological father is not known to the villagers at large, though the biological mother and the adoptive parents usually know. This situation is more apt to occur if the woman became pregnant while away from town.

8. The household picture at Old Crow lends support to Ishwaran's generalization that urbanization and industrialization do not "inevitably push the familial form in the direction of nuclearity" (1976: 26).

9. "Unmarried" here means never married. Widows, widowers, and women with children but no husbands maintained their own separate households.

10. There was a new government house-building program after my period of fieldwork. Many families moved into new houses in the 1970s. Old cabins which were not torn down appear to have been occupied by some of the single men. Stager's 1973 map shows that eight houses were then technically *owned* by single men, but he does not make clear whether the houses were actually *occupied* by these men.

11. A comparable situation among the Inuit of Pangnirtung and Frobisher Bay is discussed by McElroy (1975).

12. Since I did not interview young women who had moved away from Old Crow permanently, I am unable to report on their attitudes toward marriage. There is some discussion of this in Cruikshank (1976).

13. There is one case of an older woman who has never married, but who has several illegitimate children. She appears to be on an equal footing with married women her age, and has even held the prestigious office of president of the local church Women's Auxilliary.

REFERENCES

Acheson, Ann W.
　1977　*Nomads in Town: The Kutchin of Old Crow, Yukon Territory,* Unpublished Ph.D dissertation, Cornell University.

Ashcraft, Norman
　1968　"Some Aspects of Domestic Organization in British Honduras." In *The Family in the Caribbean,* edited by Stanford N. Gerber. Rio Piedras, Porto Rico: Institute of Caribbean Studies.

Balikci, Asen
　1963　*Vunta Kutchin Social Change.* Ottawa: Northern Coordination and Research Centre, Department of Northern Affairs and National Resources, NCRC-63-3.

Clairmont, D. H. J.
　1962　*Notes on the Drinking Behaviour of Eskimos and Indians in the Aklavik Area.* Ottawa: Northern Coordination and Research Centre, Department of Northern Affairs and National Resources, NCRC-62-4.

　1963　*Deviance Among Indians and Eskimos in Aklavik, N.W.T.* Ottawa: Northern Coordination and Research Centre, Department of Northern Affairs and National Resources, NCRC-63-9.

Cruikshank, Julie
　1976　"Matrifocal Families in the Canadian North." In *The Canadian Family* (revised ed.), edited by K. Ishwaran. Toronto: Holt, Rinehart and Winston of Canada.

Damas, David, (ed.)
 1969   Contributions to Anthropology: Band Societies. Ottawa: National Mu-
         seums of Canada, Bulletin 228, Anthropological Series 84.

Dunning, R. W.
 1959   Social and Economic Change Among the Northern Ojibwa. Toronto:
         University of Toronto Press.

Gonzales, Nancy L.
 1970   "Toward a Definition of Matrifocality." In Afro-American Anthropol-
         ogy: Contemporary Perspectives, edited by Norman E. Whitten and
         John F. Szwed. New York: Free Press.

Helm, June
 1965   "Bilaterality in the Socio-Territorial Organization of the Arctic Drain-
         age Dene." Ethnology 4(4): 361-385.

Henriques, Fernando
 1953   Family and Colour in Jamaica. London: Eyre and Spottiswoode.

Honigmann, John J.
 1965   "Social Disintegration in Five Northern Canadian Communities."
         Canadian Review of Sociology and Anthropology 2(4): 199-214.

Ishwaran, K., (ed.)
 1976   The Canadian Family (revised ed.). Toronto: Holt, Rinehart and Win-
         ston of Canada.

Jones, Strachan
 1866   "The Kutchin Tribes." Washington, D.C.: Smithsonian Institution,
         Annual Report for 1866: 320-327.

Josie, Edith
 1966   Here Are the News. Toronto: Clarke, Irwin and Co.

Lee, Richard B. and Irven DeVore, (eds.)
 1968   Man the Hunter. Chicago: Aldine.

MacGregor, Gordon
 1946   Warriers Without Weapons: A Study of the Society and Personality of
         the Pine Ridge Sioux. Chicago: University of Chicago Press.

McElroy, Ann
 1975   "Arctic Modernization and Change in the Inuit Family." In Marriage,
         Family and Society, edited by S. Parvez Wakil. Toronto: Butterworth
         and Co. (Canada).

McKennan, Robert A.
 1965   The Chandalar Kutchin. Montreal: Arctic Institute of North America,
         Technical Paper 17.

 1969   "Athapaskan Groupings and Social Organization in Central Alaska."
         In Contributions to Anthropology: Band Societies, edited by David
         Damas. Ottawa: National Museums of Canada, Bulletin 228, Anthro-
         pological Series 84: 93-114.

Morlan, Richard
  1973 The Later Prehistory of the Middle Porcupine Drainage, Yukon Terri-
        tory, Canada. Ottawa: National Museums of Canada, Mercury Series,
        Paper No. 11.

Moynihan, Daniel P.
  1965 The Negro Family: The Case for National Action. Washington, D.C.:
        Government Printing Office.

Murray, Alexander H.
  1910 Journal of the Yukon, 1847-48. Ottawa: Publications of the Canadian
        Archives, 4.

Nelson, Richard K.
  1973 Hunters of the Northern ForeSt. Chicago: University of Chicago
        Press.

Osgood, Cornelius
  1936 Ethnography of the Kutchin. New Haven: Yale University Publica-
        tions in Anthropology 14.

Queen, Stuart A., and Robert W. Habenstein
  1967 The Family in Various Cultures (third ed.) New York: J. B. Lippincott
        Company.

Savishinsky, Joel S.
  1970 "Kinship and the Expression of Values in an Athabascan Bush Com-
        munity." Western Canadian Journal of Anthropology 2(1): 31-59.

  1974 The Trail of the Hare; Life and Stress in an Arctic Community. New
        York: Gordon and Breach.

Slobodin, Richard
  1962 Band Organization of the Peel River Kutchin. Ottawa: National Muse-
        ums of Canada, Bulletin 179, Anthropological Series 55.

  1966 Metis of the Mackenzie District. Ottawa: Canadian Research Centre for
        Anthropology, Saint-Paul University.

Spindler, Louise
  1962 Menomini Women and Culture Change. American Anthropological
        Association, Vol. 64 (1) (Part 2), Memoir 91.

Stager, J. K.
  1974 Old Crow, Y.T. and the Proposed Northern Gas Pipeline. Environ-
        mental Social Committee, Northern Pipelines Task Force on Northern
        Oil Development, Report 74-21 (Information Canada, Cat. No. 72-
        139/1974).

TenHouten, Warren D.
  1970 "The Black Family: Myth and Reality." Psychiatry 33(2): 145-155.

Welsh, Ann
  1970 "Community Pattern and Settlement Pattern in the Development of
        Old Crow Village." Western Canadian Journal of Anthropology 2(1):
        17-30.

14. The Inuit Family: Past, Present, and Future

JOHN S. MATTHIASSON

Human societies have invented a variety of ingenious forms for the care and nurturance of the young, and the creation and maintenance of links between biologically related individuals and groups. Theoretically, one could conceive of an even wider range of social units designed to provide for these social needs, but empirically there are, in fact, limits which these social units, popularly called families, have taken. Anthropologists have been able to group "real" families into a typology of four classifications, one of which is termed the Eskimo type. This type obviously is named after the basic social unit found among the Inuit of the arctic regions of North America and Greenland. It is a form with which most Canadian readers will be familiar, for the typical Euro-Canadian family falls within the Eskimo category.

The Eskimo family[1] is one in which relationships are given equal importance on both the mother's and father's side. Descent and inheritance are passed on through both lines. The individual unmarried male or female, then, is the centre of a kinship unit, or family, which is only a social group for the individual, his or her unmarried siblings, and the parents, or if married, his or her spouse and their unmarried children. The classic nuclear family, then, is the basic unit of the family if the society follows the Eskimo pattern, and the Inuit do. The equal importance of both sides, father's and mother's, is dramatized by the kin terms used within the family unit, and in fact it is the use of a particular kin nomenclature which is the basis for our classifying a particular family system as being Eskimo or one of the other three basic types. In particular, the same term is used to apply to the children of the siblings of both father and mother, or those we call "cousins" in English, irrespective of the sex of the person to whom reference is being made or that of any connecting relatives. Similarly, siblings of both parents are given the same term, although a sex distinction is made, as we do in English with our words "aunt" and "uncle."

The Eskimo family, then, is one with which most readers of Euro-Canadian background will already be familiar. It is typical of the one in which they were socialized and enculturated themselves. But these are the bare essentials. A composite portrait of the traditional Inuit family of arctic Canada must be fleshed out if it is to have anything more than mere classificatory value. I will examine several matters in trying to present a fuller, yet of necessity abbreviated, picture of both the traditional and the "modern" Inuit family. There are regional variations in Inuit family structure, kinship terminology, patterns of reciprocity, and so on, and when it is felt to be necessary, these will be mentioned, but in general I shall try more to demonstrate commonalities. The materials upon which I draw in attempting this wider portrayal are, of course, taken from specific studies of particular regions, or often, small, localized communities. I hope that I shall not commit too much violence to the differences while trying to illustrate similarities. I think that most observers of the Canadian arctic will agree that variations of cultural and social forms in this vast geographical area are less apparent than constancies.

In a much-quoted phrase, Kaj Birket-Smith once said that the Inuit live on the fringe of habitation and the edge of the habitable. In this paper I will concentrate on the Inuit of arctic Canada, but it should be remembered that Inuit with almost identical cultural forms live in Greenland, mainly on the southwestern coast of that glacier-covered island; in Alaska; on islands in the Bering Sea which separates North America from Siberia; and in Siberia itself. Many of the generalizations I will make can, then, also be applied to the Greenlanders and to a lesser degree to the peoples of northern Alaska. All three—the peoples of Greenland, arctic Canada, and northern Alaska—are Inupik speakers who share a common language, although with some dialectical variations, and have cultural and social similarities. The Eskimo peoples of southern Alaska[2] are Yupik speakers and are, in many respects, culturally and socially different from the others already mentioned. Differences are also found when we look across the Bering Sea to the Siberian Eskimo.

I have emphasized similarity rather than variation among the Inuit populations of Canada. One important geographical and ecological variation should be mentioned, though, and that is between coastal Inuit and the Caribou Inuit who traditionally inhabited the interior to the west of Hudson Bay. With this exception, however, in an ecological sense the people whose family structure concerns us are coastal peoples, highly adapted to coastal living. Some cultural variation is also found along the Quebec coast in what is now called Nouveau Quebec

and into Labrador, but here again similarity is more striking than variation.

THE TRADITIONAL INUIT FAMILY

It is difficult to describe in proper anthropological perspective the
structure and functions of the traditional pre-contact and early contact
Inuit nuclear and extended families. Our earliest reports come from explorers and whalers, the first in search of the Northwest Passage, and
the latter in quest of the whale, which was so prized by nineteenth century western Europeans and North Americans. In neither instances
were these early depictors of Inuit life trained observers. Like others
who made the first forays into the regions of aboriginal peoples around
the world, they noticed and emphasized what they considered to be the
exotic and unusual. And so practices among the Inuit, such as wife exchange, are described in many early accounts, but there is little information on the more mundane and day-to-day patterns of Inuit family
life. Fortunately, these first observers of the Canadian Inuit were soon
replaced by others who had a more scientific orientation, such as Knud
Rasmussen (1927), Vilhjalmur Stefansson (1921), and Franz Boas
(1888), and because major outside intrusions into the region of the
Canadian arctic have not been extensive until the past twenty years or
so, the lifestyles recorded by these first arctic ethnographers had
changed little from those of the pre-contact period.

It was mentioned before that the basic social unit among the Inuit
was the nuclear family. Asen Balikci has criticized the interpretation
that kinship is the basic ordering principle among the Inuit, correctly
pointing out that the limiting ability of a bilateral kinship structure to
create extended alliances among individuals and groups, in an environment in which such relationships of reciprocity are critical for survival, necessitates an emphasis on other, non-kin relationships (Balikci: 1970, p. 94). Partnerships between individuals were indeed
important among all Inuit, not only the Netsilik described by Balikci.
These dyadic relationships will be discussed later, but regardless of
their importance, the individual received his or her main source of
identity from a kin-based ascribed position within the larger group,
and partnerships themselves were often predicated on connections of
kinship, or mediated within kin units.

THE INUIT NUCLEAR FAMILY

Within the nuclear family, the basic division of labour, common to
hunting societies around the world, was drawn along lines of sex.
Some observers have claimed that women in Inuit society were highly
subordinated to men, and played only a minor role in subsistence activities. After all, this is a hunting society, and women typically do not
hunt. They did take part in the basic economic activities, though, and

their labours in this area were respected and valued by males. It was the responsibility of the male to "bring home the bacon," in the form of seal, walrus, caribou, ptarmigan, arctic hare, and so on. But fishing was also a major source of food, and women collaborated in fishing activities, in particular among the interior peoples. Women helped build the stone weirs, for example, which trapped fish swimming upriver to the spawning grounds, and on occasion participated in the catch as well.

When the carcasses had been brought home by the men, if they had not been buried in caches for later retrieval during times of food shortage, it was the women who often butchered them. It was always the women who cleansed the skins and made them suitable for the manufacture of clothing or tents, and they did the sewing. When the husband, on his own or in the company of his family, went on extended hunting trips, the wife helped prepare for the expedition. When the husband returned from a trip with his seal skin boots soaked from walking through spring-time puddles, it was the wife who chewed them so that they would be soft and comfortable for his next outing. The wife was keeper of the kitchen, and prepared all food for herself and her family, although the husband would, of course, prepare his own when on hunting expeditions by himself.

The division of labour by sex was crucial for the survival of both sexes, and the part women played in economic activities was fundamental and recognized by males.[3]

Nelson Graburn, echoing Balikci, sees in the division of roles between men and women within the Inuit family and Inuit society a form of symbolic dualism (Graburn: 1973). It is a dualism symbolized by hard and soft, and exterior and interior. From this view, the Inuit wife's life is personified in the manufacture and use of the technology of skin and flesh. Her duties are cleansing skins, carving carcasses, collecting berries and grasses, sewing clothing and tents, and cooking. It is, according to Graburn, the interior of the house which is the domain of the woman. The man is concerned with manufacture of tools, weapons, maintenance of sleds or *kamatiks*, and hunting often far from the home. In such a dualistic symbolism, the two roles are then highly complementary, with a balance existing between them.

The nurturance of the young was similarly shared between Inuit spouses. As Balikci has pointed out for the Netsilik, young were not only valued as perpetuators of the identities of adults, but were a source of joy and inspiration to parents. Too many children were a burden for the individual family, but mechanisms such as adoption and, on occasion, infanticide, helped ensure that no family size would be unmanageable. Adoption was common among all Inuit. A family which had as many children as it could support would, on the discovery that the mother was pregnant again, promise the as yet unborn child to another family which may have lost children to natural catastrophes or merely wished another. The adopted child would enjoy all rights of its siblings in most instances. In the northern regions of Baffin Island I have seen adopted children take on what was almost a privileged position within the family. (There has been some suggestion, however, that adopted orphans fared less well (personal communications).) Infanticide, and in particular the killing of female offspring, was one feature of Inuit family practices which captured the imagination of early observers, and there is no question that it was a reality. Contemporary reconstructionists, on the other hand, looking for statistical data on the practice, find its prevalence to be less widespread or common than was thought in the past. The warmth which characterized Inuit nuclear family relationships should cause us to question both its prevalence as an institutional feature, and the implied callousness of its execution when it was deemed necessary.

SOCIALIZATION PRACTICES

Both parents contributed to the socialization and enculturation of the young. Jean Briggs has suggested recently that women were more instrumental in the transmission of cultural values and norms of behaviour than their spouses, calling them "makers of men" (Briggs: 1974). Her thesis is that it is not easy to be a hunter in the arctic, and socialization techniques must be used which will build into the maturing boy a will and desire to take on such an arduous and dangerous role. To a large extent, according to Briggs, it is women who do this. Her argument is intriguing and becomes compelling with her strong supporting data gained by extensive participation among land-dwelling Inuit.

To some extent, male and female children were differentially treated. When a favourite child was identified by the parents, for example, and singled out for special attention, it was usually a male. The favourite child concept was common among Inuit. Such a child was given privileges, such as greater personal autonomy than its siblings, and older siblings were usually expected to defer to its wishes. One of the puzzles of Inuit socialization is seen in this favourite child concept, in that one boy, until then favoured by his parents, might, while still quite young, be displaced by a newly born sibling. These displaced children seem to accept the change in the position within the family without overt trauma. My own observations of land-based families in the early 1960s revealed no evidence of sharp discontinuity in the behaviour of the first child when his position had been assumed by an infant. Instead of the expressions of sibling rivalry I had expected, the first child usually demonstrated a marked fondness for the younger, often doting over it, and in an uncontrived way.

The Inuit child, whether favourite or not, was, as mentioned, socialized and valued by both parents. Children were given almost unlimited freedom, although constraints on females were more obvious. Girls were expected to assist mothers in the care of younger siblings, but their time was usually spent in the company of their peers, with tiny brothers or sisters clinging to their backs in the hoods of their mothers' parkas. Boys were being socialized to become hunters, and until they had reached an age at which they might accompany their fathers on the hunt, they were allowed to express themselves in an open fashion which would rarely be tolerated by Euro-Canadian parents. The small boy would attempt acts of fearlessness and bravado, often coming close to personal injury, but a parent or older sibling would always be near to protect him in the final moment. Grandparents would tell children stories related to mythology and past events, such as hunting exploits, and instruct them in the making of string figures, which often told stories themselves. As boys in particular neared maturity, the men, often fathers and uncles, would begin to apply pressure to conformity through the use of subtle ridicule. By early adolescence, the worlds of brothers and sisters would increasingly separate as each sex prepared for sex-role defined adulthood.

Beyond the nuclear family there existed the extended family, which was important, but secondary to the former. The nuclear family was embedded within the extended family, and the latter was quite literally an extension of it. The nuclear family most often coincided with the basic residential unit, or the household, but occasionally grandparents lived with their married children. Although Inuit social structure was bilateral, preference was shown for patrilocality, a practice in which the newly married couple take up residence near the parents of the husband, or with their group. This was a preference only, in that it was by no means uncommon for the nuclear family to spend part of a year near the husband's family and the remainder near that of the wife. However, when grandparents lived with their married children, they were, because of this preference for patrilocality, usually the parents of the husband. Balikci reports instances among the Netsilik of married brothers sharing the same home with their parents and their own families (Balikci, 1970). Permutations also existed in which no nuclear family existed within the extended family residential unit. For example, a widower and his unmarried children might live with his parents and their adopted children. Balikci has described just such a household (Balikci: 1970).

INUIT RESIDENCE AND "-MIUT" GROUPS

At this juncture, some further mention should be made of traditional Inuit residential patterns. Residence was never permanent for the Inuit, a nomadic people who established residence in part because of affinities of kinship and/or partnerships, but also because of cyclical availability of game. There were no overriding tribal organizations among the Inuit. People had shared identity, and used names to identify these, always followed by the "-miut" suffix. This suffix was attached to a geographical setting, and miut groups were encapsulated within larger groupings, always having fluctuating memberships. It is similar to being a Winnipeg-miut, and yet also a Manitoba-miut, and finally a Canada-miut. Moving from Winnipeg to Brandon, where one's wife's parents live, because of new job opportunities, changes one from a Winnipeg-miut to a Brandon-miut, but the Manitoba-miut and Canada-miut identities remain. Movement of nuclear families during the year, from one setting to another, although always within circumscribed social and geographical boundaries, was both common and typical.

The extended family operated within, then, and was influenced by, residential patterns which often shifted from one season to another. There is no available statistical data on how common such movements of nuclear families were from one small miut-group to another, but the fact that they were fairly typical among the Inuit of the post-contact period, when a more sedentary life pattern had been established, suggests that they were frequent. One particular observer, such as Rasmussen (1929), might visit an area and record the composition of all households at that point in time. Returning several months later, his residential portrait may have been quite different.

With the widespread practice of senilicide, coupled with voluntary suicide by older persons who no longer regarded themselves as being economically productive, it is unlikely that extended families normally extended beyond the generation of the parents of the spouses in the nuclear family. Great-grandparents were a luxury which Inuit could ill afford. Kinship terms do suggest, however, that laterally, or in one's own generation, kinship identification did extend over several degrees of removal from the spouses in the nuclear family. Mutual obligations of reciprocity with distantly removed kinsmen, though, are unclear and appear to have been somewhat tenuous. Two hunters meeting on the sea ice some distance from both of their camps might feel more comfortable in one another's presence if they could find some connection through mutual kinsmen, but the exact nature of their newly discovered relationship did not necessarily define specifically their role relationships with one another.

In general, then, the extended family among traditional Inuit took on many forms, with some preference for patrilocality. Despite what some other writers have claimed, I find little reason for any strong emphasis on the role of the extended family in a bilateral society of nomads such as the Inuit. Extensions of the nuclear family existed, but the extended family was a composite of many variations on them.

The unit larger than the nuclear family which was more central than the extended family and provided for needs of the nuclear family on a broader scale was the basic -miut group or band. Usually on a broader scale was the basic -miut group or band. Usually it was a fairly loose association of nuclear families sharing common residential proximity. Often constituent families within it were kin-connected. The leader of the band was the *isumatag*, or "the one who thinks." He was usually the oldest still-active hunter in the group. Often other families in his band would be headed by his sons or sons-in-law. He had considerable influence over his fellow camp dwellers, and in some instances individual head-men would try to exercise coercive displays of power. To do so, however, was to face the possibility of losing those families headed by independent males, and even if successful, his position was as ephemeral as his continuing ability to make sound decisions about hunting, fishing, and other crucial activities.

ALLIANCES AND PARTNERSHIPS

One other characteristic of traditional Inuit life should be mentioned briefly, for it often involved an extension and intensification of kin ties. These were the partnerships mentioned earlier. Since this is a portrait of the Inuit family, I will only say that partnerships of a serious and joking nature were common among Inuit, and formed the basis for alliances between males, which both enhanced chances of economic survival in cases of serious ones, and reduced the likelihood of the eruption of violent expressions of interpersonal hostility through joking ones. However, two types of partnerships based on kin ties are important for our consideration of the Inuit family.

One was a partnership formed between brothers-in-law (Balikci: 1970). It did happen that, in spite of the preference for patrilocality, two individuals, married to two sisters, might reside together. There was a specific kin term for brothers-in-law in such a relationship, *angayungog-nukangor* (Balikci: 1970). The dominant relationship in such a partnership was not between the sisters, but their husbands, related to one another through marriage. They would hunt together and felt obligated to observe mutual expectations of economic and other reciprocities. A permutation, which I witnessed in the early 1960s while living with an Inuit family on northern Baffin Island, was one in which a partnership was formed between a man and the husband of his sister. It may have been common in the past, but less institutionalized than the one described before.

The second form of partnership I want to recognize is the one which more than any other relationships among traditional Inuit has fascinated outside observers often either still embedded in or only slowly surfacing from a Victorian definition of the characteristics of monogamy. That was the partnership which allowed for wife exchange.

Early visitors to the Canadian arctic were men who had, during long voyages, been isolated from the company of women. When the Inuit whom they met offered the sexual favours of their own wives in trade for metal knives, tobacco, and other trade items, they were both mildly shocked and pleasantly surprised. Graburn has provided amusing descriptions from captains' logs of these encounters. One insightful comment captures the basic structural under-pinning of these offerings of sexual relief.

"The men (of Chimo) would prostitute their women for gain very gladly with us, yet they were highly offended if their women commit a fault without their knowledge" (Finlayson, quoted in Graburn: 1969).

The practice of wife exchange was a personification in behaviour of a type of partnership between males. Anthropologists have debated its extent and significance. It is now increasingly recognized by arctic scholars that the partnership was not only one between consenting males, whose wives were participants, but between the male spouse and wife as well. The wife had a voice in the final decision, and it was, even in the casual encounteres with whalers and others mentioned before, only with her acceptance that the wife exchange was realized. Among the Inuit themselves, the partnership between two males who would share their wives was one of economic necessity; one, for example, which allowed for a man whose wife was ill, and could not accompany him on a trip to another area, to be joined on that trip by the wife of his partner. Sexual favours were a part of the arrangement, but these were only the icing on the cake of the underlying need for a man to have a female with him on a trip, which was the other side of the mutual dependency of the sexes I have discussed before.

Partnerships were a basic mechanism for alliance formation between men in traditional Inuit society, allowing for a building of relationships of reciprocity beyond the kinship structure. Partnerships between women probably existed as well, but descriptions of them are virtually non-existent. It may well have been the case, for example, that in adoptions, the arrangements were worked out between the natural mother and the adoptive mother, with husbands only giving final approval. As with ethnographic reporting on other indigenous peoples from around the world, the literature on traditional Inuit society is strongly biased toward descriptions of male behaviour. Fortunately, there are a number of excellent female anthropologists who are re-examining that literature in an effort to correct that bias, but for the early contact period, they are limited by available material.

THE INUIT FAMILY IN THE CONTACT-TRADITIONAL PERIOD

In time the period of the whalers and explorers was replaced by the presence in the Canadian arctic of contact agents who maintained at least extended residences, if not permanent. These were traders, usually employees of the Hudson Bay Company (HBC), missionaries, almost always either Roman Catholic or Anglican, and representatives of the Royal Canadian Mounted Police (RCMP). The traders usually came first, hence the irreverent arctic saying that HBC refers to "here before Christ." They established permanent trading posts at places which were accessible by supply ships from Churchill, Manitoba, or Montreal. In time, the traditionally nomadic Inuit began to establish camps located near these posts. Most present-day arctic settlements are built around early HBC sites. Although the Inuit continued to move from one place to another during different seasons of the year, as they had always done, the territories within which this movement occurred were circumscribed by the fact that they rarely moved more than two or three days' travel from the trading posts.

It is this period in recent Canadian arctic history which has been labelled the contact-traditional period. Balikci has called it the time of the arctic troika, during which the three contact agencies—traders, missionaries, and police—produced irreversible changes in Inuit life, while not being intrusive enough, whether by intent or accident, to change dramatically many aspects of traditional Inuit culture and society. This period, however, had several effects on the Inuit family structure.

In describing changes in Nouveau Quebec which resulted from the contact-traditional period and the semi-sedentariness which was a major feature of it, Arbess has suggested that the extended family began to take on new importance, at times at the expense of the nuclear family (Arbess: 1965). He was primarily concerned with the consequences of permanent year-round residence in settlement, but the roots of what he describes were also evident before.

Families living "on the land" without economic ties to trading posts moved about easily from group to group, although always within the context of their own -miut group. It was the nuclear family which moved. With the contact-traditional period, again, possibilities, or more accurately, the desire for regular movement over fairly wide geographical regions, diminished. The winter camps were base camps, and although on occasion individual nuclear families may move from one to another, they generally returned after a year or two to the earlier one. Movement was typically from a camp where the husband had kinsmen, to one where the wife had them. Regular exposure to members of the extended family was intensified, along with an increasing dependency on relatives beyond the nuclear family. Grandparents were present to assist in socialization of the young. Partnerships based on kin ties became more common, as children matured in settings where they had regular contact, and so developed affective ties, with kinsmen.

Camp residents often would pool financial resources, such as they were, to purchase Peterhead boats for whaling purposes and for transportation of several people from, for example, a summer camp to a winter one, or for visits to the settlement on special times of the year, such as "sea lift," when supply ships arrived from the south and men had an opportunity to earn extra cash. These boats replaced the traditional umiaks, or whaling boats. It was kinsmen within a single camp who contributed to their purchase, and it was usually the oldest male in the camp who also had the largest number of kin connections with individual households who became titular owner of the boat, and made decisions about its use. An investment by a household head in the boat was an investment in the camp, but this also meant making a stronger commitment to extended family ties, for the man who controlled use of the boat was both camp head-man and central figure in a camp-based extended family, whether predominantly patrilocal or matrilocal.

In general, however, the contact-traditional period was one of only moderate change for Inuit family structure. Contact with outsiders such as traders, missionaries, and police was sociologically minimal. Police made twice yearly tours of all camps surrounding a settlement. Missionaries preached Christianity, but in the settlement mission. Representatives of neither agency wished to create drastic social or cultural change. In the case of the RCMP, they usually regarded the Inuit as being basically law-abiding people who, unless they committed major crimes such as homicide or continually broke the game or liquor ordinances, were better left on their own. The missionaries feared secularization possibly more than they feared the continuation of the traditional practice of shamanism. Too much contact by their Inuit parishioners with outside influences from the south would only break down their own efforts at proselytization. The traders, of course, saw only virtue in having the Inuit continue traditional hunting practices and life on the land. Without skins and furs brought in by hunters, the posts might as well close their doors. None of the three branches of the arctic troika saw value for their own ends in extensive efforts at induced culture change among the Inuit, and so the Inuit, like many people faced with extended contact with an outside set of influences, responded by being selective about what they accepted from this new world with which they were in touch. They adapted traditions to meet new circumstances, but in the main held tenaciously to their own ways and to traditional family life.

THE INUIT FAMILY IN THE PERIOD OF CENTRALIZATION

In the recent past, the time of the 1970s, the contact-traditional way of life has in the main disappeared. There have been a few attempts by small groups to return to the land, but most Inuit now live in settlements. This major transformation was brought about as a result of a massive involvement of the federal government in the Canadian arctic. It was preceded by many concerns, such as Canadian sovereignty in its arctic territories and realization of the potentially vast oil and gas deposits to be found there, but made explicit by the creation of the Department of Northern Affairs and Natural Resources in the mid-50s. A new federal bureaucracy takes time to form itself, but by the late '60s the Canadian arctic was populated not only by representatives of the troika, but also by civil servants en masse, in the garbs of administrators, teachers, and mechanical workers.

Inuit families left the land and moved into the rapidly growing settlements, where they were given new housing, children were educated in new federal day schools, and men found employment which guaranteed a regular pay cheque instead of an often futile hunting expedition.

As had happened during the contact-traditional period, the role of the extended family was intensified once again with this process of centralization. Grandparents on both sides, along with uncles and aunts, lived within close proximity of their grandchildren, nieces, and nephews. Visiting back and forth became a regular part of settlement life. With wage work, men could come home at mid-day for lunch. In one high arctic settlement in which I have worked, I noted that at both lunch times and coffee breaks men would often visit the homes of parents or siblings. Children would regularly eat in the homes of grandparents, a continuation of a practice of the pre-contact period, but opportunities for it were more common.

There have been relatively few studies of Inuit family life in the centralization time, and so any conclusions on changes which may have resulted must be tentative. One response seems to be that family groupings have begun to act as political bodies, offering support for family members who run for local office on settlement councils, housing associations, and so on. As settlements move toward hamlet status and so achieve greater local autonomy, these positions become major sources of prestige and power. Another is related to the fact that women now have personal control over sources of cash, from wage employment, handicraft work, and family allowances. There is some evidence that they often are not putting this money into a family pool, but instead are investing it in local co-operatives or depositing it in banks for their own use and the future education of their children. This behaviour, coupled with the fact that women are increasingly running for elective office, often successfully, should lead us to question once again the traditional image of Inuit women as subservient caterers to male egos.

In several high arctic settlements men have found employment with oil companies. This work involves spending twenty or so days on the job, usually distant from the home community, and then ten days back in the settlement. This separation of fathers and husbands from their families has, of course, meant that women's roles as socializing agents have been intensified. I know of several men who have given up oil work, in spite of the high wages to be earned, because it creates a psychological hardship for them to be separated from their families for such long periods. During the contact-traditional period, men would typically leave wives and children behind in the camps while on the hunt, and I recall vividly the sadness they would express if the trips took longer than anticipated. They would speak of their families longingly, and anxiously wait for the day of return home. Each episode reflects the emotional cement which bound together traditional Inuit nuclear families.

As Inuit women develop a more solid political base, their own ideas about directions for their children become more explicit. There has been evidence for some time that Inuit women are more oriented toward modernization than their male counterparts. Young girls in the '60s demonstrated this by trying to find ways to "get south." A small number married Euro-Canadians as a means of doing so, and often they were the envy of others. Financial management of their own resources by women is one more indication of this. Another manifestation is a concern expressed by many Inuit women for the formal education of their offspring. In taking a position on this, they often must explicitly oppose the wishes of their spouses. Most settlements today have their own high schools, but in the recent past, Inuit students were taken to residential schools for secondary education. This was a hardship for them and their parents, but women tended to encourage it nevertheless, believing that modernization promised rewards which were worth the emotional costs related to the acquisition by their children of new skills. To some extent this disparity between the approaches taken to the introduction of outside influences may not bode well for harmony within the Inuit family. The women's movement, which has had such a major influence on changing sex roles in the past decade has not yet reached the Canadian arctic, but if it does, a responsive chord may be struck and a ready audience waiting.

THE FUTURE

Until more studies are carried out on the effects of centralization on the Inuit family structure, it is difficult to look into the future in anything more than a speculative fashion. It appears to be alive and well, but increasingly contact with the new dialogue between the sexes taking place in southern Canada and elsewhere may have serious implications for its on-going viability. If the family is an archaic institution in the broader world, the Inuit family may have a limited life span. It has served a people who adapted more than a thousand years ago to one of the most demanding environments in the world, and it has retained its integrity in the face of a series of socio-cultural changes almost unprecedented in human history. The Inuit themselves will decide its future.

NOTES

1. I will use the term "Eskimo" in the introduction to the paper, but only as a classificatory term. In general, the more proper name of Inuit will be used to refer to the arctic peoples whose family structure is the topic.
2. Inuit is an Inupik word, and so I use the standardized practise of referring to the Eskimo of southern Alaska and Siberia as Eskimo. Another more indigenous word would, of course, be preferable, but our concern is not with these populations in any event.
3. For a fuller discussion of relative equality between the sexes in traditional Inuit society, see Matthiasson, 1977.

REFERENCES

Arbess, Saul E.
1965   *Social Change and the Eskimo Co-operative at George River, Quebec.* Northern Co-ordination and Research Centre, Ottawa.

Balikci, Asen
1970   *The Netsilik Eskimo.* New York: The Natural History Press.

Boas, Franz
1888   *The Central Eskimo.* Sixth Annual Report of the Bureau of Ethnology, Smithsonian Institution, Washington.

Briggs, Jean
1974   "Eskimo Women: Makers of Men." In Carolyn J. Matthiasson, *Many Sisters: Women in Cross-Cultural Perspective.* Glencoe: The Free Press.

Graburn, Nelson
1969   *Eskimos Without Igloos.* Boston: Little, Brown and Company.

Matthiasson, John S.
1976   "Northern Baffin Island Women in Three Cultural Periods," *Western Canadian Journal of Anthropology,* Vol. 6, pp. 201-212.

Rasmussen, Knud
1927   *Across Arctic America.* New York: Putnam.

1929   *Intellectual Culture of the Iglulik Eskimos.* Reports of the Fifth Thule Expedition, Vol. VII, Copenhagen.

Stefansson, Vilhjalmur
1921   *The Friendly Arctic.* New York: Macmillan.

15. The Cultural Context Of Family Drinking In A Hare Indian Community

Joel S. Savishinsky and Susan F. Savishinsky

INTRODUCTION

There is a great deal of superficial, cultural resemblance between Canadian native people and the non-native populations with whom they share the continent. Similarities in dress, language, religion, and diet, shared forms of literacy and communication, the use of Western alcohol and hospitals, and attendance at Euro-Canadian movies and schools are some of the more visible cultural features they now hold in common. Yet, in four-and-a-half centuries of contact, native people have incorporated elements of Western society in a selective way. The persistence of indigenous systems of value and social structure, of environmental pursuits such as hunting, fishing, and gathering, and of distinctive types of interpersonal behaviour, continue to characterize many native communities and families. These continuities, in turn, affect the manner in which native people deal with the Western institutions that confront them.

This essay is concerned with the cultural effects on Indian people of a particular Euro-Canadian pattern, viz., alcohol consumption. It explores the impact of alcohol use upon the family life of the Hare Indians of Colville Lake, an isolated, Athabascan-speaking group of hunters, fishermen, and trappers living in the boreal forest area of the Northwest Territories. Since Colville Lake is a small settlement of approximately 70 interrelated people, and since its lifestyle centres around a nomadic, seasonal cycle during which families may spend more than half of each year in scattered "bush" encampments, ecological and social variables have a significant effect on people's drinking behaviour.[1] In this essay, a number of cultural themes that characterize Hare society will be identified, and they will be used to examine the relationship that has historically developed between native family life and alcohol consumption.[2] The particular themes to be dealt with reflect the people's concern with issues of emotional containment and expressiveness, generosity, kinship ties, individual autonomy, and responsibility.

Colville Lake's social structure is characterized by a bilateral kinship network that links its fourteen families together with an overlapping series of blood and marital ties. Households are composed of either nuclear or bilaterally extended families, and the latter may include elderly grandparents and inlaws, unmarried, adult siblings, and the adopted offspring of various kinspeople. While the people's way of life is far more secure now than it was in the aboriginal period, traditional values governing kinship, self-reliance, co-operation, and sharing remain very important. People place a high value on the autonomy of the individual, including his ability to act with independence and flexibility. This encompasses his right to choose where and with whom to hunt and live, as well as the freedom not to be interfered with in his public and private behaviour. For the Hare, such freedom has the virtue of fostering self-reliance and resourcefulness in an uncertain world, although security is ultimately seen by them as a product of group membership rather than the abilities of the individual. The family, and the wider kinship network within which it is embedded, continue to be the primary co-operative units that ensure people's survival. Historically, the fur trade has tended to increase the economic importance of the family within native communities, and so the cultural conception of kinship roles within that domestic unit remain particularly salient. The restraint and deference that characterize spouse and parent-child relations, the support that same-sex siblings are expected to give one another, and the warm, supportive relations between grandparents and grandchildren are key elements in maintaining the family as a smoothly functioning, productive, and co-operative work group in the "bush".

Even when harmony is more apparent than real in a family group, the culturally patterned repression of discord is usually effective in guaranteeing the family's viability. This pattern of repression operates, however, in a cultural context that does permit people certain opportunities for affective expression. Those cultural mechanisms which allow for the display or displacement of destructive emotions generated within families, such as the outlets provided by gossip, withdrawal, and drunken comportment, therefore constitute an important set of behaviours that are equally significant in maintaining the family system.[3]

ECOLOGICAL AND SOCIAL INFLUENCES ON DRINKING

Alcohol is one of the Western products that was introduced to the Hare Indians during the spread of the European fur trade in the Northwest

Territories. Distilled liquors are rarely consumed by the current population of Colville Lake, however, not only because of their high cost, but because the nearest government liquor store is in another community, located some 124 miles from the settlement. As a result of the logistical and economic factors that limit people's access to liquor, the prime alcoholic beverage found in the village is a native drink called *kontweh* or "homebrew." The technique for making *kontweh* was taught to the Hare by Whites, and its manufacture became widespread among the Hare in the Fort Good Hope and Colville Lake areas in the 1920s (Hurlbert: 1962). *Kontweh* is manufactured in the people's homes from a mixture of water, sugar, yeast, and a carbohydrate base that usually consists of packaged fruit, rice, or beans. These ingredients can be obtained at any trading post in the Northwest Territories, including the small store located at the settlement. Neither the illegality of brew-making in the Territories, nor opposition to its consumption by a Catholic priest stationed at Colville Lake, have dissuaded the people from using *kontweh*. Depending on how long the *kontweh* is allowed to ferment, it achieves an alcoholic content of 3 to 4% (Durgin: 1974; p. 59).[4]

Despite the constant availability of *kontweh* ingredients at the local settlement, drinking is essentially a seasonal rather than a year-round activity among the people. It coincides with those periods in the annual cycle when band members are gathered at the community, and rarely occurs when they are dispersed at their winter and spring trapping camps. The people only reside at the village in large numbers during the summer months of June through September, and at the Christmas and Easter holidays. It is at these times that the people congregate to trade their furs, purchase supplies, socialize, and attend church services at the Catholic mission. During the rest of the year, the fourteen families of the band are scattered over a radius of 100 miles from the village, living in small hunting camps comprised of one, two, or three households.

The seasonal nature of drinking at Colville Lake is the product of a number of practical considerations. The Indians' need for periodic mobility during the long, sub-Arctic winter, combined with the necessity to transport tents, traps, rifles, and other equipment, limits the amount of food supplies that the people can carry in their narrow, toboggan-style dogsleds. "Brew fruit" is a non-essential item which is therefore rarely taken to the "bush." Furthermore, most people feel that drinking promotes certain types of behaviour that are incompatible with the demands of winter survival. Alcohol consumption is usually accompanied by emotionally demonstrative and aggressive actions which violate the restrained behaviour that makes co-operative life in the bush possible. Drinking also diverts time and energy from subsistence pursuits, and impairs the cognitive skills that people rely on to hunt, travel, trap, and plan in an effective manner. As a consequence, some of the band's most ardent drinkers abstain from alcohol for months at a time while in the bush because of their perception of drinking as dangerous and counter-productive (Savishinsky: 1977).

The logistical, cognitive, and social disadvantages of drinking in the bush are much less salient in the context of village life. Survival problems are less immediate, and the needs for co-operation and harmony, both within and between families, are less pressing. Ingatherings at the settlement are also the most intensely communal periods of the year, and band members see drinking and sociability as mutually reinforcing. Brew parties are gratifying events when a large number of kinsmen and friends can participate in them, and the presence of such people at the community defines a situation in which drinking is both desirable and expected. The sharing of *kontweh* is an effective way of demonstrating one's generosity, and of reciprocating the hospitality and help that one has received from others.[5]

The reputation of individuals and families can be damaged as well as enhanced, however, by the way in which they participate in drinking. People who are regarded as stingy, or whose drunken comportment is characteristically disruptive and aggressive, are often excluded from brew parties. Families who attempt to exercise such discrimination run the risk of being abused or stigmatized themselves, however, if their exclusiveness cannot be accomplished with discretion. The difficulty of maintaining privacy and of controlling information about brew parties is aggravated by the size of the community and the nature of its visiting patterns. The casual way in which people enter one another's unlocked cabins, the proximity of houses in the compact settlement, and the ease with which the noise of a drinking session broadcasts itself tend to make the most private of brew parties a matter of public record. Unwanted visitors who impose themselves on a group of drinkers are made aware of their status as intruders: the sudden and awkward silence with which they are greeted and the removal of the brew pot and drinking cups from visibility contrasts with the "party" atmosphere and volubility that were current (and readily apparent) prior to their arrival. Drinking events are thus an occasion in which the potential for insult and animosity is as real as the rewards of hospitality. Since the people live in a cultural context that makes sharing a prime way of expressing both social cohesion and personal reputation, the selective generosity that is practised with homebrew alternately strains and strengthens the bonds between the band's families.

FAMILY RELATIONS AND DRUNKEN COMPORTMENT

The behavioural alternations that accompany drinking events affect relations within as well as between families. The Hare place a strong emphasis on emotional restraint and self-containment—a behavioural theme that is also characteristic of most other Northern Indian groups. This pattern is reinforced by a number of indirect ways that people have of coping with certain stresses and provocations: these include the displacement of hostility through beating dogs, the avoidance mechanisms of withdrawal, mobility, and residence changes, and the vicarious aggression of gossip. Drinking events, however, are regarded as occasions during which affective release in a direct manner is possible, expected, and accepted. Violence, teasing, and sexual and verbal aggressiveness may all occur on a given evening, and they display a set of emotions that are not overtly expressed at other times. Specific, hidden tensions within families may consequently become highly visible at such times: sexual jealousies between spouses may get verbalized, lingering disputes between parents and grown children may explode into a physical confrontation, and covertly antagonistic sisters-in-law may suddenly assault one another. Emotions that are normally repressed are thus articulated during these occasions, although the effective masking of such feelings over a long period of time may obscure the real roots of a hostile encounter when it finally erupts. People who hold themselves and others responsible for their actions when sober suspend this concept of accountability when drinking occurs. Brew parties thus constitute a "time out" occasion, during which behaviour that is unacceptable in other contexts is situationally excused and rationalized (MacAndrew and Edgerton: 1969, pp. 83-99). The cultural legitimacy of drunken comportment thus derives from the way in which band members redefine their notion of responsibility when alcohol is involved. It is the cultural definition of the drinking situation, then, rather than the physiological effects of the relatively weak *kontweh*, that licenses people to act out their emotions at such times.[6]

Certain aspects of cultural sex roles and husband-wife relations are made particularly visible during drinking encounters. While drinking groups are occasionally unisexual in composition, they most often include individuals of both sexes. There are significant differences, however, in the drunken comportment of males and females. Both men and women fight with people of either sex, but women characteristically take on a protective role towards their male kinsmen. When a husband, father, brother, or son is in a provocative drinking situation with other individuals, a woman will try to restrain his aggression and minimize his vulnerability. A wife, for example, will try to monitor the amount of *kontweh* consumed by her spouse, and, if necessary, will mediate or remove him from a dispute before it erupts into violence. Since female family members often act as the arbiters of male drunken comportment, they themselves must be more controlled, aware, and attentive in drinking situations than their male kinsmen. Drinking events are probably much more tense for them, therefore, because of the mediating role they assume.[7] This posture is reflective of some other kinds of deferential behaviour the women are expected to show towards men, ranging from their backstage role in family decision-making and village politics, to walking behind their husbands on paths. As has been noted elsewhere concerning their behaviour:

Women will in fact follow their husbands from house to house during a night of heavy drinking, hoping to keep them out of trouble. Females are not only concerned about the physical consequences of male drinking: they can also be visibly embarrassed by it. A drunken husband who acts in a flirtatious or foolish way is often being nervously observed by a self-conscious wife, sensitive to the spectacle being acted out before her (Savishinsky: 1977).

Interaction patterns at brew parties also reveal how the different generations within a family respond to—and learn about—the nature of drinking events. People do not attempt to segregate attendance at brew parties on the basis of relative or absolute age. Young children are given the same freedom to observe drinking events that they enjoy in moving about in all areas of the village. Since there are no standard bed-times for them, children are often awake when their parents host a brew party in their one-room homes. They consequently have the opportunity to witness the nature of drunken comportment from an early age, and this socializes them to the realities of the drinking pattern long before they become active participants in it as teenagers. This type of exposure and learning is consonant with a general thematic attitude toward socialization that characterizes Hare culture, viz., that children learn best by observation, participation, trial, error, and experience, rather than by formal or guided instruction or by being sheltered from the realities of life.

Among the Hare, people experience strong pressures from peers and others to participate in drinking: since it is one of the most ubiquitous and intensely social activities in the settlement, few people choose to exclude themselves from it as they grow up. Occasional admonitions from parents and grandparents against drinking have little effect on young adults, therefore, both because of the pervasiveness of brewing, and because these family members themselves provide a model for the very behaviour they disparage. Older siblings also provide a model for drinking behaviour that their younger brothers and sisters emulate. Augmenting this pattern of social learning is the fact that the protection and assistance that siblings are supposed to provide for one another are expressed not only in the form of food, hospitality, and labour, but in the physical and social support that siblings are expected to give one another during drunken encounters. The same siblings who fight each other at a brew party will later combine forces in a display of solidarity when another individual confronts either one of them.

Family dynamics thus tend to reinforce and transmit drinking patterns, just as the latter serve to express some of the tensions that exist within domestic groups. Children are heir to both forms of expression. Despite—or because of—their exposure to drunkenness from infancy, children are often visibly upset by the violence and disorder with which drinking parties surround them: they occasionally try to intercede in quarrels or urge a parent, sibling, or grandparent to leave a violent party. Several times children were seen to hide or destroy a brew pot in order to curtail the drinking of family members (cf. also Durgin: 1974, pp. 128-132). By their mid-teen years, however, as people participate more actively in alcohol consumption, both the *kontweh* and its consequences become more palatable. Drinking therefore becomes personally more gratifying and manageable, and so its social rewards offset its more aggravating and stressful qualities.

In learning about the predictability and rhythm of drinking events, people become aware of what they and others are capable, and this knowledge allows them ultimately to conceive of and utilize drinking as a culturally appropriate, emotional outlet. For elderly family members, drinking takes on some other meanings as well during the later years of life. Elderly parents and grandparents can no longer maintain their status and self-image through such traditional, physically demanding activities as hunting, trapping, and the sharing of food and labour. Their participation in brewing and drinking, however, does provide an opportunity for generosity, personal visibility, and community involvement in the context of a leisure pursuit. For them, the social acceptability of drinking is secondary to the use of drinking as a route to social acceptance itself. The meaning and impact of alcohol thus vary with the different age and sex groups that comprise the settlement, and yet drinking has developed into one of the relatively few, shared cultural activities that draws together such a diversified range of individuals.

Finally, despite the ubiquity of seasonal drinking at Colville Lake, it should be noted that there are some individuals and families within the community who generally abstain from this activity. Indian people rarely drink with the settlement's missionary and fur trader—the only non-native persons in their village. This is a particular instance of the ethnic segregation that characterizes residential and social patterns in most northern communities. It is also a product, at Colville Lake, of the missionary's opposition to native drinking, and to the reluctance of both white men to becoming involved in the quarrels which brew parties generate. While Indian people prefer that the whites not be privy to their disputes and gossip, they are not adverse to calling on them to interfere in fights that they themselves cannot contain.

There is also a group of four native families in the community whose members almost never drink with their fellow bandsmen. These people are among the most conservative and religious individuals in the village and, significantly, they comprise the major portion of an extended kinship network. These families are strongly oriented towards a bush way of life, and both their older and younger members find the violence and drinking of the community to be among its most distressing features. The relative lack of drinking within this network of interrelated households reflects the important role of the family and kinship group in fostering a distinctive set of attitudes and behaviours concerning alcohol use. The role of these four families in the community's drinking pattern also has a particularly ironic quality to it: it is these people who are often called upon by drinkers to intercede in violent quarrels as a result of their sobriety and their lack of direct, personal involvement in aggression. Their social distance from alcohol use thus makes them the most likely individuals to mediate its consequences.

FAMILY LIFE, DRINKING, AND CULTURAL VALUES

Family life at Colville Lake reflects a number of the cultural values and ecological realities that govern the people's existence. Concerns with survival, kinship, inter-ethnic relations, and socialization, and an interest in preserving certain forms of co-operation, generosity, self-image, personal responsibility, behavioural restraint, and family roles affect the way in which alcohol has been incorporated into the people's lives. Historically, the emotional expressiveness fostered by drinking has become a culturally legitimated outlet—one that both relieves and contributes to the tensions that develop within families as well as between them. Drinking creates both camaraderie and chaos, but its disruptive impact is bounded by fundamental needs for reciprocity and co-operation, and by the people's ability to escape from one another and their own drunken excesses and reputations by moving from the village to the bush.

People's awareness of their interdependence—the fact that security and survival depend, in part, on their ability to draw upon the help and support of others, especially kinsmen—thus limits the extent to which the gratifications and violence of drinking are permitted to rend the fabric of either the family or the larger community. Drunken excess in a socially predictable situation thus allows for the maintenance of a "reticence ethic" in other settings (Robbins: 1973, p. 115). At Colville Lake, drinking is the means by which, to borrow from Freud (1960: pp. 62,70), the group process replaces repression with regression. Regression only eliminates responsibility at an overt level, however. Responsibility may publicly be regarded as a concomitant of sobriety, but people's concern with their personal reputations and the ability of others to reciprocate abuse when they themselves become drunk constitute a way of privately enforcing a de facto system of accountability. People retain their animosities from one drinking event to the next, at which time they revive their outstanding grievances.[8] This is one of the subtler aspects of the drinking pattern that children internalize as they grow up. The Hare thus learn to experience a kind of "counter-anxiety" over revenge hostility, a pattern that Horton (1943, p. 230) identified as a factor limiting the amount of drunken disturbance that occurs in certain societies.

Of all the European goods introduced to North American native people, alcohol has clearly been one of the most problematic. Its gratifications are obvious and seductive, and yet its use has been both a source and a product of people's discontent. An ambivalent attitude toward drinking characterizes native people in a number of northern communities that have been studied.[9] While the situation at Colville Lake could be compared with these other settlements, the village has a number of unique features that set it apart from them: (1) it lacks a local outlet at which commercially manufactured liquor can be purchased; (2) it has no local police force to maintain social order and enforce liquor ordinances; (3) its population is overwhelmingly involved in "bush" activities for subsistence, rather than being dependent on wage labour or welfare for survival; (4) its native population is small and closely interrelated; and (5) it has only a handful of non-native residents.

Despite these differences, the people of Colville Lake replicate the ambivalent attitudes about alcohol found in the larger, more urbanized, and more ethnically complex communities of the north. Parents and children there both complain about one another's drinking and, at various times, all Indian people in the settlement—drinkers as well as nondrinkers—express regret over the amount and impact of alcohol consumption. Drinking nevertheless continues, and only certain families—reinforced, perhaps, by the self-deprecation of the drinkers themselves—seem exempt from the pattern. People in the village who do use alcohol echo the negative sentiments that northern whites often express about Indian drinking; in the process, they reveal their resentment over the self-fulfilling nature of their own behaviour (Clairmont: 1962, p. 8; 1963: p. 64). While none of the native people in the band are alcoholics in a clinical sense, they acknowledge that some families experience considerable economic and emotional disruption in their lives because of the drinking that does occur among their members.

Drinking has therefore been incorporated, but not integrated, into the people's lifestyle. Their use of traditional techniques for maintaining social order—gossip, public opinion, family pressure, withdrawal, mobility, aggressive displacement, and repression—are essentially noncorporate and non-political in nature. They limit the impact of drinking without—in the people's own, collective opinion—effectively controlling it.[10] On the other hand, drinking also serves to express and maintain a number of significant themes in Hare culture, and this, along with the sense of solidarity it promotes, augments the gratifications which underlie most people's participation in it. Some families have the human and motivational resources to prevent alcohol from assuming a disruptive role in their lives, but at Colville Lake, such people constitute a minority of the population. The models or mechanisms that would enable larger numbers of Indian families to exercise a comparable degree of control over drinking have yet to be discovered.[11] If they are to be developed and adopted, they will have to take into consideration the positive as well as the negative ways in which drinking is related to basic cultural values in Indian life.

NOTES

1. A more detailed ethnographic description of the community can be found in Savishinsky, 1974. Fieldwork at Colville Lake was carried out by the senior author in 1967 and 1968, and by both authors in 1971. The 1967-1968 research was done under a grant from the National Science Foundation, while the National Museum of Man of the National Museums of Canada supported our fieldwork in 1971. In this essay, the ethnographic present refers to the period 1967-1968.

2. The concept of themes is taken from the work of Opler (1945, 1946). In a number of previous publications, the senior author has delineated some of the major themes in Hare culture, and noted their similarity to those found in other sub-Arctic populations (Savishinsky: 1970, 1974, 1977). Savishinsky (1977) specifically examines the relationship between alcohol use and cultural themes in Hare society.

3. These and other coping mechanisms are discussed in Savishinsky 1974, 1976, 1977.

4. In addition to *kontweh* and commercial liquor, people occasionally drink vanilla extract, liniment, and hair spray. These products are more commonly available at stores in the larger settlements in the Territories, however, and so are infrequently consumed at Colville Lake. Durgin (1974) analyzes drinking patterns in the Hare community of Fort Good Hope, a town of several hundred people located some 140 km away on the Mackenzie River. His material reflects the situation in a more urbanized setting that the people of Colville Lake are quite familiar with, since they are related to, visit, and intermarry with the fort's population. Other studies which examine Indian and Eskimo drinking in northern settlements include those of John and Irma Honigmann (1945, 1965, 1970), Berreman (1956), Clairmont (1962, 1963), Balikci (1963), Robbins (1973), and Hippler (1973). Brody (1971) deals with an Indian skid row community in a prairie province, many of whose members come from the Northwest Territories.

5. As has been observed by Mandelbaum (1965: p. 282), alcohol addiction and solitary drinking are relatively rare in non-Western societies. At Colville Lake, no one was an alcoholic in a clinical sense, and only one individual was known as an occasional, solitary drinker. Even the latter man, despite his somewhat deviant reputation, was a frequent participant in brew parties.

6. During the course of an evening, people move back and forth between states of sobriety and intoxication with relative ease and rapidity; their behaviour is a response to changes in the immediate social context, and does not necessarily relate to the amount of *kontweh* they have drunk. Some individuals mimic a state of drunkenness even before they have finished one cup of brew. Berreman (1956), Lemert (1958), Washburne (1961), Mandelbaum (1965), MacAndrew and Edgerton (1969), Robbins (1973), and others report similar transitions during drinking in other societies.

7. The Honigmanns (1965: p. 214) make comparable observations on the unease and embarrassment experienced by Eskimo women at Frobisher Bay during drinking events.

8. Washburne (1961, p. xviii) and MacAndrew and Edgerton (1969, p. 94) note that the revival of old animosities is a prime source of drunken hostility in many societies. Durgin (1974, pp. 79-86) makes a similar observation for the Hare at Fort Good Hope.

9. See the studies cited in footnote 4.

10. Field (1962) correlates excessive drunkenness with loose, non-corporate social structures in a number of societies. Price (1975) emphasizes the lack of effective control systems as a ubiquitous problem in North American Indian drinking.

11. Hippler (1974) documents the effective role of fundamentalist Christianity in curbing alcohol abuse among some Athabascan-speaking groups in interior Alaska.

REFERENCES

Balikci, Asen
1968 "Bad Friends." *Human Organization* 27:191-199.

Berreman, Gerald D.
1956 "Drinking Patterns of the Aleuts." *Quarterly Journal of Studies on Alcohol* 17:503-514.

Brody, Hugh
1971 *Indians on Skid Row.* Ottawa: Northern Science Research Group, Department of Indian Affairs and Northern Development.

Clairmont, Donald H.
1962 *Notes on the Drinking Behaviour of the Eskimos and Indians in the Aklavik Area.* Ottawa: Northern Co-ordination and Research Centre, Department of Northern Affairs and National Resources.

1963 *Deviance Among Indians and Eskimos in Aklavik, N.W.T.* Ottawa: Northern Co-ordination and Research Centre, Department of Northern Affairs and National Resources.

Durgin, Edward C.
1974 *Brewing and Boozing: A Study of Drinking Patterns Among the Hare Indians.* Unpublished doctoral dissertation, Department of Anthropology, University of Oregon.

Field, Peter B.
1972 "A New Cross-Cultural Study of Drunkenness." In *Society, Culture and Drinking Patterns,* edited by David J. Pittman and Charles R. Snyder. New York: John Wiley and Sons.

Freud, Sigmund
1960 *Group Psychology and The Analysis of the Ego.* Translated by James Strachey. New York: Bantam Books.

Hippler, Arthur E.
1974 "An Alaskan Athabascan Technique for Overcoming Alcohol Abuse." *Arctic* 27:53-67.

Honigmann, John J., and Irma Honigmann
1945 "Drinking in an Indian-White Community." *Quarterly Journal of Studies on Alcohol* 5:575-619.

1965 *Eskimo Townsmen.* Ottawa: Canadian Research Centre for Anthropology.

1970 *Arctic Townsmen.* Ottawa: Canadian Research Centre for Anthropology.

Horton, Donald
1943 "The Functions of Alcohol in Primitive Societies: A Cross-Cultural Study." *Quarterly Journal of Studies on Alcohol* 4:199-320.

Hurlbert, Janice
1962 *Age as a Factor in the Social Organization of the Hare Indians of Fort Good Hope, N.W.T.* Northern Co-ordination and Research Centre. Ottawa: Department of Northern Affairs and National Resources.

Lemert, Edwin M.
1958 "The Use of Alcohol in Three Salish Indian Tribes." *Quarterly Journal of Studies on Alcohol* 19:90-107.

MacAndrew, Craig, and Robert B. Edgerton
1969 *Drunken Comportment: A Social Explanation.* Chicago: Aldine Publishing Company.

Mandelbaum, David G.
1965 "Alcohol and Culture." *Current Anthropology* 6:281-293.

Opler, Morris E.
1945 "Themes as Dynamic Forces in Culture." *American Journal of Sociology* 51:198-206.

1946 "An Application of the Theory of Themes in Culture." *Journal of the Washington Academy of Sciences* 36:137-166.

Price, John A.
1975 "An Applied Analysis of North American Indian Drinking Patterns." *Human Organization* 34:17-26.

Robbins, Richard H.
1973 "Alcohol and the Identity Struggle: Some Effects of Economic Change on Interpersonal Relations." *American Anthropologist* 7:99-122.

Savishinsky, Joel S.
1970 "Kinship and the Expression of Values in an Athabascan Bush Community." *Western Canadian Journal of Anthropology* 2:31-59.

1974 *The Trail of the Hare: Life and Stress in an Arctic Community.* New York: Gordon and Breach, Inc.

1976 *Vicarious Emotions as an Adaptation to Cultural Restraint: Affective Experience in a Sub-Arctic Indian Community.* Paper presented at 75th Annual Meeting of the American Anthropological Association, Washington, D.C., November 17-21, 1976.

1977 *A Thematic Analysis of Drinking in a Hare Indian Community.* Papers in Anthropology, Vol. 18, No. 2. Norman: Department of Anthropology, University of Oklahoma.

Washburne, Chandler
1961 *Primitive Drinking.* New York: College and University Press.

Bibliography

Abell, Helen C.
"Adaptation of the Rural Family to Change." In *Marriage, Family and Society*, edited by Parvez Wakil, Toronto: Butterworth and Company.

Acheson, Ann W.
1977 *Nomads in Town: The Kutchin of Old Crow, Yukon Territory*. Unpublished Ph.D. dissertation, Cornell University.

Adamski, Franciszek
1970 *Modele Malzenstwa: Rodziny a Kultura Masowa*. Warsaw: Panstwowe Wydawnictwo Naukowe.

Almond, Gabriel and Sidney Verba
1963 *The Civic Culture*. Princeton: Princeton University Press.

Anderson, Alan B.
1972 "Assimilation in the Bloc Settlements of North-Central Saskatchewan: A Comparative Study of Identity Change Among Seven Ethno-religious Groups in a Canadian Prairie Region." Ph.D. thesis in Sociology, University of Saskatchewan, Saskatoon.

1974 "Intermarriage in Ethnic Bloc Settlements in Saskatchewan: A Cross-cultural Survey of Trends and Attitudes." Research paper presented at the annual meetings of the Western Association of Sociology and Anthropology, Banff.

1975 "Ethnic Groups: Implications of Criteria for the Examination of Survival." A paradigm presented in the workshop on "Ethnicity and Ethnic-Groups in Canada," at the annual meetings of the Canadian Sociology and Anthropology Association, University of Alberta, Edmonton.

1976 "Linguistic Trends Among Saskatchewan Ethnic Groups." Research paper presented at the National Conference on Ethnic Studies and Research, University of Regina.

1977a "Ethnic Identity in Saskatchewan Bloc Settlements: A Sociological Appraisal." In *The Settlement of the West*, edited by Howard Palmer. Calgary: Comprint Publishing, University of Calgary.

1977b "Emigration from German Settlements in Eastern Europe: A Study in Historical Demography." Proceedings of the First Banff Conference on Central and East European Studies. Edmonton: Central and East European Studies Society of Alberta.

Anderson, Grace M.
1974 *Networks of Contact: The Portuguese and Toronto*. Waterloo: Wilfrid Laurier University.

Anderson, J. T. M.
1918 *The Education of the New Canadians*. Toronto: J. M. Dent and Sons Canada Ltd.

Andracki, Stanislaw
1958 "The Immigration of Orientals into Canada with Special Reference to Chinese." Ph.D. thesis, McGill University.

1972   *The Annals* of the American Academy of Political and Social Science, Philadelphia, Penn.

Arbess, Saul E.
    1965   *Social Change and the Eskimo Co-operative at George River, Quebec.* Northern Co-ordination and Research Centre, Ottawa.

Ashcraft, Norman
    1968   "Some Aspects of Domestic Organization in British Honduras." In *The Family in the Caribbean*, edited by Stanford N. Gerber. Rio Piedras, P.R.: Institute of Caribbean Studies.

Aschenbrenner, Stanley E.
    1971   "A Study of Sponsorship in a Greek Village," Ph.D. dissertation, Minneapolis, University of Minnesota.

Balikci, Asen
    1963   *Vunta Kutchin Social Change.* Ottawa: Northern Coordination and Research Centre, Department of Northern Affairs and National Resources, NCRC-63-3.

    1968   "Bad Friends." *Human Organization* 27:191-199.

    1970   *The Netsilik Eskimo.* New York: The Natural History Press.

Banfield, Edward C.
    1958   *The Moral Basis of a Backward Society.* New York: Free Press.

Bardis, Panos D.
    September 1955   "The Changing Family in Modern Greece." *Sociology and Social Research* 40:19-23.

Barnett, C. R.
    1958   *Poland*, HRAF Press.

Barringer, Herbert R., George I. Blanksten, and Raymond W. Mack
    1966   *Social Change in a Developing Area: A Reinterpretation of Evolutionary Theory 1.* Cambridge: Schenkman Publishing Co.

Bauman, Zygmunt
    1964   "Economic Growth, Social Structure, Elite Formation: The Case of Poland." *International Social Science Journal* 16: 203-216.

Beck, Kenneth E.
    1963   "Evolution, Function and Change." *American Sociological Review* 28:229-233.

Bellah, Robert N.
    1957   *Tokugawa Religion.* Glencoe, Ill.: Free Press.

Berreman, Gerald D.
    1956   "Drinking Patterns of the Aleuts." *Quarterly Journal of Studies on Alcohol* 17:503-514.

Blalock, H.
    1967   *Toward a Theory of Minority Group Relations.* New York: John Wiley and Sons.

Blaxter, Lorraine
1971 "Rendre service and jalousie." In *Gifts and Poison: The Politics of Reputation*, edited by F. G. Bailey. Oxford: Basil Blackwell.

Blishen, Bernard R. and Hugh A. McRoberts
1976 "A Revised Socioeconomic Index for Occupations in Canada." *The Canadian Review of Sociology and Anthropology* 13, 1:71-79.

Boas, Franz
1888 *The Central Eskimo*. Sixth Annual Report of the Bureau of Ethnology, Smithsonian Institution, Washington.

Boissevain, Jeremy
1970 *The Italians of Montreal: Social Adjustment in a Plural Society*. Ottawa: Studies of the Royal Commission on Bilingualism and Biculturalism.

Bonacich, E.
1973 "A Theory of Middleman Minorities," *American Sociological Review* 38:583-594.

Bonch-Bruevich, Vladimir
1954 *Zhivotnaia Kniga Dukhobortsev* (from the Book of Life of the Doukhobors. Reprint of 1910 ed. Winnipeg: Regehr's Printing.

Borrie, W. O.
1959 *The Cultural Integration of Immigrants*. Unesco.

Bott, Elizabeth
1957 *Family and Social Network*. London: Tovistock.

Brazeau, Jacques
1958 "Language Differences and Occupational Experiences." *Canadian Journal of Economic and Political Science* 49:536.

Brandes, Stanley H.
1975 *Migration, Kinship and Community: Tradition and Transition in a Spanish Village*. New York: Academic Press.

Breton, Raymond
1964 "Institutional Completeness of Ethnic Communities and Personal Relations of Immigrants." *American Journal of Sociology* 70:193-205.

Bridgeman, Rev. W.
1920 *Breaking Prairie Sod*. Toronto: Musson.

Briggs, Jean
1974 "Eskimo Women: Makers of Men." In *Many Sisters: Women in Cross-Cultural Perspective*, edited by Carolyn J. Matthiasson. Glencoe, Ill.: The Free Press.

Brody, Hugh
1971 *Indians on Skid Row*. Ottawa: Northern Science Research Group, Department of Indian Affairs and Northern Development.

Brögger, Jan
1971 *Montevarese: A Study of Peasant Society and Culture in Southern Italy*. Oslo Scandinavian University Press.

Burgess, Ernest
  May 1948   "The Family in a Changing Society," In *A.J.S.* 53:417-422.

Burgess, E. W., and H. J. Locke
  1953   *The Family.* 2d ed. New York: American Book Company.

Calhoun, John C.
  1953   *A Disquisition on Government.* Indianapolis, Indiana: The Bobbs-Merrill Co.

Caudill, William, and George De Vos
  1956   "Achievement, Culture, and Personality: The Case of Japanese Americans." *American Anthropologist* 58:1102-1126.

Cavan, R. S.
  1953   *The American Family.* New York: Thomas Y. Crowell.

Campbell, J. K.
  1964   *Honour, Family and Patronage.* Oxford: Clarendon Press.

  1964   *Honour, Family and Patronage: A Study of Institutions and Moral Values in a Greek Mountain Community.* Oxford: Clarendon Press.

Clairmont, D. H. J.
  1962   "Notes on the Drinking Behaviour of Eskimos and Indians in the Aklavik Area." Ottawa: Northern Coordination and Research Centre, Department of Northern Affairs and National Resources, NCRC-62-4.

  1963   "Deviance Among Indians and Eskimos in Aklavik, N.W.T." Ottawa: Northern Coordination and Research Centre, Department of Northern Affairs and National Resources, NCRC-63-9.

Chertkov, Vladimir
  1899   *Christian Martyrdom in Russia.* Toronto: Morang.

Chimbos, Peter D.
  1963   "The Hellenes of Missoula, Montana: Social Adjustment." Unpublished M.A. thesis, Missoula, Montana, University of Montana, pp. 44-48.

  1971   "Immigrants' Attitudes Towards Their Children's Interethnic Marriages in a Canadian Community." *International Migration Review,* Vol. 15, pp. 5-16.

  Fall
  1972   "A Comparison of the Social Adaptation of Dutch, Greek and Slovak Immigrants in a Canadian Community." *International Migration Review,* Vol. 16, pp. 230-244.

Choldin, Harvey M.
  1973   "Kinship Networks in the Migration Process." *International Migration Review* 7:163-175.

Codere, Helen
  1955   "A Genealogical Study of Kinship in the United States." *Psychiatry* XVIII: 65-79.

Connor, John W.
  1974   "Acculturation and Family Continuities in Three Generations of Japanese Americans." *Journal of Marriage and the Family* 36:159-165.

Connor, Walker
    "The Politics of Ethninationalism." *Journal of International Affairs*, Vol. 27, No. 1, pp. 1-21.

Covello, Leonard
    1967 *The Social Background of the Italo-American School Child: A Study of the Southern Italian Family Mores and Their Effect on the School Situation in Italy and America.* Leiden, Netherlands.

Cronin, Constance
    1970 *The Sting of Change: Sicilians in Sicily and Australia.* Chicago: University of Chicago Press.

Cruikshank, Julie
    1976 "Matrifocal Families in the Canadian North." In *The Canadian Family*, revised ed. Edited by K. Ishwaran. Toronto: Holt, Rinehart and Winston of Canada, Ltd.

Damas, David, ed.
    1969 *Contributions to Anthropology: Band Societies.* Ottawa: National Museums of Canada, Bulletin 228, Anthropological Series 84.

Davidson, A. M.
    1952 *An Analysis of the Significant Factors in the Patterns of Toronto Chinese Family Life as a Result of Recent Changes in Immigration Laws.* Unpublished M.S.W. thesis, University of Toronto.

Davis, J.
    Land and Family in Pisticci. London: Athlone Press.

Davis, Morris, and J. F. Krauter
    1971 *The Other Canadians.* Toronto: Methuen.

Dawson, C. A., and E. R. Younge
    1940 *Pioneering in the Prairie Provinces: The Social Side of the Settlement Process.* Canadian Frontiers of Settlement Series, Vol. VIII, Toronto: Macmillan.

Department of Manpower and Immigration
    1974 *The Immigration Programme.* Ottawa: Manpower and Immigration.

    1974 *Three Years in Canada.* Ottawa: Manpower and Immigration.

Driedger, Leo
    1955 *A Sect in Modern Society: A Case Study of the Old Colony Mennonites of Saskatchewan.* M.A. thesis in Sociology, University of Chicago.

    1968 "A Perspective on Canadian Mennonite Urbanization." In *Mennonites in Urban Canada: Proceedings of the Conference on Urbanization of Mennonites in Canada*, University of Manitoba, Winnipeg. *Mennonite Life* 23:147-159.

Driedger, Leo, ed.
    1972 "Urbanization of Mennonites in Canada." In *Call to Faithfulness*, edited by H. Poettcker and R. A. Regehr. Winnipeg: Canadian Mennonite Bible College.

1973 "Impelled Group Migration: Minority Struggle to Maintain Institutional Completeness." *International Migration Review* 7:257-269.

1975 "In Search of Cultural Identity Factors: A Comparison of Ethnic Minorities in Manitoba." *Canadian Review of Sociology and Anthropology* 12:150-162.

1977 "Mennonite Change: The Old Colony Revisited, 1955-1977." *Mennonite Life* 32:4-12.

1978 *The Canadian Ethnic Mosaic.* Toronto: McClelland and Stewart.

Driedger, Leo, and Jacob Peters
1973 "Ethnic Identity: A Comparison of Mennonite and Other German Students." *Mennonite Quarterly Review* 47:225-244.

Driedger, Leo, and Glenn Church
1974 "Residential Segregation and Institutional Completeness: A Comparison of Ethnic Minorities." *Canadian Review of Sociology and Anthropology* 11:30-52.

Dunning, R. W.
1959 *Social and Economic Change Among the Northern Ojibwa.* Toronto: University of Toronto Press.

Durgin, Edward C.
1974 *Brewing and Boozing: A Study of Drinking Patterns Among the Hare Indians.* Unpublished doctoral dissertation, Department of Anthropology, University of Oregon.

Economopoulou, Louesa
1976 "Assimilation and Sources of Culture Tension of Second Generation Greek Pre-Adolescents in Toronto." M.A. thesis, Toronto, Ontario Institute for Studies in Education.

Elkin, F.
1970 *The Family in Canada.* Ottawa: The Vanier Institute of the Family.

Engels, Frederick
1902 *The Origin of the Family, Private Property, and the State.* Chicago: Kerr.

England, Robert
1929 *The Central European Immigrant in Canada.* Toronto: Macmillan Company of Canada, Ltd.

Epp, Frank H.
1962 *Mennonite Exodus.* Altona, Manitoba: D. W. Friesen and Sons.

1974 *Mennonites in Canada 1786-1920: The History of a Separate People.* Toronto: Macmillan Company of Canada, Ltd.

Eshleman, J. Ross
1974 *The Family: An Introduction.* Boston: Allyn and Bacon.

Farber, Bernard
1964 *Family Organization and Interaction.* San Francisco: Chandler Publications.

Ferguson, T.
1975   *A White Man's Country.* Toronto: Doubleday Canada Ltd.

Field, Peter B.
1972   "A New Cross-Cultural Study of Drunkenness". In *Society, Culture and Drinking Patterns,* edited by David J. Pittman and Charles R. Snyder. New York: John Wiley and Sons.

Firth, R. F.
Forthcoming   "Studies of Kinship in London." MS. to be published by the London School of Economics.

Fitzgibbon, May (Bernard, Lally)
1899   *The Canadian Doukhobor Settlements.* Pamphlet. Toronto: William Briggs.

Foster, George M.
1960-61   "Interpersonal Relations in Peasant Society." *Human Organization* 19:174-180.

Francis, E. K.
1955   *In Search of Utopia.* Altona, Manitoba: D. W. Friesen and Sons.

Freedman, M.
Winter
1961-2   "The Family in China, Past and Present." *Pacific Affairs* 31(4):334.

Freud, Sigmund
1960   *Group Psychology and the Analysis of the Ego.* Translated by James Strachey. New York: Bantam Books.

Garigue, Philippe
1960   "The French-Canadian Family." In *Canadian Dualism—La Dualité canadienne,* edited by Mason Wade. Toronto: University of Toronto Press; Québec: Les Presses Universitaires Laval.

1971   "French-Canadian Kinship and Urban Life." In *The Canadian Family: A Book of Readings,* edited by K. Ishwaran, Toronto: Holt, Rinehart and Winston of Canada, Ltd.

Giffen, P. J.
1965   "Rates of Crime and Delinquency." In *Crime and Its Treatment in Canada,* edited by W. T. McGrath, Toronto: Macmillan Company of Canada, Ltd.

Glazer, Nathan, and Daniel P. Moynihan
1970   *Beyond the Melting Pot,* 2d ed. Cambridge: M.I.T. Press.

Gleborzecki, S. K.
1976   "Kanadyjski Wilno." *Zwiazkowiec.* Toronto, Nos. 23, 25, 27, 1957.

Gonzales, Nancy L.
1970   "Toward a Definition of Matrifocality." In *Afro-American Anthropology: Contemporary Perspectives,* edited by Norman E. Whitten and John R. Szwed. New York: Free Press.

Gordon, Milton
1964   *Assimilation in American Life.* New York: Oxford University Press.

Government of Canada
December 1975   First Annual Report of the Canadian Consultative Council
on Multiculturalism. Minister responsible for Multiculturalism, pp. iv-v.

Graburn, Nelson
1969   Eskimos without Igloos, Boston: Little, Brown and Company.

Greer, Scott
1964   The Emerging City. Glencoe, Ill.: The Free Press.

Hall, Edward T.
1959   The Silent Language. New York: Premier Book, Fawcett World Library.

Handlin, Oscar
1951   The Uprooted. New York: Grosset and Dunlap.

Harney, Robert F.
1975   "Ambiente and Social Class in North American Little Italies." Canadian Review of Studies in Nationalism 2: 208-224; "Chiaroscuro: Italians in Toronto 1885-1915." Italian Americana 1:143-167.

Hawkins, Freda
1972   Canada and Immigration: Public Policy and Public Concern. Montreal: McGill-Queen's University Press.

Hawthorne, Harry, ed.
1955   The Doukhobors of British Columbia. Vancouver: Dent and U.B.C.

Helm, June
1965   "Bilaterality in the Socio-Territorial Organization of the Arctic Drainage Dene." Ethnology 4 (4):361-385.

Henderson, M. C.
1975   "The Ethnicity Factor in Anglo-American Folkloristics." Canadian
Ethnic Studies, Vol. II, No. 2.

Henriques, Fernando
1953   Family and Colour in Jamaica. London: Eyre and Spottiswoode.

Hippler, Arthur E.
1974   An Alaskan Athabascan Technique for Overcoming Alcohol Abuse.
Arctic 27:53-67.

Hobart, Charles and C. S. Brant
1966   "Eskimo Education, Danish and Canadian." Canadian Review of Sociology and Anthropology, 3, No. 2:47-66.

Honigmann, John J.
1965   "Social Disintegration in Five Northern Canadian Communities."
Canadian Review of Sociology and Anthropology 2(4):199-214.

Honigmann, John J., and Irma Honigmann
1945   "Drinking in an Indian-White Community." Quarterly Journal of
Studies on Alcohol 5:575-619.

1965   Eskimo Townsmen. Ottawa: Canadian Research Centre for Anthropology.

1970   *Arctic Townsmen.* Ottawa: Canadian Research Centre for Anthropology.

Horton, Donald
1943   "The Functions of Alcohol in Primitive Societies: A Cross-Cultural Study." *Quarterly Journal of Studies on Alcohol* 4:199-320.

Hurd, W. Burton
1929   "The Case for a Quota." *Queen's Quarterly* XXXVI, 145-159.

Hurlbert, Janice
1962   *Age as a Factor in the Social Organization of the Hare Indians of Fort Good Hope, N.W.T.* Northern Co-ordination and Research Centre. Ottawa: Department of Northern Affairs and National Resources.

Ishwaran, K.
1959   *Family Life in the Netherlands.* The Hague: Uitgeverij van Keulen N.V.

1977   *Family, Kinship and Community: A Study of Dutch Canadians, A Developmental Approach.* Toronto: McGraw-Hill Ryerson Ltd.

Ishwaran, K., ed.
1976   *The Canadian Family* Revised ed., Toronto: Holt, Rinehard and Winston of Canada, Ltd.

Ishwaran, K., ed.
1976   *The Canadian Family* Revised ed., Toronto: Holt, Rinehart and Winston of Canada, Ltd.

1979b   "Marital Stability and Marital Commitment in a Rural Dutch Community." In *Marriage and Divorce in Canada.* Toronto: McGraw-Hill Ryerson Ltd.

Instituto Centrale di Statistica
1956   *IX Censimento Generale Della Popolozione 4 Novembre 1951.* Rome, 1, Fascicolo 79, 26.

1966   *10° censimento Generale Della Popolozione 15 ottobre 1961.* Rome, 3, Fascicolo 78, 28.

Jacobson, Nolan Pliny
1965   *Buddhism.* New York: Humanities Press.

Johnson, G. E.
1977   "Immigration and Organizational Change in Canadian Chinese Communities Since 1947." In *Multiculturalism in Canada: Third World Perspective,* edited by G. Paul. Toronto: Prentice-Hall Inc.

Jones, Strachan
1866   *The Kutchin Tribes.* Washington, D.C.: Smithsonian Institution, Annual Report for 1866, 320-327.

Josie, Edith
1966   *Here Are the News.* Toronto: Clarke, Irwin and Co., Ltd.

Kawashima, Takeyoshi
1968   *Nihon Shakai no Kazokuteki Kosei* (Familial Structure of Japanese Society). Tokyo: Nihon Hyoron-sha.

Kirkpatrick, Clifford
1955   The Family. New York: Ronall.

Kitano, Harry H. L.
1969   Japanese Americans. Englewood Cliffs: Prentice-Hall.

Komorowska, Jadwiga, ed.
1975   Przemiany Rodziny Polskiej, Instytut Wydawniczy CRZZ: Warsaw.

Kourvetaris, George A.
1976   "The Greek Family in America." In Ethnic Families in America,
       edited by Charles H. Mindee and Robert W. Hoberstein. New York: El-
       sevier, p. 176.

Krauter, J. F., and M. Davis
1978   Minority Canadians: Ethnic Groups. Toronto: Methuen.

Kravchinsky, Sergei M. (Stepniak)
1882   Russian Peasantry, Their Agrarian Condition, Social Life, and Reli-
       gion, Vol. II, London: Sonnenschein, pp. 505-549.

Kung, S. W.
Winter
1962   "Chinese Immigration into North America." Queen's Quarterly 68:4,
       pp. 612-616.

Ksiega Pamiatkowa Zwaldzku Polakow W. Kanadzie, 1906-1946.
1946   Toronto: Polish Alliance Press.

Kurokawa, Minako
1968   "Lineal Orientation in Child-rearing among Japanese." Journal of
       Marriage and the Family 30:129-136.

Lai, V.
1971   "The New Chinese Immigrants in Toronto" In Immigrant Groups,
       edited by Jean L. Elliot. Toronto: Prentice-Hall Inc.

Lam, L.
1977   Discrimination and Prejudice in Canada: Reflections on Chinese Im-
       migrants. Unpublished working paper.

1978   Achievement: How Far Can It Go? Unpublished working paper.

Lanphier, C. M.
1977   A Study of Third World Immigration. Mimeographed research report.
       Toronto: Ethnic Research Programme, York University.

Larocque, Paul, et. al.
November
1974   "Operationalization of Social Indicators of Multicultur-
       alism." Paper presented to the Fourth Departmental Seminar on So-
       cial Indicators: Department of the Secretary of State.

LaViolette, F. E.
1948   Canadian Japanese and World War II. Toronto: University of Toronto
       Press.

Lee, David T. H.
1967   A History of Chinese in Canada. Taiwan: Hai Tin Printing Co. (text in
       Chinese).

Lee, Richard B., and Irven DeVore, eds.
  1968 Man the Hunter. Chicago: Aldine Paperbacks.

Lee, S. C.
  1953 "China's Traditional Family: Its Characteristics and Disintegration."
        American Sociological Review 18:272-280.

Lee-Whiting, Brenda B.
        "First Polish Settlement in Canada." Canadian Geographical Journal
        LXXV: 108-112.

Leisler, Martin L., and B. Guy Peters
  March
  1971 The Implications of Scarcity for the Peaceful Management of Group
        Conflict. Mimeographed, University of Maryland.

Lemert, Edwin M.
  1958 "The Use of Alcohol in Three Salish Indian Tribes." Quarterly Jour-
        nal of Studies on Alcohol 19:90-107.

Lenski, Gerhard, ed.
  1961 The Religious Factor: A Sociological Study of Religious Impact on
        Politics, Economics and Family Life. Garden City, New York: Double-
        day and Co.

Lewis, Oscar
  1959 Five Families. New York: Basic Books.

Liberson, Stanley
  1970 Language and Ethnic Relations in Canada. New York: John Wiley and
        Sons.

Linton, Ralph
  1959 "The National History of Family." In The Family: Its Functions and
        Destiny, edited by Ruth N. Anthen. New York: Harper and Row.

Loewen, J. W.
  1971 The Mississippi Chinese. Cambridge, Mass: Harvard University
        Press.

Lopreato, Joseph
  1967 "Emigration and Social Change in Southern Italy." In The Sociology
        of Community, edited by C. Bell. London: Cass.

Luman, Stanford
  1971 The Asians in the West. Reno: Desert Research Institute, University of
        Nevada System.

MacAndrew, Craig, and Robert B. Edgerton
  1969 Drunken Comportment: A Social Explanation. Chicago: Aldine Pub-
        lishing Co.

MacGregor, Gordon
  1946 Warriors Without Weapons: A Study of the Society and Personality of
        the Pine Ridge Sioux. Chicago: University of Chicago Press.

Maloff, Peter
  1948 The Doukhobors, Their History, Life and Struggle. Unpublished type-

script; partial translation of *Dukhobortsi: ikh Instori'ia, Zhizn', i Bor'ba*. Thrums, B.C.

Mandelbaum, David G.
1965   "Alcohol and Culture." *Current Anthropology* 6:281-293.

Mangin, H. B.
1970   *Peasants in Cities: Readings in Anthropology of Urbanization*, Boston: Cambridge University Press.

Maraspini, A. L.
1968   *The Study of an Italian Village*. Paris: Mouton.

Marr, W.
1976   *Labour Market and Other Implications of Immigration Policy for Ontario*. Working paper no. 1/76, Ontario Economic Council.

Matthiasson, John S.
1976   "Northern Baffin Island Women in Three Cultural Periods," *Western Canadian Journal of Anthropology*, Vol. 6, pp. 201-212.

Matsumoto, Gary M., Gerald M. Meredith, and Minoru Masuda
1970   "Ethnic Identification: Honolulu and Seattle Japanese Americans." *Journal of Cross-Cultural Psychology* 1:63-76.

Maykovich, Minako K.
1975   "Japanese and Chinese in the United States and Canada." In *Politics of Race*, Westmead, England: Saxon House, pp. 95-120. Edited by Donald G. Baker.

1972a   *Japanese American Identity Dilemma*. Tokyo: Waseda University Press.

1972b   "Reciprocity in Racial Stereotypes." *American Journal of Sociology* 72:876-897.

McElroy, Ann
1975   "Arctic Modernization and Change in the Inuit Family." In *Marriage, Family and Society*, edited by S. Parvez Wakil. Toronto: Butterworth and Co. (Canada) Ltd.

McKennan, Robert A.
1965   *The Chandalar Kutchin*. Montreal: Arctic Institute of North America, Technical Paper, 17.

1969   "Athabaskan Groupings and Social Organization in Central Alaska." In *Contributions to Anthropology: Band Societies*, edited by David Damas. Ottawa: National Museums of Canada, Bulletin 228, Anthropological Series 84:93-114.

McLaughlin, Virginia Yans
1973   "Patterns of Work and Family Organization: Buffalo's Italians." In *The Family in History: Interdisciplinary Essays*, edited by Theodore K. Rabb and Robert I. Rotberg. New York: Harper and Row.

Mead, George H.
1963   *Mind, Self and Society*. Chicago: The University of Chicago Press.

Mealing, F. Mark
    1972 *Our People's Way: A Survey in Doukhobor Hymnody and Folklife.*
          Ph.D. (Folklore and Folklife) dissertation. Philadelphia: University of
          Pennsylvania.

Mendel, Charles H., and Robert W. Habenstein, eds.
    1976 *Ethnic Families in America: Patterns and Variations.* New York: Else-
          vier.

Milton, Gordon
    1964 *Assimilation in American Life.* Toronto: Oxford University Press.

Miyamoto, Shotaro F.
    1939 "Social Solidarity among the Japanese in Seattle." Seattle: *University
          of Washington Publications in the Social Sciences* 11:57-130.

Moore, Charles A., ed.
    1967 *The Japanese Mind.* Honolulu: University of Hawaii Press.

Morawska, Ewa Teresa
    1976 "The Maintenance of Ethnicity: Case Study of the Polish-American
          Community in Greater Boston." Ph.D. thesis, Boston University.

Morlan, Richard
    1973 *The Later Prehistory of the Middle Porcupine Drainage, Yukon Terri-
          tory, Canada.* Ottawa: National Museums of Canada, Mercury Series,
          paper no. 11.

Moss, Leonard W., and Stephen C. Cappannari
    1960 "Patterns of Kinship, Comparaggio and Community in a Southern
          Italian Village." *Anthropological Quarterly* 33:24-25.

Moynihan, Daniel P.
    1965 *The Negro Family: The Case for National Action.* Washington, D.C.:
          Government Printing Office.

Murdock, George
    1967 *Ethnographic Atlas.* Pittsburgh: University of Pittsburgh Press.

Murray, Alexander H.
    1910 *Journal of the Yukon, 1847-48.* Ottawa: Publications of the Canadian
          Archives, 4.

Nagata, Judith A.
    Fall
    1969 "Adaptation and Integration of Greek Working Class Immigrants in
          the City of Toronto, Canada: A Situational Approach." *International
          Migration Review,* Vol. IV, pp. 44-67.

Nakane, Chie
    1970 *Japanese Society.* Berkeley: University of California Press.

Nelli, Humbert S.
    1970 *The Italians in Chicago, 1880-1930: A Study in Ethnic Mobility.* New
          York: Oxford University Press.

Nelson, Richard K.
    1970 *Hunters of the Northern Forest.* Chicago: University of Chicago
          Press.

Okolowicz, Josef
1913 *Kanada; Garstka Windomosci dla Wychodzcow.* Krakow: Polski Towarzystwo Emigracyjne.

Opler, Morris E.
1945 "Themes as Dynamic Forces in Culture." *American Journal of Sociology* 51:198-206.

———.
1946 "An Application of the Theory of Themes in Culture." *Journal of the Washington Academy of Sciences* 36:137-166.

Osaka, Masako M.
1976 "Intergenerational Relations as an Aspect of Assimilation: the Case of Japanese Americans." *Sociological Inquiry* 46:67-72.

Osgood, Cornelius
1936 *Ethnography of the Kutchin.* New Haven: Yale University Publications in Anthropology, 14.

Palmer, Howard
1971 *Pamietniki Emigrantow: Kanada.* Warsaw: Ksiazka i Wiedza.

1972 *Land of the Second Chance: A History of Ethnic Groups in Southern Alberta.* Lethbridge: The Lethbridge Herald, p. 246.

Parsons, Talcott
January-March
1943 "The Kinship System of the Contemporary United States." *American Anthropologist,* 45:22-38.

1975 "Some Theoretical Considerations on the Nature and Trends of Change of Ethnicity." In *Theory and Experience,* edited by Nathan Glazer and Daniel P. Moynihan. Cambridge, Mass.: Harvard University Press, pp. 56-71.

Parsons, Talcott, and Robert F. Bales
1965 *Family Socialization and Interaction Process.* Glencoe, Ill.: The Free Press.

Parsons, Talcott, et.al., eds.
1961 *Theories of Society.* New York: Free Press.

Patterson, E. P.
1972 *The Canadian Indians: A History Since 1500.* Don Mills: Collier-Macmillan.

Peacock, Kenneth
1966 *Twenty Ethnic Songs from Western Canada.* Ottawa: National Museum.

———.
1970 *The Songs of the Doukhobors.* Ottawa: National Museum of Man.

Perkowski, J. L.
1971 "Folkways of the Canadian Kashubs." In *Slavs in Canada,* Vol. III,

edited by Cornelius J. Jaenen. Toronto: Ukrainian Echo Pub.

Pitt-Rivers, J. A.
1961   The People of the Sierra. Chicago: University of Chicago Press, p. 85-6.

Porter, John
1965   The Vertical Mosaic. Toronto: University of Toronto Press.

Price, C. A.
1958   "Report on the Greek Community in Toronto." M.A. thesis, Toronto, York University.

Price, John A.
1975   "An Applied Analysis of North American Indian Drinking Patterns." Human Organization 34:17-26.

Queen, Stuart A., and Robert W. Habenstein
1967   The Family in Various Cultures, 3d ed. New York: J. B. Lippincott & Co.

1974   The Family in Various Cultures. Philadelphia: J. B. Lippincott & Co.

Radecki, Henry
1970   "Polish-Canadian, Canadian-Polish, or Canadian?" Mimeograph. Toronto, York University.

1974   "How Relevant Are the Polish Part-Time Schools?" In Past and Present, edited by B. Heydenkorn. Toronto: Canadian Polish Research Institute, pp. 61-72.

1975   "Ethnic Organizational Dynamics: A Study of the Polish Group in Canada." Unpublished Ph.D. thesis, York University.

1975   "Leaders and Influentials: Polish Ethnic Group in Toronto." In From Prairies to Cities, edited by B. Heydenkorn. Toronto: Canadian Polish Research Institute, pp. 43-59.

1976   "Cultural Mosaic: A Micro View." In Topics on Poles in Canada, edited by B. Heydenkorn. Toronto: Canadian Polish Research Institute, pp. 127-140.

Radecki, Henry, with Benedykt Heydenkorn
1976   A Member of a Distinguished Family: The Polish Group in Canada. Toronto: McClelland and Stewart Ltd.

Ramu, G. N.
1976   "The Family and Marriage in Canada." In Introduction to Canadian Society, edited by G. N. Ramu and Stuart D. Johnson. Toronto: Macmillan Company of Canada, Ltd.

Rasmussen, Knud
1927   Across Arctic America. New York: Putnam.

1929   Intellectual Culture of the Iglulik Eskimos. Reports of the Fifth Thule Expedition, Vol. VII, Copenhagen.

Reitz, J.
August
1974 "Language and Ethnic Community Survival." The *Canadian Review of Sociology and Anthropology*. Toronto: University of Toronto Press.

1970 Report of the Royal Commission on Bilingualism and Biculturalism, *The Cultural Contribution of the Other Ethnic Groups*, Book IV, Table A-1. Ottawa: Queen's Printer, pp. 230-245.

Reymont, Wladyslaw S.
1970 *Chlopi*, 4 vols. Warsaw: Panstwowy Instytut Wydawniczy.

Rhoades, Jonathan
1900 *A Day with the Doukhobors*. Pamphlet. Philadelphia.

Richmond, Anthony H.
1967 *Immigrants and Ethnic Groups in Metropolitan Toronto*. Toronto.

1976 "Recent Development in Immigration to Canada and Australia: A Comparative Analysis." *International Journal of Comparative Sociology*, XVII, 3-4, pp. 183-205.

1977 "Factors Associated with Commitment to and Identification with Canada." In *Identities*, edited by N. Isajiw. Toronto: Peter Martin Associates Ltd.

Richmond, A. H., and W. Kalbach
1979 *Immigrants in Canada*. Forthcoming, Statistics Canada, Ottawa.

Rideman, Peter
1962 "Rechenschaft unsrer Religion, Zehre and Glaubens. Von den Bruedern, die man die Huterischen nennt." Cayley, Alberta, pp. 48-52.

Robbins, Richard H.
1973 "Alcohol and the Identity Struggle: Some Effects of Economic Change on Interpersonal Relations." *American Anthropologist* 7:99-122.

Rosen, Bernard C.
February
1959 "Race Ethnicity and the Achievement Syndrome." *American Sociological Review* 24, p. 52.

Stafilios-Rothschild, Constantina
May
1967 "A Comparison of Power Structure and Marital Satisfaction in Urban Greek and French Families." *The Journal of Marriage and the Family*, 29, p. 349.

Said, Abdul A., and Luis R. Simmons, eds.
1967 *Ethnicity in an International Context*. New Brunswick, N.Y.: Transactions Press, p. 10.

Saloutos, Theodore
1964 *The Greeks in the United States*. Cambridge, Mass.: Harvard University Press, pp. 313-314.

Savishinsky, Joel S.
1970 "Kinship and the Expression of Values in an Athabascan Bush Community," *Western Canadian Journal of Anthropology* 2:31-59.

1974　*The Trail of the Hare: Life and Stress in an Arctic Community*. New York: Gordon and Breach, Inc.

1976　"Vicarious Emotions as an Adaptation to Cultural Restraint: Affective Experience in a Sub-Arctic Indian Community." Paper presented at 75th Annual Meeting of the American Anthropological Association, Washington, D.C., November 17-21.

1977　"A Thematic Analysis of Drinking in a Hare Indian Community." *Papers in Anthropology*, Vol. 18, No. 2. Norman: Department of Anthropology, University of Oklahoma.

Schermerhorn, R. A.
1970　*Comparative Ethnic Relations: A Framework of Theory and Research*. New York: Random House.

Schneider, D. M., and G. C. Homans
1955　"Kinship Terminology and the American Kinship System." *American Anthropologist*, LVII: 1194-1208.

Sedgewick, C. P.
1973　*The Context of Economic Change and Continuity in an Urban Overseas Chinese Community*. Unpublished M.A. thesis, Vancouver: University of British Columbia.

Shibutani, Tamotsu, and Kian M. Kwan
1965　*Ethnic Stratification: A Comparative Approach*. New York: Macmillan Co.

Simic, Andrei
1973　*The Peasant Urbanites: A Study of Rural-Urban Mobility in Serbia*. New York: Academic Press.

Sidlofsky, Samuel
1969　*Post-War Immigrants in the Changing Metropolis with Special Reference to Toronto's Italian Population*. Ph.D. thesis. Toronto: University of Toronto.

Slobodin, Richard
1962　*Band Organization of the Peel River Kutchin*. Ottawa: National Museums of Canada, Bulletin 179, Anthropological Series 55.

1966　*Métis of the Mackenzie District*. Ottawa: Canadian Research Centre for Anthropology, Saint-Paul University.

1972　"The Socio-Political Dynamics of the October Events." *The Canadian Review of Sociology and Anthropology* 91:33-56.

Spindler, Louise
1962　"Menomini Women and Culture Change." *American Anthropological Association*, Vol. 64(1) (Part 2), Memoir 91.

Stager, J. K.
1974　*Old Crow, Y.T. and the Proposed Northern Gas Pipeline*. Environmental Social Committee, Northern Pipelines Task Force on Northern Oil Development. Report 74-21, Information Canada, Cat. 72-139/1974.